The Love Debate Poems of Christine de Pizan

The Love Debate Poems

University Press of Florida

Gainesville

Tallahassee

Tampa

Boca Raton

Pensacola

Orlando

Miami

Jacksonville

Barbara K. Altmann

of Christine de Pizan

Le Livre du Debat de deux amans
Le Livre des Trois jugemens
Le Livre du Dit de Poissy

Copyright 1998 by the Board of Regents of the State of Florida
Printed in the United States of America on acid-free paper
All rights reserved

03 02 01 00 99 98   6 5 4 3 2 1

LIBRARY OF CONGRESS CATALOGING-IN-PUBLICATION DATA
Altmann, Barbara K., 1957–
The love debate poems of Christine de Pizan / Barbara K. Altmann.
p. cm.
Includes bibliographical references and index.
ISBN 0-8130-1578-2 (alk. paper) 0-8130-2490-0 (pbk)
1. Christine de Pisan, ca. 1364–ca. 1431—Criticism and interpretation.
2. Debate poetry, French—history and criticism. 3. Love poetry,
French—History and criticism. I. Title.
PQ1575.Z5A44 1998   97-43642
841.'2—dc21

The University Press of Florida is the scholarly publishing agency for the State
University System of Florida, comprised of Florida A & M University, Florida
Atlantic University, Florida International University, Florida State University,
University of Central Florida, University of Florida, University of North Florida,
University of South Florida, and University of West Florida.

University Press of Florida
15 Northwest 15th Street
Gainesville, FL 32611
http://nersp.nerdc.ufl.edu/~upf

To LLA and ALL,
my all and backwards.

Contents

Acknowledgments

INTRODUCTION

  I. Text and Context: Background to the Poems
    The Author 3
    The Poems 6
    Synopses 7
    Christine's Debate Poems and Their Place in
      the Literary Tradition 12
        The Late Medieval Debate Poem in Relation
          to Established Forms 12
        Generic Transformations: Christine's Challenges
          to the Form of the Debate 16

  II. Theme and Variations: Interplay of Form and Content
    Sociohistorical Contextualization of the Debate:
      The Case of the *Dit de Poissy* 18
    Transtextual Readings: A Debate among Debates 24
    The Self-Destructing Love Debate: Women's Voices
      as Agents of Dissent 28
    Orality, Reading, and Writing in the Debate Poems 31

  III. Philology and Codicology
    Manuscripts 36
    Previous Editions and Base Text 43
    Language 47
    Versification 51
    Miniatures 54
    Establishment of the Text 58

  IV. Notes to the Introduction 63

TEXTS

Le Livre du Debat de deux amans
Introduction   81
Text   84
Variants   135
Notes   139

Le Livre des Trois jugemens
Introduction   153
Text   155
Variants   194
Notes   197

Le Livre du Dit de Poissy
Introduction   203
Text   206
Variants   259
Notes   264

Glossary   275

Bibliography of Works Cited   284

Illustrations follow page 54.

Acknowledgments

I am grateful for the research time and funds provided by the Social Sciences and Humanities Research Council of Canada, the National Endowment for the Humanities, and particularly the University of Oregon, through its Summer Research Fellowship program and through the Oregon Humanities Center. I would like to acknowledge as well the research collections and manuscript libraries in which I had the pleasure of working, in particular the Bibliothèque Nationale, the Bibliothèque Royale Albert Ier, the British Library, and the Musée Condé.

There are those who will not be surprised that the completion of this book turned out to be infinitely more involved than I had ever imagined. The weak spots are unquestionably my own. However, there would have been many more without the unstinting help of colleagues in the field. In particular, I most humbly appreciate the expertise, erudition, and generosity of William Calin, Thelma S. Fenster, William W. Kibler, James Laidlaw, and Nadia Margolis, from all of whom I still have much to learn.

One could not ask for better, more astute assistants than Erika Hess and Suzanne Kocher.

Personal debts are the hardest to define and impossible to repay. My thanks to the friends and colleagues who bore with me and offered invaluable advice. Anne M. Altmann, a wise and generous woman, gave most graciously of her time. And I thank with all my heart Charles Lachman, without whose unwavering support this project simply would not have seen the light of day.

Introduction

I

Text and Context: Background to the Poems

The Author

Christine de Pizan (1364–ca. 1431) and her writings have recaptured scholarly attention in the last few decades among those investigating issues of gender, genre, and poetics in the late Middle Ages. Recent research is resulting in new editions of her works, major advances in codicological and art-historical studies of her manuscripts, and a much more thorough appreciation of her literary production. Both author and corpus merit this increased scrutiny. Her poetry and prose show the hand of a master poet who participated actively in the elaboration of literary genres and techniques. Moreover, her work presents a unique female voice in courtly literature, raised in counterpoint to the male chorus that dominates the learned discourse of her age.

The basic facts of her biography need be rehearsed only very briefly here.[1] The name *Pizan*, often incorrectly spelled *Pisan* in earlier titles, derives from the Italian village of Pizzano, near Bologna.[2] Her father, Tommaso di Benvenuto da Pizzano, moved to France at the request of Charles V in 1364, as the king's astrologer and counselor. His wife and young daughter joined him in Paris in 1368. Christine thereby grew up in and around the French court and inherited from her scholar-father a desire and aptitude for learning. At the age of fifteen, she married Etienne de (or du) Castel, who became notary and secretary to the king. Their partnership was a love match, and Christine never remarried after Etienne died in 1389. Left to provide for herself and her extended family, she experienced considerable hardship, and it took many years to settle confused and litigious financial affairs. The obstacles she encountered during this difficult period are reflected in the poetry she began to write in the 1390s. The plight of widows became a recurring theme in her work, as did the virtues of a good marriage and her great sorrow at her husband's death.

By the end of the century, she had undertaken serious study to fill the gaps in her education and had completed her first collections of lyric poetry, using the fixed forms of the *rondeau, ballade,* and *virelay*. By the early 1400s, she had gained enough confidence and prestige to engage eminent Parisian scholars in the famous epistolary battle over Jean de Meun's *Roman de la Rose,* a key text in the vernacular courtly tradition, and his misogynist views. The years 1400–1403 saw rapid production, including the *Epistre d'Othéa,* several *dits* and *débats,* among which were the three love debate poems in this volume, plus more lyric poetry. From this point on, however, she became increasingly concerned with political and moral issues, and the early forms gave way to longer verse and prose works of a didactic nature, often using allegory. These include the *Livre de la Mutacion de Fortune,* the *Livre du Chemin de long estude,* and *L'Avision-Christine,* all completed by 1406. Her biography of Charles V, the *Livre des Fais et bonnes meurs du sage roy Charles V,* was written in 1404 on commission from Philippe, duke of Burgundy. The very popular *Livre de la Cité des dames* and the *Livre des Trois vertus,* a companion volume of sorts, were composed between 1405 and 1407. A final *ballade* cycle, the *Cent balades d'amant et de dame,* dates from 1409 or 1410. Thereafter, apart from the *Epistre de la Prison de vie humaine* and the *Heures de contemplacion,* both of which appear between 1416 and 1429, we have only the *Ditié de Jehanne d'Arc,* which was finished July 31, 1429. In short, Christine was very prolific, and a full bibliography would include numerous other works, many of a political and some of a religious nature.[3]

Christine's corpus lends itself to a division into two types of work, the lyric love poetry and the generally later, more erudite works. So far, the learned works have received the lion's share of critical notice, particularly because they contain the most explicit statements in her defense of women and therefore provide excellent terrain for the investigation of premodern feminism. Accordingly, recent translations, editions, and criticism have focused on the letters and poetry associated with the debate concerning perceived misogyny and the use of language in the *Roman de la Rose,* for example, and on allegorical works such as the *Cité des dames*. Her love poetry—the lyric poems and the shorter narrative works written early in the fifteenth century—have suffered from their status as more "conventional" literature,[4] even though she was appreciated by her contemporaries for these very works. In an interesting twist on Christine's own *Cité des dames,* Martin Le Franc (ca. 1410–1461), for example, sings Christine's praises as one of the worthy women in his didactic treatise, the *Champion des dames* (1440–1442).[5] He speaks of the fame attained by *dame Cristine,* an author whose name *a trompe et a cor ... va par tout et ne fine*.⁶ Concerning the quality of her work, he states:

> Loer assez je ne la puis
> Sans souspirs, regrets et clamours,
> Non porroient ceux qui aux puis
> Servent le gay prince d'Amours;
> Car vraiement toutes les flours
> Avoit en son jardin joly
> Dont les beaux dictiers longs et courts
> Fait on en langage poly.

In this passage, Le Franc admires her rhetoric, the polished nature and ornamentation of her language so suitable for emulation by other love poets; some lines later, he adds a testimonial to her eloquence and wisdom, comparing her to Cicero (Tully) for the former and Cato for the latter.⁷

In our day and age, more attention is being paid to her lyric poetry as critics realize that both in spite of and because of its conventional nature, it demonstrates Christine's considerable talents and manifests her innovative attitudes. As a result of increased discussion concerning Christine as a feminist writer, more critics have focused on the woman's point of view she displays in her courtly love poetry as well as in the more obviously erudite works. This recognition of new motifs in old forms helps attenuate earlier assessments of Christine's courtly poems as derivative or formulaic. Pierre Le Gentil's re-evaluation of Christine's poetry may be considered a groundbreaking analysis in this vein.⁸ Since his article appeared in 1951, Charity Cannon Willard and others have carried such analysis much further. Looking at the *ballade* cycles in particular, they have discovered there a repeated illustration of the pitfalls awaiting the lady who participates in an illicit love affair. These stories obviously complement the more explicit warnings to women that are incorporated into the *Livre des Trois vertus* and elsewhere. Once these parallels have been identified, it becomes clear that there is a greater coherence of themes and attitudes in Christine's corpus than had previously been acknowledged.⁹

A study of the debate poems, all of which continue to employ the models established by Guillaume de Machaut, furnishes additional proof of the coherence of her corpus. Here, as elsewhere, Christine reworks literary tradition and embellishes inherited forms, in this case establishing a critical distance from the content, which allows her simultaneously to engage and dismiss the topic of courtly love.

The Poems

Christine de Pizan's three debate poems show her in mid-career, an accomplished dialectician on the topic of love and a master at manipulating the conventional literary forms and topoi in which such discussion was couched. Her *Livre du Dit de Poissy*, *Livre des Trois jugemens*, and *Debat de deux amans*, all composed in 1400 or shortly thereafter, fall squarely into the paradigm of the *débat amoureux* made popular by Guillaume de Machaut half a century earlier.[10] While only the *Dit de Poissy* can be dated precisely—the text itself gives its date of composition as April 1400 (ll. 37–39)—the other two may well have been written the same year.[11]

Christine's examples of judgment poetry are much in keeping with the spirit of courtly vernacular literature of her day, particularly given the renewed enthusiasm for love casuistry that resulted in the founding of the Court of Love in 1400 under the auspices of Charles VI.[12] Her debates take up a subject matter very similar to that in two of her other works from the same period, the *Epistre au dieu d'Amours* (1399), Christine's first long poem, and the *Dit de la Rose* (1402). Exploiting a tried-and-true subject (what she had earlier called *Le sentement...qui mieulx plaist a tous de commun cours*)[13] the three debates are like prisms, each illuminating a different aspect of the endlessly fascinating topic of love among young nobles. The *Deux amans* stages a debate between an enthusiastic, idealistic young squire and a rather world-weary knight in his prime who argue whether love brings more good or harm. The *Trois jugemens* recounts the disputes of three separate couples who question the reasonable limits of fidelity. The *Dit de Poissy*, finally, reports a debate between a knight and lady, each of whom passionately asserts the right to be called the more unhappy as a result of their disappointments in love; somewhat paradoxically, their discussion takes place on the homeward journey after a visit to the priory of Poissy, where a group of friends organized by Christine have called on the nuns.

Christine was clearly writing to please a particular audience: all three debates are dedicated to a patron whom Christine the narrator asks to judge the case(s) she is presenting. *Deux amans* addresses the duke of Orléans in its prologue, while *Trois jugemens* states that it is composed in honor of Jean de Werchin, the Seneschal of Hainaut.[14] *Poissy* is not quite so explicit: Maurice Roy assumed, as many modern critics do, that it, too, was dedicated to Jean de Werchin, but Charity Cannon Willard points out that this conclusion is inconsistent with information given in the poem. She suggests that it was likely sent instead either to the marshal Boucicaut or to Jean de

Châteaumorand.[15] Whoever the actual dedicatee, Christine profited from her connections in and around the royal household to place these works in the hands of noblemen well-disposed to rewarding literary gamesmanship. The economics of patronage help explain why an ambitious but relatively untried author would take up this genre and also throws into relief the daring nature of her sometimes ironic tone.

A synopsis of each poem appears in the following section. The section entitled "Theme and Variations: Interplay of Form and Content" discusses a variety of issues concerning the literary nature of the debates taken singly and as a group, while "Philology and Codicology" addresses linguistic and technical aspects of the poems and this edition. Each text is also preceded by a short introduction of its own.

Synopses

Debat de deux amans

The poem opens with a dedication to the duke of Orléans, for whom Christine, to bring some joy to his heart, will recount a debate she witnessed (ll. 1–81). The debate takes place at a party held in a splendid private residence in Paris. The guests are young, beautifully dressed, and bent on enjoying themselves. They dance joyfully and exchange many flirtatious glances (ll. 82–143). Christine sits alone in the midst of this gaiety, observing from a hidden corner, removed from the festivities by the sorrow of her widowhood (ll. 144–61). She notices a most attractive squire who is clearly enamored of a certain lady there (ll. 162–208). Then Christine becomes aware of a pensive figure near the bench where she sits, a careworn knight who appears smitten with another lady in the room (ll. 209–85). He notices that Christine has spotted him, and begins to converse with her (ll. 286–344). The squire comes to join them, and their discussion turns to the nature of love and specifically whether it brings more joy or sorrow. The young man suggests that they move outside to the garden to pursue the debate, which they do in the company of two other women whom Christine asks to join them (ll. 345–92).

After inviting the ladies to speak first (ll. 407–11), the knight begins his argument that love is a destructive force (l. 422 ff.). Speaking from personal experience as well as hearsay, he states that love robs its victims of all reason (ll. 447–52) and is a seductive siren (l. 459) who lures a man to his death. Fortune prepares a hard path for the lover, who becomes enslaved to Amour despite the grief it brings him (ll. 486–533). Even those whose love is requited are beset by the inescapable force of Jealousy (ll. 533–640). The knight begins to list famous lovers to demonstrate that even the best loved, who did not fall prey to jealousy, lost soul and body for their pains. His examples are drawn from classical mythology and literature and from medieval French sources (ll. 641–779). Rehearsing once more all the ill effects love can cause, he warns young people to flee its temptations, using himself as an example to be avoided (ll. 780–886). He ends his speech by saying that he makes his statement, not because he is averse to serving love himself or to criticize those who choose to do so, but to explain how one must proceed in order to pledge one's loyalty to love (ll. 886–92). He then gives a quick summary and cedes the floor (ll. 893–908).

The lady now proffers her conviction that while love is fine as a pastime, its ill and desirable effects are highly exaggerated and those who profess to be driven to despair by love are insincere (ll. 909–1000).

The squire begins immediately after the lady has finished, addressing his remarks to the knight. He begins by expressing dismay over the knight's contention that love brings only suffering; in his opinion, love is responsible for all the good that comes to man (ll. 1001–55). Bonne Esperance will sustain even the rejected lover, who must not be unreasonable (ll. 1056–68). He lists all the ennobling qualities and pleasures of love (ll. 1069–1133, 1134–1244). He denies that jealousy inevitably accompanies love, insisting that true love does not, in fact, allow for it (ll. 1245–80). Instead, jealousy belongs to abusive conjugal relations or is born of fearful, suspicious, or disdainful hearts (ll. 1281–1364). He counters the knight's list of *exempla* with a similar list of his own, citing cases of those who were wise enough to profit from love to improve themselves (l. 1365 ff.). Whereas the knight maintains that many worthy men have lost their lives because of love, the squire points out that those who suffer from love have only themselves to blame (ll. 1374–84), for all good things can be misused (l. 1385 ff.). He chooses examples of famous lovers to counter those in the knight's speech and recasts some of the same exemplars, such as Tristan (ll. 1441–50). He concludes with praise of some noblemen of his own day (ll. 1560–1718). A short recapitulation of his major points ends his disquisition (ll. 1719–48).

The knight offers a short rebuttal, concluding that the love free of jealousy described by the squire must be a less serious one than that which leads a lover to despair (ll. 1749–1824). The squire, in turn, restates his position and suggests they seek a judge for their dispute (ll. 1825–81), to which the knight agrees (ll. 1882–1912). They discuss many possible choices (ll. 1913–33), and Christine intervenes when it becomes clear that they cannot reach a decision, suggesting her patron as the best possible arbiter (ll. 1934–76). The knight and squire agree, praise Christine's skill as a writer, and request that she compose a *dit* recounting their debate (ll. 1977–92).

She consents and addresses the duke, humbly dedicating her work to him (ll. 1993–2017). She then closes the poem with an anagram (ll. 2018–23).

Le Livre des Trois jugemens

Introduction: Christine appeals to her patron, the Seneschal of Hainaut, to pronounce on the debate of some lovers who have asked her to decide their cases. She undertakes to report their tales to him word for word (ll. 1–32).

First case: a hard-hearted lady refuses to take pity on her smitten suitor until Amour wounds her with the spark of love. She then grants him her love, saying she knows he is worthy of her trust; in return, he promises repeatedly to love no one but her. Soon, however, her lover begins to visit less and less frequently. The lady is devastated. She complains to him and expresses the hope that other ladies will take her example as a warning not to believe those who claim to love them. He pleads that he has been very busy and that he is wary of harmful gossip, but he promises to remain faithful and to visit more often. Despite these assurances, he does not change his ways, and the lady languishes in despair (ll. 33–336).

Slowly the lady comes to her senses and abandons hope that he will return. Another suitor begins to press his case with her. She is reluctant to accept him, given her unhappy experience, but he serves her so well that she finally retains him as her lover (ll. 337–507).

News finally reaches her first lover, who returns and accuses the lady of being unfaithful to him. She counters that she is entitled to take a new lover because he left her before she considered accepting the second (ll. 508–693).

Second case: two lovers hold each other very dear. They are constrained, however, by the prying eyes of gossips. Eventually the married lady forgets to act prudently, and word reaches her husband. He contrives to find the lovers together, and although the knight is able to save the lady's honor by finding a plausible excuse for their meeting, the husband forbids his wife ever to see the knight again, on pain of death (ll. 693–832).

In secret the lover continues to enquire after the lady and send her messages, including a "Complainte" (ll. 898–1012). This missive tells at length of his unhappiness and gives her advice about how to remain steadfast and avoid despair, despite the severe constraints placed on them. The lady replies with a "Complainte" of her own. She suggests that he divert himself with suitable activities such as hunting, and leave the grieving to her (ll. 1022–92).

This state of affairs lasts for some time. The lovers do not see each other for two winters and a summer. Finally, the knight begins to forget about the lady and finds another (ll. 1093–1131). One day, he and his first love encounter each other by chance. She reproaches him, and he insists that he has done nothing wrong. They agree to put the case to a judge. First they ask Christine, but she recommends her patron, a choice they are happy with (ll. 1131–1268).

Third case: a knight is devoted to a lady who is perfect in all ways, other than that she is very young. They love each other steadfastly until he begins to think that he is too elevated in status for her and would prefer someone of loftier social standing. Accordingly, he finds and begins to serve a powerful lady, but their love does not last long (ll. 1269–1340).

The young lady, meanwhile, is very upset by his change of heart. In reply to her pressing messages, he promises that he will come see her, but never does. She realizes in time that he loves someone else and that her grief was pointless. Thereafter, she no longer tries to contact him and has no desire to love anyone else (ll. 1341–99).

Meanwhile, he renounces his new love after less than a year and begins to recall the pleasure he took in his love of the first young woman. He comes to his senses and decides to love her again. He therefore asks her to forgive him. He suggests that she take whatever vengeance she might want in exchange for his infidelity, but asks that she grant him her love again (ll. 1400–1441).

She is no longer interested, however, either in him or in love. She refuses to consider his entreaties, saying that he is entitled to suffer if he likes, but he has proven himself to be so fickle that his love will surely not last long (ll. 1442–59). The knight requests a judge, insisting that no man was born perfect enough not to commit mistakes and that if a judge were to pronounce him in the wrong, he would go away. She consents but desires that the case be put to other ladies for their opinion. They agree to find a judge and go to Christine for help, who sends them to her patron (ll. 1460–1531).

Le Dit de Poissy

Christine, the narrator, appeals to her patron to judge the case of two lovers who have asked her to find someone to arbitrate their dispute (ll. 1–28). She explains how the debate took place: she and a group of friends undertake an expedition to visit her daughter, a nun at the convent at Poissy (ll. 29–59). They ride through the forest, enjoying the pleasures of the spring day (ll. 60–211). The group arrives at Poissy and makes its way to the convent, where the nuns welcome them (ll. 212–31). The narrator greets her daughter and they attend mass (ll. 232–38). The nuns offer their visitors some refreshment and the prioress, Marie de Bourbon, invites them to speak with her in her apartments. There they also meet the princess Marie and the noble ladies who accompany her (ll. 239–96). Life in the convent is described (ll. 297–342). At the suggestion of the prioress, the guests are served lunch (ll. 343–70). Christine's party takes leave of the prioress and is given a tour of the premises (ll. 371–577).

The guests depart, promising to return after dinner. They dine and rest at their inn before returning to the convent, where they converse with the sisters in the gardens (ll. 577–678). The visit ends, and Christine says goodbye to her daughter (ll. 678–708). The group returns to their lodgings for the night (ll. 709–64). Over supper, the topic of conversation turns to knights of renown. Christine's patron is praised, and she promises again to write a poem for him, which a messenger agrees to deliver (ll. 765–867). After a stroll by the river, the group retires for the night (ll. 868–89).

The next morning, they set out on the journey home (ll. 890–904). One of the ladies rides apart from her companions, looking pensive. Christine notices her unhappiness and, together with a young squire, approaches her (ll. 905–38). The lady is reluctant to divulge the source of her unhappiness but agrees to do so if the squire promises to keep her story a secret and tell her, in turn, why he is sorrowful, too (ll. 939–1068). The lady begins her tale of woe, opening with a portrait of her lover (ll. 1069–1256). She explains that her troubles began when her knight was taken prisoner during the crusade to Nicopolis. Although she attempts to hide her grief in public, it is overwhelming (ll. 1257–1388). The squire recounts his unhappy love affair, explaining how he met his lady in a garden and describing her great beauty (ll. 1389–1661). He tells how he became well acquainted with her, frequenting her home and keeping company with her friends. He could not bring himself to declare his love but served her well (ll. 1662–1760). Without explanation, he says, his lady's reception of him changed; suddenly, she no longer welcomed his presence. He was crushed and still suffers greatly (ll. 1761–1876). The squire and the lady each assert that his/her own pain is greater than the other's (ll. 1877–2005).

The debaters decide that they need a judge to resolve the issue and ask Christine to name one. She suggests her patron and again states her request to him (ll. 2005–52). The group approaches Paris. They dine at Christine's house, and before leaving, the debaters ask her to settle the matter of their dispute quickly (ll. 2053–64). Christine says she started writing the poem at once, and gives her name in an anagram in the last line (ll. 2065–75).

Christine's Debate Poems and Their Place in the Literary Tradition

The qualification of these works by Christine as "debates" is in some ways rather cavalier. Indeed, in attempting to label these three studies on love, one enters fully into the minefield of medieval generic specificity or, more precisely, the lack thereof. Of central importance to an understanding of their composition is the notion that late medieval literary forms were dynamic and evolving.

The Late Medieval Debate Poem in Relation to Established Forms

The titles of the works in question are sufficient to show the state of flux that surrounded such designations.[16] In the *Debat de deux amans*, the term *dit* is used self-referentially to describe the text in lines 10 and 46, and is therefore equated with *rommans* (l. 53). The work called the *Livre des Trois jugemens* in the incipit of manuscript *D* (Bibliothèque Nationale f.fr. 835, 606, 836, 605) becomes the *Dit des trois jugemens* in the explicit, and *Dit* is used also in the incipit of manuscript *L3* (B.N. f.fr. 604). The incipit for *Poissy* in manuscript *D* reads *Livre du dit de Poissy*, while the explicit gives simply *Dit de Poissy*. In contrast, manuscript *R* (British Library Harley 4431), the base manuscript of this edition, begins by calling it the *Livre de Poissy* and ends with the *Dit de Poissy*.

While there was obviously a fair degree of variety and overlap in the names assigned to these works, they do belong to two recognizable categories: the *dit*, and the *débat amoureux*, also known as the *jugement*. The *dit* might be considered an overarching category, because the designation implies more a technique or aesthetic of composition than a subject matter, while the *jugement* is more closely tied to the poem's formal properties and to the topic of love casuistry itself.

The *dit*

The medieval *dit* is an extremely elastic construction allowing the association of multiple distinct formal units as well as the mingling of several kinds of content. As a result, most attempts to define it are unsatisfactory; they undertake the impossible task of identifying general principles that can account for the enormous variety to be found in the many poems called *dits*. In trying to pin down its fundamentally hybrid nature, some resort to a double-barreled label, such as Pierre-Yves Badel's "genre mi-narratif, mi-didactique" and Pierre Le Gentil's often quoted "genre lyrico-narratif."[17] Both of these are inadequate. Many *dits* do have a didactic element, often expressed by use of allegory, but some do not; and while it is fair to say that all *dits* combine lyricism and narrative, it has been pointed out that not all texts that do so are *dits*.[18]

Even within the corpus of one author, the title *dit* is applied to very different works. Machaut's *Dit dou vergier*, for example, is of a totally different order than his *Voir dit*. Christine's *Dit de la pastoure* is essentially a *pastourelle*, the *Dit de la rose* belongs to Christine's series of polemical works opposing the mistreatment of women, and the *Dit de Poissy*'s affinities clearly lie more closely with the other *jugement* poems. In this regard the label is similar to that of *livre* and other general terms.[19]

The constants of the *dit* that one can glean among the variety, however, are the following: it is essentially narrative; as its name implies, it is written to be read aloud, not to be sung; it often deals in the dialectic of love; and it is usually of considerable length. Beyond these generalizations, one must conclude with Paul Zumthor that the *dit* "n'est bien définissable ni sur le plan thématique ni sur le plan formel."[20]

In perhaps the most useful attempt to date to determine distinct criteria for discussion of this fluid and expansive form, Jacqueline Cerquiglini lists three characteristics that in combination distinguish the *dit* from other genres: first, it operates on a principle of discontinuity; second, it falls within the domain of first-person narration in the present tense, and the narrator figures in the text; and third, the "I" is a writer-clerk, with the result that the work is didactic.[21] Given the infinite permutations possible even within the constraints of these constants, she stresses that the *dit* can be defined only in terms of the "mise en présence" of its various elements and not in terms of the nature of those elements.[22]

The "mise en présence" or "montage" Cerquiglini isolates is a process of exterior structuring, a selection of components and the arranging of them. In other words, it operates on a level once removed from the events of the narrative itself.[23] Often this principle of construction includes the deliberate rupture of the narrative's formal structure by the insertion of independent, variously organized units. In the case of Machaut's *Voir dit*, for example, letters written in prose and lyric poems of the "fixed form" variety are intercalated into a running narrative written in octosyllablic couplets, a pattern Christine follows by integrating poems into the *Dit de la pastoure* and the *Dit de la rose*.

Christine's love debates conjoin elements somewhat differently, drawing on "la technique énumérative"[24] to elaborate a series of examples. In *Deux amans* and *Trois jugemens* one finds an externally imposed numeric organization, as is evident from their titles. In *Deux amans*, there are two major participants, who argue the only two possible conclusions to the question they choose, namely, whether love is beneficial or harmful. Their arguments are presented serially, however, rather than being interwoven, dividing the text into two major sections. In the *Trois jugemens*, more strikingly, the three cases presented one after the other in fact constitute entirely autonomous blocks of texts linked only by the narrator's interventions (*ancor or en droit / Ij. autres cas diray*, ll. 682–83; *Et du tiers cas sicomme il me souvient, / Je vous diray le fait*, ll. 1269–70).

Disjunction operates somewhat differently in the *Dit de Poissy*. This text hints at the formal rupture involved in the intercalation of lyric poetry into narrative by quoting the titles or first lines of two songs that are performed by the young people in the garden of the inn after the company's visit to the priory (one lady sings the song which begins *Tres doulx ami de bien amer penson*, l. 739, and a squire follows with *Gente de corps et de beauté louée*, l. 747). The rhythm of the text's quatrains is never broken, however: there is no break on the formal level. In *Poissy* the variation on the discontinuity characterizing the *dit* consists instead of the linking of two very nearly antithetical subject matters, namely, the trials and tribulations of love in courtly circles and the productive and peaceful existence of a community of women devoted to the service of God. I have argued elsewhere that this apparently paradoxical combination of preoccupations results in the exposure of courtly life as hollow and unhappy.[25] Certainly Christine plays with the potential invested in the fictional construct of the narrator to unify and bring coherence to a conjunction of diverse elements. Her particular narrator, complete with a professional interest in the life of the nobility, a personal affiliation with the priory of Poissy, and considerable religious devotion, provides a unique focalizer through which to reconcile apparent contradictions between the two realms. By its inclusion in a larger narrative, the love debate, a set-piece in its own right, transcends its textual and thematic boundaries and functions ironically as emblematic of attitudes Christine criticizes. The flexibility of the *dit* thus serves her purposes well, and any endeavor to evaluate it in terms of post-medieval notions of coherence runs the risk of obscuring the very expansive, adaptable nature that allows this narrative form to succeed in an infinite variety of permutations.

The *débat amoureux*

As opposed to the *dit*, the *débat amoureux* or *jugement* appears to have had relatively stable genre markers and a traceable evolution from earlier forms. Christine chose to follow the model of the *débat amoureux* or *jugement* established in the mid-1300s by Guillaume de Machaut. He, in turn, was drawing on the well-established tradition of debate poetry that flourished in the Middle Ages, encouraged by teaching practices that emphasized dialectical exchange.[26] Literary debates in the vernacular had existed for some time before him in the form of the Provençal *tenso* and *partimen*.[27] Of more direct influence on Machaut, however, were the Latin and Old French *débats du clerc et du chevalier*, also called *jugements d'amour*, and the trouvères' *jeux-partis*.

The label *débat du clerc et du chevalier* is actually a misnomer for a half dozen late twelfth- and early thirteenth-century poems in which knights and clerks (meaning "clerics" or "scholars") are the subjects of the debate rather than its participants.[28] It is generally two ladies who discuss the relative merits of loving a clerk or a knight, and a judgment on the question is either rendered by the god of love or determined by a judicial duel between two champions who each defend one side of the argument. The oldest of these poems is probably the *Altercatio Phyllidis et Florae*. The other Latin example is the *Romarici montis concilium* (more commonly known as the *Concile de Remiremont*), in which a group of nuns debate the question in a council held at their convent. Four French poems on the same topic exist: the *Jugement d'amour* (often referred to as *Florence et Blancheflor*), *Hueline et Aiglantine*, *Blancheflour et Florence*, and *Melior et Ydoine*. One of the most important aspects of these poems for the subsequent development of courtly poetry is the description of the god of love and his surroundings that they standardized and passed on.

The *jeu-parti* was a shorter poem that hit the peak of its popularity in the second half of the thirteenth century at Arras.[29] Artur Långfors, in his *Recueil général des jeux-partis français*, describes its main characteristics:

> Le jeu-parti, dans son type normal, est une pièce lyrique de six couplets suivis de deux envois: dans le premier couplet, l'un des deux partenaires propose à l'autre une question dilemmatique et, celui-ci ayant fait son choix, soutient lui-même l'alternative restée disponible. Dans les deux envois, chacun des deux partenaires nomme un juge. Il n'y a dans les textes aucune trace d'un jugement que ceux-ci auraient prononcé. (pp. v–vi)

The subject of the *jeu-parti* was almost always a point of love doctrine. Approximately two hundred of these poems remain, in which the debaters argue their positions in alternating stanzas. As Långfors states, no decisions on the questions under discussion have been recorded. He suggests that the naming of a judge "était plutôt une manière d'hommage rendu à des personnages de marque" (p. vii).

Machaut's two judgment poems, the *Jugement dou roy de Behaigne* and the *Jugement dou roy de Navarre*, obviously incorporate many of the essential elements inherited from these earlier genres.[30] From the knight versus clerk debates he adopted the narrative aspect of the story, the use of allegorical figures, and the recording of a decision in the case. From the *jeux-partis* he took the irresolvable nature of the issue and the idea of submitting the question to a nobleman for arbitration. He rejuvenated the old conventions enormously, however, by rounding out the scenario with several of the hallmarks of his *dits amoureux*. As Ernest Hoepffner points out, Machaut's narrator assumes a much greater role in the proceedings. Rather than remaining a witness, he proposes the judge and leads the debaters to him. In *Navarre*, he himself takes part in the debate. As well, the allegorical aspect of the court scene is played down in favor of a more realistic setting and tone. The many concrete details provided give the poem "le caractère d'une aventure vraie et vécue."[31]

Machaut's new formula was clearly a success: his first judgment poem, the *Jugement dou roy de Behaigne*, engendered the *Jugement dou roy de Navarre* as a sequel, and both poems took their places as major works in collections of Machaut's narrative poetry. Christine was therefore invoking a powerful model when she cast her three poems concerning love dilemmas in the form of Machaut's judgment poems, one which many authors up to and including Alain Chartier would imitate.[32] Rather than following the prototype in every detail, however, she operated significant changes on it, and to good effect.

Generic Transformations: Christine's Challenges to the Form of the Debate

Christine's poems challenge the "horizon of expectations"[33] applicable to Machaut's exemplar of the late medieval judgment in two telling ways. Her most obvious change to generic conventions is certainly the reduction of the debate proper in each of her three works: for argumentation, she substitutes storytelling. Of the three, only *Deux amans* constitutes a true debate both in its content and structure. It is the most scholastic by far, demonstrating the rhetorical-legal technique of marshaling evidence in the form of *exempla*. The amount of discussion or argument that actually takes place in *Trois jugemens* is, in contrast, quite minimal. Here, argumentation has yielded in large measure to the history behind the dispute in which each couple is involved. The same can be said of *Poissy:* the exchange between the knight and lady at odds consists mainly of the first-person recounting of their unhappy histories. Unlike the scenario in *Trois jugemens*, the debaters here are not each other's love interest, with the result that they cast their arguments with a somewhat higher degree of detachment. However, surrounding their two stories in the framework of the visit to the convent (which takes up fully half of the text) and making their discussion coterminous with the journey home relegates the debate to the function of an amusement, a way to pass the time, rather than making it the focus of the work as a whole. With its layers of embedded discourse, *Poissy* is emblematic of the whole genre of debate as entertainment, verbal sparring that distracts momentarily from the "real" life in which the debaters and spectators alike are engaged.

A second telling change Christine made to Machaut's model follows on the first: the amount of debate proper having been reduced, its significance is further undercut by the absence of judgments at the end of each poem. None of them renders a decision on the points in contention. Such an obvious shift of emphasis away from the conclusion of a *jugement*, the resolution of a point of doctrine, displaces a concomitantly larger interest onto other parts of the process. One of these is the dynamic between patron and writer. Recalling Långfors's comments on the *jeu-parti*, which also lacks resolution, the naming of an arbitrator becomes much more a question here of honoring a worthy nobleman than of relying on his wisdom. Indeed, all three of Christine's debates are subordinated on a discursive level to an elaborate appeal to the chosen recipient. The patron, along with Christine herself as agent, emerges as the most prominent, if least active, participant in the production. In other words, extratextual and extradiegetic elements are given precedence over the stories themselves: to a considerable extent, these debates are about the act of writing and the art of offering. The miniatures accompanying the texts bear out this interpretation, as many of them depict Christine in the process of presenting the dispute to her patron, with the debaters themselves relegated more or less to the literal margins. The medium becomes the message.

The results of Christine's innovations are to introduce a much greater degree of narrative into a previously static genre, to open a space for critical irony within each text, and to capitalize on its suitability as a commodity for exchange. The next sections address various aspects of these properties.

II

Theme and Variations: Interplay of Form and Content

Sociohistorical Contextualization of the Debate:
The Case of the *Dit de Poissy*

The use of realistic detail to lend a certain verisimilitude to *dits amoureux* was well established before Christine's day. Machaut's *Jugement dou roy de Behaigne* contains several examples of this sort. The scenario that leaves the narrator hidden in some bushes to overhear the knight's and lady's disagreement is plausibly motivated. Clever opening gambits (such as the lady's curious little dog) are constructed to allow the characters to fall naturally into conversation with each other. There is also a detailed and concrete description of the castle at Durbuy, to which Guillaume the narrator leads the disputants in their quest for a judge. Christine's *Debat de deux amans* employs similar techniques, setting the stage for the debate with a realistic scene wherein the debaters and Christine the narrator are all guests at a brilliant social gathering held in a Parisian town house (ll. 82–383). However, neither of these careful backdrops prepares us for the documentary-style opening of the *Dit de Poissy*, which is unique in the way it anchors its debate in an historical construct so elaborate and accurate that it ceases to function as background material and constitutes a major focus—if not *the* major focus—of the poem. The abundance of keenly observed mimetic detail infuses the academic and arid nature of traditional debate with the lifeblood of concrete and recognizable characters and settings, and with a much more vibrant, if still limited, personal voice.

The prologue introducing the trip to the convent in Poissy leads the reader to expect a brief description of the physical site, with the debate to follow shortly. The narrator, speaking to the patron-judge, tells him how, when, and where the case to be judged took place (ll. 29–33). There is nothing surprising in the springtime idyll that follows, either. As in many a conventional opening, the assembled company make an excursion into the countryside, are delighted by the birds and flowers, and turn their conversation to the subject of love.

What is unexpected, however, is the purpose of the outing and the personal motivation for undertaking it: Christine wishes to visit her daughter, who is a nun at the Dominican convent in Poissy, and has gathered some friends to ride there with her.[34] Precedents for mixing descriptive reportage with dramatic dialogue can be found both in Machaut's *Jugement dou roy de Navarre* and in Boccaccio's *Decameron*, for example. In both works the bleak and detailed picture of the ravages of the plague contrasts starkly with the lighthearted entertainments that the protagonists undertake to refresh the spirit. The visit to the convent in *Poissy* differs from those models in that it develops a topic bearing no immediately obvious thematic or causal connection to the story that follows; moreover, it extends this passage to such length that it occupies almost as many lines of the text as the debate, which is, after all, the supposedly primary subject matter.

The description of the priory at Poissy and of the life of the nuns there is not a chronicle because it does not recount any events of historical significance. The visit is made for personal reasons, and Christine is reporting on the day-to-day functioning of the convent. Nevertheless, she gives what passes as an eyewitness account of an important and prestigious institution of the day and writes with such concern for detail and accuracy that her *dit* should be considered an early foray on her part into the writing of annals or history. In an article on the development of Christine as an historian, Nadia Margolis points out that Christine's interest in such subject matter is evident even in her earliest poems.[35] By the beginning of the fifteenth century, when the judgment poems were composed, she was manipulating historical constructs for didactic purposes. The fictional founding of a chivalric order in the *Dit de la rose* (1402) allows an admonition to men to defend the honor of women. One hundred short historical narratives in the *Epistre d'Othéa* (around 1400) were used to instruct her son and other readers. She also freely mixed history with other sorts of material: the *Epistre's* examples are each followed by a gloss and an allegory; the *Mutacion de Fortune* of 1403 is a "24,000-line journey through Christine's life in relationship to the history of the world."[36] The allegorical tale of the building of a fortress in the *Cité des dames* (1404–5) affords the opportunity to give the life stories of both real and legendary women. Unlike Froissart, Christine did not abandon lyric poetry to turn to didactic works only in the later stages of her career. Her most purely historical work, the *Fais et bonnes meurs du sage roy Charles V,* was written in 1404 and was followed by more lyric poetry, including the *Livre du Duc des vrais amans* and the *Cent balades d'amant et de dame.*

The autobiographical elements of the *Dit de Poissy* cannot be fully confirmed. The information that Christine's daughter was a Dominican sister at the cloister in Poissy is corroborated by a passage in *L'Avision Christine* in which Dame Philosophie reviews for Christine the blessings of the latter's life, including the children of whom she should rightfully be proud.[37] But did Christine actually undertake a visit to this daughter in April 1400? Whether or not the trip took place as described, Christine's account of the priory is extremely accurate and could well be based on firsthand knowledge. The *Dit de Poissy* is frequently cited as an authority in descriptions of the priory and independent historical and archival sources confirm the information she gives.[38]

Some background information might be useful before discussing the conditions Christine described in 1400. The house was founded by Philippe IV (le Bel) in 1304, in honor of the recently canonized Saint Louis, who had been born in Poissy. The church, consecrated in 1330 and dedicated by Philippe VI de Valois, was built to proportions suitable for a cathedral; in size and elevation, it apparently rivaled Tours, Poitiers, and Bayeux.[39] The convent maintained an apartment for the use of royal visitors, and the prioress, chosen by the elder sisters of the house, also had her own suite of rooms separate from the dormitories. The institution, well endowed and maintained by the kings of France, controlled considerable revenues and properties.

The women allowed to enter were a select group. The plans originally called for a total of 120 nuns, with the number to increase to two hundred, but the community never grew to be that large. During Philippe le Bel's lifetime, he exercised the prerogative of approving the admittance of each young woman who wanted to enter. After his death, the charter stated, the sisters themselves could admit suitable candidates of noble families. For admission of commoners, however, royal permission was required.[40] The nuns would therefore have certainly been what the text calls *de belles sortes* (*Poissy,* l. 226). Philippe had intended them to be learned as well. In a letter written in 1299 to the Dominican "Provincial" of France, whom he addresses as brother Guillaume, the king stated that especially in the early stages it was important to choose women who knew how to read and sing, were of good health, could withstand the rigors of the religious life, and would be capable of instructing by word and example the novices who would join them.[41] Hinnebusch adds that when founding Poissy, Philippe sought to provide for the intellectual welfare of the nuns by sending at least four friars on book-hunting expeditions to copy or commission the copying of works for the sisters' library. He also founded a small priory near the monastery for thirteen friars who would be the spiritual and intellectual mentors of the nuns.[42] Some nuns brought books into the convent with them, as part of their dowry, and the sisters themselves copied and illuminated manuscripts primarily for their own use.

The information Christine provides about the convent in the *Dit de Poissy* paints an accurate and fairly complete picture of life within its walls. A brief review of some of the details she mentions shows how precise her descriptions are. For example, Christine indicates in line 225 that she and her party needed special permission to enter the convent and visit with the nuns, as the law of enclosure was quite strictly enforced. As Christine says, the sisters themselves never left the premises: *Ne je ne sçay se il leur va grevant, / Mais jamais jour pour pluye ne pour vent / De la n'istront et ne voient souvent / Les gens estranges* (ll. 309–12). The privilege of entering the convent was, in fact, extended on occasion to royalty, higher clergy, and friends and benefactors of the establishment,[43] but it must indeed have been an unusual request, to visit twice in one day (*d'entrer ens .ij. fois n'est pas usage, / N'a estrangiers ne a ceulx du lignage, / Non en un jour*, ll. 646–48). The special privilege extended to Christine's group would be plausible as an indication of their close ties with the court. It is not surprising that the gentlemen in the party were not allowed to see the dormitories (ll. 453–56); as she says, no men were allowed in to serve the nuns in any capacity (ll. 299–308), and the law of cloister actually stated that no one was to enter those parts of the monastery inhabited by the nuns. The sisters would have spoken to outsiders through the *treillices / De fer doubles a fenestres coulices* (ll. 328–29) in their parlor.

Marie de Bourbon, named in line 251, was the seventh prioress of the convent, holding that position from 1380 until her death in 1401.[44] At the time that Christine's daughter was in residence, the prioress had under her care the royal princess Marie de France (l. 281), daughter of Charles VI and Isabeau de Bavière. Charity Cannon Willard speculates that Christine's daughter entered at the same time as the princess, in 1397: "As it was the custom for the king to provide dowries for a certain number of young women to enter with his daughter, this would have provided Christine's daughter with a welcome opportunity."[45] The reference to the *gentil[s] femme[s]* (ll. 283–89) who kept the princess company there is in keeping with the high standards set for those allowed to join the community.

The layout of the convent, which Christine describes as the nuns take their visitors on a tour, corresponds closely to a late eighteenth-century plan that both Edmond Bories and S. Moreau-Rendu reproduce. The large cloister where the visit began (ll. 383–404) opened off the refectory, to which they went next (ll. 405–13). This refectory was a splendid hall of very large dimensions, vaulted with Gothic arches; it was used as a chapel until the church was finished and thereafter often served as a meeting place for assemblies.[46] The fountains that so impressed Christine (ll. 422–33) were an important convenience for the establishment. King Philippe had assured the water supply in 1303–4 by granting the convent possession of the springs at Migneaux, a small neighboring village, and pledging that he and his successors would maintain the system of pipes that led the water into the nuns' residence. Bories quotes a document relating to the position of *plommier*, which states that running water was provided:

> Dedenz le couvent des dites soeurs et par toutes les branches où elles se dirigent, en la cuisine, en la despense et au lavoir du grand cloître des soeurs, entre le grand cloître et le cloître de l'infirmerie des dites soeurs, dans la tour dedans et dehors sus les frères du dit lieue, et entre les deux chambres du roy et retournant vers la piscine.[47]

Records show that the repair and maintenance of the water conduits was seen to by Charles VI in 1396 and 1407, around the time that Christine's visit would have been made.

The church must have been as impressive as Christine describes it (ll. 462–513). Built in High Gothic style, it was approximately one hundred meters long, forty-five meters wide at the transept, with thirty-meter vaults supported by flying buttresses. The public entrance was on the north side, into the crossing that gave access to the nave. The nuns entered by a door in the south end of the crossing that opened onto the cloister. The *closture* (l. 489) that Christine mentions as separating the public and private sides of the church was a feature of Dominican churches in general, where a screen hid the friars or nuns from the other worshipers. The decoration was sumptuous. Christine speaks of *maint chef . . . de maint saint* entombed there (ll. 465–66); over the centuries, indeed, many noblemen and illustrious members of the convent were buried in that location, including Louis and Jean, sons of Saint Louis, the princess Marie, daughter of Charles VI, and Marie de Bourbon, whose tomb was to the right of the screen that separated the choir from the nave. Philippe le Bel's heart was buried in the choir, although he had died at Fontainebleau. The high altar was placed on the spot where Saint Louis was said to have been born; in the late fourteenth century, it was decorated with an ivory altarpiece that was a gift of Jean, duke of Berry, and is now preserved at the Louvre.[48] Also at the Louvre is a black-and-white marble statue of Marie de Bourbon that used to stand on the spot where she was interred.

Further corroboration of Christine's account is unnecessary. Despite the occasional hyperbolic and lyrical embellishments, it is obviously written with an appreciation for precision and factual reporting. The sheer length of this section and the wealth of information it contains should not obscure the fact that Christine's concern for anchoring her *Dit* realistically to the world outside the text is manifested elsewhere as well. Her predilection for concrete and topical detail pervades the conventional springtime-outing topos, for example, in references such as the *bel chastel qui a nom Saint Germain / Qu'on dit en Laye* (ll. 167–68): to reach Poissy from Paris in the Middle Ages, one would, in fact, come upon the Seine with its green islands (ll. 131–36) and traverse the forest of Laye that Christine's group rides through (ll. 169–213).

In a more thematically charged vein, however, historical detail also enters the debate sequence in a way that infuses the dramatic situation with a great deal more immediacy than can be found in prototypes of poems with historically grounded settings. In comparison with Machaut's *Jugement dou roy de Behaigne*, for example, which *Poissy* so resembles, the circumstances regarding the lady's lover have changed: in *Poissy* what prevents her from seeing him is not that he has died but rather that he has been imprisoned as a hostage. While she might have chosen any number of unspecified foreign skirmishes and countries, Christine makes him one of those held as a result of the ill-starred campaign at Nicopolis in 1396, a defeat recent and devastating enough still to rankle in French circles at the turn of the century.

Christine's brief summary of the crusade and its results (ll. 1261–96) recalls passages in the works of other writers of the period. Eustache Deschamps wrote several poems on the subject; Jean Froissart treated it at length in his *Chroniques*, as did the author of *Le Livre des Fais de Bouciquaut*.[49] The lament of Christine's lady in particular finds echoes in Boucicaut's memoirs. Having described the grief experienced by the parents of the victims and prisoners, Boucicaut compares it with the enduring devastation of their wives, mentioning various noblewomen by name. Christine's heroine would fit well among their number. According to Boucicaut,

> La fille au seigneur de Coucy ... avoit cause de dueil avoir; ... et tant d'autres dames et damoiselles du royaume de France que grant pitié estoit d'ouÿr leurs plains et regrais, les quieulx ne sont mie a plusieurs d'elles, quoy que il ait ja grant piece, ancore finez, ne a leur vie croy que ilz ne fineront; car le cuer qui bien aime de legier pas n'oublie.[50]

The tone of this prose as well as its content resembles closely that of *Poissy*, including the axiomatic nature of the final phrase. Neither the love nor the unhappiness that Christine's lady feels has been dimmed by the years elapsed since she last saw her lover, even though the argument against her in the debate holds that time and absence will surely make her forget. Such parallels between the two texts remind us that certain scholars have speculated that Christine might be the author of the *Livre des Fais de Bouciquaut*. The theory was first put forward by Kervyn de Lettenhove and was revived by Jean-Louis Picherit, although most critics, including Denis Lalande, the work's latest editor, disagree.[51]

Whether or not one subscribes to the idea, it is undeniable that Christine had a perceptive annalist's (as well as analyst's) eye and proved her capacity to write accurate factual material. The nugget of information about Nicopolis, the many details of topography near Paris, and the privileged, insider's view of the religious house at Poissy must have made the *Dit* much more vivid and topical to her patrons and readers and raised its entertainment value considerably; what might have passed for timeworn material was rendered much more immediate by its contextualization within their own time and place. In Christine's hands the device of the realistic backdrop allows her both to breathe new life into an old formula and to challenge the cohesive limits of the *dit*.

Transtextual Readings: A Debate among Debates

Despite Christine's large debt to Machaut and regardless of the many traits the three judgment poems share, they are far from lacking in individuality: each plays on the rich heritage of the "historical family"[52] that they belong to by privileging certain generic traits over others, and each capitalizes on this differentiation to treat quite different perspectives on the intricacies of love. I am proposing here that the varying generic models invoked in each case redeploy the subject matter to expose its varying facets.

One simple and mildly provocative formula might be to say that *Deux amans* treats love from a theoretical viewpoint, *Trois jugemens* from a practical viewpoint, and *Poissy* from the comparative perspective of contemplative versus courtly life. These capsule summaries reflect affinities in each work with very different traditions of poetry. *Trois jugemens*, for example, is very reminiscent of the *jeu parti* and could be considered, in fact, a "narrativized" elaboration of that older genre. It replaces the stanzaic structure with freewheeling octosyllables and embodies the abstract issues debated by dueling poets in the form of unhappy lovers, yet draws on exactly the same list of delicate relationship questions in need of resolution. Because the ill-used lovers in *Trois jugemens* speak for themselves, there is no pretense of objectivity or neutrality, and the argument is much more highly personalized than the academic exercise in rhetoric that constitutes the *jeu parti*. In choosing to rehearse the arguments of three couples, the narrator actually presents six different opinions, effectively multiplying the plurivocal nature of such a debate. Putting even conventional complaints and quibbles in the mouths of vexed lovers renders them more intimate and more piquant in a gossipy way. But the clerkly voice of the fictionalized Christine intervening between stories and commenting occasionally in a caustic tone distances the reader or listener from too much involvement with the protagonists. As a result, the issues are trivialized: they become vicissitudes in the love lives of individuals rather than subjects worthy of debate by learned authorities. The accumulation of three such case histories each following on the heels of the other emphasizes their interchangeable nature, particularly as all the ladies complain of the same problem, namely, infidelity. Devalorizing the subject matter, in turn, has the effect of giving more prominence to Christine-the-narrator's role, as her commentary and task as court reporter are what cement the autonomous parts into a larger whole.

We have noted that the amount of debate as such is much reduced in both *Trois jugemens* and *Poissy*. In contrast, however, it constitutes the major portion of *Deux amans*. Here, debate is represented as a serious intellectual exercise and gives Christine a format that allows her to establish her credentials within the academic style. The two major debaters are men. Both speak only in theoretical terms. It is implied that each has had his own love experience (in fact, at the social gathering where the story begins, we see the young squire in thrall to the compelling attractions of the lady he loves), but when they present their respective sides of the case, they build their evidence on historical, mythological, and legendary lovers of various kinds, not on personal history.

Aside from the references to prominent contemporary figures (and a dissenting voice to which I will return), the arguments of this debate would not be out of place in the *Roman de la Rose* or in Machaut's *Jugement dou roy de Behaigne*. The issue itself, the style of argumentation, and the evidence adduced by the contestants place *Deux amans* squarely in the tradition of the opposition between rational maturity and hot-blooded youth. Both protagonists—one brimming with youthful exuberance and charm, the other the embodiment of seasoned power and reason—are carefully described as ideal specimens, fully worthy lovers in their own right, and each can therefore speak with an authoritative voice. They stand only for their respective stages in life, however, and are so little individualized that they lack only the abstract noun for a name that would make them allegorical figures. Were this a debate *à la* Machaut, the squire would undoubtedly be Jeunesse, and the knight, perhaps Las-du-monde, the world-weary one, or simply Expérience.

Certainly *Deux amans* is much more explicitly didactic than either *Trois jugemens* or *Poissy*. In a prologue that also sets the tone of a *consolation*, one reads that this work will be all about love,[53] preparing the ground for a modest *ars amatoria* of sorts. The major speeches are examples of very learned discourse: the young man's argument is full of rhetorical questions as he moves through lists of lovers ennobled and strengthened by Love. He is obviously conscious and proud of his tactics, claiming to have proven his point irrefutably.[54] The poem's didactic quality is reinforced by the ornamentation in the manuscripts containing the text. In British Library Harley 4431 (the base manuscript for this edition), for example, paragraph markers in the margin to the left of the text draw attention to places where proper names are used by either speaker to enumerate worthy examples.[55] Erudition is thus displayed to dazzle and impress both the ear and the eye.

The *Deux amans* may well be the earliest of the three debates. Its stock elements, its thematic scope, and its elevated style all make this debate more reminiscent of the inherited model than either of the others. Such a hypothesis is supported by its position as the first of the three debates in each of the manuscripts that contain all of them, especially in light of the fact that Christine's presentation manuscripts of collected works are generally organized according to date of composition. Nevertheless, as the first treatment of the theme the reader encounters, *Deux amans* also enjoys a certain primacy of place. As a set piece discussing romantic love in its largest dimensions, it makes a suitable introduction and backdrop to the other two debates, which, in the wake of *Deux amans*, read like variations on a theme and seem somewhat whimsical or idiosyncratic in nature.

Although *Deux amans* provides a useful yardstick against which to measure *Trois jugemens* and *Poissy*, the interpretive force moves in both directions and requires that one consider each of Christine's judgment poems in the context of the others. When the frame of reference is widened to include all three, the reader gains additional insight into them individually and collectively.

To understand the larger perspective attained by reading them as a group, one can begin again with their lack of resolution. None of them answer the questions they pose, at least not explicitly. But in the absence of an intra- or extratextual decision made by a judge, these poems provide their own arbiters and answers. Take, for example, the request made by the unhappy woman in *Trois jugemens* that her case be heard by "other ladies" before a judge pronounces on the case.[56] Her jury of ladies is not provided for; instead, Christine suggests that they appeal to Jean de Werchin for a decision. But the female jury does exist in the form of the lady spectator of the *Deux amans*, she who speaks at the midpoint to debunk the seriousness of all such tortured debate and decry the posing of men who moan a little too loudly about the pain of love.

Likewise, the knight and squire in *Deux amans* have presented their cases equally well by the end of their contest, and there is no indication of whom the duke of Orléans, Christine's choice of judge in this instance, would declare the winner. The evidence of *Trois jugemens* and *Poissy* tips the balance, however, if the young noblemen and women heard lamenting therein count as further examples of *les bons vaillans* mentioned by both the knight and the squire (ll. 1108 and 1563). These contemporary lovers prove without a doubt that love is painful. *Trois jugemens* and *Poissy* provide the anecdotal evidence needed to shore up the side of the knight; his carefully constructed roster of unhappy legendary and mythological lovers finds corroboration in the lived experience of his own (albeit fictional) peers.

In the three debate poems, then, the characters find their inscribed judges just outside the confines of their own work, and Christine, as the author of them all, writes the ultimate judgment in the form of cautionary tales. Based on experiential evidence, she answers the question posed in theoretical terms in *Deux amans*, proving incontrovertibly that love causes more grief than pleasure. The overall conclusion of the group as a whole—that love is definitely not the ennobling force that callow youth and most preceding poetry would have it be—is no surprise to Christine's readers, who can discern this attitude in many of her poetic works. What we do learn in considering these poems together is to look beyond the boundaries of any single text in her corpus, for she often appends a final word or rumination, a parallel text or sequel to her works, short or long. One can argue that like the debate poems, indeed like much late medieval French literature in general, every one of Christine's poems has others it plays off against, and that the dynamic of such transtextuality brings much more to the poem than when it is considered in isolation.

These debate poems cover the same ground—try the same case, one might say—from three very different perspectives. When taken together, as their shared thematic and formal elements and their manuscript arrangement suggest we should read them, they stand in what can be understood as a dialogic relationship to one another, replicating on a transtextual level the aesthetic and structure of the individual pieces, creating a debate among debates. There is movement from each autonomous poem outward, toward the extradiegetic world in the form of a patron. However, even without the explicit generation of one text by the next in a linear progression, as in Machaut, there is also movement among the poems, pointing from one to another, raising the interest of the listener for more and sending the reader back to the manuscript. Given how close their dates of composition are, given the intertextual references among them, the debate poems are designed to be read against one another, as well as in the context of the love debate tradition or the rest of Christine's corpus. Much like her groupings of *formes fixes*, they constitute a block of text with its own logic and with articulations on several levels, one to be heard or read in part or in whole.

The Self-Destructing Love Debate: Women's Voices as Agents of Dissent

So far we have discussed the effects of the changes Christine brings to the *jugement* tradition by the way in which she manipulates its generic conventions and inscribes each discrete example into a larger group of three. Now we must consider the implications of the novel perspectives she brings to the subject matter in the form of voices usually excluded from such deliberations. These voices are female voices, principally those of a rebellious narrator found throughout the three poems and of an impertinent, skeptical observer in the *Deux amans*; moreover, the very presence of the nuns in *Poissy* and the sensible objections of the women in *Trois jugemens* introduce in the text heteroglossic layers that help undermine to a significant degree the assumptions on which the whole genre is predicated.

As mentioned, the lack of a verdict in Christine's debates leaves the reader with an overriding impression of strife, unhappiness, and thwarted desire. Because no decision is forthcoming, the disputants are locked in a stalemate with the hope of resolution endlessly deferred. The ensuing picture of love as the debaters have experienced it is mostly gloomy. They are mired in a static, unproductive, contentious situation, and the sheer weight of evidence from their stories points out that the gratification and joy of any new relationship will most probably degrade into a similar morass of dissatisfaction. The knight of the *Deux amans* makes this point specifically, in his direct address to the audience of *jeunes gens* outside the frame of the story, saying: *Quieulx que soient d'amours les commençailles / Tous jours y a piteuses deffinailles. / Fuyez, fuyez, / Yceste amour, jeunes gens! et voyez / Comment on est pour lui mal avoyez!* (ll. 834–38). The notable exception to the collective unhappiness is the knight's opponent in debate, the squire, who is still in the first full flush of love's excitement. The knight's greater experience, however, suggests that just as the young man must age, so, too, must his naive optimism give way to the realization that love inevitably entails grief.

In the end then, the debates present *fin'amor* in the same jaundiced light as it is portrayed in Christine's other writings: love of this kind is a folly that leads to disaster and despair, particularly for the woman involved.[57] While there are no explicit statements to this end in any of our three texts, various factors conspire to reinforce the lessons of the debaters' stories. Reason, the traditional adversary of love, is praised as a desirable quality, one that alleviates and counteracts the damage love can do.[58] The sort of dalliance the young nobles are involved in is often referred to as foolish love (*fole amour*), and they suffer from "loving excessively" (*trop amer*).

Counter once again to the standard model provided by male authors of love poetry, Christine's narrator chooses significantly to present herself not as a lover nor in any way a servant of love. Rather, she goes to considerable lengths to disassociate herself from personal experience of idle or illicit love, using a variety of distancing techniques. In *Trois jugemens*, this distance is rendered chiefly by a refusal to take on any role in the debate beyond that of intermediary between the judge and the couples in need of arbitration; the narrator, despite a reputation for wisdom, will not play moderator herself. In *Deux Amans*, her distance from the debate is dramatized in physical terms by her removal from the action. In the prologue, she chooses to remain on the sidelines of the elegant soirée where the knight and the squire meet in a company of urbane, flirtatious guests; during the debate itself, she virtually effaces herself to let the principals take the floor. In *Poissy*, finally, her detachment from the world of sensual, romantic love is manifested by her commitment to two parallel realms of experience, the maternal love she bears her daughter and the spiritual love of God that mother and daughter share with the nuns at the priory of Poissy.

One can conclude that Christine's love debates hardly promote the very stuff they speak of, a contradiction which on the face of it produces an unlikely and unproductive literary agenda. In one sense, however, she is simply returning the debate to its roots in the *jeu-parti*, a genre intended as a rhetorical exercise and an amusement. She is writing to please her patrons, supplying them with well-written samples of the kind of disputes entertained at the courts of love. The outcome is unimportant; rather, the pleasure derives from the poignancy of each deliciously difficult situation and the dilemma of choosing between equally unsatisfying alternatives.

The debates also challenge the validity of the pursuit they depict on a much bolder level than simply that of formal properties. Through the use of women's voices, which produce both verbal and structural irony, they force the reevaluation of a highly stylized and literary phenomenon in light of lived experience. In this regard, Christine might be described as a pragmatist of the first water. Many of her courtly writings evoke the practical exigencies of a noblewoman's life to throw light on the idealized *fin'amor* of romance and lyric, revealing the faultlines that make illicit alliances such treacherous terrain for a lady dependent on her good name as a guarantor of social standing and a productive life. In the *Duc des vrais amans*, for example, written a few years after the debates, the stern moral voice of the governess Sebile de Monthault, Dame de la Tour, admonishes her former charge regarding *[l]es perilz et dangiers qui sont en tele amour, lesquieulx sont sans nombre.*[59] Not only does the young lady risk offending God, but she also—and, dare one say, more important on the quotidian level—risks compromising her respectability and her authority over those she governs. In even more stentorian tones, the voice of the narrator Christine exhorts in *La Cité des dames:*

> Enfin, vous toutes, mesdames, . . . [r]epoussez ces hypocrites enjôleurs qui cherchent à vous prendre par leurs beaux discours et par toutes les ruses imaginables votre bien le plus précieux, c'est-à-dire votre honneur et l'excellence de votre réputation! Oh! fuyez, mesdames, fuyez cette folle passion qu'ils exaltent auprès de vous! Fuyez-la! Pour l'amour de Dieu, fuyez! Rien de bon ne peut vous en arriver.[60]

Her words recall the admonition to flee uttered by the knight in *Deux amans,* as quoted above. But the warning has moved beyond the dry, schoolmasterish dictum proffered as general wisdom by maturity to callow youth, taking on an urgency and a specificity that make it much more compelling. The lady is informed of just exactly what she stands to lose, the pleasures of love are reduced to pretty speeches (*beaux discours*) and tricks (*toutes les ruses imaginables*), and seductive suitors are labeled as nothing more than hypocritical flatterers (*hypocrites enjôleurs*). From the subversion of romance topoi in the *Duc* to the overt didacticism of the *Cité*, Christine is engaged, to use Roberta Krueger's phrase, in "demystifying the masculinist love ethos."[61]

Such demystification is articulated most clearly in the debates by the lady who speaks at the midpoint of *Deux amans*. Her very presence as a spectator in the story is motivated by Christine's concern with propriety: she suggests that two female companions go with her into the garden to witness the debate, because, as she states, *qui racoise / De mesdisans le murmure et la noise / Moult sages est* (ll. 390–92). When first invited by the knight to declare her position on the nature of love, the lady demurs, deferring to the knight and insisting that he can speak better than she (ll. 412–21). After having heard him out, however, she no longer hesitates: in her opinion, the suffering of men for love is greatly exaggerated, as are the reports of their death from such ills. Such excesses are recounted in romances such as the *Roman de la Rose*, she states, although in that work one also finds Reason, who tries to show the lover the error of his ways (ll. 958–77).[62] In *Deux amans*, the lady represents the voice of reason. In a pointed display of dry humor, she states that she has never been told the location of those cemeteries where all the martyrs for love are buried (ll. 987–93). The crucial distinction, then, is between fact and fiction, between real life and a parlor game. Men's protestations are nothing more than a hyperbolic form of entertainment.

She adds in a conciliatory tone that it is not her intent to undermine the knight's speech nor to deny the possibility that what he says might be true: *Pour desdire voz dis et vo complaint / Ne le dy pas, / Sauve vo paix, ne je ne me debas / Qu'estre ne puist* (ll. 995–98). But in fact she has done just that. Significantly, the men do not rise to the challenge; they neither engage nor rebut what the lady says, despite—or because of—the fact that she throws into question the entire raison-d'être of their debate. They speak only to each other, and as a result the lady's words constitute a speech act *outside* the debate, a metadiscursive commentary addressed to quite a different audience than the debate itself. She launches a new discourse, one which invalidates the terms of the old matrix. She does not go as far as Chartier's *Belle dame sans mercy* or Christine's narrator in the *Cité*; nevertheless, the logical implications of her speech hint broadly at the harsh assessment her fictional successors make concerning the perils specific to women in courtly love and at the redefinition of the lady's role that they propose as a result.

Orality, Reading, and Writing in the Debate Poems

In their dynamic relationship with both oral performance and textual tradition, these poems are a marvelous example of the multifaceted nature of literary experience in the late Middle Ages. On the one hand, they draw attention to oral and aural transmission on two fronts, first by purporting to record a spoken debate, and second by assuming that the audience will hear the poem read aloud. On the other hand, they simultaneously valorize the written word, both in their self-conscious references to the process of composition and the role of the writer, and in their carefully designed presentation in the codex, which demonstrates a fine awareness of visual appeal and intertextuality. Other critics have commented on the complex interaction of the written, the spoken, and the heard in late medieval texts like Christine's debates. Because of its aesthetic based on rupture, the *dit* has been isolated as representative of a new type of text: according to Cerquiglini, "Le *dit* marque ... l'apparition d'un nouvel âge pour le texte médiéval, âge où celui-ci passe progressivement du status d'objet auditif, qu'il était aux époques antérieures, à un status d'objet auditif et visuel."[63] In a broader view, Joyce Coleman has recently challenged most convincingly the widely accepted theory of a progression in medieval literature from "oral" to "literate" and the mutually exclusive nature of those two modes of reception. She proposes instead that the "mixedness" of a stable written text intended to be read aloud to an audience—that is, of aurality—represents much more than an intermediate stage. Public reading, she argues, constituted a favored and common practice among privileged audiences of France and England.[64]

The prologue of *Deux amans* explicitly addresses the pleasure to be derived from hearing good material read aloud. In an ingenious twist on the topos concerning David and his ability to calm the wrath of God with his lyre, Christine places the sound of reading on a par with instrumental music:

> ... et j'ay leu en un livre
> Que quant David, qui la loy Dieu volt suivre,
> Vouloit estre de tristece delivre,
> Lors de sa lire
> Moult doulcement jouoit, et souvent l'ire
> Il rappaisoit de Dieu; et oÿr lire
> Choses plaisans font souvent joye eslire
> Aux escoutens. (ll. 33–40)

The narrator's knowledge of the David story, we might note, comes from an authoritative written source, which she read to herself. But the effect on the emotions is here associated with the aural. These lines strongly recall a passage from Machaut's *Prologue* which employs the lyre/wrath (*lire/l'ire*) rhyme.[65] Her addition of *lire*, "to read," to the list of rhyme words evokes the notion of "musique naturele" introduced by Eustache Deschamps less than a decade earlier in his *Art de dictier*; what he meant by "natural music" was the sonorous, musical quality of spoken language and more specifically of poetry.[66] A pleasing text well read, she says, can bring joy to the hearts of the listeners. So confident is she of the worth of her work that she is sure it will be "heard" by French, German, and other audiences, by anyone who understands *rommans* (ll. 54–55).

On the codicological level, however, quite apart from the content of the poems, numerous paralinguistic elements in the manuscripts support the notion that these texts were meant to engage the eye as well as the ear. Each debate is decorated with a well-realized miniature at the head of the first column of text, always with a scene appropriate to the content of the poem and often foregrounding, quite literally, the narrator/author figure's role as intermediary and reporter. Paragraph marks signal the beginning of direct discourse as the first-person voice shifts from one character to another, indicate transitions in the narrative or argument, and direct attention to lines which contain the names of illustrious exemplars. Running titles above the text allow the reader to locate a particular item with ease, as does the table of contents found at the beginning of several manuscripts. Taken together, these elements constitute an interpretive schema superimposed on the linguistic body of the text.

A comparison of the markings in different versions of a text can reveal their importance as a hermeneutic tool. One small example concerning paragraph marks will suffice to demonstrate how paralinguistic features can influence the reading of the text. In the *Deux amans*, the lady who delivers rebellious remarks at the midpoint of the poem is indisputably a minor character. Despite her limited role, however, her skeptical opinions sit uneasily between the two long disquisitions, which never question the centrality of love in the life of noblemen and women. Given her troublesome interventions, the manner in which her role is treated visually, in the form of paragraph marks, is instructive in understanding how much importance she should be accorded. The manuscripts appear to display three levels of awareness of her presence: the three *L* manuscripts (Chantilly, Musée Condé 492; Bibliothèque Nationale f.fr. 12779 and f.fr. 604) give her the least attention, marking the transition at the end of the knight's passage shortly before the lady begins to speak, but not the lady's own words; manuscripts *R* (British Library Harley 4431), *D* (Bibliothèque Nationale f.fr. 835, 606, 836, 605), *S1* (Brussels, Bibliothèque Royale 11034), and *S2* (Bibliothèque Nationale f.fr. 1740), by contrast, mark the spot where her direct discourse starts, just as they do for both male debaters; beyond that, however, *S1* alone marks the points much earlier in the poem where she is first introduced (l. 385) and where the knight first asks her to pronounce on the issue (l. 412), flagging her as a significant figure and anticipating her active role later. The effect is to raise the status of the lady to one much more on a par with the other speakers than in the other versions, which allow her to disappear more thoroughly into the text. The extra paragraph marks in *S1* throw her dissenting words into relief, upsetting the symmetry and the self-satisfaction of the exchange between the men. The visual interacts intimately with the linguistic at these spots, transmitting the interpretation that the scribe of manuscript *S1* wanted to bring to light.

Punctuation marks thus reveal a layer of mediation between the words on the vellum and us, the reader or hearer, thereby forcing us to consider the filters through which we understand the works. In a speculative realm, however, they should also be considered in light of the performative space opened by the text. The original function of punctuation was, in the words of M. B. Parkes, a "form of direction for the oral performance of the written text."[67] Given that *Deux amans* explicitly addresses the question of how the text is communicated, one might posit that the position of paragraph marks in the text influenced the way in which the text was read aloud. In any text, markers cause the reader to pause in her delivery, to emphasize what is highlighted by means of changes in intonation patterns or pitch of voice. Vocal stress, too, can underline a character's presence, bringing it much more to the fore and giving it much more life than when it is subsumed by the flow of the narrative.

Christine's *dits* thus operate in a middle ground between *oïr* and *lire*, in the space of *oïr lire*, or hearing something read. This state of overlapping orality and literacy has been studied more for the vernacular text of the High Middle Ages in Europe than for the fourteenth and fifteenth centuries, about which much remains to be said.[68] But to close this introduction, I would like to shift focus briefly from modes of transmission to modes of production, to point out another current in the texts that speaks to their reception. As with other late medieval French authors conscious of their writerly status, the hearing/reading conjunction in Christine is complemented by a third term. The verbs *oïr* and *lire* are linked unavoidably with *écrire*, meaning both the art of composition and the use of ink and paint to give shape to the text and the book to be read. The listener or reader is frequently reminded of the physicality of the object in which the stories they hear are inscribed, of writing as a form of communication, and of the author as medium and creator.

Oral communication lies at the heart of these poems because of the very nature of debate and the rhetorical tradition: they manifest what Walter Ong calls the "academic orality" that permeates much medieval literature.[69]

The final product of Christine's (fictional) mandate to report on debates held in her hearing consists, to a significant extent, of transcribed rhetorical performances, particularly in *Deux amans* and *Poissy*. However, Christine also sometimes shifts the medium of debate to a written form: the quarreling lovers of the *Trois jugemens* communicate at times by means of letters, anticipating the epistolary romance in the *Cent balades d'amant et de dame* and even her own instigation of the *querelle* concerning Jean de Meun's *Roman de la Rose*.

Her self-representation in the text, however, is the key element in bringing the process of writing to the forefront; although a character in the story, her narrator is associated almost exclusively with the textual element, with the process of writing, which she stresses as her principal function in relation to the works. Christine is present primarily *en escrit*, an anagram she employs at the end of the *Cent Balades*, the first work in the manuscripts containing the debate poems.[70]

Furthermore, Christine's notion of the role of the author includes that of editor, compiler, and designer. She writes with an awareness of her corpus as a whole, as is evident in other works, for example, in the self-referential remarks that identify the governess's letter in *Le Livre des Trois vertus* as a passage borrowed from the *Duc des vrais amans*.[71] Similarly, the mutually illuminating nature and complementary properties of the debate poems are further evidence of Christine's evolving publishing project, that nascent phenomenon of late medieval manuscript culture.[72] More specifically in the case of our base text for this edition, the project is the book, now Harley 4431, which she had carefully written, ordered, and ornamented for Queen Isabeau de Bavière, with an eye to its internal coherence as well as to its completeness.

The fourteenth and fifteenth centuries were an age in which vernacular book culture took on a new life.[73] Christine's texts, like others of her day, reflect interplay between orality and literacy on many levels and dramatize the relationship of author to codex just as they do the relationship of text to intended audience. The literary experience they embody includes that of production as well as reception. By virtue of such preoccupations, Christine and her near contemporaries participate in the emergence of modern notions of authorship and literature as a fixed product attributable to a particular creative mind.

III

Philology and Codicology

Manuscripts

The *Dit de Poissy* and the *Livre des Trois jugemens* are preserved in five manuscripts, while *Deux amans* survives in the same five, as well as in two additional copies as a single work. The assessment of existing copies for these as well as for Christine's other works has been greatly facilitated by recent and ongoing codicological investigation into the manuscripts produced by her workshop. Several thorough descriptions of the major manuscripts are available,[74] and much has been done to clarify their dates of compilation and the hands in which they are written.

For the purposes of this edition I have adopted the *sigla* established by Laidlaw for the principal collections of Christine's works, rather than other designations such as those of Maurice Roy or Eric Hicks. In Laidlaw's explanation of the early manuscripts as compendia of Christine's works, *D* stands for the "Collection du duc," *L* for the "Livre de Christine," and *R* for the "Collection de la reine." These labels are more descriptive and express more clearly than the earlier designations the content of the manuscripts and the relationship among them. As Laidlaw states, "The possible confusion which results from using a new set of abbreviations is more than outweighed by the advantage of a system which is unambiguous and readily comprehensible."[75]

For the two single-work copies of *Deux amans*, I have established my own *sigla*. These are *S1* for Brussels, Bibliothèque Royale 11034, and *S2* for Paris, Bibliothèque Nationale f.fr. 1740. I have chosen to represent them as members of the same family because, while they are not identical (despite Roy's assertion), they bear more of a resemblance to each other, by virtue of their format and decoration, than to any of the other manuscripts individually or as a group. The letter *S* stands for single-text, single-column, and small-format manuscript, descriptors that apply to both of them.[76]

The illuminations accompanying the texts in each manuscript are described in the section "Miniatures" below.

S1 [Roy *C1*], Brussels, Bibliothèque Royale 11034

This codex is one of the few surviving manuscripts containing a single work by Christine. While there is no concrete indication of when it was made, Laidlaw suggests that it is an early one, like Bibliothèque Nationale f.fr. 1740 (=*S2*; see infra), dating from between 1399 and 1404 and quite possibly before any of the other extant versions of the *Deux amans*.[77] In the opinion of Gilbert Ouy and Christine Reno, it is written in the *X* hand, that is, in the hand they identify as Christine's.[78]

This manuscript, like *S2*, differs in layout from the other five versions of *Deux amans* in that the text is written in a single column. It is of smaller format than the volumes of collected works, measuring approximately 280 by 190 millimeters. The text block, containing twenty-seven lines per side (with the exception of folios 2v° and 24v°, which have twenty-eight), measures 170 by 105 millimeters and therefore leaves wide margins. It is composed of thirty-nine folios, with *Deux amans* occupying numbers two to thirty-nine. The introductory capital is decorated, as are four intermediate capitals. There is one miniature, executed in grisaille and situated at the beginning of the text at the top of folio 2r°, which measures approximately 100 by 105 millimeters.[79]

A dedicatory *ballade* of thirty-four lines appears on the verso of folio 1, a single sheet that does not form part of the quires containing the text. Copied under the heading *balade*, written in red at the top of page, the poem addresses *Deux amans* to Charles d'Albret as an *étrenne*, or New Year's gift. The text is as follows:

> Bon jour, bon an et quanque il puet souffire
> De bien, d'onneur et de parfaite joye,
> Mon redoubté seigneur, d'Alebret sire,
> Charles puissant, pri Dieu qu'il vous envoye
> Ce jour de l'an qui maint bon cuer resjoye,   5
> Et vous presente
> Cestui livret, que j'ay fait par entente,
> Ou est descript et la joye et la paine
> Qu'ont ceulx qu'Amours met d'amer en la sente;
> Si le vueilliez recevoir pour estraine.   10
>
> Et s'il vous plaist a l'oÿr ou le lire,
> De .ij. amans orrez qu'Amours maistroye,

> Si a entre eulx debat, car l'un veult dire
> Qu'Amours grieve trop plus qu'elle n'esjoye,
> L'autre dit non, et que plus bien envoye;   15
> Et a l'attente
> De jugement, lequel a miendre entente
> Se sousmettent et a sentence plaine;
> C'est nouvel cas a journee presente,
> Si le vueilliez recevoir pour estraine.   20
>
> Et non obstant qu'ayent voulu eslire
> Mon seigneur d'Orlïens qui leur fait voye
> Et juge en soit, ne vueilliez escondire
> Leur bon desir, car chascun d'eulx vous proye
> Tres humblement, s'il vous plaist toutevoye, 25
> Et se guermente,
> Que vous disiez vostre avis, se dolente
> Vie est qu'amer ou tres joyeuse et saine.
> Cestui dittié leur fait vous represente;
> Si le vueilliez recevoir pour estraine.   30
>
> Mon redoubté seigneur des milliers trente,
> Me recommend a vo bonté hautaine
> Cui mon service ottroy sanz estre lente;
> Si le vueilliez recevoir pour estraine.

Various signs indicate that in all likelihood the text of the debate was written out before Christine decided to send a copy of it to Charles d'Albret. In terms of codicological evidence, the dedicatory poem was inserted at the beginning of the manuscript, having been copied on a single folio quite separate from the quires containing the debate. Moreover, while Albret's name is evoked in the text (ll. 1653–64) as an illustrious example of knights ennobled by love, the passage containing this reference is not marked either visually or rhetorically in any special way in this manuscript, something one might have expected if the copy had been prepared specifically with him in mind. As for the *ballade*, it reappears in Christine's collected works as part of the group of poems called *Autres balades*. Roy reproduces it as item 21 of that grouping and points out that while the poem is contained in manuscripts *D* and *R*, it is not included in manuscripts of the *L* family.[80] This fact supports the notion that the *ballade* was composed and sent to Albret somewhat after the *Deux amans* itself was written, after the earliest years of the century, by which time *L1* and *L2* had been completed, and before 1405 or a few years later, the period during which *D* was prepared.

The format of the *ballade* is appropriate to the metrical structure of the debate, given its mixture of a predominant long line (albeit decasyllabic rather than octosyllabic, as in the text) with a much shorter one, which here introduces a new rhyme midway through the stanza. In terms of its content, there are some differences between the poem as Roy transcribes it among the *Autres balades* and the version that figures at the beginning of *S1*. Most notably, line 29 as it appears in the *Autres balades* version reads, *Et le livret le fait vous represente*, whereas in the dedicatory poem of the Brussels manuscript a different noun phrase at the beginning of the line, *Cestui dittié*, links the poem more directly to the text it introduces, adding immediacy to the reference. A second significant variant occurs in the envoi. Lines 31–32 in the collection version read, *Mon redoubté seigneur, des meilleurs trente / Me reçoivent a vo bonté haultaine*, whereas the stronger version in *S1* (*Mon redoubté seigneur des milliers trente, / Me recommend a vo bonté hautaine*) is both more flattering to the patron (who is the *seigneur des milliers trente*) and more straightforward as an expression of Christine's devotion to his service.

The dedicatory *ballade* attempts to reconcile sending a presentation copy of the poem to Charles d'Albret despite the fact that the text itself contains a dedication to Louis, duke of Orléans. The third stanza finesses this potentially delicate question, asking Albret not to reject the case out of hand because it names Louis as judge and patron. The lovers, we read, are soliciting Albret's opinion, as well. Two verbs in the present tense (*proye*, l. 24, and *se guermente*, l. 26) mediate any gap between the time frame of the argument and the moment of its presentation to this particular nobleman, bringing the new dedication and the original text into the same present. It also merges fiction and reality much as the debate itself does, by referring to the speakers as if they were historical characters and by recasting Albret as one of the original *destinataires* or interlocutors. As a tactical approach to the recycling of old material, this rededication is deftly handled.

S2 [Roy C2], Paris, Bibliothèque Nationale f.fr. 1740

Much of the information given regarding *S1* pertains here as well. Like *S1*, this manuscript contains only the *Debat de deux amans*. Roy assigns it no date, but Laidlaw places it between 1399 and 1404.[81] Reno and Ouy identify it as among those manuscripts written in the X hand.[82]

Its dimensions are somewhat smaller than those of the collected-works manuscripts: the parchment measures 284 by 206 millimeters, and it contains only the thirty-two folios occupied by the text plus one blank leaf (folio 33). The text is written in a single column, on sides (other than the first and last) that average thirty-three lines apiece. The six-line introductory capital is decorated in blue, gold, and red, and four intermediate capitals in the body of the poem are executed two in blue and two in red. The prefatory miniature, 110 by 107 millimeters, is rendered in grisaille.

The relationship of the text in this manuscript to that in *S1* and the other witnesses is not easily summarized. While they present very closely related readings, they are not what Roy called "absolument identiques pour le texte."[83] In some details, *S1* and *S2* agree with each other against all the other manuscripts. For example, they both place a paragraph mark at several lines where the others have none (ll. 570, 836, 886, 1077). They also share a few unique readings: at line 665, they read *Pour tel amour*, against several other variants, and, perhaps most significantly, at line 1158 they both repeat the pronoun *chascun* from the preceding line rather than using *le monde* like the other five manuscripts.

However, each at times agrees with one or more of the other witnesses. The more significant lines are listed here. At line 681, *S2* uses the *R* reading *peri*, against all the other manuscripts, including *S1*, which read *mouru*. At line 975, it is *S1* that agrees with *R* to the exclusion of all the others, which give a variety of minor variants. In line 1956, *S2* shares an error with *L* that *S1* does not have (*Se* for *De*, repeated from the beginning of the preceding two lines). In line 619, *S2* leaves out the same word as *L2* but then corrects the mistake by adding the missing negative particle (*ne*) above the line. In one case, *S1* corrects a common error: at line 15, where *S2* shares with *L1* and *L3* the reading *empris* at line end, *S1* has an obvious correction removing extraneous letters before its final word *pris* (which it shares with *RDL2*).

There seems to be a special affiliation between *S* and *D*. At line 783, *S2* and *D* share a correction (which consists of the word *en* written in over the line). In line 1493, *S2* and *D* share the reading *reschappes* where the others read *eschappes*. However, *S1* and *D* share a variant in line 1787 (*nous* for *vous*). Both *S1* and *S2* share an error with *D* at line 1357, where the word *point* has been crossed out. All three share a variant (*en* for *de* [*R*] or *n'en* [*L*], l. 510) and one unusual spelling (l. 1740) where they read *faames*, which in *S1* has been rendered by adding the second *a* above the line.

In summary, on the question of the relationship between *S1* and *S2* and between them as a group and the other manuscripts, one can conclude, first, that they are more closely linked with each other than with the text of *Deux amans* in any of the collection manuscripts, and, second, that they show roughly equal but separate affinities with the *L* family and with *D*. Beyond that, their exact place in the stemma awaits further clarification.

D [Roy *A1*, Hicks *B2*] Paris, Bibliothèque Nationale f.fr. 835, 606, 836, 605

This collection contains most of Christine's shorter lyric poetry as well as several of her longer works.[84] There is some dispute as to the number of volumes originally included in this collection and whether these volumes were originally intended to form a whole.[85] It is richly decorated, having been prepared as a presentation copy, possibly for Jean, duc de Berry, sometime between the end of 1405 and 1408 or 1409. There is no doubt that Christine herself supervised the production of these volumes. The quality of the text is excellent, and the manuscript is well preserved.

The debate poems appear in the first volume, f.fr. 835. Like the others, this codex is made of vellum. It measures 352 by 261 millimeters and contains 103 folios. The debate poems constitute items 10, 11, and 12: *Deux amans* occupies folios 52r°a to 64r°a; *Trois jugemens*, folios 64r°b to 73v°a; and *Poissy*, folios 74r°a to 86v°b. The texts are written in double columns, with an average of 41 lines per column. Each text is decorated with a prefatory miniature, a rubric, and a four-line decorated capital at the beginning of the text. Paragraph marks appear frequently in the left margins throughout, each executed in gold and surrounded by a field of pink or blue with white tracing. Consistent with the rest of this volume, running titles identify each text in the top margin of each folio. Occasional inaccuracies occur in the titles: in *Poissy*, for example, the verso of each folio reads *Le Livre du dit*, while the recto sides complete this with *de Poissy .xij*. On folios 76, 77, 78, and 79 verso, however, the first part of the title is mistakenly given as *Le Livre des .iij.* (or *trois*), in confusion with the *Livre des Trois jugemens*, which immediately precedes *Poissy*.

Maurice Roy's late nineteenth-century edition of Christine's *Oeuvres poétiques* is based on *D*.

L1 [Roy *B3*, Hicks *A2*] Chantilly, Musée Condé 492

Together with the other two *L* manuscripts, this Chantilly codex represents Christine's first collection of her works. Manuscript *L1* is now thought to be the earliest of the three, dating from shortly after 1400. It is made of vellum, contains 182 folios, and measures 290 by 239 millimeters. A table of contents at the front of the volume gives an accurate list of the lyric poetry and longer pieces included.

The texts are written in double columns of thirty-two lines per column. *Deux amans* occupies folios 51v°a to 67r°b, *Trois jugemens*, folios 79v°a to

91v°a, and *Poissy,* folios 92r°a to 108r°b. Each is ornamented with one miniature at the head of the text, as well as with a decorated capital for the first letter of each work. Paragraph marks appear in the left margin, although there are fewer of these than in *D* and *R*. They are also less elaborate, each consisting of the paragraph mark alone, in solid red or blue, with no border surrounding it and no gold used in its execution.

L2 [Roy *B2*, Hicks *A1*] Paris, Bibliothèque Nationale f.fr. 12779

This manuscript is made of vellum, has 172 folios, and measures 323 by 255 millimeters. It, too, dates from the very early fifteenth century.

The texts are written in double columns with an average of 32 lines per column. *Deux amans* occupies folios 50r°a to 65r°. The text of *Deux amans* begins at line 51; the first 50 lines must have been copied on folio 49, now missing from the manuscript.[86] *Trois jugemens* appears on folios 77v°a to 89v°a, and *Poissy* on folios 90r°a to 106r°b (leaving one and a half columns blank between the two texts). *Trois jugemens* and *Poissy* are both decorated with an illumination and a decorated capital at the beginning of the text and *Deux amans* presumably displayed both these same design elements. There are paragraph marks throughout all three texts.

There are two copies of *L2* in Paris, made by Lacurne de Sainte Palaye (to whom this manuscript once belonged);[87] one is Arsenal 3295, the other B.N. Moreau 1686.

L3 [Roy *B1*, Hicks *A3*] Paris, Bibliothèque Nationale f.fr. 604

This manuscript is now recognized as the latest of the *L* family and is thought to be a copy of *L1* (or of a very similar manuscript), to which its readings are almost identical. It probably dates from the first third of the fifteenth century, and certainly after 1407.[88]

The texts of the debate poems are written in double columns of approximately 40 lines per column. *Deux amans* begins on folio 39v° (after the last five lines and the explicit of the *Gieux a vendre*) and ends at the bottom of 51v°a. *Trois jugemens* begins on folio 60v°b (following the last seven lines and the explicit of the *Dit de la rose*) and ends on folio 70r°a. *Poissy* begins on folio 70r°b, directly after *Trois jugemens*, and finishes on folio 82v°a.

There are many indications that this manuscript was hastily prepared, among them the lines and half-lines left blank above the beginning of the texts, space intended for miniatures and decorated capitals that were never added. Similarly, preparations are visible in the margins for paragraph marks that were never executed.

A partial edition of *Poissy*, published by Paul Pougin in 1857, is based on *L3*, although Pougin was also aware of *D*.[89]

R [Roy A2, Hicks B3] London, British Museum Harley 4431

A manuscript well known for its lavish and beautiful illuminations,[90] R, like D, was prepared as a presentation copy; Christine offered it to Queen Isabeau de Bavière (wife of Charles VI) between 1410 and 1415. The dating of it is based on its inclusion of several lyric pieces that do not appear in D.[91] Recent research has established that the Harley manuscript is in all probability an autograph copy, that is, written in Christine's hand.[92] This discovery has led to a reassessment of R as a final version or "edition" by the author of the works contained. It is on the text of R that this edition is based.

This vellum manuscript is bound in two volumes, comprising 398 folios, each measuring 380 by 280 millimeters. The debate poems appear in volume one. *Deux amans* occupies folios 58v°a to 71r°b; *Trois jugemens*, folios 71v°a to 81r°a; *Poissy*, folios 81r°b to 94r°a.[93] The texts are written in double columns of approximately 40 lines per column. Each poem is decorated with a prefatory miniature and a rubric, a decorated four-line capital beginning the text, several intermediate capitals in the body of the text (with the exception of *Poissy*, which has none), and paragraph marks throughout. Running titles, in red, identify the texts at the top of each folio.

For purposes of transcribing the text, the following characteristics of the hand in R were important: i is distinguished in a series of minims by a diagonal stroke above the line (resembling an acute accent); initials b and v are easily confused, as are the pairs u and n and finals s and e. Barely visible virgules are used in many lines to separate the fourth and fifth syllables and, occasionally, to separate either individual items in a list of adjectives or nouns or two words that have been run together.

Previous Editions and Base Text

Before Roy's edition, now long out of print, the debate poems were not widely distributed in published form. His is the first modern edition of *Le Livre des Trois jugemens*. An excerpt of *Deux amans*, consisting principally of lines 1520–1688, had been published in the first half of the nineteenth century by Paulin Paris in his *Manuscrits françois de la Bibliothèque du roy*.[94]

Paulin Paris also reproduced a short passage of the *Dit de Poissy*.[95] Shortly thereafter, P. Pougin published a much longer portion of the poem in his article, "Le Dit de Poissy de Christine de Pisan. Description du prieuré de Poissy en 1400."[96] As his title implies, he edited primarily the section dealing with the convent. The portion of the poem that he does not edit is paraphrased, with considerable editorial comment. In his description of the travelers' journey from Saint-Germain to Poissy, he quotes four lines of poetry that are obviously not from the *Dit* (they are each of six syllables, and rhyme *abab*), but no other attribution is indicated. There are numerous errors in his transcription of *L3*, and he appears to have made some emendations without signaling them to the reader.[97]

Roy's texts of the poems, in contrast, are very reliable: the errors in transcription are few (a half dozen have been corrected in the errata).[98] His edition does have shortcomings, however, which are found principally in the critical apparatus and in his assessment of the manuscript tradition. The failings of the former include the absence in the variants of any readings from *L1* (Chantilly 492)[99] and the frequent omission of variants from the other three manuscripts.[100]

As mentioned above, Roy's edition of Christine's *Oeuvres poétiques* is based on *D* (B.N. f.fr. 835, 606, 836, 605), and a case for using this manuscript as the primary witness can certainly be made. Roy's reasons for choosing it, however, are flawed. In justifying his choice he states:

> Il est facile ... d'invoquer en sa faveur les meilleures considérations, tirées non seulement de son origine bien établie, mais surtout de l'excellence de son texte. Enfin une dernière raison, et elle a bien son importance, il est de tous les mss. que nous ayons retrouvés, celui qui se rapproche le plus de la date de composition des différentes pièces dont il donne le texte.[101]

The first two features Roy cites—the manuscript's excellent quality and its sterling provenance—are undeniable. Nevertheless, he admits that *R* compares in quality to *D*.[102] As for its origins, it appears that *D* may well have been written for Louis, duke of Orléans, to whom several texts in the collection bear dedications, rather than for Jean de Berry, as Roy assumes. Jean probably bought it from Christine after Louis's assassination, in November 1407, had deprived her of the intended patron.[103] But in terms of pedigree, too, *R*, the queen's manuscript, is certainly the equal of *D*.

Roy's justification is most seriously undermined, perhaps, by his mistaken assessment of the *L* family (Musée Condé 492, B.N. f.fr. 12779, B.N. f.fr. 604) and the ensuing fallacious assumption that *D* is the extant manuscript most nearly contemporaneous with the composition of the poems. As a group, the *L* collections were described by Roy as "exécutés vers le milieu du XVe siècle" and "[b]ien inférieurs sous tous les rapports" when compared with *R* and *D*. As the manuscript descriptions above make clear, however, Roy's dating has been superseded; the consensus of more recent codicologists places both *L1* and *L2* in the early years of the fifteenth century, and only *L3*, the latest of them all, in the mid-fifteenth century.

Even discounting the new information brought to light recently, Roy's reasoning in arriving at his conclusions is not clear. If the *L* family is later than *D* or *R*, why does he speak of the "lacunes" and "vers faux" found in the *L* manuscripts as "*rectifiés* dans les mss. A [i.e., *D* and *R*]"?[104] He also disregards the notice introducing the table of contents, written on an endpaper in *L1* and *L3* (which Roy mistakenly attributes to *L2* as well). It states clearly:

> Cy commencent les rebriches de la table de ce present volume, fait et compilé par Cristine de Pizan, demoiselle, commencié l'an de grace mil .ccc. IIII^{xx} xix. eschevé et escript en l'an mil quatre cens et deux, la veille de la nativité saint Jehan Baptiste.[105]

Hicks and Mombello agree with Roy that *L1*, *L2*, and *L3* are all somewhat corrupt copies of the lost original that included this table of contents and that must therefore have been completed by 1402.[106] But they both conclude, as do most other researchers who have recently studied these manuscripts, that all three are older than Roy was willing to admit, and that their readings should not be dismissed quite so readily.[107]

All three *L* manuscripts are now regarded as representatives, whatever their actual date of production, of the earliest collection of Christine's poetry as compiled by the author herself. Together they give the readings of a first version of those works. Manuscript *D* constitutes a second version, and *R* the third and final version.

The changes made to particular poems from one collection to the next have been examined by Félix Lecoy and Laidlaw, who agree that Christine deliberately modified her work in successive "editions," an opportunity afforded her by the control she maintained over the production of her manuscripts. Lecoy has studied the evolution of a certain number of *ballades* and concludes that in each new version the pieces are stylistically refined.[108] Laidlaw has examined the shorter lyric poems as well as several longer pieces and demonstrates convincingly, in support of Lecoy, that Christine used the preparation of a new collection as a chance to revise and correct her work.[109]

Consequently, the autograph manuscript *R* is now widely considered the culmination of Christine's career and certainly the author's definitive version of the poems included. Laidlaw is therefore convinced that "[i]t is essential that critical editions of the works of Christine de Pizan be based on the latest version known to have been copied under her supervision." In other words, in the case of the debate poems and many other texts, new editions should be based on *R*.[110]

Recent editions have favored *R* for various reasons. Varty, in his anthology *Christine de Pisan's Ballades, Rondeaux, and Virelais*, chose it rather than *D* "partly because it has never before been reproduced and partly because it is the most complete,"[111] containing nine poems of the *Encore aultres balades* that *D* does not include, plus the *Cent balades d'amant et de dame*. He also believes *R* to be "slightly more accurate" than *D*.[112] In accordance with Laidlaw's principle, the recent translation by Earl Jeffrey Richards of *Le Livre de la Cité des dames* is based on the readings of *R* precisely because "the text to be used ... should correspond to the final version Christine proposed."[113] Richards also prefers the Harley text for the "largely aesthetic reason" that the orthography is more Latinate than in the other manuscripts, a stylistic element that he considers a small additional argument "on Christine's part for the affinity of women and learning."[114] Cerquiglini's recent publication of the *Cent balades d'amant et de dame* uses *R* of necessity, as no other manuscript preserves this text. She offers a revised reading, however, differing in significant details from Roy's edition, and has augmented the critical apparatus by adding textual notes, a glossary, and a table of proper names.

Textual evidence corroborates the choice of *R* as base manuscript. Manifestly incorrect passages are infrequent, as witnessed here in the variants by the small number of readings rejected from the *R* text. While occasional lapses do occur (such as the inexplicable repetition of ll. 1804–15 in *Deux amans*), the manuscript was carefully proofread, and corrections are evident in several forms, including expunctuation marks beneath extraneous syllables, erasure and replacement of letters or words, lowercase letters in the margin at line beginning to correct the order of lines copied out of sequence, and some simple barring of mistakes. Manuscripts *D* and *R*, the latest chronologically of the witnesses, sometimes correct the reading in *L* (as in *les* for *leurs*, *Deux amans*, l. 1075, which avoids an awkward repetition). Manuscript *R* occasionally differs from the reading of all other versions, often with a visible correction of the text, suggesting authorial emendation. At line 1433 of *Deux amans*, for example, the words *Sur toute riens* replace *Plus qu'autre riens*, which strengthens the description of the power of Lancelot's love; at line 107 of *Trois jugemens*, *R* visibly corrects the first letter of *vueil* to read *dueil*; again in *Deux amans*, the change in order and substance in lines 1922 and 1923 makes *R* the better reading by replacing a standard line of formulaic flattery with additional description more closely tied to the topic of the passage, the lovers' suffering. (Other examples will be clear from the variants and are signaled in the notes to each poem.)

While the readings of the extant copies of the debate poems do not differ greatly, it seems appropriate, to reason with other recent editors, that the debate poems be presented in the final and most polished version left by the author. In summary, then: this edition uses manuscript R as its base text because it offers a reading of the debate poems superior in several ways to that in manuscript D, the base text used by Roy in the only preexisting complete critical edition of these poems.[115]

Language

The debate poems do not yet display the masterful word craft to be found in Christine's later polemical prose writings. While their language presents no particular problems, however, the vocabulary of the poems is rich.[116] Christine's tendency to use a large variety of adjectives and concrete nouns in descriptive passages is a characteristic displayed most prominently, perhaps, by the *Dit de Poissy*, in passages such as the otherwise conventional springtime opening (ll. 83–112). The diversity of the language in *Poissy* is due also to the somewhat technical nature of the narrator's report on the visit to the priory, which includes, for example, descriptions of architectural details of the cloister (ll. 386–95), the refectory (ll. 405–12), the church (ll. 481–513), and vestimentary details of the nuns' habits (ll. 518–34). *Deux amans* and *Trois jugemens* demonstrate less lexical variety, although the description of the social event setting the scene for the discussion in *Deux amans* is specific and vivid in its portrayal of the activities in which the guests engage (ll. 101–40).

In their morphology and phonology, the debate poems manifest the hallmarks of the Middle French period.[117] Some vestiges of the Old French case system can be found. One such example is the occasional occurrence of *li*, the old form of the masculine definite article in the nominative case, which was used only infrequently at this period.[118] In manuscript R, it is used ten times in *Deux amans* (ll. 61, 497, 911, 947, 952, 988, 1048 in the masc. pl.; ll. 757, 1350, 1410 in the masc. sing.), three times in *Trois jugemens* (ll. 498 and 705 in the masc. pl.; l. 846 in the masc. sing.), and eight times in *Poissy* (ll. 78, 189, 483, 1126, 2063 in the masc. pl.; l. 462 as a collective masc. sg.; twice in l. 817 as part of the pronoun *li quieulx*). Consistent with the breakdown of the declension system, however, one finds that in a significant number of the contexts where the old form appears, it is used incorrectly. In line 497 of *Deux amans*, for example, it coexists with the more modern form *les*, used with a noun elsewhere in the line, and is followed by a noun and adjective that take the *-s* of the modern plural.

Other archaic traits include the use of the old nominative plural possessive adjective *si* (*si sourcilz*, P1493; *si oeil*, P1497); *ouÿl* for *oui* (P541); *o* for *avec* (e.g., DA1634; P208, P283, P727); *truis* for *trouve* (P1021); and old forms instead of the newer form *estoit*, third-person singular imperfect of *estre*: *ere* (TJ703) and *ert* (DA699, P166, P1878).[119]

It is in Middle French that first-person singular present indicative verbs begin frequently to take new endings by analogy with the second- and third-person singular, and the debate poems reflect this transition by manifesting both old and new forms. The first-person singular *aim* appears in *Poissy* ll. 233, 1697, 1981, 1998, and *Trois jugemens* ll. 154, 906, but *aime* is found in *Poissy* l. 1947 and *Trois jugemens* l. 1029. Likewise one reads *cuid* in *Poissy* ll. 429, 933, 1085, and *Deux amans* ll. 582, 1973, but *cuide* in *Poissy* l. 199 and *Deux amans* ll. 883, 1307, 1346, passim, *jur* in *Poissy* ll. 967, 1219, and 1871 but *jure* in *Poissy* ll. 1291, 1639. Other examples of the old conjugation are *port* (P1026) and *doubt* (P929, P1023); *tiens* with flexional -*s* (P233, P538, P1564, P1697) represents the new.

In the preterite, some weak forms of verbs were at this time in the process of being remodeled by analogy with the strong forms, so that for *venir*, for example, the form *venimes* was slowly changing to modern French *vînmes*. As well, the preterite first-person plural ending -*mes* is rivaled by -*smes*, a form that had become popular by analogy with the second-person plural and that, alongside -*mes* endings, Christine uses liberally (as in *DA*383–400, where in one short passage we find *levasmes*, l. 384; *appellasmes*, l. 385; *menasmes*, l. 387; *partismes*, l. 393; *entrasmes*, l. 394). Consequently, it is not surprising to find several variations on any given preterite form. In the case of *venir*, we find, for example, *veismes* (P213, P345) as well as the more traditional *veni(s)mes* (P131, P699), and in addition to these forms, the other manuscripts use *vimes* (DL2L3, l. 213) and *vinsmes* (L1, l. 213; L1L3, l. 345). The preterite *vosmes*, first-person plural of *voloir*, is found three times in *Poissy* (ll. 240, 465, 466) but not in the other texts; it appears to be a hybrid form that participates in the tendency to adopt the -*smes* ending and the evolution of *voloir* from its various strong stems to an irregular form on the model of *estre* and *avoir* (for which one finds in the first-person preterite *fusmes*, ll. 217, 258, and *osmes*, ll. 246, 346, 545, 869, 899).[120]

The same state of flux is evident in the handling of former epicene adjectives: for the feminine singular, *Poissy* alternates between *grant* (ll. 60, 1147, 1185) and *grande* (ll. 610, 1025, 1123), whereas *Deux amans* and *Trois jugemens* use only *grant*, the older form. All three texts alternate between feminine singular *grief* (DA679, DA1804; TJ50; P610, P1025, P1123) and *grieve* (DA1816, DA1818; TJ84, TJ431, TJ738; P1290). The adjective *vert* qualifies a feminine noun in *Poissy* ll. 84, 93, 194, but *vertes* is used in line 102 for a feminine plural. The feminine form is often verified by syllable count (e.g., P102, P1025, P1123, P1290), proof that it is not simply an orthographic variant. No doubt the flexibility inherent in this period of development let the choice of form depend on the demands of meter and rhyme.

In their phonology, the texts do not manifest any true dialectal forms; neither orthography nor rhyme show traits that deviate from standard Parisian literary usage of the period. The language of the text is very much a product of its time as far as vowels in hiatus and the reduction of diphthongs are concerned, demonstrating the progressive reduction and the resulting unpredictable quality that mark fourteenth- and fifteenth-century French by using both the old and new forms.[121]

Some of these vowel combinations require brief commentary. The vowel groups *ia* and *io*, disyllabic in Old French, remain so here. The verbs *riant* and *oublia* and the noun *especiaulté* (DA189, TJ1117, TJ957) therefore count as two, three, and five syllables, respectively. The reader should keep in mind, however, that after *g*, the appearance of *i* signals simply that the consonant is fricative rather than guttural (e.g., *mengiames*, P683). The letter *i* should also be recognized as part of a diphthong (in the process of reduction) when combined with -*au(l)x* (e.g., *biaulx*, DA139; *chappiaulx*, P899; *aviaux*, DA399).

The group *io* is also reliably disyllabic. The sole exceptions are the noun *gorgions* (P433), in which the *i* indicates a soft rather than a guttural *g*, and verb forms using the -*ions* of the first-person plural verb ending (found in the imperfect indicative, the present conditional, and the present and imperfect subjunctive), as well as a single occurrence of the *ion* ending in a present participle, *plungion* (DA711). In these cases *io* is monosyllabic.

Christine is conservative in her treatment of two other instances of vowels in hiatus in the three debate poems. While *eoi* is sometimes reduced to a monosyllable in other authors of the late-fourteenth and early-fifteenth centuries (and, indeed, in other texts by Christine), here this combination is consistently disyllabic. Verbs such as *veoir* retain the disyllabic vowel both in the infinitive (e.g., DA253, DA569) and in conjugated forms (e.g., *veoye*, DA227; *veoit*, TJ470, TJ786; *seoit*, P1222, P1594). The combination *ea*, too, is always disyllabic here (e.g., *agreable*, DA4; *leal*, TJ557; *leans*, P298).

In contrast, the debate poems manifest the Middle French tendency to use the formerly disyllabic combination *ee* as both one and two syllables. It is conserved as disyllabic in *vëez* (P1895), and that is the norm, but the same spelling elsewhere represents a monosyllable (*creez*, P729; *veez*, TJ568, P927). Our texts display the same fluctuation in other cases. The group *ei* is in the process of reduction: *veist* counts for one syllable (DA124; P99), and the verb *deist* is monosyllabic in *Poissy*, ll. 114 and 1114, but the same form is disyllabic (*deïst*) in *Poissy*, ll. 954, 1215, and 1595. The vowel combination *eu* also can represent either one syllable or two, as is evident from various past participles: for example, at line end, *esleüe* counts for three syllables in

Poissy, l. 278, but two (*esleue*) in l. 1599; the forms *deüe* (P279), *veüe* (TJ1454), and *meüe* (TJ1455) count for two syllables, but *receue* (P1147) and *deceue* (TJ360, TJ1452) also for two; one finds forms of disyllabic *veü* in *Poissy*, ll. 386, 402, 1174, 1596, but *veu* in l. 1549.

Another combination which can count as either one syllable or two is *aou*. We find *säouler* as well as *saoulz* (P418 and P294, respectively), *aournemens* (P505) as well as *äouree* (DA829) and *päour* (DA1353). The spelling *aa*, in contrast, always represents a monosyllable (e.g., *Paaris*, DA826; *aage*, TJ1279).

The spelling -*ie* in the adjective *lie* represents two distinct possibilities, reflecting a shifting accent; the vowel represented can be either *ié* or *ie*. The word *lie/lié*, meaning "happy," is appropriate to the context of joyful young lovers and appears frequently. The texts can therefore benefit from its versatility at line-end (e.g., rhyming with *é* in DA584 ff. and TJ148 ff. but with *ie* in P724 ff. and P1047 ff.) as well as internally, where it can count as one syllable (e.g., *lié* TJ189, P1659) or as two (*lie* before initial consonant, making the final atonic *e* count; e.g., TJ507, P134). In the one instance where either would assure the correct syllable count (before initial vowel: *Or soies lie, et ne pensez qu'a bien*, TJ142), I have chosen to leave it as *lie*. The same flexibility appears to apply to the adverbial form: the form *liement* counts for three syllables (e.g., DA174, DA355; TJ153) but so must *liéement* in P67, rather than for four as one might expect.

The distinction at the rhyme between word endings in -*ié* and -*é* is most often respected (e.g., TJ1516-23, in which a quatrain in -*ier* is followed by one in -*er*). Occasionally, however, they are paired at the rhyme, a fairly frequent Middle French practice. A good example of flexibility in this usage occurs at *Poissy*, ll. 28–31. In that quatrain, manuscripts *D* and *L* maintain the -*ier* ending for each of the infinitives found at line-end, but *R* renders at least two of them in -*er*. (See note to P28–31.)

One last orthographical trait deserves mention. Christine's autograph manuscripts show that she shared the taste for Latinized spelling common in the works of many writers of the day, who reintroduced unpronounced consonants into words in an attempt to make them resemble more closely their Latin roots.[122] There were multiple reasons for this phenomenon, including the objective of making French legible for foreigners and a general concern with *bele escripture*. Using such spellings certainly displayed the author's (or scribe's) erudition, and they are thus consonant with Christine's desire to present herself as learned.[123] A few examples will suffice to represent Latinized spelling in manuscript *R*: the letter *l* is restored in words such as *mieulx* (e.g., DA118, DA375, DA387; P74, P77, P79), *joyaulx, nouviaulx, oysiaulx, biaulx* (P684–87),[124] *hault* (e.g., DA2, DA139, DA1918;

TJ466, TJ1326), *haultement* (e.g., *DA102; TJ1329; P581*), *doulx* (a word occurring with high frequency, e.g., *DA116, DA119, DA192*), and *chappiaulx* (which also shows reinstated the simplified double *p* of L. *cappa* [derivative of *capellus*], *P899*); letters *b* and *c* are frequently restored (e.g., in *Poissy, soubmis,* l. 11, *dicte,* l. 619, and *soubz,* l. 766), while forms of *escript* (e.g., *DA75, DA958, DA959, DA1567; P3, P491, P1522*) add both *p* and *s*. Manuscripts other than *R* also use these learned spellings, although perhaps not as consistently or to such a degree. Manuscript *D* (and *L*, intermittently) presents one particularly interesting type of spelling that is not found in *R*, in what Pope calls the "deliberate attempt to preserve to the eye the connection between the masculine and the feminine [forms of adjectives]";[125] these are *souuefve* (*P1170* in *D* and *L3*) and *griefve* (*P1290* in *D* and *L2*), used as feminine equivalents of *souef* and *grief*.

Versification

The three debate poems are written in a strophic form consisting of quatrains containing three decasyllabic lines built on the same rhyme, followed by one line of four syllables that introduces the next rhyme.[126] The rhyme scheme is thus: *a10 a10 a10 b4 / b10 b10 b10 c4*, etc.

Guillaume de Machaut employed this meter for his *Jugement dou roy de Behaigne* and in various shorter pieces (notably his "Complaintes").[127] It proves to be a very good format for both description and debate. Hoepffner remarks in his edition of Machaut's works that because of the interlocking rhymes, "[l]es strophes ... sont indissolublement enchaînées l'une à l'autre en une suite ininterrompue d'après le principe qui préside au système plus ingénieux encore de la *terza rima* de la *Divine Comédie*."[128] Indeed, this verse structure is very fluid. Syntactic units sometimes end with the short line (e.g., in *DA40, DA100; TJ12, TJ32; P20, P28, P52, P56*). Occasionally, a new sentence begins in midline (e.g., in *DA49, DA103, DA258; TJ23, TJ187; P39, P323, P574*; due allowance must, of course, be made for the decisions of individual editors as to punctuation).

Enjambment from line to line and from one quatrain to the next is very frequent. In some cases, enjambment is pushed to considerable lengths; proper names, for example, are frequently divided over two lines (*DA1641–42: Bon chevalier est l'Ermite et valables / De la Faye ...; DA1532–33: Et le Gallois / Durmas vaillant ...*). Monosyllabic words that are usually unstressed can appear at line end: the contraction *des* ends a quatrain (*P827*), while the rest of its noun cluster (*Beaulx vassellages*) is held over into the next line; similarly, in *Poissy* l. 1958 the negative adverb *ne* falls at line's end, although it must be contracted with the preceding adverb *si* in order to maintain the rhyme. In an extreme case, the suffix of an adverb is separated from its root word and pushed into the next line (*DA*1568–69: *veritable- / Ment*).

The decasyllables are long enough to allow for considerable narrative development within one line, while the shorter four-syllable line provides rhythmic relief and often highlights a phrase of thematic importance; in *Deux amans*, for example, ll. 246–48 (*les tres ameres armes / Qu'Amours livre a ceulx qu'il rent trop enfermes / Et maladis*) reinforce the message regarding the unhappiness caused by love by ending with the strong and multisyllabic *maladis*, while in *Poissy*, ll. 23–24 (*pour achoison / Du bien de vous*) stress the worthy qualities of the poem's patron in the association of *bien* and *vous* in the short line.

Hoepffner also pointed out that given the demands of this particular strophic form in which four consecutive lines must rhyme, it was difficult for the poet to use rich rhymes.[129] Accordingly, rhyme in the debate poems is not of great complexity, and no attempt is made to alternate masculine and feminine line endings. Rhyme is carefully respected, however, with few exceptions. Some liberty is taken in rhyming words ending in *-bre* with *-dre* (*P*280–83, *chambre: tendre: remembre: mendre*; *P*356–59, *chambre: estendre: tendre: attendre*). As in other late medieval texts, *ueil* rhymes with *eil* (e.g., *TJ*1036–39, *dueil: vueil: merveil: vueil*). The rhyming of *-orme* with *-om(me)* (*P*1292–95, *homme: Romme: somme: forme*) is evidence of the weakening of r before another consonant. Likewise, the coupling of *-arme* and *-ermes* is a trait that had become general in Middle French (*DA*244–47, *lermes: fermes: armes: enfermes*). Rhymes linking *-eure* with *-ure* (*TJ*592–95, *injure: parjure: gageure: jure*; *P*1404–7, *heure: labeure: seure: sequeure*; *P*1552–55, *asseure: charneure: mesure: creature*) illustrate the instability in the early fourteenth century of the pronunciation of *eü* in the process of reducing to *u*.[130]

Syllable count is very regular as well, capitalizing on syntactic and phonological flexibility of the language to maintain a strict metrical accuracy. As expected, unstressed *e* counts in word-final position before a word beginning with a consonant. The *-ent* ending of third-person plural present indicative verbs must be counted in the interior of a line but not at line's end (e.g., *D*55 and *D*64, respectively). In the interior of words, however, between consonants or after another vowel, we see proof of the instability of so-called mute *e* in this period. Thus the adverbs *jugement, durement, chierement* (*P*13, *P*14, *P*15) count for three syllables. In comparison, the word *guerredons* (*DA*1623) counts for two syllables, as do the following: *seremens* (*TJ*281);[131] *souveraine* (*TJ*706); *clement* (*TJ*1473); *derrenier* (*TJ*1526); likewise, the verb forms *guerredonner* (P693) and *guerredonnez* (TJ436) count for three. Another good example of the shifting value of interior *e* occurs at *Trois jugemens*, l. 1473, which reads *Car par raison veult monstrer tout clerement*. In manuscript R, the word *par* is added above the line, with the result that the adverb *clerement* must count for only two syllables in that text, whereas in manuscripts D and L, which present a different word order and omit the adverb *tout*, it must count for three.

On the question of where the cesura falls within the decasyllablic verses of the debates, there is no one predominant structure. Often there is a discernible break after the fourth syllable, and it is clear from the frequent use of a virgule at this spot in the line in manuscripts L and R that this division was intended to mark at least a breath group. On occasion this 4/6 cesura is used effectively to emphasize a rhetorical structure that mirrors the quatrains' emphatic short, four-syllable line: for example: *Qu'en diroie?* and *Tant y fait bel* (P574, P577). However, there are also a great number of lines in all three poems that break 6/4 (e.g., *De cil que je portë en ma memoire*, DA151, and *Plus ne te plains d'Amours, disant, 'Aymy!'* TJ147); many that break 5/5 (*Ou enfouÿ sont ceulx qu'amours entiere*, DA989; *Ains enquismes tout et leur demandasmes*, P666). Others have no discernible cesura.

The poems occasionally make use of the hiatus lyric cesura at the fourth syllable, in which an *e* that would normally elide before another vowel (or non-aspirate *h*) counts as a syllable. There are seven examples of this hiatus lyric cesura in *Deux amans* (ll. 290, 451, 1521, 1583, 1642, 1854, 2007); five examples in *Trois jugemens* (ll. 591, 647, 667, 899, 1055); and ten examples in *Poissy* (ll. 593, 649, 942, 1143, 1491, 1573, 1655, 1710, 1725, 1759). As in other contexts where unstressed *e* does not elide before a vowel, it is marked in the text with a diaresis.

One might also argue that Christine also occasionally uses the epic cesura, in which the mute *e* before a following consonant does not count in the versification (just as it does not count at line's end). In three cases, the flexibility inherent in the line allows one to read either an epic cesura or a standard 4/6 break. These are: *Joyeux et lyé, ne que ja tant mefface* (DA1311); *Cil qui si lié qu'a peu qu'il ne voloit* (TJ189); and *Dont l'un a l'autre les cuers s'entre embloient* (P1450). Because there are so few of these constructions, I have chosen to avoid the epic cesura: in the first two lines, I use an acute accent on *lyé* (*lié*), making it unequivocally monosyllabic, and in the third, I use *s'entre* rather than *s'entrë*, allowing it to elide with the following *embloient*. Certainly this is an editorial decision that could well have been resolved the other way.[132]

Miniatures

The layout of all three debate poems was intended to include an illumination in all the surviving copies, although in some cases the miniature has not been executed in the space reserved for it. That the debate poems are illustrated at all argues for their relative importance among the shorter texts in these volumes.

Few of these miniatures have been reproduced. The descriptions below are therefore intended to provide some idea of the content of each one, as well as of the similarities among many of them. Descriptions of individual illuminations include notes specific to that particular image. Considerable art-historical material is available for specific works and specific manuscripts.[133]

S1 Brussels, Bibliothèque Royale 11034

Deux amans (f.2r°): the miniature shows the duke of Orléans seated under a canopy decorated with the fleur de lis. Two retainers stand behind him. Christine kneels before him and is handing him a scroll while gesturing to the two debaters behind her. These two men are engaged in conversation. One of them, clearly the older, has a beard and wears a hat covering his eyes, and one foot is visible beneath his clothing. The hat and the exposed foot recall ll. 237–39 of the text. The illumination is executed in grisaille, with touches of color to indicate flesh tones, some shading in the folds of the figures' garments, and a yellow-green floor.[134]

Pierre Cockshaw points out that this miniature closely resembles those in two other Bibliothèque Royale manuscripts containing Christine de Pizan's *Livre du Chemin de longue étude* (MSS 10982 and 10983).[135] One salient difference distinguishing this presentation miniature in *Deux amans* from the other two in the Brussels collection (both of which show Christine presenting her work to Charles VI) is that the object Christine hands to her patron is a scroll rather than a book.

S2 Paris, Bibliothèque Nationale f.fr. 1740

The one miniature in this manuscript of *Deux amans* is very similar to that in *S1*. It is done in grisaille with touches of color (yellow-green for the floor, pinkish tones on skin), and depicts the same presentation scene in which Christine presents her volume to the duke of Orléans. While the composition is identical to that in *S1* in its main elements, it is less carefully rendered and less detailed; there are no figures standing behind the duke's chair

Le Livre du Debat de deux amans. Copyright Royal Library Albert Ier, Brussels, B.R. 11034, f.2r°.

Le Livre du Debat de deux amans. By permission of The British Library. Harley 4431, f.58v°a.

Le Livre des Trois jugemens. By permission of The British Library. Harley 4431, f.71v°a.

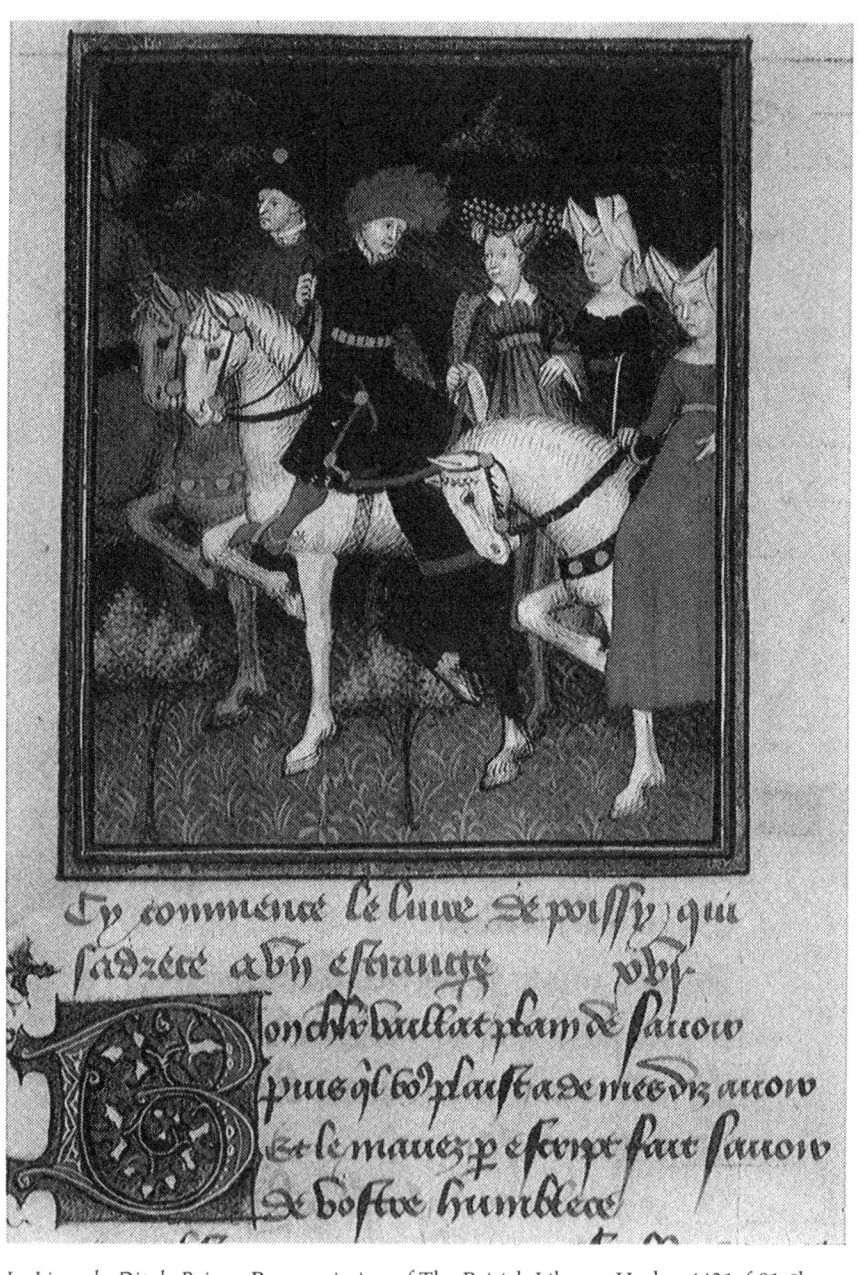

Le Livre du Dit de Poissy. By permission of The British Library. Harley 4431, f.81rºb.

in this miniature, there is no attempt to show writing on the scroll, and the debaters are more generic in character, lacking the details which differentiate them in *S1*.

D Paris, Bibliothèque Nationale f.fr. 835, 606, 836, 605

There are only six illuminations in the first volume (835) of this anthology. The debate poems, each of which is illustrated with a prefatory miniature, thus collectively contain half of them and gain in prominence as a result. In their content the miniatures are similar to those in Harley 4431 (MS *R*).

Deux amans (f.52r°a): the duke of Orléans is seated at left, with two retainers, on a dais ornamented with the fleur de lis. Christine is kneeling before him, front and center. Behind her kneel the two debaters. It is difficult to distinguish which is the knight and which the squire. Christine gestures toward her patron with her left hand and back toward the two men with her right. The figures are contained in an architectural setting, consisting of a chamber with white and gold floor tiles, two Gothic windows on the wall behind the debaters, and a gold roof that trangresses the frame.

Trois jugemens (f.64r°b): the patron is seated at left in a chair. Christine is in the middle, pointing with her left hand at the patron and with her right hand at the six debaters beside her at the right side of the illustration. This group consists of three women in the front row and three men behind them. The men's faces and headgear carefully individualize them. The women all wear the same type of headdress (like Christine's), but each has a different color dress, and two wear necklaces. The clothing and floor are colorful, while the architectural setting is mostly gray and white, with touches of mauve.

Poissy (f.74r°a): the miniature shows Christine riding in the woods with four men and two women. She appears in the foreground, wearing a gray dress, and seems to be indicating the direction the party should follow. The ladies and gentlemen appear to be admiring something outside the frame to the right. In the background, distant towers and spires are visible.[136]

L1 Chantilly, Musée Condé 492

Deux amans (f.51v°a): the duke of Orléans is seated at left, under a canopy ornamented with a coat of arms showing the fleur de lis at the top. He holds a scroll. Christine is kneeling center foreground, gesturing toward the scroll and the duke. Behind her on the right are the two debaters, one visibly older than the other by virtue of his beard. The two men are engaged in conversation.

This illumination has much in common with those in *S1* and *S2;* the scroll being exchanged between patron and author is particularly significant, suggesting a possible connection between this manuscript and the *S* family. The scroll emphasizes the oral nature and the immediacy of the interchange, represented in the miniatures of the other manuscripts by Christine's hand gesture, and contrasts with other presentation miniatures in Christine's work in which the object she hands to the patron is a bound book.

Trois jugemens (f.79v°a): the patron is seated at left, in a large chair. A retainer stands beside and a little behind the chair, toward the center of the frame. The patron gestures toward Christine, who stands front and center. She, in turn, points with her right hand toward the debaters at the right of the picture. With her left hand, she holds the arm of a young woman. Only four debaters are depicted, two women (drawn as noticeably smaller figures) standing in front of two men.

Poissy (f.92r°a): three gentlemen and two ladies, one of whom is Christine, ride on horseback from right to left across a grassy surface.

L2 Paris, Bibliothèque Nationale f.fr. 12779

Deux amans: the beginning of this poem (on what must have been folio 49) is missing in the manuscript, and one cannot therefore be sure that there was an illumination here. Details of the layout argue that such a miniature did exist, however. Most important, both *Trois jugemens* and *Poissy* have illuminations; furthermore, the fifty lines of text missing from the beginning of *Deux amans* correspond closely to the block of text following the miniature on the first folio of each of the other two debates and would have left room for a miniature here, too.

Trois jugemens (f.77v°a): the patron is seated at left, while Christine stands in the middle, and six debaters, three women in front and three men behind, stand at the right. Christine gestures toward the judge with her right hand and toward the debaters with her left. The debaters are differentiated by details of their apparel and seem to be talking or quarreling among themselves. The background is a beautifully textured red-and-gold brocade-like surface. The paint has been lightly applied on the figures' robes; ruling for lines of text is visible through parts of the illumination.

Poissy (f.90r°a): the illumination depicts a group of four ladies and six gentlemen riding from right to left on a grassy field with trees behind them. The background is a flat red and the human and animal figures are painted with minimal coloring.[137]

L3 Paris, Bibliothèque Nationale f.fr. 604

There are no illuminations in this manuscript, although space has been left for them before each of the three debate poems (and in other texts). The blank is a fourteen-line space before *Deux amans* (f.39v°a, in which has been added, in a later hand, the notation, *Duorum Amantium Contentio*), a sixteen-line space in *Trois jugemens* (f.60v°b), and an eleven-line space in *Poissy* (f.70r°b).

R London, British Library Harley 4431

Deux amans (f.58v°a): the illumination introducing this poem emphasizes the formal, hierarchical quality of the debate. The duke of Orléans is seated left, in a grand chair with a canopy lined in a fabric on which appears the royal fleur de lis. Christine is kneeling, facing her patron. She points behind her, where there are two men, each down on one knee. Of the two, one appears older: he has a goatee, while the younger man is curly haired and beardless. The older man, dressed in red, wears a cloak that covers his legs to the ankle, while the younger man, in green, has a cloak that falls to the knee. The room in which the figures appear contains a large chest in the background and an elaborate geometric pattern of tiles on the floor. A checkerboard pattern executed in gold and color fills the background.

Trois jugemens (f.71v°a): much as in the miniature for *Deux amans*, this painting shows Christine presenting the debaters to their judge. Dressed in blue with a white headdress, she stands alone in the center of the frame, facing the Seneschal, who is seated on the right side of the picture wearing a red robe. Christine addresses him while gesturing with her left hand to a group behind her consisting of three women and three men, arranged in a tight group at the left of the frame. Each of the debaters is somewhat individualized, but they are less prominent than either Christine or the judge.[138] The background behind the standing figures consists of diagonal rows of squares in gold, red, and blue, and the floor tiles are green and black. Again, like that in *Deux amans*, this miniature reflects the formal structure of the poem in its rigidity and compartmentalized quality, placing prominence on the communication between Christine and her patron (and therefore indirectly on the commodity they exchange) with correspondingly less attention to the substance of their interaction.

Poissy (f.81r°b): the prefatory miniature incorporates both major aspects of the poem, the excursion to the priory as well as the debate. It shows a group of young nobles on horseback passing through an idealized landscape, while the two central figures, no doubt the squire and the lady, are talking as they ride. Christine, in her characteristic blue dress, follows closely behind them and appears attentive to the discussion. This central group of three is flanked by another man on the left and another woman on the right. The scene depicted has a spontaneous, lively quality that enhances the sense of motion as this company rides along. A half-lit figure disappears from the frame on the left, with only his back and the rear quarters of his horse still visible, while the woman on the right is just entering the pictorial space, her mount and body also only partially seen. The result is a more fluid, less static composition than in the miniatures accompanying the other judgment poems, despite the structured arrangements and symmetry of the figures.

Establishment of the Text

My policy in establishing the text has been to intervene as little as possible in the readings of my base manuscript, *R* (British Library Harley 4431).

Use of diacritical marks generally follows the conventions codified by Mario Roques and further refined by Alfred Foulet and Mary Blakely Speer.[139] The only three marks used, therefore, are the acute accent[´], which distinguishes tonic from atonic *e*, the diaresis (or trema [¨]), which indicates hiatus in a group of two or more vowels, and the cedilla on *c* [ç], which distinguishes it as a sibilant.

In Middle French there is flexibility regarding atonic final *e* before a word beginning with a vowel (or a nonaspirate *h*): it can be elided or retained as a syllable. Wherever it must be counted as a syllable, it is marked here with a diaresis (e.g., *në en chemin* and *Quë il ama, TJ267, TJ1120*). In some instances, there is a choice to be made regarding which atonic *e* to retain (e.g., the phrase *Que autre amoit, TJ1380*, which I have chosen to render, *Que autrë amoit*, allowing the *e* on *Que* to elide). For cases of this sort, I have chosen where to place the diaresis based on the rhythm of the line and on the reading of the other witnesses, while recognizing, of course, that other readings are possible.

As noted earlier (see "Language"), there is considerable flexibility and hesitation at this stage of Middle French regarding vowels in hiatus. To avoid confusion and to aid the reader in scanning the line, the diaresis is used to mark hiatus in any vowel combinations that can be either mono- or disyllabic in these texts.

Abbreviations in the text have been resolved with reference to the spelling found in *R* itself and in the other manuscripts. The abbreviation *q* plus a bar has always been rendered as the full form *que*, even when the final *e* elides before another vowel. Spelling of the base text has been retained except for the substitution of *v* for consonant *u* and *j* for consonant *i*, which have been regularized in accordance with modern orthography. Following Omer Jodogne, *u* is used instead of *v* in the verb *pouoir*.[140] Roman numerals have been retained as written in the manuscript rather than being spelled out. Most of these numerals are preceded and followed by a period; in cases where one or the other period is missing in the manuscript, I have added it to regularize use of the convention, whereby the period separates numerals from letters preceding or following. Punctuation has been added with an eye to guiding the reader through the sometimes intricate syntax of the original while preserving the author's long sentences. Direct discourse has been set off with double quotation marks, and capital letters have been used for proper names and the start of sentences within a line. All the manuscripts capitalize the first word of each line, and these capitals have been retained. Apostrophes have been added to separate elided articles from the following word.

Many compound words and expressions appear in the manuscript either as agglutinations or divided into their components (e.g., *non pourtant* and *non pour tant*). I have chosen to reproduce the form as it most frequently appears in *R*. The tendency of the manuscript is to split them, often counter to more modern spelling (e.g., *tous jours* rather than *toujours*, *non obstant* rather than *nonobstant*). Exceptions to the rule include *sicom(me)* and *toutevoye*, which are written with their elements joined.

Every fourth line is numbered in the right margin in this edition, following the model of Roy's edition. As a result, numerical divisions correspond to the visual breaks provided by the short fourth line of the poem's meter. Also marked in the right margin are folio and column numbers referring to the *mise-en-page* of the poem in *R*.

Variants are listed immediately following each poem, keyed by line number and appropriate *siglum*. They include both rejected readings from the base manuscript *R*, as well as readings from the other manuscripts that differ from the base text. Variants of a purely orthographic nature are not given. In cases where more than one manuscript is cited, the spelling used is usually that of the first text listed. *Sigla* and editorial comments are italicized. Where *L1*, *L2*, and *L3* agree, the short *siglum L* is used to represent all three. Where *S1* and *S2* agree, the *siglum S* is used to represent both.

Rejected readings from *R* are listed before the other variants for each line. Very few emendations have been made. The text has a tendency to use *c* and *s* interchangeably, as in *se/ses* for demonstrative *ce/ces*, or *ce/ces* for reflexive *se* or possessive *ses*. Although these are, in fact, simply orthographic variants, they have been changed here when necessary to conform to modern usage because they are morphologically misleading for the reader (e.g., in *DA*352, *DA*593, *DA*1209, *DA*1902; *TJ*151, *TJ*438, *TJ*1079, *TJ*1397). Substitutions of *c* for *qu* and vice versa have been left as written. *Que* for *qui* in subject position is quite common in Middle French; this usage has therefore been retained as found in manuscript *R*, with *qui* in other manuscripts noted as a variant. In all but three cases where the *R* reading was rejected, at least one of the other witnesses offers an appropriate alternative and was thus used as a basis for the correction. The exceptions are in *Trois jugemens*, l. 957, where manuscript *R* differs from all the others, and *Poissy*, ll. 984 and 1573, where all manuscripts lack the feminine final *e* necessary for the rhyme (l. 984) or for the syllable count (l. 1573). In all three cases my correction is enclosed in square brackets.

In order to remain as faithful as possible to the original, readings from *R* remain unchanged in several places where the variants provided by *D* and *L* might be considered preferable. In line 1802 of *Poissy*, for example, *couardement* is a better reading in the context of the squire's timid avowal to his lady than the *R* alternative *couvertement*, but the latter is syntactically and logically possible.

An asterisk in the text refers the reader to the notes following each poem. These notes provide more information on historical, linguistic, or literary points of interest in the line(s) so marked. Roy's edition was of considerable help regarding information on historical figures mentioned in the texts. Details of codicology regarding the presentation of the text in the base manuscript (that is, *R*) are included, especially where they may relate to variants.

A note is necessary to elucidate the use of paragraph or capitulum marks sprinkled along the left-hand margins of the text blocks in all of the debate poem manuscripts. The configuration of these marks is consistent and distinctive. It consists of a colored *C* shape, which a vertical slash distinguishes from the regular uppercase letter. These marks are rendered in the debate poems in red or blue, or in gold in the more deluxe manuscripts, surrounded by a field of pink or blue. Where the decoration of the manuscript is incomplete (as in *L*3), the preparation for the paragraph marks stands in for them, in the form of quickly executed, double diagonal lines.

The functions of the paragraph mark are consistent with the double locus of its production: it was the scribe who determined where the mark would be placed but the rubricator who painted it.[141] In keeping with the job of the latter, the paragraph mark obviously has a display function. It stands out clearly both by adding a touch of color to the page surface and by breaking the otherwise empty plane of the margin. Its presence lends a certain visual rhythm to the pages, interrupting otherwise quite regular and undifferentiated columns of lines. As a form of punctuation, the responsibility of the scribe, its genesis lies in the conflation and transformation of a variety of marks used to indicate the *paragraphus* and the *capitulum*. True to these origins, the symbol indicates some kind of division in the text. In Christine's short lyric poetry, it often appears at the beginning of poems or occasionally at the head of each strophe within a poem. In her narrative works, by contrast, it has an indexing function; it is used to mark new stages of the story, indicate a change of speaker, draw attention to aphorisms or turning points in the articulation of an argument, or highlight lines containing proper names used as *exempla*.

Given these functions as their primary purpose, the paragraph marks found in the manuscripts of the debate poems form relatively coherent systems. Often all copies of any of the three texts use a paragraph mark at the same line. Certain manuscripts, including *R*, use them more copiously than others do.[142] Occasionally it is difficult to understand the rationale behind their placement; some fall mid-sentence or where none of the other manuscripts use them, or are left floating between two lines. This apparently idiosyncratic usage seems much more frequent in *Poissy* than in the other texts, especially in the first section, which details the visit to the priory.[143] The reason might well be that the descriptive portion of the text has fewer of the rhetorical formulae that so often signal a transition in the debate proper (commonly beginning with *ainsi, adonc,* or *mais or,* for example). As a consequence, one can speculate that the paragraph marks in the first half of *Poissy* serve primarily in their decorative function, to break the text for the eye rather than to indicate key lines and passages in the narrative.

Whatever their function, paragraph marks, like other paralinguistic devices in medieval manuscripts, cannot be eliminated without the loss of an interpretive tool. As a system of labeling, paragraph marks provide information on aspects of the work that at least one agent active in the production of the manuscript considered particularly noteworthy. As such, they must be treated as meaningful signifiers in both the editing and analysis of late medieval texts. They are consequently reproduced here as found in *R* in order to represent as accurately as possible one witness to the textual tradition.

IV

Notes to the Introduction

I. Text and Context: Background to the Poems

1. Several full-length bibliographical studies of Christine have been published. The best and most recent is *Christine de Pizan: Her Life and Works* by Charity Cannon Willard. Also useful is Marie-Josèphe Pinet's book *Christine de Pisan, 1364–1430: Etude biographique et littéraire*. Enid McLeod's *The Order of the Rose: The Life and Ideas of Christine de Pizan* is a more popular account. For further references on all aspects of Christine de Pizan's career, consult Angus J. Kennedy, *Christine de Pizan: A Bibliographical Guide*, his update, "A Selective Bibliography of Christine de Pizan Scholarship, circa 1980–1987," in *Reinterpreting Christine de Pizan*, as well as his *Christine de Pizan: A Bibliographical Guide, Supplement 1*. See also Edith Yenal, *Christine de Pizan: A Bibliography*. Autobiographical material in Christine's own writing can be found in the *Livre de la Mutacion de Fortune*, the *Livre du Chemin de long estude*, and in *L'Avision-Christine*.

2. The formerly common spelling, *Pisan*, seems to have stemmed from the misapprehension that Christine's family came from Pisa. Christine herself, however, spelled her name with a z in presentation copies of her work, and this is by now the accepted version. Kennedy's 1984 bibliographical guide clarifies this issue (see p. 12 and items 235 and 128.1).

3. More complete information on Christine's works can be found in the biographies listed in note 1 and in the informative entry on Christine by Suzanne Solente in the *Histoire littéraire de la France*.

4. Notable exceptions to this generalization are the collection edited by Kenneth Varty, *Christine de Pisan's Ballades, Rondeaux, and Virelais: An Anthology*, and the articles by James Laidlaw in *Modern Language Review* concerning Christine's reworking of her poetry through several "editions": "Christine de Pizan: An Author's Progress," and "Christine de Pizan: A Publisher's Progress." More recently, literary aspects of the *ballade* cycles in particular have attracted critical attention; see, for example, Altmann, "L'art de l'autoportrait littéraire"; Liliane Dulac, "Dissymétrie et échec de la communication"; Laidlaw, "The *Cent Balades*: The Marriage of Con-

tent and Form"; Françoise Paradis, "Une polyphonie narrative"; Willard, "Christine de Pizan: *Cent ballades d'amant et de dame*: Criticism of Courtly Love" and "Lovers' Dialogues in Christine de Pizan's Lyric Poetry."

5. Gaston Paris, ed., "Un poème inédit de Martin le Franc." All quotations of Le Franc's text are taken from this source.

6. This quotation as well as the following passage are from G. Paris, "Un poème inédit," p. 415.

7. *Mais elle fut Tulle et Cathon: / Tulle, car en toute eloquence / Elle eut la rose et le bouton; Cathon aussy en sapience;* in G. Paris, "Un poème inédit," p. 416. The name Tulle (Tully) comes from that rhetorician's full name, Marcus Tullius Cicero. The Cathon that Le Franc refers to is likely the *Disticha Catonis,* a collection of moral sententiae well known in medieval France and spuriously attributed to the famous model of Roman virtue, Cato—whether the Elder or the Younger is uncertain.

8. Pierre Le Gentil, "Christine de Pisan, poète méconnu."

9. Willard has published several articles that illustrate this point, among them "Christine de Pizan: *Cent ballades d'amant et de dame:* Criticism of Courtly Love," "Concepts of Love According to Guillaume de Machaut, Christine de Pizan, and Pietro Bembo," and "Lovers' Dialogues in Christine de Pizan's Lyric Poetry from the *Cent Ballades* to the *Cent ballades d'amant et de dame.*" Also relevant are the introduction by Jacqueline Cerquiglini to her edition of the *Cent ballades d'amant et de dame* and two articles by Liliane Dulac, "Dissymétrie et échec de la communication dans les *Cent ballades d'amant et de dame* de Christine de Pizan" and "Christine de Pisan et le malheur des 'vrais amans'."

10. For the sake of consistency, the full titles of the works have been retained as Maurice Roy presented them in the first modern edition of Christine's poetic works (*Oeuvres poétiques de Christine de Pisan*) and by which titles they are now known in literary histories and bibliographies. Roy took the names from the rubrics preceding the texts in MS D (B.N. f.fr. 835, 606, 836, 605), his base text; in other manuscripts, the titles vary somewhat. In this introduction, as elsewhere in the book, the poems are referred to by shortened forms of their titles.

11. Dating must remain approximate for lack of documentation. Enid McLeod, however, states that the *Debat de deux amans* can be dated to 1401 on the basis of internal evidence (p. 58). Roy also decides from traceable facts in the text that *Deux amans* must date from between 1400 and 1402: the former is the year in which Châteaumorand fought at the head of a small troup in Constantinople, an event to which Christine alludes in ll. 1627–37; the latter corresponds to the death of Louis de Sancerre ("le connestable de Sancerre"), whom Christine mentions at ll. 1593–94 as still among the living. See Roy, vol. 2, p. xiii.

12. See Arthur Piaget, "La cour amoureuse dite de Charles VI"; Daniel Poirion, *Le poète et le prince,* pp. 37–38; Cerquiglini, "1401, St. Valentine's Day"; and in French, Cerquiglini-Toulet, *La couleur de la mélancholie,* pp. 49–56. For the actual composition of the Court of Love, see Carla Bozzolo, Hélène Loyau, and Monique

Ornato, "Hommes de culture et hommes de pouvoir parisiens à la cour amoureuse."

13. This quotation comes from a statement in the fiftieth of her collection of *Cent Balades* (ll. 11–12), in which she describes love as the lightest (*le plus legier*) and the most popular topic at the disposition of poets.

14. Werchin himself wrote a poem a few years later that might be construed as an answer to the cases Christine presents him with in *Trois jugemens*. Entitled *Le songe de la barge*, it was composed in 1404 and consists of approximately 3,500 lines. The only existing edition is the partial one published with an introduction and commentary by Arthur Piaget in *Romania*. In her biography of Christine (p. 67), Willard suggests that Werchin's poem "gives every evidence of being a reply to Christine" because it imitates features found in *Trois jugemens,* namely its formal properties (three decasyllabic lines followed by a four-syllable line introducing the next rhyme) and its narrative framework (in Werchin's case a maritime expedition, involving a fleet assembled at the port of Brest before setting off for England). Although Werchin writes about the question of loyalty, which is the essential theme of each of the lovers' disputes in the debate Christine sent him, he in no way attempts to settle their specific complaints. His poem therefore takes its place alongside Christine's as an example of the genre but does not constitute a direct response to her work. Influences other than *Trois jugemens* are evident in *Le songe:* Piaget also names Christine's *Dit de Poissy* (which, he believes, is also dedicated to Werchin) as well as Oton de Granson's *Complainte de saint Valentin* as sources of Werchin's literary inspiration. Piaget's opinion of the poem is not high; he characterizes the *Songe* as "fort médiocre, d'une psychologie rudimentaire, sans aucun souci de la forme" (p. 110), an assessment which the excerpts he prints would tend to confirm.

15. The question turns on which patron was absent from Paris when *Poissy* was written, because the text stresses that it is addressed to someone who is *loings de ci* (l. 10). Willard draws attention to the fact that Werchin's pilgrimage to Santiago de Compostela, which he is said to have undertaken at the time the poem was composed, did not take place until the summer of 1402. Boucicaut and Jean de Châteaumorand, however, were both in Constantinople in the spring of 1400. See Willard, *Christine de Pizan: Her Life and Works*, pp. 64–65, 68.

16. Some of the material in this and the following section has appeared in an earlier version in Barbara K. Altmann, "Reopening the Case: Machaut's *Jugement* Poems as a Source in Christine de Pizan."

17. Badel, *Introduction à la vie littéraire du moyen âge,* p. 162; Ernest Hoepffner gives the same kind of definition in describing Machaut's *dits;* he calls them "poésies narratives et didactiques" (*Oeuvres de Guillaume de Machaut*, vol. 1, p. lii). The source of the quotation from Le Gentil still eludes me, after considerable searching. It is attributed to Le Gentil by Cerquiglini in "Le clerc et l'écriture," p. 158, and by Daniel Poirion, "Traditions et fonctions du 'dit poétique' au XIVe at au XVe siècle," p. 148. However, neither of them gives a complete reference.

18. Cerquiglini, "Le clerc et l'écriture," p. 158. She gives the example of Jean Renart's works.

19. In his introduction to *Jean Froissart: Dits et Débats*, Anthime Fourrier examines the word's etymology and its relationship to *ditié, traitié,* and *livre/livret*, and suggests that *dit* is loosely synonymous with these other terms. See pp. 14–22.

20. Paul Zumthor, "Rhétorique et poétique latines et romanes," p. 88. Paul Imbs offers a similar, more recent formulation: "Il semble que le dit ne soit pas autre chose que le nom commun par lequel on désigne une forme littéraire qui précisément offre cette particularité de ne pas obéir à des règles strictes: le dit permet en effet de réunir des éléments divers selon des seules exigences de la matière...." See Imbs, *Le Voir-Dit de Guillaume de Machaut*, p. 213.

21. See Cerquiglini, "Le Dit." Other, older discussions of the *dit* include Le Gentil, *Littérature française du moyen âge*, pp. 160–61, in which he lists in a clear and concise manner the many genres from which a *dit* may borrow, its potential for either allegorical or realistic exposition, and an enlightening explanation of the two different aspects the lyrical element can take.

22. Cerquiglini, "Le Dit," p. 87.

23. Cerquiglini explains this in "Le clerc et l'écriture" as a "jeu au second degré" (p. 158); "un jeu de distanciation" (p. 159); and "une méta-écriture" (p. 155).

24. Cerquiglini, "Le Dit," p. 89.

25. See Altmann, "Diversity and Coherence in Christine de Pizan's *Dit de Poissy*."

26. For background information on the factors accounting for the popularity of debates, see Michel-André Bossy's introduction to *Medieval Debate Poetry*, particularly pp. xi–xvi. On vernacular debate forms (especially those of the twelfth century) as a literary manifestation of formal debate, see R. Howard Bloch, *Medieval French Literature and Law*, p. 167 ff.

27. On the history of the *dit* and its relation to the *tenson*, see Rudolf Zenker, *Die provenzalische Tenzone*, pp. 58–66. Zenker cites *Trois jugemens* as an important fifteenth-century example of this style of poem (but without mentioning Machaut's *Roy de Behaingne*).

28. On the *jugement d'amour*, see Edmond Faral, *Recherches sur les sources latines des contes et romans courtois du moyen âge*, pp. 191–250; Marc-René Jung, *Etudes sur le poème allégorique en France au moyen âge*, especially pp. 192–226; Paul Meyer, "Notice du ms. 25970 de la Bibliothèque Phillipps (Cheltenham)" and "Melior et Ydoine"; and Charles Oulmont, *Les débats du clerc du chevalier*, which includes the texts of these poems, although the readings are not reliable.

29. On the *jeu-parti*, consult Artur Långfors, *Recueil général des jeux-partis français*. Georges Lote, in *Histoire du vers français*, vol. 2, pp. 215–17, provides specifications concerning the metrical structures and rhyme schemes used.

30. Hoepffner, vol. 1: *Behaigne*, pp. 57–135; *Navarre*: pp. 137–291. There are also two recent editions of *Behaigne*; see William W. Kibler and James I. Wimsatt, *Le jugement du roy de Behaigne; and Remede de fortune*, and R. Barton Palmer, *Gui-*

llaume de Machaut. All line references for Machaut's poems refer to Hoepffner's edition.

31. Hoepffner, vol. 1, p. lxiii.

32. On the late medieval French debate genre, see the article "Le débat" by Pierre-Yves Badel in *La littérature française aux XIVe et XVe siècles*. Badel establishes a typology that distinguishes three subsets of this genre—the dialogue, the *jugement*, and the debate itself—using as criteria the importance of the conflict under discussion and formal structure (p. 100). By these guidelines, Christine's poems, like Machaut's, are in the *jugement* category, primarily because they are written in verse but not in strophes, but also because the dialogue is largely reduced to successive long speeches (pp. 103–4). Badel emphasizes, however, that because of the large role given the narration of events, which does more than simply set the stage for the debate, both Machaut's and Christine's *jugements* are more truly to be considered *dits* (on Christine, p. 98; on Machaut, p. 104). He makes the perceptive statement that with Christine's *Trois jugemens*, "nous sommes fort près de la nouvelle italienne" (p. 98, note 12).

33. The phrase is a translation of Hans Robert Jauss's *Erwartungsrichtung*. One of several works by Jauss that employs and explains this concept is *Toward an Aesthetic of Reception*, particularly p. 79.

II. Theme and Variations: Interplay of Form and Content

34. While often referred to as the "abbey" of Poissy, the institution was actually a priory.

35. Nadia Margolis, "Christine de Pizan: The Poetess as Historian."

36. Ibid., p. 367.

37. Philosophie asks Christine:

> Nas tu enfans beaulx gracieux et de bon sens ton premier fruit qui est une fille donnee a dieu et a son service rendue par inspiracion divine de sa pure pure [sic] voulente / et oultre ton gre en leglise et noble religion de dames a poyssi / ou elle en fleur de ionnece et tres grant beaute se porte tant notablement en vie contemplative et devocion que la ioye de la relacion de sa belle vie souventes fois te rend grant reconfort Et quant de elle meismes tu recoips les tres doulces et devotes lettres discretes et sages que elle tenvoye pour ta consolacion esquelles elle ieunette et innocente te induit et amonneste a hair le monde et desprisier prosperite. (f°66v°–67r°)

This passage is quoted from the edition by Sister Mary Louis Towner, *Lavision-Christine*, p. 174.

38. On the convent itself, see the relevant chapters in Edmond Bories, *Histoire de la ville de Poissy*; S. Moreau-Rendu, *Le Prieuré royal de Saint-Louis de Poissy*; Octave Noël, *Histoire de la ville de Poissy*. Also helpful for background on the Do-

minican order is William A. Hinnebusch, *The History of the Dominican Order*, particularly Chapter XIII, vol. 1, "The Second and Third Orders." The information in my brief history of the institution is based on these sources. An unpublished paper by Willard, entitled "A Visit to the Dominican Abbey of Poissy in 1400," gives a useful summary of the history of the convent and the visit described in the *Dit de Poissy*.

39. Moreau-Rendu, p. 52.

40. As quoted by Moreau-Rendu: "Elles ne pourront les recevoir sans en avoir demandé la permission de nos successeurs roy de France," p. 315.

41. Ibid., p. 39.

42. Hinnebusch, p. 385.

43. Ibid., pp. 135, 398.

44. For more complete information on the inhabitants of the convent whom Christine mentions by name, see the notes following the text of the poem.

45. Willard, "A Visit to the Dominican Abbey," p. 5.

46. Moreau-Rendu, pp. 66–68.

47. Quoted by Bories, p. 39.

48. Millard Meiss reproduces a photograph of this altarpiece in *French Painting in the Time of Jean de Berry: The Limbourgs and Their Contemporaries*, vol. 2, fig. 383.

49. See Denis Lalande, *Le Livre des Fais du bon messire Jehan le Maingre, dit Bouciquaut*. Note to line 1261 of the *Dit de Poissy* gives further details on contemporary sources.

50. Lalande, pp. 119–20.

51. The problem of attribution for the *Livre des Fais* is discussed by Lalande in his edition of the text, pp. xlii–lvii. Jean-Louis Picherit argues his case in "Christine de Pisan et le *Livre des Faicts du bon messire Jean le Maingre*." More recently, Hélène Millet argues in favor of Nicholas de Gonesse as author of *Le Livre des Fais;* see her article "Qui a écrit *Le Livre des Fais du bon messire Jehan Le Maingre, dit Bouciquaut?*"

52. Again, the term is taken from Jauss, p. 80.

53. Christine tells her patron that she has composed the work *A celle fin que vo cuer avoyez / A soulacier / Aucunement* (ll. 47–49) and adds, *Car tout d'amours sera cilz mien rommans* (l. 53). One finds a very similar passage at the end of the poem: *Ce dictié fis pour vous duire a memoire / Joye et solas par ouÿr ceste hystoire / Qui d'amours fait mencion et memoire* (ll. 2009–11).

54. *Si ay prouvé* ... (l. 1742).

55. For such passages see, for example, ll. 641 ff., 722.

56. *Elle veult toutevoye / Que ains que l'en rende / Le jugement, aux dames on demande / Leur bon avis* (ll. 1491–97).

57. Willard has written a number of articles on this topic. See, for example, "Concepts of Love" and "Lovers' Dialogues."

58. See, for example, *Trois jugemens*, ll. 356–60, in which the lady comes "back to reason" (*le sien cuer a raison se revint*, l. 358) when she abandons her inconstant lover, and ll. 845–52, in which reason saves the lady from despair.

59. Thelma S. Fenster, *Le Livre du Duc des vrais amans*, p. 177, ll. 204–5.

60. Thérèse Moreau and Eric Hicks, *Cité des dames*, 3.19, p. 277.

61. Roberta Krueger, *Women Readers and the Ideology of Gender in Old French Verse Romance*, p. 226. See chapter 8, "A Woman's Response: Christine de Pizan's *Le Livre du Duc des Vrais Amans* and the Limits of Romance," pp. 217–46. In what is obviously a structural parallel to the endings of the debates, Krueger points out the "conspicuous lack of resolution" in Christine's romance, which "invites the reader's critique of the *vrais amans*" (p. 242).

62. Despite Christine's vehement objection to other aspects of the *Roman de la Rose*, as embodied particularly in her epistolary debate on the topic (with Jean Gerson, the Col brothers, and Jean de Montreuil), she is clearly prepared to endorse the figure of Raison in an alliance on the side of dispassionate good sense. One finds indirect corroboration for this approval even in the *Epistres*; for example, the following from *Le Débat sur le Roman de la Rose*, edited by Eric Hicks: "Je ne reppreuve mie Le Rommant de la rose en toutes pars, car il y a de bonnes choses et bien dictes sans faille" (p. 21). For a comparison of Christine and Jean de Meun, see Douglas Kelly, "Amitié comme anti-amour."

63. Cerquiglini, "Le Dit," p. 92.

64. I regret that Coleman's book, *Public Reading and the Reading Public in Late Medieval England and France*, came to my attention too late to be taken into consideration more fully in this discussion. The reader is referred for background to Coleman's first chapter, which reviews and critiques the evolution of orality/literacy theory. In building her case for the importance of aurality, Coleman cites Christine de Pizan among other French authors, and in particular her *Livre de la Paix* (pp. 61–62), her letters concerning the *Roman de la Rose* (p. 113), and her biography of Charles V, the *Livre des Fais et bonnes meurs* (pp. 118, 121). Another provocative analysis of the oral mentality and its pervasive presence in fourteenth-century English philosophical, political, and poetic discourse is Jesse Gellrich's book, *Discourse and Dominion in the Fourteenth Century*. Literary texts are the focus of chapters 6, on *Sir Gawain and the Green Knight*, and 7, on Chaucer's *Knight's Tale*.

65. Machaut's *Prologue* can be found in Hoepffner's *Oeuvres de Guillaume de Machaut*, vol. 1, pp. 1–12. The lines in question (126–34) are as follows:

> David li prophetes jadis, / Quant il voloit apaisier l'ire / De Dieu, il acordoit sa lire, / dont il harpoit si proprement / Et chantoit si devotement / Hympnes, psautiers et orisons, / Einsi comme nous le lisons, / Que sa harpe a Dieu tant plaisoit / Et son chant qu'il se rapaisoit.

66. Deschamp's *L'Art de dictier* is available in a recent critical edition and translation by Deborah M. Sinnreich-Levi.

67. M. B. Parkes, *Pause and Effect: An Introduction to the History of Punctuation in the West*, p. 34.

68. A recent example is the book by Sandra Hindman on Chrétien de Troyes, *Sealed in Parchment: Rereadings of Knighthood in the Illuminated Manuscripts of Chrétien de Troyes*. Major theorists to be considered on questions of orality and

literacy must include Walter J. Ong, *Orality and Literacy: The Technologizing of the Word*; Brian Stock, *The Implications of Literacy: Written Language and Models of Interpretation in the Eleventh and Twelfth Centuries*; Jeffrey Kittay, "Utterance Unmoored: The Changing Interpretation of the Act of Writing in the European Middle Ages"; and Paul Zumthor, "Le texte médiéval entre oralité et écriture."

69. A brief introduction to this point can be found in Ong's article "Orality, Literacy, and Medieval Textualization."

70. Cerquiglini concisely analyzes Christine's anagrams in her preface to the *Cent Ballades d'amant et de dame*, pp. 22–23. The significance of *creintis* as an anagram is discussed comprehensively in Christine Laennec, "Christine Antygrafe," pp. 35–49. See also my article on the definition in the *Cent Balades* of Christine's role as author: Altmann, "L'art de l'autoportrait littéraire dans les *Cent Balades* de Christine de Pizan," and, again, on the word *creintis*, Claire Nouvet in "Writing in Fear."

71. See on this topic Kevin Brownlee, "Romance Rewritings: Courtly Discourse and Auto-Citation in Christine de Pizan."

72. Laidlaw, "Christine de Pizan—An Author's Progress" and "Christine de Pizan—A Publisher's Progress."

73. On the new aspects of book culture in late medieval France, see Jacqueline Cerquiglini-Toulet, *La couleur de la mélancolie*, and "L'amour des livres au XIVe siècle."

III. Philology and Codicology

74. The most helpful are those in Hicks, *Le Débat sur le Roman de la Rose*, pp. lxx–lxxxi; see also Roy, vol. 1, pp. v–xxi, and vol. 2, pp. xiii–xiv (although, as will be shown, some of his information has been proved incorrect); and Gianni Mombello, *La Tradizione manoscritta dell'"Epistre Othea" di Christine de Pizan*, pp. 9–13, 16–22, 63–70, 106–16, 199–200. Laidlaw provides details of the contents, decoration, collation, and signatures of the five manuscripts containing all three debates in the tables following his article "Christine de Pizan—A Publisher's Progress." Other descriptions will be mentioned with reference to specific manuscripts.

75. Laidlaw, "Christine de Pizan—An Author's Progress," pp. 532–50. An explanation of his *sigla* and the quotation given can be found on p. 534.

76. The difficulty of choosing new *sigla* for the two single-work manuscripts will be apparent. Several of the more obvious choices (*D* for *Deux amans*, for example, or simply *A* for *Amans*) are ruled out because of *sigla* used by Roy and others. A single letter is preferable for ease of reference and for consistency, which eliminates the possibility of combinations such as *BR* for Brussels and *B.N.* for Bibliothèque Nationale (itself undesirable, because that abbreviation could apply to several other witnesses). The *siglum S* is intended to set these manuscripts apart from the others while giving them a label that is meaningful in terms of their format. The distinction between $(S)_1$ and $(S)_2$ is not intended to be hierarchical; both appear to date from the same range of a few years, and they contain equally good texts. One might arguably give primacy to S_1, however, on the basis of its more thoroughly docu-

mented provenance and the superior quality of its miniature, as compared with that of S2. See the respective manuscript descriptions for more detail on their readings, and the section "Miniatures" for a discussion of their illuminations.

77. Laidlaw, "A Publisher's Progress," p. 41. Roy lists it simply as "du XVe siècle," vol. 2, p. xiii. Other mentions of the manuscript can be found as follows: In the article "Christine de Pizan, the Earl of Salisbury and Henry IV," Laidlaw uses S1 as one of several examples to demonstrate that Christine varied her judgments according to political expediencies. Camille Gaspar and Frédéric Lyna, in *Les principaux manuscrits à peintures de la Bibliothèque royale de Belgique*, 2ème partie, p. 10, number 202 and pl. CXVIb, posit a date of circa 1410 for S1. Their dating must be revised, given the evidence provided by the dedicatory *ballade*. That information would support a date more or less contemporary with BR 10983, another Christine manuscript containing a miniature to which they compare the one in S1. (See the section "Miniatures" and note 135 below for more information on these illuminations.) Georges Doutrepont, in his book *La littérature française à la cour des ducs de Bourgogne*, lists the titles by Christine de Pizan that were in the collection of Philippe le Bon (1396–1467), among which was this copy of *Deux amans*. Doutrepont posits that the manuscript must have come from Charles d'Albret; see vol. 2, p. 292, note 10. See also Georges Dogaer and Marguerite Debae, *La librairie de Philippe le bon*, number 151, pp. 103–4, for a brief description of the manuscript and miniature (no reproduction).

78. Gilbert Ouy and Christine Reno, "Identification des autographes de Christine de Pizan."

79. The illumination is reproduced in Lucie Schäfer, "Die Illustrationen zu den Handschriften der Christine de Pizan," pl. 57, and in Pierre Cockshaw, *Miniatures en grisaille*, pp. 14–15.

80. Roy, vol. 1, pp. 231–32.

81. This manuscript is described briefly by Roy in vol. 2, p. xiv. For Laidlaw's dating, see "A Publisher's Progress," p. 41. See page 42 of the same article for additional details concerning the decoration of the manuscript and characteristics of the hand in which it is written.

82. Ouy and Reno, "Identification des autographes de Christine de Pizan," p. 227.

83. Roy, vol. 2, p. xiv.

84. There are thirteen items in the first volume, B.N. f.fr. 835, numbered consecutively. They are (1) *Cent balades*; (2) *Virelais*; (3) *Ballades d'estrange façon*; (4) *Lais*; (5) *Rondeaux*; (6) *Jeux à vendre*; (7) *Balades de divers propos*; (8) *Epistre au dieu d'amours*; (9) *Complainte amoureuse*; (10) *Le debat de deux amans*; (11) *Le Livre des Trois juge-mens*; (12) *Le Livre du Dit de Poissy*; (13) *Les epistres sur le Roman de la Rose*. The list of contents and order of items is similar in the other two collections, R and L. In the five manuscripts that contain all three judgment poems, they always appear in the same order: *Deux amans, Trois jugemens, Dit de Poissy*. *Poissy* always follows *Trois jugemens* directly. In L, the *Epistre au dieu d'amours* and the *Dit de la rose* intervene between *Deux amans* and *Trois jugemens*.

85. In "The Second 'Autograph' Edition of Christine de Pizan's Lesser Poetical Works," Hicks and Ouy have suggested that the four volumes listed were created separately and put together later. Maureen Curnow, in her dissertation, pp. 360–71, suggests that B.N. f.fr. 607, which contains the *Livre de la Cité des dames*, forms the fifth and last part of the compendium. In "A Publisher's Progress," Laidlaw throws doubt on Hicks and Ouy's theory but gives new codicological evidence that supports Curnow's view (see pp. 52–59). Laidlaw's article contains a very useful, highly detailed discussion of the composition of all five compendia in which the judgment poems are included, in an illustration of how Christine the "publisher" organized the production of her manuscripts.

86. Laidlaw speculates that folio 49 was taken from the manuscript because of the miniature it must have contained. See "A Publisher's Progress," p. 46.

87. See Hicks, p. lxxi.

88. On the dating of *L3* and its similarity to *L1*, see in particular Laidlaw's two articles: "An Author's Progress," p. 533, and "A Publisher's Progress," p. 42 and note 24.

89. These manuscripts were known at the time as Bibliothèque Impériale 7087-2 (fonds de la Mare) and 7217 (ancien fonds), respectively. See Pougin, p. 535.

90. For a detailed description of this manuscript and its history, see Paul Meyer, "Note sur le manuscrit offert par Christine de Pisan à Isabeau de Bavière."

91. See Sandra L. Hindman, "The Composition of the Manuscript of Christine de Pizan's Collected Works in the British Library: A Reassessment."

92. See Ouy and Reno, "Identification des autographes de Christine de Pizan," which identifies the three hands in which Christine's manuscripts are executed. Further details are given in Ouy and Reno's subsequent article, "Les hésitations de Christine."

93. In vol. 1, there are two sets of foliation numbers after f. 50. For details, see Laidlaw, "A Publisher's Progress," note 55, p. 60, and Hindman, "The Composition of the Manuscript of Christine de Pizan's Collected Works," note 15, p. 121. The pencil foliation has been used here, which discounts two blank leaves following f. 50.

94. Paris, vol. 5, pp. 162–67. Earlier, according to Roy (vol. 2, Notes, p. 306), a very few lines had been reproduced by the Abbé Sallier in *Mémoires de l'Académie des inscriptions*, vol. 17, p. 515.

95. Vol. 5, p. 171 ff.

96. Pougin presents ll. 1–14, 35–52, 57–59, 65–69, 167–68, 212–731, 773–94, and 1397–1400.

97. Errors in transcription (or typesetting) include *la* for *me*, l. 58; *arrivent* for *aviennent*, l. 69; *La* for *Le*, l. 380; *Ecuismes* for *Es cuisines*, l. 431; *ou* for *qui*, l. 437; *chenal* for *cheval*, l. 445; *antieulx* for *autieulx*, l. 507; *blanchie* for *blanche est*, l. 521; *roison* for *raison*, l. 619; *saintes* for *faites*, l. 675; *demes* for *dames*, l. 786; *Hors* for *Lors*, l. 791. He changes *prieuse* to *prieure* in l. 251 (although it no longer rhymes with the other lines in the quatrain), l. 291, and l. 645, but not in l. 773. *Leans* is regularly changed to *ceans* (ll. 298, 377, 500, 555, 589).

98. Using *Poissy* as an example, the following errors occur in Roy's edition: in l. 233, D does not read *tres*, but *tiens* (abbreviated in the manuscript with a nasal bar over the *e*). He is incorrect in noting that R and D omit *s'est* in l. 1645, when in fact both read *c'est*. The rejected reading for D in l. 1686 is not *Qu'en voulsisse*, but *Que* [in abbreviated form] *n'en voulsisse*, the same reading he gives for R. The D reading in l. 1822 is *racropis*, not *raccopis*, which he rejects. Manuscript D does not omit *ja* in l. 1958, as he indicates.

99. The omission is made clear in vol. 2, p. xvii.

100. Among the variants for the first 200 lines of *Poissy*, for example, he does *not* note that L as well as R omits *du dit* from the rubric; R reads *je tendray* for D *j'entendré* in l. 7; L reads *Bien vueilliez* for D and R *Si en vueilliez* in l. 27; L2 reads differently than L3 in l. 55; R reads *Qui . . . qui* for D *Qu'il . . . qui* in ll. 19 and 109; R reads *chantant a* for D *chantant de* in l. 119; R agrees with L against D in ll. 121 and 174; R reads *les* for D *ces* in l. 141; L2 reads *veoir et* for D *veoir ou* in l. 174.

101. Roy, vol. 1, p. xvii.

102. See ibid. It has been suggested that Roy's insistence regarding the primacy of D, even in the face of his own assessment of R, may well stem simply from French nationalism. Margolis demonstrates how Roy tinkered with rubric representation and the placement of individual poems in editing the *Complaintes amoureuses* among Christine's early lyric poetry, thus "subtly relegating to secondary status the Queen's Ms. [R] itself." See "Clerkliness and Courtliness in the *Complaintes* of Christine de Pizan."

103. This hypothesis is strengthened by evidence in inventories of the Duke of Berry's possessions, that other manuscripts were added to Jean's collection from Louis's library at about the same time. On this point, see Millard Meiss and Sharon Off, "The Bookkeeping of Robinet d'Estampes and the Chronology of Jean de Berry's Manuscripts," p. 228.

104. Vol. 1, p. xx (my emphasis).

105. Quoted from L1 with punctuation and diacritical marks added.

106. See Roy's "Généalogie probable des manuscrits," vol. 1, p. xx; Hicks, p. lviii; Mombello, p. 306.

107. As mentioned above, L1 is now unanimously dated from the first decade of the fifteenth century, and L3 is recognized as the latest of the three. Roy is mistaken in dating L2 as later than L1 and L3: Hicks dates L2 from "le commencement du XVe siècle" (p. lxx), while Mombello allows only "Prima metà del sec. XV" (p. 349). Laidlaw, in the most recent reworking of this subject, states categorically but without further explanation that L1 and L2 were copied under Christine's supervision and can be dated between 1402 and 1405; see "An Author's Progress," p. 533. (Laidlaw is supported on the question of L2 by Ouy and Reno, "Identification des autographes de Christine de Pizan," p. 224.) He is also more explicit with regard to L3, dating it from "the first third of the fifteenth century and after 1407 (o.s.)" (p. 533).

108. Félix Lecoy, "Note sur quelques ballades de Christine de Pisan." His study also has important implications for the dating of the L manuscripts. Roy assumes

that one of the *Ballades d'estrange façon* (no. 16, vol. 1, p. 122) is dedicated to the *connétable* Charles d'Albret, who held that position as of February 1403; it is unclear whether this is the cause or effect of his reasoning that the L family of manuscripts could not be the original(s) produced before the end of 1402. Lecoy constructed an interpretation that leaves the dating of those texts open, in suggesting that the *ballade* in question was actually dedicated to Charles d'Albret's predecessor, Louis de Sancerre (see p. 109 of Lecoy's article).

109. See Laidlaw, "An Author's Progress."

110. Ibid., p. 550.

111. Varty, pp. xxxvii–xxxviii.

112. Ibid., p. xxxviii.

113. Richards, *Christine de Pizan: The Book of the City of Ladies*, p. xiv. See also n. 38, p. li.

114. Ibid.

115. In the sections "Language," "Versification," and "Establishment of the Text," the titles of the three debate poems will be shortened even further when in parentheses to simplify the many line numbers given as examples. The title *Deux amans* is rendered as *DA*, *Trois jugemens* as *TJ*, *Poissy* as *P*. The number(s) of the line(s) follow directly after the abbreviation.

116. Although no systematic study of Christine's language has yet been undertaken, the following sources deal with specific aspects of the topic: A.M. Binias, "Glossaire des vieux mots employés par Christine de Pisan dans le *Livre du Dit de Poissy*"; J. E. Bruins, *Observations sur la langue d'Eustache Deschamps et de Christine de Pisan*; Bernard Combettes, "Une notion stylistique et ses rapports avec la syntaxe"; Lucy M. Gay, "On the Language of Christine de Pisan"; Jean-Claude Mühlethaler, "'Les poètes que de vert on couronne'." On the very learned style and vocabulary of her *Cité des Dames*, see Richards, "Christine de Pizan and the Question of Feminist Rhetoric."

117. See Robert-Léon Wagner, *L'ancien français*, pp. 26–28, who gives as the two major characteristics differentiating Old from Middle French the declension of nouns and adjectives and the high incidence of hiatus, both of which break down in the later period. For an overview of Middle French phonology, orthography, morphology, and syntax, consult Peter Rickard's *Chrestomathie de la langue française au quinzième siècle*, pp. 19–35; his anthology (pp. 58–62) includes an excerpt from Christine's *Livre des Fais et bonnes meurs du sage roy Charles V*. Two much more detailed studies are Christiane Marchello-Nizia, *Histoire de la langue française aux XIVe et XVe siècles*, and Robert Martin and Marc Wilmet, *Manuel du français du moyen âge*. I have relied particularly on Marchello-Nizia, whose work is frequently referred to below.

118. On this topic, see Marchello-Nizia, p. 112.

119. On these archaic forms, see Marchello-Nizia as follows: possessive adjectives, pp. 136–37; *ouÿl* for *oui*, p. 255; *o* for *avec(que)*, still a relatively common form, p. 274; forms of *trouver* (*truis* being very unusual here), p. 221; old forms of *estre* in the imperfect, pp. 218–19.

120. For the morphology of the preterite, see Marchello-Nizia, especially pp. 215–16, and Mildred K. Pope, *From Latin to Modern French*, §1037, for more on analogical formations.

121. On this topic, see Marchello-Nizia, pp. 57–61.

122. For a discussion of this phenomenon and the letters most likely to be added, see Marchello-Nizia, p. 93, and Pope, §707.

123. Richards discusses this aspect of the language found in *R* with respect to his choice of that manuscript as the base text for his translation of the *Cité des dames*; see *The Book of the City of Ladies*, p. xlv.

124. The spelling *iau*, which might be construed as a northern trait, was in fact geographically generalized. See Jacques Chaurand, *Introduction à la dialectologie française*, p. 72: "L'aboutissement IAUS, de *ellus*, est, à peu de chose près, général; ... [cette forme] a cédé la place, en moyen français, à la forme EAU, tandis que la première devenait populaire." Note that the poem also uses the newer *eau* spelling: for example, *beau(l)x* (P22, P317, P326); *nouveaulx* (P506).

125. Pope, §785.

126. The first three lines of each poem, all of which are decasyllabic, constitute the only incomplete quatrains. The fourth line, which has four syllables, then introduces the rhyme for the second quatrain.

127. Hoepffner discusses this form in his introduction to the "Complainte" contained in the *Remede de Fortune;* see *Oeuvres de Guillaume de Machaut*, vol. 2, pp. xxxviii–xxxix. Note 1, p. xxxviii, speculates on the origin of the form and gives a list of all the works in which Machaut made use of it. Pinet points out that it is mentioned in a fifteenth-century treatise on the "Règles de seconde rhétorique," p. 245, note 1). The anonymous work to which she refers, edited by Ernest Langlois in *Recueil d'arts de seconde rhétorique*, calls this particular configuration of lines the "Taille de trois et un" and identifies it as suitable for "complaintes amoureuses ou grans lays" (p. 33) and for "diz, rommans ou orisons" (p. 98; Pinet misquotes from the text). Jean Molinet also lists it as the form used in "Complaintes amoureuses" (Langlois, p. 225). For a more recent treatment of the form, see Robert Deschaux, "Le lai et la complainte."

128. Hoepffner, vol. 1, p. lx.

129. Hoepffner states, with regard to Machaut's *Behaigne*: "La même rime paraît quatre fois de suite; il était donc bien plus malaisé pour le poète de construire des vers à rime riche, et on ne saurait raisonnablement comparer les rimes de ce poème à celles des autres dits" (vol. 1, p. lx).

130. For further information on the phonological traits mentioned here in connection with rhyme, see Marchello-Nizia: *ueil* and *eil*, p. 70; weakening of *r* before consonant, pp. 83–84; rhyming of *arme* with *erme*, pp. 73–4; instability of *eü*, pp. 58–59.

131. Proof that the internal *e* of *seremens* sometimes elides can be seen from the readings of several manuscripts. In the line cited here (*TJ*281), *R* uses an abbreviation which resolves to give the spelling *seremens* (compared with the *D* reading of *sermens*). If this were an unusual occurrence, it could be corrected as an error. However, the usage is borne out by other examples, such as in *L1* and *L2*, which spell out

seremens at l. 604 of *Trois jugemens*, where again it must count for only two syllables. The *L* family also agrees with *R* in *Poissy*, l. 693 in using *guerredonner* as compared with the *D* reading of *guerdonner*.

132. I am indebted to William W. Kibler for pointing out to me the possibility of epic cesura in these lines, as well as for his help on many other points of philology.

133. In general, for discussions of the miniatures in Christine's works and particularly the copious and renowned illuminations of Christine's presentation copies, see Lucie Schäfer, "Die Illustrationen zu den Handschriften der Christine de Pizan"; Millard Meiss, *French Painting in the Time of Jean de Berry: The Boucicaut Master, The Limbourgs and Their Contemporaries*, and *The Late XIV Century and the Patronage of the Duke*; Patrick M. de Winter, "Christine de Pizan, ses enlumineurs et ses rapports avec le milieu bourguignon," and *La bibliothèque de Philippe le Hardi*.

134. The miniature is reproduced in several sources, among them Lucie Schäfer, pl. 57. See also the following note.

135. Cockshaw, pp. 14–15. Gaspar and Lyna suggest that the miniature might have been inspired by that in BR 10983, which they date to "vers 1403-04" (p. 10, no. 202 and pl. CXVI*b*).

136. This miniature ("Christine travels to Poissy") is ascribed by Meiss to the Egerton Master and is said to show the strong color characteristic of the Egerton workshop. See *The Limbourgs and Their Contemporaries*, vol. 1, p. 38, and vol. 2, pl. 139. See also Schäfer, pp. 170–71.

137. Laidlaw considers the *L2* miniature more successful than that in *L1*. See "A Publisher's Progress," p. 47.

138. This miniature is reproduced with a misleading caption in *From Workshop to Warfare: The Lives of Medieval Women*, by Carol Adams et al. The image is used as an illustration in Section 6, "Women Law-breakers," and is labeled as showing "women prisoners being brought before the Seneschal of Hainault" (p. 31). I am grateful to Charity Cannon Willard for the reference to this reproduction.

139. Mario Roques, "Etablissement de règles pratiques pour l'édition des anciens textes français et provençaux," and Alfred Foulet and Mary Blakely Speer, *On Editing Old French Texts*.

140. Omer Jodogne, "Povoir ou Pouoir?" Jodogne uses Christine's poetry, among other examples, to prove his case.

141. This discussion concerning the history of the paragraph mark is heavily indebted to the work by M. B. Parkes, *Pause and Effect*. See particularly pp. 41–44, pl. 25–27, and the definitions of *capitulum*, p. 302, and *paraph* and *paragraphus*, p. 305. The mark as one finds it in Christine's manuscripts corresponds to Parkes's definition of the paraph.

142. In the text of *Poissy*, for example, there are 78 paragraph marks in *R*, 38 in *D*, 23 in *L1*. Manuscript *S1* of *Deux amans* also uses paragraph marks freely, containing 102 occurrences, compared with 98 in *R*.

143. This idiosyncratic usage of the paragraph marks in *Poissy* may be true more of manuscript *R* than the others. For example, the first two marks in *R* appear at ll.

13 and 38; in both cases, they call attention to a line that falls in the middle of a sentence, and they in no way signal a division in the text. The next three, at ll. 57, 75, and 83, at least coincide with the beginning of sentences; loosely speaking, the passages that begin at these marks may introduce new topics within the larger description of springtime and the company with whom Christine is traveling. Eventually, *R* places a paragraph mark at l. 217, the first line so indicated in *D* and *L*. This line does constitute a significant division, signaling the moment when the company has arrived at Poissy. The next two marks in *R*, however (ll. 241, 248), again fall mid-sentence and mid-passage.

Texts

Le Livre du Debat de deux amans

Introduction

> Dites, ma dame,
> Vo bon avis de l'amoureuse flame,
> Se joye en vient ou dueil a homme et fame.
>
> (ll. 412–14)

The question at issue in this scholastic debate between a young and idealistic squire and his older, wiser interlocutor is quite simply whether love is more burden or boon to those who are smitten by it. Sparked by the atmosphere of the soirée at which they find themselves, their discussion is both an enquiry into the rationale behind the flirtatious behavior of the assembled guests and an entertainment in itself. The debate is largely an academic one, although each speaker has sufficient experience in the realm of love to know whereof he speaks. It is obviously the knight's own previous misfortunes and ill-advised behavior in this arena (see ll. 430–31, 853–60, 899–904, for example) that motivate him to take up the negative side of the argument.

While the two men are to a large degree stock characters, more representative of stereotyped points of view than of individuals, Christine has taken the trouble to give them some shading, a little depth. The knight wears a hat that obscures his eyes; this concealment, emblematic of the tortured and wounded lover, makes it difficult even for the perceptive observer to see his gaze wander frequently in the direction of one particular lady. He limps but is graceful enough to disguise this impediment. And despite his own unhappiness, he is most courteous in his behavior, drawing out the solitary lady beside him in his hidden corner. The squire, for his part, is impetuous and impassioned, high-handed and somewhat pompous in his rhetoric. So impatient is he to get to the heart of the debate that the knight must school him in etiquette: it is custom, says the older man, to allow the ladies present to speak first. This gentle rebuke introduces a note of humor into the text, directed at the great seriousness of purpose with which the squire attempts to promote with objectivity the benefits of the love that holds him in its thrall.

The two men are, of course, not speaking only to each other. Christine, the narrator, is invited by the squire to join them in a quiet spot away from the party, and she in turn, for reasons of propriety, invites two other women. We learn next to nothing about these guarantors of respectability; one is *la dame* introduced in line 385, who later speaks her mind in a forthright manner between the speeches of the knight and the squire, the other *une bourgeoise*, mentioned exclusively in lines 388–89. The second woman remains silent throughout the work, possibly because her social rank is incongruent with the conventions of courtly poetry. But while the bourgeoise does not speak and is often overlooked by critics, her presence underscores the importance of symmetry to the structure of the debate poems, in which the principles are arranged by pairs, both in the text and in the miniatures illustrating them. Given that here, as in the other judgments, Christine limits her role to that of disinterested onlooker and intermediary between discussants and judge, it seems entirely likely that the balance be maintained, even if in a cursory fashion, by the inclusion of two other women as witnesses.

The inclusion of the lady who does indeed speak when the knight solicits her opinion adds a second level of discourse that most effectively undermines the very foundations of the debate. While the dispute between the squire and the knight quantitatively dominates the poem, her eighty-five-line contribution, falling conspicuously at the midpoint (l. 915 ff.), undermines the validity of the question they are arguing so passionately. Adopting the voice of reason, she praises Dame Raison of the *Roman de la Rose* (ll. 961–77), a nice irony in the face of Christine's major offensive during her career against that work in some of its principal elements. Launching what is veritably an objection to the larger enterprise behind the debate as a whole, she refutes both the pain and the ecstasy of love. The highlight of her speech is perhaps the dryly humorous remark that she has not yet heard tell of the cemeteries where one might discover the remains of those who have died for love (ll. 987–93). Her commentary, while directly refuting the knight's statement, could just as well be addressed to personae outside the text, most obviously Christine the author, or her patron. Her disquisition is, in fact, a jewel of a *mise en abyme* of Christine's own position on love as it emerges from her corpus as a whole. Confirmation that the lady's speech is intended to function at this level is found in the failure of the knight and squire to engage with her in any real way. Neither replies to or acknowledges her comments; the squire, who speaks immediately after her, ignores her altogether. She and he are involved in different debates, and he cannot endorse her agenda in any way without invalidating his own entirely.

The essence of the knight's speech is well captured in the Ovidian image he employs of love as a wound so serious that it deprives the victim of all reason. He contends that jealousy invariably accompanies love and elaborates on this theme at considerable length, while his interlocutor, the squire, asserts that on the contrary, love's primary attribute is its power to polish and perfect its adherents. Both illustrate their arguments using examples drawn from the compendium of legendary and mythological figures of Greek and Roman antiquity as well as French literary heroes and historical figures, including noblemen of their own day. The squire's list closely follows the knight's; true to the symmetrical forms at play in these works, he replies to the latter's speech point for point, refuting each in turn. Christine's final appeal to her patron then brings the poem full circle, bringing to mind the opening lines concerning David, his lyre, and the pleasures of listening to enjoyable poetry (ll. 38–40) when she states the hope that hearing her *dictié* will bring the Duke some joy and comfort (ll. 2009–11). These and other features in the composition reveal that the structure of *Deux amans*, like that of the other two debates, is a model of balance and careful closure: dedication as frame, major bi- or tripartite divisions with interventions disrupting the fiction in between, all in the control of a first-person voice that fuses authoritative eyewitness and authorial hand.

Le Livre du Debat de deux amans*

        Ci commence le livre du debat des .ij. amans

Prince royal, renommé de sagece,*   [58v°a]
Hault en valeur, puissant, de grant noblece,
Duit et appris en honneur et largece,
    Tres agreable   4
Duc d'Orlians, seigneur digne et valable,*
Filz de Charles, le bon roy charitable,
De qui l'ame soit ou ciel permanable,
    Mon redoubté   8
Seigneur vaillant, par vostre grant bonté
Mon petit dit soit de vous escouté,
Ne par desdaing ne soit en sus bouté
    Par pou de pris;   12
Si ne l'ait pas vo haultece en despris
Pour ce que j'ay pou de savoir appris
Ou pour ce qu'ay foible matiere pris
    Et hors l'usage   16
De vo bon sens, qui n'escoute lengage
Que tout ne soit tres vertüeux et sage.*
Mais a la foiz point ne tourne a domage
    A ouÿr choses   20
De divers cas en textes ou en gloses,
Et mesmement ou matieres encloses
Joyeuses sont, soient rimes ou proses;   [58v°b]
    Et par ouÿr   24
Choses qui font par nature esjouïr
On fait souvent tristece hors fouïr,
Car trop grant soing tolt souvent a jouÿr
    Cuer occuppé   28
D'avoir solas quant trop enveloppé
Est es choses ou il s'est entrappé,
Ne corps humain tant soit bien attrempé
    Ne pourroit vivre   32
Toudis en soing; et j'ay leu en un livre
Que quant David, qui la loy Dieu volt suivre,
Vouloit estre de tristece delivre,
    Lors de sa lire   36
Moult doulcement jouoit, et souvent l'ire

Il rappaisoit de Dieu; et oÿr lire
Choses plaisans font souvent joye eslire
Aux escoutens. 40
Si n'est nul mal et en lieu et en temps
Lire et ouÿr de choses esbatans.
Et pour ce, Prince excellant, mal contens
Vous ne soiez 44
De moy, pour tant, s'ay desir que voyez
Un petit dit, lequel ay rimoyez
A celle fin que vo cuer avoyez
A soulacier 48
Aucunement. Si vous vueil commencier
A raconter, Dieu m'en vueille avancier,
Un grant debat dont j'ouÿ fort tencier*
A .ij. amans, 52
Car tout d'amours sera cilz mien rommans,
Si l'entendront François et Allemans
Et toute gent s'ilz entendent rommans.
Mais jugement 56
Y appartient, si supplie humblement
Vo noble cuer qu'il daigne bonnement
Droit en juger sicomme sagement
Le sara faire, 60
Car li amant, ou il n'a que refaire,
Le requierent et de tout cest affaire
Ilz vous chargent, noble Duc debonnaire, [59r°a]
Et si se tiennent 64
A vostre dit, car bien scevent et tiennent
Que droituriers les jugemens qui viennent
De vous tous sont, nez ceulx qui appartiennent
Es fais d'amours, 68
Qui aux jeunes font souvent changer mours
En bien ou mal, en joyes ou clamours;
Mais naturel est a tous cil demours,
Tant comme il dure, 72
Si ne le doit nul tenir a laidure,
Car tout ce qui est donné de nature,
Nul ne le peut tolir, dit l'Escripture.*
¶ Si vous diray 76
Le grant debat, ne ja n'en mentiray,

De .ij. amans que je moult remiray,
Car leur descort a ouÿr desiray
Et leur tençon 80
Gracïeuse, non mie en contençon.
Ce fu en may en la doulce saison
Qu'assemblee ot en moult belle maison
Et gracïeuse 84
Qui a Paris siet, en place joyeuse,
Compaignie jeune, belle et songneuse
De solacier; creature envïeuse
N'ot en la route 88
Fors de jouer, sicom je croy sans doubte.
Tres belle fu la compaignie toute,
Ou mainte dame ot qui d'amer n'ot goute,
Et mainte gente 92
Damoiselle paree et par entente,
Mainte gentil pucelle, et que ne mente,
De chevaliers y avoit plus de .xxx.
Et d'autre gent 96
Beaulx et gentilz, papillotez d'argent,
Gays et jolis, assesmez bel et gent;
Si furent tous et toutes diligent
De joye faire. 100
La ot moult bons menestreulx plus d'un paire,
Qui haultement faisoient le repaire
Tout retentir. Si devoit a tous plaire
Celle assemblee, [59r°b] 104
Car feste et joye y estoit si comblee
Qu'a cent doubles fu plus qu'aultre doublee,
N'elle n'estoit de discorde troublee
Mais tres unie; 108
Toute tristece en estoit hors banie.
Et en place bien paree et onnie,
Grant et large, nette, non pas honnie,
Menoient tresche, 112
Joyeusement, par dessus l'erbe freche.
Maint joli tour, maint sault, mainte entreveche*
Y veïst on, et lancier mainte fleche
A doulx regart, 116
Tout en requoy traire par soubtil art,

Et qui mieulx mieulx chacun faisoit sa part
De ce que doulx Deduit aux siens depart.
Ainsi dançoient 120
Tous et toutes, ne point ne s'en lassoient,
Et en dançant leurs cuers entrelaçoient
Par les regars quë ilz s'entrelançoient.
Qui veist jolyes* 124
Femmes dancier a contenances lies,
Si gayement de manieres polies,
A chapeaulx vers de fleurs et d'acolies,
Par mignotise 128
Bien avenant, doulcetement assise,
Rire, jouer, elles plaindre en faintise,
Parler, atrait de maniere rassise,
Les contenances 132
De ces amans, a chacun tour des dances
Müer coulour, faire maintes semblances,
Moult en prisast les doulces ordonnances.
Et puis aprés 136
Les menestreulx, qui bien jouoyent tres
Par my chambres et par my ces retrés,
Ouyst on chanter hault et cler, a biaulx trais
Bien mesurez. 140
A brief parler, tant furent procurez
La ris et gieux qu'il sembloit que jurez
Fussent d'ainsi estre a feste adurez
A tous jours mais. 144
¶ Et moy, en qui tout ennui est remais [59v°a]
Depuis le jour que Mort de trop dur mais
M'ot servie, dont je n'aray jamais,
C'est chose voire, 148
Plaisir joyeux au monde, ains aré noire
Pensee adés pour la dure memoire
De cil que je portë en ma memoire
Sans nul oubly, 152
Dont l'esperit soit ou ciel establi,
Qui seulete me laissa, n'entroubli*
Ne fait mon dueil, ou que soye, affoibli
En nulle guise, 156
Fus sus un banc en cellui lieu assise*

Sans mot sonner, regardant la devise
Des fins amans gentilz, plains de cointise,
Tant renvoysiez 160
Que de mener solas furent aysiez.
Mais je, qui os l'esperit accoisiez,
Consideray que de tous les prisiez*
De celle place, 164
Un escuier bel de corps et de face
Y ot jolis, mais tant fu en sa grace
Qu'il sembloit bien qu'il eüst plus grant masse
De toute joye 168
Qu'autre qui fust ou lieu, se Dieux me voye;
Car mon regart a lui toudis avoye
En remirant la gracïeuse voye
De son maintien, 172
Car il dançoit et chantoit si tres bien,
Si liement jouait, je vous di bien,
Quë il sembloit que le monde fust sien.
Tant resjouÿ 176
Forment estoit, ou qu'il eüst jouÿ
De tous les biens dont oncquë hom joÿ,
Tant par estoit son gay cuer esjouÿ,
A droit voir dire, 180
Car ne finoit de jouer et de rire
Ou de chanter et dancer tout a tire.
Mais de ses gieux nul ne peüst mesdire,
Tant lui seoient, 184
Car les autres tous resjouÿr faisoient,
Et ses soulas si gracïeux estoient [59v°b]
Qu'a toute gent communement plaisoient;
N'il ne parlast 188
Fors en riant, et sembloit qu'il volast
Quant il dançoit; mais quoy que il se celast,
A peine un pas de nul costé alast
Que de doulx oeil 192
Ne regardast simplement, sans orgueil,
Tele qui fu present ou tout son vueil
Estoit assis, mais par soubtil recueil,
Comment qu'il fust, 196
Son regarder gitoit que on n'apperceust*

Qu'a celle, plus qu'a autre, pensee eust.
Si ne cuidoye pas que pou lui pleust,
Car bien sembloit 200
Que pour elle fust en amoureux ploit,
Tout non obstant que de gens tant s'embloit
Comme il pouoit, mais l'amoureux esploit
Fort a celler 204
Est aux amans, qu'Amours fait affoller
Par trop amer et venir et aler;
Ainsi surpris d'Amours, a brief parler,
Cil sembla estre. 208
¶ Mais pres du banc ou je seoye a dextre
Avoit assis decoste une fenestre
Un chevalier qui sus sa main senestre
Tint appuyé 212
Son chief enclin, comme tout anuyé
Et tout pensif, et pou ot festoyé;
Në il n'estoit joyeux ne desroyé,
Në esbatant 216
Ne sembla pas, mais n'estoit pas pour tant
Lait ne viellart, ains de beauté ot tant
Com nul qui fust et moult entremettant
En gentillece 220
Et en honneur sembla, et de jeunece
Assez garni, jolis et sans parece.
Mais bien sembloit que pou eust de lëece
Et pou de joye, 224
Car moy, qui lors dessus le banc seoye,
Songneusement son maintien regardoye
Pour ce que si pensif je le veoye [60r°a]
Et sans solas; 228
Par maintes fois lui ouÿ dire, "Helas!"
Bassettement, n'estre ne pouoit las
De souspirer comme homme qui en las
Est enserré; 232
Et avec ce tant ot le cuer serré
Quë il sembloit qu'on l'eüst deterré
Tant palle estoit, ou qu'il fust enferré
D'un fer tranchant. 236
Et non obstant qu'il s'alast embrunchant

D'un chapperon dessus ses yeulx sachant,
C'on n'apperceust le pié dont fu clochant
Ne son malage, 240
Et tout fust il loyal, secret et sage,
Sicom je croy, si faindre son courage
Ne pot qu'il n'eust tout au lonc du visage
Souvent les lermes; 244
Tant ne pouoit estre constans ne fermes
Que couvrir peust les tres ameres armes
Qu'Amours livre a ceulx qu'il rent trop enfermes
Et maladis. 248
Ainsi cellui fu la, com je vous dis,
Morne, pensif et petit esbaudis;
Mais, si me doint Jhesu Crist paradis,
Telle pitié 252
Me fist de lui veoir si dehaitié,
C'onques homme, tant y eusse amistié,
Ne m'atendri le cuer a la moitié
Comme cellui 256
Me fist, que la je veoye, a par lui,*
Morne, pensif, lermoier. Ne nullui
N'appercevoit, je croy, l'ennui de lui
Fors moy, sans plus, 260
Car les autres toudis de plus en plus
S'ebatoient, et cil estoit reclus
Entre la gent, plus simple qu'un reclus,
Ne ne pensoit 264
Que le maintien qui triste le faisoit
Nul perceüst, car chacun y dançoit
Fors lui et moy, et pour ce ne cessoit
D'estre pensifs. [60r°b] 268
Mais la cause qui si le tint rassis
Apperceu bien, car des fois plus de .vj.
Mua couleur quant pres de lui assis
Le corps gentil 272
D'une dame belle et gente entre mil
Estoit; adont tout se tresmuoit cil,
Si la suivoit aux yeulx, mais si soubtil
Fu son regart, 276
Qu'appercevoir ne le peust par nul art

Nul ne nulle, n'avoit l'ueil autre part,
Dont j'apperceu et vi tout en appert
Que le meschief 280
Qui lui troubloit et le cuer et le chief
Venoit de la, je ne sçay par quel chief,
Mais sans cesser souspiroit de rechief.
¶ Ainsi se tint 284
La longuement, dont trop de mal soustint.
Mais or oyez aprés qu'il en avint:
Quant ot songié assez, il se revint
Un pou a soy, 288
Comme homme qui un pou a sa grant soy
Estancheë. Et je, qui l'apperçoy,*
Le regarday, mais, s'onques nul bien soy,
Me fus advis 292
A son regart et au semblant du vis
Qu'il apperceut que tout son maintien vis,
Et comme la estoit sicom ravis,
Si lui greva 296
Que veü l'oz. Ne sçay comme il en va,
Mais assez tost de ce lieu se leva
Et vers moy vint et achoison trouva
De m'aresner; 300
Et moy, qui moult me voulsisse pener
De l'esjouïr, se g'i sceusse assener,
Pour la pitié qu'oy eu, dont atourner
En tel conroy 304
L'avoye veu, quant devers la paroy
Le vy venir, adont sans nul desroy,
Je me levay; mais s'il fust filz de roy
Ou duc ou conte, 308
Sçot il assez que gentillece monte [60v°a]
Courtoisie, qui les bons en pris monte
Et qui apprent, enseigne, duit et dompte
Tout bon courage 312
Lui ot appris; adont le doulx et sage*
Si me rassist, et, sanz querre avantage
De nul honneur, humblement, sanz haultage,
Dessus le banc 316
Decoste moy s'assist, cil qui fu blanc

Et palle ou vis, ou n'ot couleur ne sanc
Par trop amer. Son bras dessus le flanc
Adont me mist 320
Courtoisement, et bellement me dist,
"Que pensez vous cy seule? Car il n'ist
De vous nul mot, bien croy qu'il vous souffist
De cy penser 324
Sans autre esbat. Pour quoy n'alez dancer?"
Et je respons, "Mais vous, sire, avancer
Pou vous en voy et ne deussiés cesser
De vous esbatre, 328
Ce m'est avis, car en ce lieu n'a .iiij.
Qui plus soient jeunes, mais pou embatre
Je vous y voy. Ne sçay qui fait rabatre
Si vo pensee." 332
Et cil, qui volt la douleur qu'amassee
Avoit ou cuer moy celer, a pesee
Parole dist: "En pou d'eure est passee
Certes ma joye. 336
Tant suis rudes que dancer ne saroye
Në autrement jouer, et toutevoye
N'ay je courroux, ne chose qui m'anoye,
Mais c'est ma guise 340
D'estre pensif; ce n'est pas par faintise.
Dieux a en moy tel condicion mise;*
Ou qu'il m'anoit ou que bien me souffise,
C'est ma nature." 344
¶ Ainsi parlions a bien basse murmure
Et ja avions conté mainte aventure
Quant vers nous vint cellui tout a esture,
Dont j'ay parlé 348
Ja cy dessus, qui n'ot cuer adoulé [60v°b]
Ains fu joyeux; si a l'autre acolé
Tout en riant, et a lui rigolé
S'est bellement, 352
Et d'un et d'el parlerent longuement,
Mais sus amours tourna le parlement.
Si dist adonc l'escuyer liement,
"A ma requeste, 356
Parlons d'amours un pou, et, sans arreste,

D'entre nous .iii. de devisier s'appreste*
Son bon avis chacun, et s'amour preste
Plus joye ou mains 360
Aux vrays amans, vous pry a jointes mains
Qu'en devision, que nul ne l'oye; au mains
Pouons parler de ce dont joye ont mains.
¶ Si faisons conte 364
Que c'est d'amer, de quoy vient, n'a quoy monte
Ycelle amour, qui le cuer prent et dompte,
A quoy c'est bon, s'onnour en vient ou honte;
Chacun en die 368
Ce qu'il en scet, ou se c'est maladie
Ou grant santé, ou se l'amant mendie
Qui dame sert. Le corps Dieu le maudie
Qui mentira 372
De son avis, et qui tout ne dira
Des tours d'amours ce qu'il en sentira.
Or y perra qui le mieulx en lira.
¶ Mais je conseil 376
Que nous yssions trestous .iii. hors du sueil
De cel huis la et alions en ce brueil,
Ou il fait vert, nous seoir en recueil
Joyeusement, 380
Pour deviser la plus secretement,
Que nul n'oye l'amoureux plaidement
Fors que nous .iij." Et adont vistement
Nous nous levasmes; 384
Mais par mon los une dame appellasmes
Avecques nous qui het mesdis et blasmes;
Encore avec pour le mieulx y menasmes
Une bourgeoise* 388
Belle, plaisant, gracïeuse et courtoise; [61r°a]
Par mon conseil fu fait, car qui racoise
De mesdisans le murmure et la noise*
Moult sages est. 392
Si partismes de la, et sans arrest
Ou bel verger entrasmes, qui fu prest
A deduire, plus dru q'une forest
D'arbres moult beaulx, 396
Qui en saison portent bons fruis nouveaulx,*

Ou en printemps se deduisent oyseaulx,
Et en beau lieu, qui y fist ses aviaux,
Fumes assis. 400
¶ Adonc cellui qui fu le mains pensifs
Dit a l'autre, qui ot plus de soulcis,
"Dittes, sire, car plus estes rassis
Et le plus sage, 404
Vo bon avis de l'amoureux servage,
S'il en vient preu, joye, honneur ou dommage."
Et cil respont, "Beaulx amis, c'est l'usage
Selon raison, 408
Qu'en trestous cas et en toute saison,
Honneur porte aux dames tout gentilz hom;
Premier diront, beau sire, et nous taison.
Dites, ma dame, 412
Vo bon avis de l'amoureuse flame,
Se joye en vient ou dueil a homme et fame."
Et celle dit et respont, "Par mon ame,
Je ne saroye 416
Qu'en dire au fort; quant est de moy, louroye
Que vous dissiez et voulentiers l'orroye,
Car proprement certes n'en parleroye.
Dites, beau sire, 420
Car je sçay bien que mieulx en sariés dire."
Et cil respont, "Ne vous doy contredire,
Ne vueille Dieux qu'a ce ja mon cuer tire
Que vous desdie. 424
Puis qu'il vous plaist, ma dame, que je dye*
Ce qu'il m'est vis, quoy qu'autre contredie,
Des fais d'amours et de la maladie
Qui vient d'amer, [61r°b] 428
Se plus en vient de doulx et moins d'amer,
Selon que sçay et que puis extimer
Par essayer et par m'en informer,
J'en parleray 432
Ce que j'en sens, ne ja n'en mentiray.
Combien qu'autre trop mieulx que ne saray
En parleroit, toute foiz en diray
Tout mon advis, 436
S'onques je sos congnoistre ne ne vis

Les tours d'amours, par qui cuers sont ravis.
C'est un desir qui ja n'est assouvis,
Qui par plaisir 440
En jeune cuer se vient mettre, et choisir
Lui fait amours; de ce naist un desir
De franc vouloir, qui le cuer vient saisir
De tel nature 444
Qu'il rent amant le cuer et plain d'ardure
Et desireux d'estre amé tant qu'il dure.
Mais tant est grant celle cuisant pointure
Qu'elle bestourne 448
Toute raison et tellement attourne
Cil qui est pris, que du joyeux fait morne
Et le mornë en joyeuseté tourne;
Souvent avient. 452
¶ C'est une riens de quoy l'omme devient
Tout tresmüé, si qu'il ne lui souvient
De nulle honneur, ne de preu ne lui tient.
Souventes fois 456
Oublïer fait et coustumes et drois,
Fors voulenté n'i euvre en tous endrois.
C'est seraine qui endort a sa voix
Pour homme occire; 460
C'est un venim enveloppé de mirre
Et une paix qui en tous temps s'aÿre,
Un dur lïen ou desplaisir në yre
N'a nulle force 464
Du deslïer; c'est vouloir qui s'efforce
De nuire a soy, une pensee amorse
A desirer, par voye droite ou torse, [61v°a]
Avoir aysance 468
De ce en quoy on a mis sa plaisance;
Et quant on l'a, n'y a il souffisance,
Car le las cuer est toudis en balance
S'il aime fort. 472
Car s'il avient que l'amant tant au fort
Ait fait qu'il soit amé, et reconfort
Lui soit donné, si me rens je bien fort
Qu'icelle joye 476
N'yert ja si grant qu'Amours ne lui envoye

Mille soucis contre une seule voye
D'avoir plaisir, ne que ja son cuer voye
Asseüré, 480
Et tout soit il ou jeune ou meüré,
Ou bel ou bon, ja si beneüré
Ne se verra que tres maleüré
Il ne se claime* 484
Souventes fois, se parfaictement aime.
Car Fortune, qui les discordes seme,
En plus perilz que nef qui va a reme
Par maintes voies 488
Le fichera; mais le las toutevoyes
Tout le peril ne prisera .ij. oyes,
Mais qu'il ne perde aucunes de ses joyes
Chier achetees. 492
¶ Haÿ, vray Dieux, quantes douleurs portees
Sont es las cuers ou amours sont boutees!
Quant m'en souvient, de moy sont redoubtees
Les dures larmes, 496
Les durs sanglous et li mortelz vouacarmes,
Et les souspirs plus poignans que gisarmes.
Et se parler en doy comme clerc d'armes,
Ce scet bien Dieux, 500
Et quel dangier et quel tourment mortieulx
Porte l'amant, ou soit jeunes ou vieulx,
Pour faire tant qu'il lui en soit de mieulx
Devers sa dame, 504
S'il est a droit espris de l'ardant flame,
Qui par desir l'amant art et enflame, [61v°b]
Avant qu'il soit amé, je croy, par m'ame,
Qu'assez endure 508
De griefs ennuys; je ne sçay comme il dure
En tel tourment de si mortel pointure.
N'il n'a en soy autre soing n'autre cure*
Que celle part 512
Ou il aime; si acquite sa part
De tous les biens que Fortune depart,
Pour cellui seul qui pou lui en espart*
Certes peut estre. 516
Ainsi le las son paradis terrestre

A fait de ce qui son cuer plus empestre,
Et tout soit il roy ou duc ou grant maistre,
Fault qu'il s'asserve 520
Ou vueille ou non, et que sa dame serve
Et vraye amour, ains que joye desserve.
Et puis y a encor plus dure verve
S'on l'escondit: 524
Or se tient mort le las, or se maudit
Et puis Espoir autre chance lui dit,
Puis Desconfort revient et l'en desdit;
Ainsi n'a paix. 528
En tous endrois le sert de divers mais
Ycelle amour, qui ne laroit jamais
Avoir repos le cuer ou est remais
Cellui vouloir. 532
¶ Mais suppose qu'a l'amant tant valoir*
Lui vueille Amours que cause de douloir*
N'ait en nul cas, ne lui doye chaloir
Fors de lëece, 536
Et qu'a son gre du tout de sa maistresse
Il soit amé, qui lui tiengne promesse
Et loyauté; ne croyez qu'a destrece
Pour tant ne soit, 540
Car Faulx Agait, qui moult tost apparçoit
Le couvine des amans, et conçoit
Par leur semblans leur fait comment qu'il soit,
Ne s'en taist pas; 544
Si resveille moult tost, plus que le pas [62r°a]
Les mesdisans, cui Dieu doint mau repas,*
Qui font gaiter Jalousie au trespas
Et mettre barres 548
Es doulx deduis des amans et enserres.
Lors commencent et murmures et guerres
Souventes fois, trop plus grans que pour terres
Ne pour avoir. 552
¶ Beaulx sire Dieux, qui pourroit concevoir
Le grant tourment qu'il couvient recevoir
Au povre amant, qui ne peut bien avoir
Pour le parler 556
Des mesdisans qui lui tolent d'aler

Devers celle qu'il aime et veult celer!
Trop durement font l'amant adouler
Les mesdisans 560
Ou le jaloux, qui trop lui est nuisans.
Ceulx lui tolent ses doulx biens deduisans,
Dont tel dueil a, qu'au lit en est gisans
En desespoir 564
Souventes fois, ou il se met a poir,*
En grant peril de mort, s'il n'a pouoir
De soy chevir autrement, n'a espoir*
Qu'autrement puist 568
Celle veoir pour qui le cuer lui cuist.
¶ Encor y a une chose qui nuist
Trop aux amans et qui a dueil les duist:
C'est jalousie, 572
Qui oublïer fait toute courtoisie
Au las amant, qui si fort se soucye
Qu'il est aussi comme homme en frenasie
Et loing et pres. 576
S'il s'apperçoit qu'un autre amant en gres
De celle amer soit, ou son cuer est tres,
Sachés de voir, s'il y voit nulx attrés
Qu'elle lui face, 580
Il en muera sens et couleur et face
Ne je ne cuid qu'autre meschief efface
Si mortel soing, quoy qu'il se contreface
Joyeux ne lié. 584
C'est mort et dueil, qui estre appallïé [62r°b]
Certes ne peut, n'en paix estre alïé,
Le cuer qui est de tel tourment lïé.
C'est une rage 588
Trop amere, qui met l'omme en courage
De faire assez de maulx et de dommage;
Plusieurs en ont honneur et heritage
Souvent perdu. 592
Qui jaloux est, a meschief s'est rendu;
Mieulx lui vauldroit gesir mort estendu,
Mais grant amour lui a ce bien rendu
En guerredon, 596
Car trop amer si empetre ce don

Au pouvre amant, qui de son cuer fist don.
Si lui semble que trop perderoit don
S'un autre avoit 600
Le bien que si cher comparer se voit.
Mais certes se le las mourir devoit,
N'en partiroit nez s'il ores savoit
Que relenqui, 604
Et delaissié l'eüst sa dame, en qui
Son cuer a tout, puis qu'amours le vainqui
Par un regart, qui du doulx oeil nasqui
Quë il tant prise, 608
Et qu'a celle qui tant est bien apprise
Il s'est donné et qu'elle a s'amour prise.
Jamais nul jour n'en doit estre desprise,
Comme il lui semble, 612
Pour riens qui soit, mais tous les maulx assemble
En son las cuer, qui d'aÿr sue et tremble
Et souvent het et puis amour rassemble;
C'est dure dance 616
Et moult estrange vie et concordance,
Et tout d'amour en vient la deppendance.
Ainsi en soy n'a ne paix n'acordance,
Ains derve d'ire 620
Le las amant jaloux, quant il oyt dire
Ou apperçoit qu'a autre amour se tire
Celle de qui ne peut oÿr mesdire
Et si le laisse. 624
Si est plus serf que chien c'om maine en laisse, [62v°a]
Que le veneur tient, n'aler ne le laisse;
Ainsi le tient celle qui pou l'eslaisse
En son danger. 628
¶ Ha, quel amour, qu'on ne peut estranger
Du dolent cuer, tant sache dommager!
On s'en doit bien de dueil vif enrager
Quë il couviengne 632
A force amer, ce dont fault que mal viengne,
Et que subget obeïssant se tiengne*
Le las amant, quelque mal qu'il soustiengne,
C'est grant merveille. 636
Amours, amours! nul n'est qui ne s'en dueille.

Cil qui te sert pou repose et moult veille,
Et trop pener lui fault, vueille ou ne vueille,
Qui tu accointes.   640
¶ Mais regardons encore les plus cointes,
Les mieulx amez et ceulx qui n'ont les pointes
Qu'ont les jaloux, qui sont d'amertume ointes.
Sont ilz dehors   644
Ses grans meschiefs? Je croy que non ancors,
Ains y perdent plusieurs et ame et corps,
S'il m'en souvient, et se j'en ay recors,
Quant sont peris   648
Par tel amour en France et a Paris
Et autre part. Ainsi furent meris
Jadis plusieurs amans; meismes Paris,*
Qui dame Helaine   652
Ot ravie en Grecë, a moult grant peine,
Dont Troye, qui tant fu cité haultaine,
Fu puis arse, detruite et de dueil plaine,
Ou fu perie   656
La plus haulte et noble chevalerie
Que ou monde fust, et si grant seignorie,
Mesmes a Paris durement fu merie
L'amour sans faille,   660
Car Thelamon l'occist en la bataille.
Et .ij. amans autres, que je ne faille,
¶ Receurent mort, comme Ovide le baille*
En un sien livre,   664
Par telle amour qui les folz cuers enyvre
Car moult souvent pour joyeusement vivre   [62v°b]
S'assembloient, et leur vouloir en suivre,
En uns bocages   668
Qu'a nom Limaulx: la, les bestes sauvages
Devourerent l'amant, dont fu dommages.
¶ Et Piramus, l'enfant courtois et larges,*
Et la tres belle   672
Doulce Thisbé, la jeunette pucelle,
Ne s'occirent ilz sus la fontenelle
Soubz le murier blanc? Il mourut pour elle
Et elle aussi   676
S'occist pour lui, dont le murier noircy,

Pour la pitié dont moururent ainsi.
Ainsi grief mort les .ij. enfans quorsi*
Par trop amer.   680
Piteusement aussi peri en mer
⁋ Lehander, qui pour garder de blasmer*
Belle Hero, qui le volt sien clamer,
Par nuit obscure,   684
Le las amant, prenoit celle aventure
De mer passer en sa chemise pure,
Dont une fois, par grant mesaventure,
Y fu noyez   688
Par tempeste de temps. Voiez, voyez
Comment les las amans sont avoyez,
Qui par Amours sont pris et convoyez.
Qu'ont ilz de peine!   692
⁋ Et Achilles aussi pour Polixene,*
Ne mourut il quant en promesse veine
Il se fia, dont mort lui fu prochaine?
Ne fu dont mie   696
Raison en lui bien morte et endormie
Quant il eslut pour sa dame et amie
Celle qui ert sa mortel ennemie?
Mal lui en prist.   700
Ce fist Amours, par qui maint en perist,
Mais quant mal vient aux gens, il s'en sourrist.
Et ceste amour trop durement surprist
⁋ Aesacus,*   704
Filz au bon roy Priant, qui si vaincus
Fu d'amer trop, que sans querir escus   [63r°a]
En mer sailli, comme trop yrascus
Que reffusé   708
L'ot celle a qui lonctemps avoit musé,
Dont les fables, qui le cas encusé
Ont, tesmoignent qu'en plungion fu rusé
Et tresmüé.   712
Si com se fu dedens l'eaue rüé
En cel oysel fu tantost remüé;
Pour amours fu en tel forme müé,
En tel maniere   716
Son corps gentil oncques n'ot autre biere.

Veoir le peut on en mainte riviere
Ou de noyer encor monstre maniere.
Les dieux de lors 720
Pour memoire changierent si son corps.
¶ Mais regardons d'autres amans encors
Qui pour amer furent peris et mors
Et exillé: 724
Ypys aussi en fu tant traveillié*
Par telle amour, qui si l'ot bataillié
Qu'il s'en pendi, comme mal conseillié,
A l'uis de celle 728
Qui reffusé a responce crüelle
L'ot durement, et pour celle nouvelle
Le las s'occist; mais les dieux de la felle
Vengence en prirent, 732
Car ymage de pierre dure en firent
Son corps crüel devenir; si la virent
Plusieurs dames, qui exemplaire y prirent,
Ce fu raison. 736
¶ Et a Romme, pour autelle achoison,
Un jouvencel s'occist qui sa raison
Ot comptee, ne sçay en quel saison,
A son amee. 740
Mais la felle, comme mal informee,
Le refusa, et cil en la fumee
Tout devant elle a sa char entamee
D'agus couteaulx, 744
¶ Ainsi fina. Mais de temps plus nouveaulx,
Or regardons, de Tristan qui fu beaulx,* [63r°b]
Preux et vaillant, amoureux et loyaulx,
Quelle la fin 748
En fu, pour bien amer de vray cuer fin.
Ne le gaita son oncle a celle fin,
Qu'il l'occisist, et mort a la parfin
Il lui donna? 752
Mais celle amour Yseult si ordena,
Qu'entre les bras de son ami fina;
Par mon serment, cy piteuse fin a
De .ij. amans. 756
¶ Et Quahedins, sicom dit li rommans,*

Ne mourut il plus noirci qu'arremens
Pour tel amour? Si fu ses testamens
Plain de pitié. 760
¶ Encor depuis, regardons l'amistié
Du chastellain de Coucy, se haitié*
Il fu d'amours. Je croy qu'a grant daintié
En avoit bien, 764
Mais la dame du Fayel, qui pour sien
Tout le tenoit, je croy, l'acheta bien,
Car puis que mort le sçot, ne volt pour rien
Plus estre en vie. 768
¶ Et du Vergi la tres belle assouvie
Chastellaine, qui de riens n'ot envie*
Fors de cellui a qui avoit pleuvie
Amour loyale; 772
Mais elle et lui orent souldee male
Par trop amer, car mort en iurent palle.
Si ont fait maint, et en chambre et en sale,
A grant doulour 776
Par tel amour, qui fait changer coulour
Souventes foiz, ou soit sens ou folour,
Süer en froit, et trembler en chalour.
Mais je m'en passe 780
Pour plus briefté, et se tous vous nommasse,
G'y mettroye, je croy, un an d'espace.
Mais des perilz il y a si grant masse*
Que c'est sans nombre 784
Pour telle amour, qui passe comme un ombre,
Et le las cuer si empeche et encombre, [63v°a]
Que ses meschiefs il ne compte ne nombre!
¶ En quantes guises 788
Sont les peines des amoureux assises;
Les uns si ont voyes couvertes quises
Pour bien avoir, mais douleurs ont acquises
Estrangement, 792
L'un pour rapport, l'autre pour changement,
L'autre ne peut avoir allegement,
L'autre par non soy mener sagement
En gist pasmé, 796
Par divers cas, et tieulx qui ont amé

Trop haultement, dont ont esté clamé
Faulx desloyaulx, et en chartre enfermé
Ou detranchez, 800
¶ Et de tieulx qui en ont perdus les chiefs
Diversement, et mains autres meschiefs
En sont venus a ceulx qui atachez
En tel maniere 804
Sont tous les jours, c'est chose coustumiere.
Pour tel amour sont maint porté en biere
Qui comparent yceste amour trop chiere,
En maint endroit. 808
¶ Qui tous les cas deviser en vouldroit
Qui aviennent, lonc temps y couvendroit.
Mais trop souvent avient, soit tort ou droit,
Dont c'est dommages. 812
¶ Quantes noises sourdent es mariages
Pour ceste amour, qui dompte folz et sages,
Car ou s'esprent, il n'est si fors courages
Qu'elle ne change. 816
Si fait amer souvent le plus estrange
Et delaissier le privé en eschange,
Estrangement les cuers entremeslange
Sans que raison 820
Clamee y soit, si n'y vise saison
Ne temps ne lieu. C'est l'amoureux tison
Qui mesmement fait mainte mesprison
Faire au plus sage. 824
C'est le piteux et mal pelerinage
La ou Paaris ala par mer a nage,* [63v°b]
Ou il ravi Helaine au cler visage
Qui comparee 828
Fu durement par Venus l'äouree,
Et Cupido son filz, qui procuree
A mainte amour, dont plusieurs la couree
Et les entrailles 832
Ont eus perciez; ne sont pas devinailles.
Quieulx que soient d'amours les commençailles
Tous jours y a piteuses deffinailles.
¶ Fuyez, fuyez, 836
Yceste amour, jeunes gens! et voyez

Comment on est pour lui mal avoyez!
Ses promesses, pour Dieu, point ne croyez,
Car son attente 840
Couste plus chier que ne fait nulle rente.
Nul ne s'i met, qu'aprés ne s'en repente,
Car trop en est perilleuse la sente,
Sachés sans doubte, 844
Et moult en est de leger la foy route.
C'est un trespas obscur, ou ne voit goute
Cil qui s'i fiert et nissement s'i boute,
N'est pas mençonge; 848
Tant de meschiefs en vient, que c'est un songe,
Si tient plus court que l'esparvier la longe,*
Et mal en vient, le plus de ce respon ge,
C'est fait prouvé. 852
¶ Croyez cellui qui bien l'a esprouvé:
Si ne suis je mie pour tant trouvé
Sage en ce cas, mais nice et reprouvé,
C'est mon dalmage. 856
Mais a la fois, un fol avise un sage,
Et qui esté a en lointain voyage
Peut bien compter comment on s'i hebarge,
En mainte guise. 860
Qui s'i vouldra mirer, je l'en avise,
Car tous les jours avient par tel devise,
Mais du peril ne se gaite ny vise
L'amant musart, 864
Qui sa vie met en si fait hasart,
Et n'escheve le grant feu et tout s'art; [64r°a]
Ainçois le suit et celle amour de s'art*
L'amant esprent 868
Par le plaisir qui a amer le prent.
Si le tient si qu'il ne scet s'il mesprent
Ou s'il fait bien, et, s'aucun l'en reprent,
Il s'en courrouce 872
Ne gre n'en scet; tant a plaines de mousse
Ses oreilles, qui de raison escousse
Sont si que ouÿr lui semble chose doulce
De chose amere, 876
Et sa marrastre il retient pour sa mere;

Felicité lui semble estre misere,
Et de misere et servage se pere;*
Est il bien bugle?* 880
¶ Ainsi amours fait devenir avugle
Le fol amant, qui se cueuvre d'un cruble*
Et bien cuide veoir en temps de nuble
Le cler souleil, 884
Et juge bon ce qu'il lui plaist a l'ueil,
Ainsi est il. Pour tant, dire ne vueil
Ce que je di pour ce que n'aye vueil
D'amours servir, 888
Ne pour blasmer qui s'i veult asservir,
Mais pour dire comme il s'i fault chevir
Qui a amours veult loyauté pleuvir
De cuer certains. 892
¶ Ainsi, ma dame, et vous, beau doulx compains,
Ouÿr pouez que l'amant a trop mains
De ses plaisirs, s'il est a droit attains,
Qu'il n'a de joye; 896
Ce scevent ceulx qu'amours destraint et loye
En ses lïens, ou maint homme foloye.
Savoir le doy, car griefment m'en douloye
Quant en ce point 900
Estoye pris; encor n'en suis je point
Quitte du tout, dont dessoubz mon pourpoint
Couvertement ay souffert maint dur point
A grant hachee. 904
Mais je ne croy que a nul si bien en chee*
Que tel peine ne lui soit approuchee, [64r°b]
Com je vous ay ycy dicte et preschee;
¶ Ce n'est pas fable." 908
Quant le courtois chevalier aimable*
Ot finee sa parole nottable
Que li plusieurs tendroient veritable
Et bien comptee, 912
¶ Dite a beaulx trais, ne peu ne trop hastee,
La dame adont, qui bien l'ot escoutee,
Recommença et dit, "Se j'ay nottee
Vostre parole, 916
Bien a son droit Amours a dure escolle

Tient les amans, qui n'est doulce ne molle,
Sicom j'entens, et qui maint homme affolle
Sans achoison. 920
Mais quant a moy, tiens que mie foison
Ne sont d'amans pris en tele prison,
Tout non obstant que plusieurs leur raison
Vont racontant, 924
Puis ça puis la, aux dames, mais pour tant
N'y ont le cuer, ne ne sont arrestant
En un seul lieu, combien qu'assez gastant
A longue verve 928
De leur mos vont; mais que nul s'i asserve
Si durement ne croy, ne que ja serve
Si loyaument de pensee si serve
Amours et dame; 932
Et sauve soit vostre grace, par m'ame,
Ne croy que nul espris de tele flame
Soit qu'il ait tant de griefs doulours pour femme.
Mais c'est un compte 936
Assez commun, que aux femes on racompte
Pour leur donner a croire, et tout ne monte
Chose qui soit; et celle qui aconte
A tel lengage, 940
A la parfin on la tient a pou sage.
Et quant a moy, tiens que ce n'est que usage
D'ainsi parler d'amours par rigolage
Et passer temps, 944
Et s'il fu voir, ce que dire j'entens,
Qu'ainsi fussent vray en l'ancïen temps [64v°a]
Li amoureux, il a plus de cent ans,
Au mien cuidier 948
Que ce n'avint, ce n'est ne d'ui ne d'yer
Qu'ainsi attains soient; mais par plaidier
Et bien parler se scevent bien aydier
Li amoureux, 952
Et se jadis et mors et langoureux
Ilz en furent, et mains maulx doulereux
Endurerent mesmes les plus eureux,
Comme vous dites, 956
Je croy qu'adés leurs douleurs sont petites.

Mais es rommans sont trouvees escriptes
A droit souhaid et proprement descriptes
A longue prose. 960
Bien en parla le Rommant de la Rose*
A grant proces, et auques ainsi glose
Ycelle amour, com vous avez desclose
En ceste place, 964
Ou chapitre Raison, qui moult menace,
Le fol amant, qui tel amour enlace,
Et trop bien dit que pou vault et tost passe
La plus grant joye 968
D'icelle amour, et conseille la voye*
De s'en oster; et bien dit toutevoye
Que c'est chose qui trop l'amant desvoye,
Et dur flëaulx, 972
Et que c'est la desloyauté loyaulx
Et loyauté qui est trop desloyaulx,
Un grant peril ou nobles et royaulx,
Et toute gent 976
Sont perillé s'ilz en vont approuchant.
Ainsi fu dit, mais je croy qu'acrochant
Pou s'i vont, mais tous n'aiment fors argent*
Et vivre a ayse. 980
Et qui pourroit ainsi vivre ou mesaise*
Qu'avez compté? Je croy, par saint Nicaise,*
Qu'omme vivant n'est, a nul n'en desplaise,
Qui peust porter, 984
Tant soit il fort, les maulx que raconter
Vous oy ycy, sans la mort en gouster.
Mais je n'ay point, ou sont, ouÿ compter [64v°b]
Li cemetiere 988
Ou enfouÿ sont ceulx qu'amours entiere
A mis a mort et qui pour tel matiere
Ont gieu au lit ou porté en litiere
Soient au saint 992
Dont le mal vient; et quoy que dïent maint,
Je croy que nul, fors a son ayse, n'aimt.
Pour desdire voz dis et vo complaint
Ne le dy pas, 996
Sauve vo paix, ne je ne me debas

Qu'estre ne puist, mais je croy qu'a lent pas
Sont trouvez ceulx qui ont si mal repas
Par trop amer." 1000
Adont cellui qui ja n'esteut nommer,
C'est l'escuyer ou n'ot goute d'amer,*
Parla ainsi, com m'orrez affermer
Et briefment dire: 1004
B eau doulx compains et amis, et cher sire,
Je me merveil, n'il ne me peut souffire,
Dont vous dites que c'est des maulx le pire,
Que cil qui vient 1008
De par amours amer; s'il m'en souvient,
Vous avez dit que l'amant tout devient
Morne et pensif quant celle amour survient
En ses pensees, 1012
Et qu'aux plus lyez ses joyes sont passees
Souventes fois et doulours amassees
En lieu de ris. Et de vous sont taussees
Moult pou les joyes 1016
Qui a l'amant viennent par maintes voyes,
Par doulx desirs, et par pensees quoyes,
Et en mains cas autres, et toutevoyes
Tout le plaisir 1020
Envers le mal, qui avient par desir
Et par servir sa dame a lonc loisir,
Petit prisiez. Qui vous orroit choisir
Il sembleroit 1024
Que le loyal amant, qui aimeroit*
De tout son cuer, jamais nul bien n'aroit;
Espoventé seroit qui vous orroit
D'amer a certes, [65r°a] 1028
Quant si payé seroit de ses dessertes.
S'ainsi estoit, ja nul n'aimeroit certes,
Quant tieulx peines lui seroient offertes
Et nul loyer. 1032
Homs ne seroit qui se voulsist loyer*
En tel lïen; mieux lui vauldroit noyer
Que soy aler soubmettre et avoyer
A tel contraire. 1036
Mais de tout ce que ouÿ vous ay retraire,

Sauve vo paix, je tien tout le contraire,
Et que plus bien par amer sans retraire
Il peut venir 1040
Au vray amant que mal, qui maintenir
Si veult a droit et loyauté tenir.
Quant est de moy, je tiens et vueil tenir
Que d'amours viennent 1044
Tous les plaisirs qui homme en joye tiennent
Et tous les biens qui aux bons appartiennent.
En sont appris, et tout honneur retiennent
Li amant fin 1048
Qui loyaument aiment a celle fin
De mieulx valoir et d'avoir, en la fin,
Joye et plaisir; ne croy qu'a la parfin
Mal leur aviengne. 1052
¶ Je consens bien que de franc vouloir viengne
Ycelle amour, mais que l'amoureux tiengne
Morne et dolent, n'est drois qu'il appartiengne.
Et supposé 1056
Qu'amé ne soit, ne tant ne soit osé
Qu'a celle en qui tout son cuer a posé
Le die, et que ja ne soit reposé
D'amer sans ruse, 1060
S'il fait le droit, n'est raison qu'il s'amuse
A dueil mener. Poson qu'on le reffuse:
Quant en ce cas, se de raison n'abuse,
Bonne esperance 1064
Le doit tenir, ou qu'il soit, en souffrance,
Ne doit pour tant s'enfouïr hors de France
Ou par despoir son corps mettre a oultrance
De mort obscure. 1068
¶ Si ne vient point tant de male aventure,
Sauf vostre honneur, ne reçoit tant d'injure, [65r°b]
A homs qui met en bien amer sa cure
Comme vous dites; 1072
Ainçois Amours paye si grans merites*
A ses servans, que toutes sont petites
Leurs peines vers les grans joyes eslites*
Qu'il leur en rent. 1076
Car quant l'amant a vraye amour se rent,

    Qui le reçoit et lui promet garent
    Contre tous maulx comme prochain parent,
    Il le remplist   1080
    D'un doulx penser qui trop lui abelist,
    Qui ramentoit la belle qu'il eslist
    A sa dame, et la doulçour qui d'elle ist
    Et tous ses fais.   1084
    La est l'amant de joye tous reffais
    Quant lui souvient du gent corps tres parfais
    De la tres belle, et c'est ce qui le fais
    D'amour parfaicte   1088
    Lui fait porter, et espoir qui l'affaite
    Et qui lui dist qu'encore sera faite
    L'acointance, sans ja estre deffaite,
    De lui et d'elle.   1092
 ¶ Et ainsi sert, en esperant, la belle
    Et bonne amour qui souvent renouvelle
    Ses doulx plaisirs; car se quelque nouvelle
    Ouÿr il peut,   1096
    Dont esperer puit avoir ce qu'il veult,
    Ou regardé en soit plus qu'il ne seult,
    Sachés de vray que ja si ne s'en deult
    Que le confort   1100
    Ne soit plus grant que tout le desconfort,
    Ne ja desir ne le poindra si fort
    Qu'il n'ait espoir et doulx penser au fort
    Qui le conforte.   1104
 ¶ Ycelle amour toute pensee torte
 ¶ Tolt a l'amant, et tout bien lui ennorte;
    Si met grant peine a estre de la sorte
    Aux bons vaillans.   1108
    S'il aime a droit, courtois et accueillans
    En devendra, et a tous bienvueillans;
    Si het orgueil në il n'est deffaillans   [65v°a]
    En nul endroit,   1112
    Nul villain tour ja faire ne vouldroit,
    Tous vices het, si est larges a droit,
    Joyeux et gay, cointe, appert et adroit
    Est devenu.   1116
    Ja n'ara tant esté rude tenu

Qu'il ne lui soit lors si bien avenu
Quë on dira que de tout vice est nu
Et de rudece. 1120
Si est appris en toute gentillece
Et aime honneur et vaillance et proece
Et la poursuit affin que sa maistresse
Oye bien dire 1124
De tous ses fais; son cuer est vuide d'ire
Et du peché d'avarice qui tire
A maint meschiefs, et gentement s'atire
En vestement, 1128
Et entre gent se tient honnestement,
Liez et appert, et saillant vistement;
Joyeux, rÿant, gracïeux, prestement
Appareillié 1132
Est a tous biens, songneux et resveillié.
Et vous dites qu'il est si traveillié
Par celle amour qui l'a desconseillié
Et mis en trace 1136
D'estre plus serf que chien qui suit a trace,
Plain de meschief; mais, Sire, sauf vo grace,
Ains est entré en voye plaine et grace
Et plantureuse 1140
De tous les biens, beneuree et eureuse,
Doulce, plaisant, tres sade et savoureuse.
¶ Ne fu il dit de la vie amoureuse,
Tres assouvie, 1144
En amer a plaisant et doulce vie
Jolye, qui bien la scet sans envie
Maintenir, qui le vray amant renvie
A tous soulas? 1148
Et il y pert, car ja si fort le las
N'estraint l'amant quë il puit estre las
D'icelle amour; combien qu'il dye, "Helas!," [65v°b]
Tant lui agree 1152
La pensee tres loyale et secree
Qu'il a au cuer, qui tant lui est sucree,
Qu'il ne vouldroit pour riens que desancree
De lui ja fust. 1156
¶ C'est un doulx mal; chacun amer deüst,

Ne blasmee, se le monde le sceust,
Ne deüst estre femme, qui m'en creust,
Car c'est plaisance   1160
Trop avenant, et de gaye naissance
Vient celle amour, qui oste desplaisance
Du jolis cuer et remplist tout d'aisance
Et de baudour.   1164
¶ Beaulx sire Dieux! quel tres soueve ardour
Rent doulx regart au vray cuer amadour
Quant il s'espart sus l'amant! Onque oudeur
Tant precïeuse   1168
Ne fu a corps d'omme si gracïeuse,
Ne viande, tant fust delicïeuse.
Si n'en doit pas estre avaricïeuse
A son amant   1172
Dame qui paist cellui en elle amant,
Qu'elle a s'amour tire com l'aÿmant
Attrait le fer, et com le dyament
Est affermé   1176
En seue amour, et des armes armé
Qu'Amours depart a ceulx qu'il a charmé
Pour lui servir et du tout confermé.
¶ Mais or dison   1180
Quelle joye reçoit le gentilz hom,
Le fin amant, qui est en la prison
De sa dame sans avoir mesprison
En riens commise.   1184
Së il avient qu'il ait tel peine mise
Que sa dame son bon vouloir avise
Tant que s'amour lui donne par franchise
En guerredon,   1188
Je croy qu'il soit bien enrichi adon,
Car plus joye a, se Dieux me doint pardon,
Je croy, que s'il eust le monde a bandon,   [66rºa]
Voire plus, certes.   1192
S'il aime bien et la desire a certes,
Or est il bien meri de ses desertes,
Car ne prise ne ses deulx ne ses pertes,
Or est il ayse.   1196
¶ Quelle est la riens qui peust mettre a mesaise

Le fin amant, que sa dame rappaise
Et doulcement l'embrace et puis le baise?
Que lui fault il? 1200
N'est il ayse? N'a il plus de cent mil
De doulx plaisirs? Je le tendroie a vil
Se plus vouloit! Certes, eureux est cil
Qui en tel cas 1204
A eu pour lui Amours pour avocas;
Il n'a garde d'estre flati a cas.
Joyeux est cil, ne doit pas parler cas
Në enroué; 1208
Bien l'a gari le saint ou s'est voué.
¶ Mais dit avez, se ne l'ay controuvé,
Que Faulx Agait, qui maint homme a trouvé
En recellee, 1212
Par qui mainte grant oeuvre est decellee,
Ne s'en taist pas; par lui est pou cellee
La chose, car parlant a la vollee
L'amant accuse. 1216
Si resveille Jalousie, qui muse
Pour agaitier et a l'amant refuse
Son doulx solas; si ne le tient a ruse
Ne s'en depporte, 1220
Ainçois le las amant s'en desconforte
Que joye et paix dedens son cuer est morte,
Et mesdisans, qui resont a la porte,
De l'autre part 1224
Le grievent tant qu'il a petite part
De ses soulas; et ainsi lui depart
Amours cent maulx pour un tout seul espart
De ses desirs. 1228
¶ Quant en ce cas, je consens que souspirs
Au povre amant sourdent, et desplaisirs,
Quant empeschié lui sont ses doulx plaisirs.
¶ Mais vrayement [66r°b] 1232
Quant il bien pense et scet certainement
Que sa dame l'aime tres loyaument,
Ce reconfort lui fait paciemment
Porter son dueil, 1236
Et s'un doulx ris, regardant de doulx oeil,

Lui fait de loing par gracïeux accueil,
Il souffit bien pour avoir joyeux vueil,
Qui mieulx ne peut.   1240
Si est trop folz l'amant qui tant se deult
Com vous dites, car en tous cas, s'il veult,
Assez de bien et de doulçour recuelt
Pour s'esjouÿr.   1244
¶ Mais merveilles je puis de vous ouÿr!
S'ainsi estoit, mieulx s'en vauldroit fouÿr
Qu'en tel langour son cuer laisser rouÿr,
N'en tel courroux,   1248
Que nous dites que l'amant est jaloux*
S'il aime bien, et plus derve qu'uns loups,
S'il voit qu'autre pourchace ses biens doulx,
Et souspeçon   1252
Sur sa dame a, dont a tel cuisançon,
Qu'ester ne peut n'en rue n'en maison,
Et dont il lit mainte laide leçon
Sans courtoisie.   1256
¶ Si suis dolent quant vous tel heresie
Sur vraye amour mettez, qui jalousie
Y adjoustez qui tant est desprisie
Et tant maudite.   1260
Si nous avez or tel parole dite
Que d'amours vient jalousie despite;
Dieu! de l'amour, certes, elle est petite.
Ne sçay entendre   1264
Qu'estre ce puist, ne je ne puis comprendre
Que souspeçon et amour on puist prendre
Parfaictement ensemble, sans mesprendre
Vers amours fine,   1268
Car vraye amour toute souspeçon fine,
Et qui mescroit, certes l'amour deffine,
Car loyauté, qui tout bon cuer affine,
On doit penser   1272
Estre en celle qu'on aime sans cesser,   [66v°a]
Et qu'en nul cas ne daigneroit fausser;
Ne tel penser en son cuer amasser
En nulle guise   1276
Amant ne doit, car chacun croit et prise

Ce qu'il aime, c'est communal devise,
Si est bien droit qu'a l'amant il souffise
Sans autre preuve. 1280
¶ Et que d'Amours ne viengne, le vous preuve,
Jalousie, que tout homme repreuve;
Ouÿr pourrés la raison que g'i treuve
Sans variance: 1284
Chacun veoir peut, par experïence,
Que mains maris plains de contrarïence,
Rudes et maulx et de grant tarïence
Sont, et divers 1288
A leurs femmes, et jaloux plus que vers
Sont, ou que chien, et tous jours en travers
Leur giettent mos et frappent a revers,
Et tant les battent 1292
Souventes fois qu'a leurs piez les abatent,
Tant sont jaloux, et non obstant s'esbatent
D'autres femmes, et en mains lieux s'embatent
De vilté plains. 1296
Diront ilz puis, 'Ma femme, je vous aims!,'
'Mais vo gibet, Sire, tres ort villains,'
Respondre doit, et s'elle n'ose, au mains
Penser le peut. 1300
Doncque est ce amour, qui ainsi les esmeut?*
Mais tele amour tire a soy qui se veult,
Car quant a moy, celle dont on se deult,
Je n'en prens point. 1304
¶ Si vous respons pour vray dessus ce point,
Que qui bien aime et est d'amours compoint,
Je ne cuide que coup ne buffe doint,
Ne nul mal face 1308
A soy mesmes n'a autre, dont defface
Ycelle amour qui lui tient cuer et face
Joyeux et lyé, ne que ja tant meffasse
Que jaloux soit 1312
De celle dont maint plaisant bien reçoit, [66v°b]
Et toute riens a bonne fin conçoit
Quanqu'elle fait; et s'ores s'apperçoit
Quë un ou deux 1316
Ou mains autres en soyent amoureux,

N'en ara il ne pesance ne deulx,
Ains pensera qu'il est amé tous seulx
Et que lëece 1320
Doit bien avoir quant il a tel maistresse
En qui tel bien et tel beauté s'adresse
Que chacun veult amer pour sa noblesse
Et grant valour. 1324
¶ Si n'a l'amant ne cause ne coulour
D'estre jaloux ne de vivre en doulour
Pour bien amer, mais maint par leur folour
Mettent la rage 1328
Sus a amours, mais c'est leur fol courage
Qui recevoir ne prendre l'avantage
Ne scet d'amours; si sont de tel plumage
Et de tel sorte, 1332
Et puis dïent qu'en eulx est joye morte
Par trop amer, qui tant les desconforte,
Mais ce n'est que leur condicion torte
Qui si les tient. 1336
Si a grant tort, sanz faille, qui maintient
Que doulce amour, a qui joye appartient,
Rende l'amant jaloux, car point ne vient
Tel maladie 1340
For de failli, lache cuer, quoy que on die,
Et d'envie triste et accouardie,
Qui personne fait estre pou hardie
Et mescreant, 1344
Et soucïer fait l'omme de neant.
Si cuide estre plus lourt et pis seant
Que les autres, et quant il est veant*
Jolis et gays 1348
Jeunes hommes, lors est en male paix,
Car il cuide estre de tous li plus lais,
Si ne lui plaist ne souffreroit jamais
Qu'acointes fussent 1352
De ses amours, de päour que plus plussent.
Si sont tristes tieulx gens et se demussent [67r°a]
Pour agaitier qu'apperceü ne fussent.
Dont par nul tour 1356
Ne dites que jalousie d'amour

Viengne. Ainçois vient de cuer plain de cremour,*
Ou souspeçon et desdaing fait demour
Par mal vouloir 1360
Pour ce qu'autre ne cuide pas valoir,*
Et c'est ce qui le cuer fait tant douloir
Au maleureux qui n'a autre chaloir
Par folliance. 1364
¶ Aussi ne doy pas mettre en oubliance
Ce qu'avez dit qu'amoureuse aliance
A fait perir par sa contralïence
Maint vaillant homme 1368
Ou temps jadis et en France et a Romme
Et autre part; si en nommez grant somme
Qui dure mort receurent toute somme,
Com vous comptez, 1372
Par tele amour. Mais un pou m'escoutez:
Je di pour vray, et de ce ne doubtez,
Que s'il fust vray que ainsi fussent matez
Et mis en biere, 1376
Blasme n'en doit en nesune maniere
Amour avoir, car leur fole maniere
Les fist mourir, non pas amour entiere.
¶ Je vous demande,* 1380
N'est pas bonne, doulce et sade, l'amande?
Mais se cellui qui la veult et demande*
S'en ront le col ou a l'arbre se pende
Vault elle pis? 1384
¶ Le vin est bon, mais s'aucun tant ou pis
S'en est fiché qu'yvre soit accrouppis,
Ou comme mort gisant com par despis,
Ou une bigne 1388
Se fait ou front par yvrece folligne,
Ou il s'occist ou un autre l'engigne,
On doit, je croy, pour ce arracher la vigne
Qui tel fruit donne? 1392
Ne peut on pas de toute chose bonne
Tres mal user? De une bonne personne [67r°b]
Peut venir mal a qui mal s'en ordonne.
Ainsi sans faille 1396
Est il d'amours, ce n'est pas controuvaille,

Car il n'est chose ou monde qui tant vaille,
Mais cil est folz qui tel robe s'en taille
Dont pis lui viengne. 1400
C'est droit qu'amant a une amour se tiengne,
De tout son cuer aime et toudis maintiengne
Foy, loyauté, et verité soustiengne.
Mais pour ce faire, 1404
N'est pas besoing s'occire et soy deffaire;
Amour faite fu pour l'omme parfaire,
Et non pas pour lui grever et meffaire,
C'est chose voire. 1408
¶ Mais pour ce que ramenteu mainte histoire
Avez ycy que li comptes avoire
Des vrays amans, dignes de grant memoire,
Qui moult souffrirent 1412
Par grant amour et qui a mort s'offrirent,
Ainsi compter vueil de ceulx qui eslirent
Le mieulx du gieu, et pour amours tant firent
Que renommee 1416
Par le monde fu de leur bien semee
Par vaillans fais en mainte grant armee
Faire, par quoy a tous jours mais semee
Sera leur grace 1420
Tres honorable, et rien n'est qui ne passe
Fors bon renom, mais aprés qu'on trespasse
Demeure loz; sages est qui l'amasse.
¶ Or regardons 1424
Se Lancelot du Lac, qui si preudoms*
Fu en armes, receut de nobles dons
Pour celle amour de quoy adés plaidons.
Fu il vaillant? 1428
Qu'en dites vous? S'ala il exillant
Pour celle amour ne son corps besillant?
Je croy que non; ains plus que son vaillant
Lui fu valable 1432
Sur toute riens, et bonne et prouffitable,*
Car par ce fu vaillant et agreable, [67v°a]
Dont ne lui fu ne male ne nuisable,
Je croy au mains. 1436
Si ne s'occist, ne fu par autres mains

Mort ne blecié; ains de joye en fut plains.
¶ Aussi d'autres encores en est mains,
Et mesmement 1440
Tristan, de qui parlastes ensement,*
En devint preux, se l'istoire ne ment.
Pour amours vint le bon commencement
De sa prouece, 1444
Et non obstant qu'il mouru a destresse
Par Fortune, qui maint meschiefs adresse,
Tant de bien fist pour sa dame et maistresse
Qu'a tous jours mais 1448
Sera parlé de ses haultains bienfais;
Ce fist Amours, par qui il fu parfais.
Si avez dit que de l'amoureux fais
Fors mal ne vient; 1452
Or regardons, pour Dieux, s'il m'en souvient,
Së a chacun d'amours si mesavient.
¶ Jason jadis, sicom l'istoire tient,*
Fu reschappé 1456
De dure mort, ou estoit entrappé
Se du peril ne l'eüst destrappé
Medee, qui de s'amour ot frappé
Le cuer si fort 1460
Que le garda et restora de mort
Quant la toison d'or conquist par le sort
Que lui apprist en Colcos, quant au port
Fu arrivé; 1464
Qui qu'en mourust, cellui fu avivé
Par tele amour, mais trop fu desrivé
Quant faulte fist a celle qui privé
L'ot de peril. 1468
¶ Et Theseüs, du roy d'Athenes fil,*
Quant envoyé fu en Crete en exil,
Adriane par son engin soubtil
Le reschappa 1472
De dure mort; si le desveloppa
De la prison Minos quant s'agrappa
A son fillé, et la gorge coppa [67v°b]
Au crüel monstre. 1476
Ne nuisi pas Amours, je le vous monstre,

A cestui cy, car l'istoire demonstre
Qu'il eschappa par mer plus tost que loustre
Gué ne trespasse. 1480
¶ Et Eneas, aprés qu'ot esté arse*
La grant cité de Troye, a qui reverse
Fu Fortune, qui maint royaume verse,
Quant il par mer 1484
Aloit vagant a cuer triste et amer,
Ne ne finoit de ses dieux reclamer;
Mais bon secours lui survint pour amer,
Car accueilli 1488
Fu de Dido la belle et recueilli.
S'elle ne fust, esté eust maubailli,
Dont ot grant tort quant vers elle failli.
Si n'en moururent 1492
Mie ces .iij.; ains eschappez en furent,
Et mains autres assez de biens en eurent.
¶ Et si est vray, com les histoires jurent,
Que Theseüs* 1496
Dont j'ay parlé, qui tant fu esleüs
Qu'avec le fort Hercules fu veüs
En grans effors, en mains lieux fu sceüs,
Quant enfançon 1500
Estoit petit, il estoit lait garçon,
Boçu, maufait, sicom dit la chançon
De l'istoire; mais il changia façon
Pour belle Helaine, 1504
Pour lui fu preux et emprist mainte peine.
Vous le vëez en ces tappis de laine
En un aygle d'or, qu'on conduit et maine,
Ou fu mucié 1508
Tant qu'il se fu a la belle annoncié.
Puis la ravi, dont furent courroucié
Tous ses parens, si ne lui fu laissié
La mener loings. 1512
¶ Si n'est on pas exillié de tous poins
Pour ceste amour quant on apprent les poins
D'estre vaillant par honnourables soings.
¶ Autres histoires [68r°a] 1516
Si racontent assez de choses voires

Des vrays amans, dont les haultes memoires
A tous jours mais seront par tout nottoires.
¶ Et Florimont 1520
D'Albanië, il n'ot en tout le mond*
Nul plus vaillant, mais dont lui vint tel mont
De vaillances fors d'Amours qui semont
Ses serviteurs 1524
A estre bons, tant anoblist les cuers?
Pour Rome de Naples mains grans labeurs*
Il endura, non obstant a tous fuers
Il conquestoit 1528
Pris et honneur; son temps dont ne gastoit
En bien amer, par qui il acquestoit
Les vaillances qu'Amours lui apprestoit.
¶ Et le Gallois* 1532
Durmas vaillant, qui fu filz au bon roys
Danemarchois, cellui ot si grant voix
De proueces que plus n'en orent trois.
Je vous demande 1536
Quë il perdi quant roÿne d'Irlande
Prist a amer et tout en sa commande
Il se soubmist, dont passa mainte lande
Pour lui conquerre 1540
Son royaume, et demena si grant guerre
Qu'il le conquist et lui rendi sa terre,
Dont il dot bien par droit honneur acquerre?
¶ Cleomadés,* 1544
Fu il vaillant pour amours et adés
Armes suivoit? Aussi Pallamedés;*
Vous souvient il des proeces et des
Grans vaillantises 1548
Qu'on dit de lui assez en maintes guises?
Tout pour Amours faisoit ses entreprises;
Si vous suppli ne soient voz devises
Que mal en preigne. 1552
¶ Aussi Artus, qui fu duc de Bretaigne,*
Pour Flourance, qui puis fu sa compaigne,
Il chevaucha et France et Allemagne [68r°b]
Et maintes terres, 1556
En mains beaulx fais et en maintes grans guerres,

Tout pour Amours, qui le mettoit es erres
D'avoir honneur; pour ce emprenoit ses erres.
¶ Mais sans aler   1560
Plus loing querir, encor pouons parler
De notre temps. Ne devons pas celer
Les bons vaillans qui, sans eulx affoller
Në eulx mal mettre,   1564
Vouldrent leur cuers en parfaite amour mettre.
Ne me fault ja autre preuve promettre
N'autre escript pour tesmoing, në autre lettre,
Car veritable-*   1568
Ment le scet on, le vaillant connestable
De France, dont Dieux ait l'ame acceptable,
Le bon Bertran, le preux et le valable*
Du Gueaquin,   1572
Qui aux Anglois fist maint divers hutin,
Dont ot honneur; leur chasteaulx a butin
Mettoit souvent, ou fust soir ou matin,
Et renommé   1576
Sera tous jours et des bons reclamé;
Premierement pour Amours fu armé,
Ce disoit il, et desir d'estre amé
Le fist vaillant.   1580
De bonne heure le fist si traveillant
Amours, qui fait chacun bon cuer veillant
A poursuivrë honneur s'il est vueillant
Loz qui mieulx vault   1584
Que riens qui soit. Et le bon Bouisicault*
Le mareschal, qui fu preux, sage et cault,
Tout pour Amours fu vaillant, large et bault,
Ce devenir   1588
Le fist ytel; celle voye tenir
Ses .ij. enfans veulent, et maintenir
D'armes le faiz, pour le temps avenir*
Louange acquerre.   1592
¶ Et a present ancore vit sur terre,
Dieux lui tiengne, le vaillant de Sancerre*
Connestable, si ne couvient enquerre   [68v°a]
De chevalier   1596
Meilleur de lui; en son temps batailler

  L'a fait Amours, qui moult bon conseiller
  Lui a esté, quant par soy travailler
  A tant conquis   1600
  Quë il a loz entre les bons acquis;
  S'a fait Amours, qui lui a ce pourquis.
¶ Aussi d'autres, sicom j'en ay enquis,
  En ce regné   1604
  En a esté qu'Amours a gouverné;
  Encore en est, le gieu n'est pas finé,
  Qui en armes se sont si bien mené
  Qu'a tous jours mais   1608
  Sera retrait de leurs beaulx et bons faiz.
¶ Des chevaliers ne sçay pourquoy me tais
  Qui sont adés en vie, qui le fais
  D'armes porter   1612
  Pour bien amer a fait en pris monter.
¶ Des trespassez encore puis compter:
  Du bon Othe de Grançon racompter*
  Avez assez   1616
  Ouÿ comment de bien ne fu lassez;*
  En lui furent tous les biens amassez.
¶ De Vermeilles Hutin mie effacez*
  D'entre les bons   1620
  Ne doit estre, Dieu lui face pardons.
¶ Mais aux vivans chevaliers regardons
  S'il en y a qui doivent grans guerredons
  Par esprouver   1624
  A bonne amour, que l'en peut bons trouver
  Vaillans, sages, courtois et non aver.
¶ Le bon Chasteau Morant, que Dieu sauver*
  Et garder vueille,   1628
  Qui en armes sur les Sarrasins veille
  En la cité Constantin, qu'il conseille,
  Ayde et garde, pour la foy Dieu traveille;
  Cil doit avoir   1632
  Pris et honneur, car il fait son devoir,
  Et ceulx qui sont o lui, a dire voir,
  Loz acquierent, qui trop mieulx vault qu'avoir, [68v°b]
  Et aux François   1636
  Font grant honneur. Et encor m'apperçois

De maint vaillant sages en tous endrois
Qu'Amours a fais bon, courtois et adrois
Et honnourables. 1640
₵ Bon chevalier est l'Ermite et valables*
De la Fayë, et d'autres tieulx semblables
En est assez de vaillans et louables,
Mais pour briefté 1644
M'en tais; mais, se Dieu vous envoit santé,
₵ Or regardons, s'en trouverons planté
Des plus jones, qui plus bien que griefté
Ont et conduis 1648
Sont pour Amours, qui si bien les a duis
Qu'a toute honneur poursuivre sont aduis;
Courtoisie, vaillance est leur reduis
Ce n'est pas fable. 1652
₵ De Monseigneur d'Alebret, tres valable*
Charles, qui est a chacun agreable,
Qu'en dites vous? Vous semble il point louable,
Ne que son pris 1656
Soit bien digne qu'il soit en tout pourpris
Ramenteü? Est il sage et appris,
Duit aux armes? Peut il estre repris
En nul endroit? 1660
Qui vouldroit mieulx souhaiter, il fauldroit,
Je croy, que lui, car raison aime et droit,
Et tout bon fait Amours lui a a droit
Et avoyez. 1664
₵ Le Seneschal de Haynau, or voyez,*
Est il d'Amours a droit bien convoyez?
Ses jeunes jours, sont ilz bien employez?
Est il oyseux? 1668
Va il suivant armes, est il parceux?
Que vous semble il? N'est il bien angoisseux
D'aquerir loz? Dieu lui doint, et a ceulx
Qui lui ressemblent; 1672
Je croy qu'en lui assez de biens s'assemblent,
Courtoisie, valeur ne s'en dessemblent;*
N'est pas de ceulx a qui tous les cuers tremblent [69r°a]
De couardie. 1676
₵ Et de Gaucourt, que voulez que je die?*

Il m'est advis qu'en maniere hardie
Armes poursuit, nul n'est qui en mesdie,
Tant bien s'i porte; 1680
Ce fait Amours qui lui euvre la porte
De vaillantise. Et tout par autel sorte,
Le bon Charles de Savoisi ennorte*
Et fait vaillant, 1684
Si que son corps n'espargne ne vaillant
Pour avoir loz com preux et traveillant,
Ou soit de lance ou d'espee taillant,
En armes faire. 1688
¶ Castelbeart et autres plus d'un paire*
En qui bonté et vaillance repaire,
Ce fait Amours, qui leur fait tout ce faire
Pour loz acquerre, 1692
Car chevaliers meilleurs ne couvient querre.
¶ Aussi Clignet de Breban, qui enquerre*
Vouldroit de lui, en France et autre terre
Est renommé, 1696
Car en mains lieux pour Amours s'est armé,
Par quoy il est et sera renommé.
Si sont jolis, jeunes et assesmé,
Et pour leur dames 1700
Vont com vaillans en mains lieux faisant armes,
Dont, quant les corps seront dessoubz les lames,
D'eulx remaindra louanges et grans fames
En tout empire. 1704
Mais que toudis se gardent de mesdire,
Car c'est chose qui trop noble homme empire,
Si feront ilz, car leur bon cuer ne tire
Qu'a fuïr vice 1708
Et a suivir toute chose propice;*
Amours le fait, car c'est son droit office,
Dont leur rendra loyer et benefice,
S'ilz le desservent. 1712
¶ Si ne dites jamais qu'amans s'asservent
Pour bien amer quant un tel maistre servent
Qui les fait bons, et se bien le perservent, [69r°b]
Sachés de voir, 1716
Qu'ilz acquerront, en faisant leur devoir,

Proece, honneur, sens, louange et avoir.
¶ De tieulx assez, ce povez vous savoir,
  En est, sans doubte; 1720
  Mais qui vouldroit nommer la somme toute
  Des bons et beaulx amans toute la route
  Dureroit trop, car souvent qui escoute
  Un trop lonc compte 1724
  Il ennuye; mais ceulx dont je vous compte
  Et d'autres tant dont je n'en sçay le compte
  Sont gracïeux, car il n'est duc ne conte,
  Prince ne roy, 1728
  S'il aime a droit, qu'il ne hee desroy
  Et tout mesdit, et qu'en tout son arroy
  Ne vaille mieulx, car l'amoureux conroy
  Les fait apprendre. 1732
¶ Donc, beaulx amis, se bien voulez entendre,
  Ouÿr povez que se l'amant veult tendre
  A joye avoir, Amours lui est plus tendre
  Qu'elle n'est dure, 1736
  Se doulcement et quoyement endure
  En esperant, combien que ycelle ardure
  Lui soit poignant; mais trop fait grant laidure
  Qui tant mesprent 1740
  Que le mieulx voit et le pis pour soy prent.*
  Si ay prouvé qu'en amours on apprent
  Bien et honneur et a faire on se prent
  Toute vaillance. 1744
  Si ne dites plus que si grant dueillance
  Ait en amours, et tele deffaillance
  De reconfort, ne si grant traveillance
  Ne si penible." 1748
Quant l'escuyer, qui fu sage et sensible,
  Qui verité ot dit comme la Bible,
  Ce lui sembla, adoncques fu taysible*
  Sans plus mot dire, 1752
  Le chevalier un pou prist a soubsrire
  Et en pensant sans parler le remire,
  Et puis vers lui courtoisement se tire [69v°a]
  Et dit a trait: 1756
¶ "Par Dieu, Sire, vous avez cy retrait

Grans merveilles et qui vers vous se trait
Pour medicine avoir et pour bon trait
A tost tarir 1760
Les maulx d'amours, bien en savez garir
Et bon conseil donner pour tost perir
Toute doulour, pour servant remerir
Bien a son ayse, 1764
Mais qu'on vous creust. Mais de petit s'apaise
Qui pou a dueil et qui n'a nul mesaise;
Ainsi l'avez gaigné, mais que je tayse,
Sanz mot sonner, 1768
Les grans raisons que je puis assener
Contre les dis que vous oys raisonner,
Car vous voulez droitement ordonner
A droit souhaid 1772
Les fais d'amours et chacun a son haid
Pou ou assez a voulenté en ait,
Si que le bien en preigne et le mal lait.
Ne plus ne mains 1776
¶ Mettre voulez et la tenir aux mains
Bride a Amours et, fors en poins certains,
Le faire aler et qu'on n'en soit atains
Fors a sa poste. 1780
Autrement va, compains, qui a tel hoste,
A son vouloir ne le met pas decoste.
Avez vous cuer qui joye met et oste
A voulenté? 1784
Dont n'amez vous, dire l'ose, planté.
Aussi ne font tous ceulz qui sont renté
De tel plaisir, com vous avez compté,
Sans dueil avoir; 1788
Estre ne peut. Il est bon a savoir
Que qui aime de cuer sans decevoir,
Parfaictement, qu'il ne lui faille avoir
Mainte durté, 1792
Ou vueille ou non, ja si bien ahurté
Ne se sera qu'il y ait seürté
Et que toudis il ait beneürté [69v°b]
En sa querelle. 1796
Mais vous comptez cy d'une amour nouvelle*

A vo vouloir, ne sçay comme on l'appelle,
Dont nous avez compté longue nouvelle.
¶ Mais ancor dis je 1800
Que l'amant qui est vray, et subgiet lige,
Tres grant amour son cuer si fort oblige
Qu'estre le fait jaloux, et tant engrige
Celle grief peine 1804
Qu'il n'a repos nul jour de la semaine
S'il s'apperçoit que un autre amant se peine
A acquerir l'amour qui le demaine
En maint endroit. 1808
¶ Et vous cuidez nous prouver cy endroit
Que qui jaloux seroit, amours fauldroit,
Et je vous di qu'amours ne peut a droit
Sans jalousie. 1812
Si soit de vous vo pensee accoisie,
Car je vous dy que trop plus se soussie
Un cuer amant, et mains est adoulcie*
Sa peine grieve 1816
Quë un autre qui de leger s'en lieve.
Mais vous parlez d'une amour qui pou grieve,
De qui ne chault s'elle est ou longue ou brieve
Et se tost passe, 1820
Mais elle sert de dire, "Amours m'enlace,
J'en suis joli, de servir ne me lasse,
Et si n'en ay nulle pensee lasse [70r°a]
C'est avantage." 1824
¶ Adont respont l'autre et ront le lengage
Et dit, "Par Dieu, estre cuidez trop sage!
Autrement va et tout d'autre plumage
Sont amours fines, 1828
Et nous serions ycy jusqu'a matines;
Mais je vous di que plus sont enterines
Vrayes amours, et mieulx en sont les signes
Et plus certains, 1832
Quant un amant qui d'amours est atains
Est liez et bault et de gayeté plains,
Pour la joye qu'il a, dont est attains,
D'amours loyale. 1836
Quant lui souvient de la haulte royale

Dame qu'il sert, toute pensee male
Pour sa valeur de son cuer se ravalle,
Si s'en tient gay 1840
Et envoysiez en avril et en may
Et en tout temps; si n'a doulour n'esmay
Par vraye amour qui de son luisant ray
Tout l'enlumine. 1844
¶ Quoy que dissiés, encor dy et termine,
Que c'est plus grant et trop plus parfait signe
De grant amour parfaicte et enterine
De soy fÿer 1848
En ses amours que de s'en deffïer,
N'estre jaloux; j'ose bien affïer
Que plus aime cil qui sans soussïer,
Argent ou or 1852
Baille a garder, ou aucun grant tresor,
A un autrë, et si lui dist, 'Trés or*
Me fie en vous, garde vous fais encor
De mon avoir,' 1856
Que cil qui veult grant seürté avoir
Et le conte veult chacun jour savoir
Qu'on fait du sien, de paour que decevoir
L'autre le vueille. 1860
Ainsi est il, a qui que plaise ou dueille,
Du fait d'amours, car cil qui se despueille
De son vray cuer, et tel fiance accueille, [70r°b]
Que il le donne 1864
A un autre et du tout lui abandonne
Sans marchander, ne que plus en sermonne,
C'est mieulx signe que la personne a bonne
Il tient sans faille, 1868
Que cellui qui en marchandant le baille
Et qui tous jours se doubte que on lui faille
Ou que bonté et loyauté deffaille
Aucunement. 1872
Car qui aime se fie entierement,
Comme j'ay dit, ne seroit autrement
Parfaite amour, et le vray jugement
En ose attendre, 1876
S'il est aucun qui sache bien entendre

Noz .ij. raisons et tous les poins comprendre.
¶ Si vous suppli que juge vueillés prendre
　Tout a vo guise, 1880
　Et tout sur lui soit ceste cause mise."
¶ Le chevalier respont: "Et sans faintise
　Le jugement conseil, a vo devise
　Soit juge pris 1884
　Et esleü, mais qu'en lui ait tel pris
　Qu'il soit vaillant, preux, sage et bien appris,
　Noble et gentil, et des amans surpris
　Sache juger. 1888
　Et quant a moy, sans plus tant lengager,
　Je dis et tiens que plus comparer cher
　Le bien d'amours couvient sans aleger
　C'on n'en a joye, 1892
　Et pour un bien plus de cent maulx envoye,
　Et que l'omme qui a amer s'avoye
　De tous perilz il se met en la voye.
　Et du seurplus, 1896
　Je di ancor que cellui aime plus
　Qui pour amours devient mat et reclus,
　Pensif, pali, morne, taysant et mus,
　Que cil qui lyez 1900
　Plus en devient; ne point n'est si lïez
　Le cuer qui a joye s'est alÿez
　Comme est cellui qui est contralïé [70v°a]
　Par tel amour, 1904
　Et qu'il couvient qu'en lui face demour
　Jalousie, dont les yeulx plains d'umour
　On a souvent faisant mainte clamour;
　Se sanz retraire 1908
　Il aime a droit, tel mal lui couvient traire.
　Et vous dites et tenez le contraire;
　Or nous doint Dieux vers loyal juge traire
　Prochainement." 1912
　　A dont les .ij. amans leur parlement
　　　Ont affiné, mais en grant pensement
　De juge avoir furent, qui proprement
　Sentence a droit 1916
　Leur sceust donner justement selon droit.

Maint hault baron choisirent la endroit,
Maint chevalier, cointe, appert et adroit,
Gay et jolis, 1920
Y nommerent, et de la flour de lis
Eslisoient de tieulx qui sont palis
Par fort amer, dont n'ont pas tous delis,
Soubs leur chappeaulx, 1924
Pour ce que pas ne font tous leurs aveaulx
Es fais d'amours, qui depart ses tourteaulx
Diversement, et amaigrir les peaulx
Fait a maint bons 1928
Souventes fois; et ainsi a leurs bons
Choisissoient et nommoient les noms
De maint vaillant, disant, "Cellui arons!"
Et puis disoient 1932
Que mieulx valoit un autre qu'ilz nommoient.
¶ Et quant je vy qu'en tel descort estoient
Qu'a leur droit gre nul juge ne trouvoient,
Lors m'avisay 1936
Tout en pensant et pris mon avis ay
Que pour leur fait un bon juge visay.
Quant pensé l'oz, ainsi leur devisay
Com vous pourrés 1940
Ycy ouïr; si me tiray plus pres
Et si leur dis: "S'il vous plaist, vous orrés
Ce qu'il m'est vis et me pardonnerés [70v°b]
Se je m'avance 1944
De mettre accort en l'amoureuse tence
Dont vous plaidiés, et croyez sans doubtance
Que j'en desir droituriere sentence
Et si le fais, 1948
A bonne fin; et, se charger le fais
Et ce descort voulez et soit parfais
Selon mon los, vous en serés reffais
Et tous contens 1952
Et assouvis a droit gre a tous temps.
Se le tres hault noble duc que j'entens
S'en veult charger et estre consentans
De ce juge estre, 1956
¶ Bon juge arés, vaillant, sage et grant maistre,

C'est le tres hault, puissant, de noble ancestre,*
Duc d'Orlïens, qui ait joye terrestre
Et paradis; 1960
Cellui est bon, sage en fais et en dis
Juste, loyal, et aux bons de jadis
Veult ressembler, car maintenir toudis
Lui plaist justice. 1964
Si est humain, humble, doulx et propice
En trestous cas, et meismes en l'office,
De droit jugier; si n'est mie si nice
Qu'il n'ait appris 1968
Les tours d'amours, non obstant son hault pris.
Si vous conseil que de vous il soit pris
Et esleü a juge, et bien empris
Arés, sans faille, 1972
Car je ne cuid que nul autre le vaille,
Mais qu'il lui plaise et que tant en travaille
Son noble cuer que sentence il en baille,
Ne pourriés mieulx." 1976
¶ Adont les .ij. amans, haulçans les yeulx,
Respondirent: "Et louez en soit Dieux,
Vous nous avez assis en noble lieux
Et ramenteu 1980
Juge loyal et par nous esleü;
Së il lui plaist, sera le cas veü,
En jugera a son vueil et sceü [71r°a]
S'a gre lui vient. 1984
¶ Si vous prions, puis que tant vous souvient
De notre bien, que vous, a qui avient
Et bien et bel faire dis, dont seurvient
En mainte place 1988
Maint grant plaisir, que de vo bonne grace
Faciés un dit du fait et de l'espace
De no debat; si nous ferés grant grace
Et grant lëece." 1992
¶ Adont respons: "Je ne suis pas maistresse
De faire dis; non pour tant, sans parece
Je le feray, pour la haulte noblece
Du bon vaillant 1996
Prince royal, qui nul temps n'est faillant

De bien juger, d'estre bien conseillant,
Et en tous fais adroit et traveillant,
Pour mettre en joye 2000
Son noble cuer, së il daigne qu'il l'oye.
Or me doint Dieux, ainsi com je vouldroie,
Faire chose dont esjouïr se doye
Et faire feste." 2004
⁋ Et ainsi, hault Prince de noble geste,
Mon redoubté Seigneur, a qui Dieu preste
Longue vië et puis a l'ame appreste
Sa vraye gloire, 2008
Ce dictié fis pour vous duire a memoire
Joye et solas par ouÿr ceste histoire
Qui d'amours fait mencion et memoire,
Dont je supplie 2012
Vo haultece qu'elle tant s'umilie
Qu'en bon gre l'ait, ne le tiengne a folie,
Car voulenté et vray desir me lie
A moy pener 2016
De vous servir, se g'i sceusse assener.
Et or est temps de mon oeuvre affiner;
Mais de trouver, s'aucun au deffiner
A voulenté, 2020
Quel est mon nom, sans le querir planté,*
S'il le cerche, trouver le peut enté
En tous les lieux ou est Cristïenté.* [71r°b]
          Explicit le debat des .ij. amans

Variants

Rubric *D* Le debat de deux a., *L1L3* Ci c. le debat des d. a., *L2 is missing the beginning of the text and begins at line 50*, *S* Ci c. le debat de .ij. amans

2   *L1L3* g. prouesse
15 *L1L3S2* m. empris
17 *R* q. m'escoute l.
18 *DL1L3S* Qui
21 *S2* Ne
24 *S1* Et a o.
45 *S1* t. se d.
69 *L3* s. chanter m.
86 *D* et joyeuse
93 *DLS* paree par entente
97 *D* et jolis p.
122 *D* d. les c.
129 *L* B. a. et doulcement a.
130 *DL2S* R. et j.
133 *L* t. de d.
143 *L* F. ainsi d'estre a f.
155 *LS2* N'en f.
163 *RDL1S omit* de
166 *LS2* m. tout fu
169 *D* ou bien se
173 *L* il chantoit et dançoit si
174 *L* Et l. j.
177 *L* Tant fort e.
178 *L* d. onq homme j.
181 *L* j. ne de
190 *R omits* se
199 *DLS* ne cuide je pas
202 *DLS1* que des g.
204 *R* Fors a
209 *L3* du blanc ou
219 *DLS* qui y f.
234 *S2* l'e. descerré
236 *S1* De f.
245 *S2* e. contens
247 *L omit* trop
266 *LS2* N. n'apperceust c.
270 *DLS* J'apperceu b.
273 *L1L3 omit* et
274 *DLS* se transmuoit c.
277 *D omits* le
281 *L1L3* t. tout le
285 *L* Moult l.
303 *LS2* p. qu'ay eu
306 *DLS* vy v. vers moy s.
307 *R* m. cil fu f.
313 *R omits* et
315 *D* s. hauçage, *L* s. hontage
319 *DLS* a. et son b. par le f.
343 *R* qu'il m'amoit ou
349 *DLS1* Y cy d.
352 *R* C'est
357 *L1L3* P. un peu d'a.
362 *S2* Que d.
365 *S1* c'est d'amours de
374 *L3* De t.
391 *DL* m. la m.
399 *L* f. les a.
435 *L3* Et p.
439 *L3* ja n'yert a.
462 *L1L2* en tout t.
469 *S2* ce a q.
476 *D* Que celle j.
495 *R* m'en souvent
510 *DS* t. t. en si, *L* t. t. n'en si
513 *D* si a quitté
515 *D* en depart
529 *R* s. deduis m.
531 *LS* c. en est
542 *R* Les c., *L2S2* La c.
543 *L* qu'il voit
557 *L1L2S* De m., *DLS* t. l'aler
567 *DLS* a. ne e.
575 *L2L3S2* est ainsi c.
582 *L2* ne cuid pas qu'autre, *L3* Je ne c. pas qu'autre
583 *DLS* Ce m.
593 *R* m. c'est r; *L1L3* m. est r.
597 *S1* a. lui e.
599 *L* lui sembla, *L1L3* perdroit le don
619 *L* n'a paix, *L1L3* p. në a.

621	L Le l. j. a.	866	D n'e. l'ardent f., L2 omits grant, L1L3 le f. ou t. së art
626	DLS ne delaisse		
637	S1 n'est nul q.	867	RD de sa art
648	RL1L3 perilz	869	DL1L3S a a. l'aprent
650	L f. peris	875	S1 Est si, S2 Et si
652	LS Qui belle H.	883	D v. ou t.
657	L p. n. et h. ch.	885	S2 ce qui l.
658	LS1 Qui ou	905	R omits ne
665	DL1L2 Pour t., L3 Pour celle a., S Pour tel a.	933	LS2 Mais s.
		934	DLS n. tant espris de tel fl.
669	DS1 Qu'ot n.	951	R p. ce s.
670	DLS l'a. ce fu	957	L3 omits sont
681	DLS1 a. mouru en	965	D c. traison q.
685	D p. telle a.	975	D p. aux n. et loyaulz, L1L3 p. et n., S2 n. ot r.
690	L omit las		
694	L q. pour pr.	979	DLS P. y v.
698	D omits sa	981	DS2 p. aussi v.
710	DLS le fait e.	983	R omits n'en
713	R c. ce fu	986	L V. voy y.
714	L2L3 En tel o.	990	L1L2S2 tel martire, S1 tel maniere
719	R n. encore m.		
720	L1L3 d. des l.	998	L c. qu'au l.
725	D Y. a. tant fort fu tr., LS Y. fu si durement tr.	1011	L1L3 omit et, DL2L3S q. telle a.
		1023	L v. octroit c.
733	DLS omit en	1031	L3 Q. celz p.
741	S2 la folle c.	1033–35	DLS Ou bien petit. Il n'est nul qui loier / En tel liain se voulsist. Mieux noier / Trop lui vauldroit quë ainsi s'avoier
746	D Or regardez de		
751	DL3 Q. l'occist		
782	R c. bien an		
783	DLS p. en y a	1052	LS l. en viengne
785	DLS1 Par t.	1058	L Que c.
788	D en maintes g.	1073	DLS si haulx m.
795	D m. mausagement	1075	L v. leurs g.
797	DLS1 t. qu'ilz o.	1079	S1 comme a p.
801	R omits en, S1 Ou de t., L1L3 p. leurs c.	1089	R q. la faite, LS et c'est ce qui
		1097	L omit avoir
806	L3 Pour celle a.	1123	LS2 q. la m.
818	D p. pour es.	1133	L et esveillié
846	RL ob. on ne	1141	DLS b. benoite et
847	L n. se b.	1147	DLS M. et qui vray a.
849	L2L3 de meschief en	1158	L1L3 m. ne s., S se chascun le
860	D Et m.	1159	D N'en d.
863	L2L3S2 ne si g., L2L3 g. ne v.	1199	L1 d. embrace et

1207 L1 c. et ne doit parler, L2 omits pas, L3 c. et doit parler
1209 R ou c'est v.
1210 L a. si ne
1211 L A. que m.
1214 L3 omits pas, L pour l.
1217 L Si s'esveille
1221 DLS las si fort s'en
1227 S1 omits tout
1233 L omit bien
1235 S1 Et r.
1254 S1 Q. n'en p.
1257 D d. dont v.
1277 S2 A. n'en d.
1281 DLS v. je v.
1287 DLS Maulx et felons et
1291 DLS m. en frappant a.
1322 L1L2 et loyauté s'a.
1331 L2S2 Ne sot, DLS s. d'amer si
1350 R omits li, L1L3 de trestous li
1357 L1L3 d. plus que
1361 R ne cuident pas
1377 L3 en n. matiere
1387 DLS1 c. porc g.
1389 D fr. et par
1399 L1L3 M. il est
1402 D et s'i m.
1407 D g. ne m.
1414 S Aussi c.
1433 DLS Plus qu'autre r.
1439 DLS d'a. en fu encore est m.
1458 D Et du
1461 L Qu'elle le, L3 le garde et, S2 Qu'el le g.
1478 D c. histoire d.
1479 L e. de m.
1485 D A. najant a
1493 DS2 a. reschapez en
1513 L1L3 n'est il pas, L2 omits on
1526 D P. roÿne de N. m. l.
1537 L Qu'il p. q. la r.
1541 L1L3 et mena si
1543 LS2 il doit b.
1552 L en viengne
1559 DL1S2 e. ces e.
1567 DL1L3S2 Në a., n'aultre l.
1572 D De Clequin, LS2 De Gleaquin
1583 D si est v.
1587 L v. saige et
1590 R Ces .ij.
1594 D D. l'i t.
1598 L3 Le f.
1602 DL Ce f.
1617 LS Comment onques de b.
1618–19 reversed in L
1634 L3 s. a l.
1658 L2L3 Il est s.
1666 DLS S'il est d'A.
1670 L2L3S2 omit N'.
1687 R lancee
1694 D de Berban
1697 R A. c'est a.
1709 R a fuïr t.
1726 DLS2 t. que j.
1733 LS b. compains se
1741 RL1L2 Qui
1759 DLS et b. entrait
1760 LS Pour t.
1765 L M. d'un p., S2 M. du p.
1773 D Les maulz d'.
1786 R t. seulz q.
1787 DS1 c. nous a.
1794 D a. ja s.
1795 D il y ait
1797 R c. si d'une; LS1 omit d'.
1801 D est droit vray s., LS1 v. droit s.
1813 DLS2 de ce vo
1817 DLS Qu'a un, L l. se l.
1827 D A. est et
1830 D di qui p.
1835 L1L2S2 est ençains
1838 DL3 D. qui s.
1841 L1L2 Et renvoisiez en
1844 L omit l'.
1860 S1 L'a. ne v., S2 L'a. se v.
1864 L3 omits le

1871 *D* Ou qu'en b.
1876 *L3* Et n'ose a.
1883 *DL2L3S* j. consens a
1887 *LS2* N. g. et
1889 *DLS* Car q.
1891 *D* Les biens d'.
1898 *R* mate
1902 *R* j. c'est a.
1905 *R* qu'on
1907 *DL2L3S* En a
1922 *DLS* Que dieu maintiengne en joye et tous delis
1923 *LS* Eslisoient de telz qui sont palis, *D* Choisissoient de t. q. s. p.
1930 *D* et nommerent l.
1935 *L1L2S2* g. bon j.
1950 *L2L3S2* Se ce
1956 *LS2* Se ce
1958 *R* S'est
1977 *D* a. haulcent l.
1979 *LS2* en nobles l.
2001 *L1L3* c. que il
2005 *DLS* Ainsi treshault P.
2018 *L3* Car or
2021 *DL2L3* s. y q.
2022 *D* Si le c.
Explicit *D* d. de .ij., *L1L3* Cy fine le, *S* read Explicit *only*

Notes

Title and rubric. In the table of contents at the beginning of MS *R*, the text is listed as: *Item le livre du debat de deux amans .xiiii.* On the folios containing the text itself, that is, f58v° to 71r°, the running title *Le debat de deux amans* plus the item number appear across the top margin of facing pages. There are numerous small errors: the preposition *de* is repeated on both sides in four cases and is omitted entirely in three.

1. Underneath the miniature adorning the beginning of the text (see Introduction) and the rubric, the initial *P* of the first word, *Prince*, is a four-line-high, elaborately decorated capital executed in pink with white filigree. Its gold border sprouts ivy foliage, which extends up and down (approximately 5–6 millimeters) in the left margin. Inside the letter, a vine decoration in pink, blue, white, and black appears on a gold background.

5. The *Duc d'Orlians*, Christine's chosen patron and judge for this poem, was Louis I, son of the French king Charles V (as mentioned in l. 6) and thus the younger brother of the future Charles VI. Christine also dedicated to him her *Epistre d'Othéa* and the *Dit de la rose*, as well as making mention of him in several lyric poems. Willard argues that Christine took considerable trouble to cultivate the duke as a patron partly in the hope of placing her son in his service, although in the end the young man joined the household of the duke of Burgundy instead. (See Willard, *Christine de Pizan: Her Life and Works*, pp. 166–67.)

18. *Que:* the use of the relative pronoun *que* for *qui* in subject position is quite common. (See Marchello-Nizia, p. 161.) Consequently, *que* is retained here, even though MSS *DL1L3S* all use *qui*. The same usage can be found in this poem at ll. 658 and 1741.

51. In MS *R* the word *debat* is added above the line.

75. I have found no corresponding Scriptural passage concerning the question of the legitimate and indelible quality of attributes given by Nature. Christine may well be indulging in a somewhat ironic or even satirical call to acknowledged authority in order to establish the validity of writing about, and pronouncing opinions on, matters of love. The mention of such an unimpeachable source authorizes both her enterprise in writing up this debate for her patron and his in accepting and considering it.

114. From the context it appears that l. 114 refers to various dance steps performed by the guests at the party. The words *tour* and *sault* can be read simply as "turns" and "jumps," but the term *entreveche* is more specialized. Extrapolating from dance vocabulary still in use (e.g., *entrechat*), one can speculate that such a movement involves quick and intricate footwork in which the feet cross. That possibility is supported by related entries in Huguet's dictionary of sixteenth-century French; he lists the verb *entrevescher*, meaning "to intermix, to entangle," and the derivative feminine noun *entreveschure*, meaning the action of mixing or mingling something. Unfortunately, little is known today of medieval dances.

124. The third-person singular, present subjunctive *veist* can count as either mono- or disyllabic. In this line, it counts as only one syllable, but in l. 115 (*Y veïst on*), it counts as two.

Line 124 begins a long sentence that includes a description of the appearance and behavior of the guests assembled at the party. Its main thrust, however, is contained in 124 and 135: "He who could have seen [the handsome company present and their entertainments] would have prized highly their pleasing demeanor."

154. *Seulete:* Christine is given to the use of diminutives in descriptions of her own persona, and particularly with regard to her emotional state after the death of her husband. The most striking example of such usage in purely stylistic terms is surely the much anthologized eleventh *ballade* of her *Cent Balades*, in which twenty-four of the twenty-five lines in the poem begin with *seulete* (Roy, "Seulete suis," in *Oeuvres poétiques*, vol. 1, p. 12). On this lexical usage more generally and its importance in Christine, see Margolis, "Elegant Closures: The Use of the Diminutive in Christine de Pizan and Jean de Meun."

157. The word *banc* in MS *R* has been corrected.

163. In MS *R* the word *prisiez* has been corrected. MSS *D, L1, L3,* and *S1* read *proisiez* at this spot.

197. In MS *R*, the *er* of the infinitive *regarder* has been added above the line in abbreviated form.

257. In MS *R*, the word *je* is added above the line.

290. This line, beginning with a past participle completing a compound verb tense begun in the preceding line, provides a good example of Christine's penchant for enjambment. (For an extreme example, involving a hyphenated word, see ll. 1568–69.) Referring to the knight, who is recovering from the reverie induced by watching the lady he admires, the passage (ll. 287–90) means, "When he had dreamed long enough, he recovered himself a little, like a man who has somewhat quenched his great thirst."

313. MS *R* omits *et*, although there is a rubbed patch where something has clearly been erased after *doux* and before *sage*. A preparation in the text, in the form of an abbreviation above the word *sage*, suggests that the correction was intended but not realized.

342. In MS *R*, the word *en* is added above the line.

358–61. The squire suggests that he, the knight, and the narrator all prepare to give their opinions as to how much joy love brings. This is the first statement of the debate's theme, which will be repeated again several times. One finds it again almost immediately, in ll. 364–67, and then in ll. 403–6 and 425–29, for example.

388. Below this line in MS *R*, the catchwords *belle plaisant gracieuse* appear in the bottom margin in a cursive script, indicating the end of a quire in the makeup of the manuscript and corresponding to the first line at the top of the following folio (f.61).

391. The noun *murmure* is generally masculine in Old French and feminine in Middle French. The different readings here reflect the shift in gender occurring in some nouns in the late Middle Ages.

397, 399. These lines are reversed in MS *R*. Small cursive letters *a* and *b* appear in the left margin to indicate the correct order.

425. The uppercase *P* at the start of this line in MS *R* is the first of four two-line ornamented letters that mark major transitions in the text. Along with the miniature found at the beginning, the large, ornamented capital on the first word of the text, and the paragraph or capitulum marks scattered throughout, these intermediate capitals constitute the decorative program in this and the other debates. The *P* resembles in its colors the capitulum marks, although it is somewhat larger. The letter itself is executed in gold, blue, and pink, accented with white filagree, and surrounded with a black border. MSS *D*, *L1*, *L2*, and *S* all use very similar capitals. In *L3*, the letter is missing, although the necessary two-line space has been left empty, and a tiny, lowercase *p* is visible as a preparation. The manuscripts are largely consistent in their use of such capitals; one also finds them (or, in the case of *L3*, the preparation for them) in l. 1005 and l. 1913 in all seven manuscripts, and at l. 1749 in *R* and *D*, where the other five place a paragraph mark. All manuscripts other than *R* use an intermediate initial at l. 909; because of their unanimity on this point, and because of the transition that occurs at this point from the knight's speech to the lady's, such an initial has been added in this edition as a correction to *R*.

In the case of l. 425, the decorated capital signals the start of the knight's long disquisition, following the lady's refusal of his suggestion that she speak first.

484. In MS *R*, the *i* in the word *claime* is added above the line.

511. In MS *R*, one letter, apparently an *n*, has been erased at the beginning of *autre*.

515–16. The phrase *qui pou lui en espart / Certes peut estre* means, "Little of which certainly will be apportioned him." In other words, this lover relinquishes his share of Fortune's spoils for that one thing (*cellui seul*, l. 515, that is, his lady's favors), of which he will certainly have but little.

533. In MS *R*, the *a* in *qu'a* is a correction.

534. In MS *R*, the final *s* on *Amours* is added in light ink above the line.

546. In MS *R*, the word *cui* is a correction.

565. *A poir:* this curious locution is used elsewhere in Christine's works. It appears three times in *Trois jugemens* (ll. 162, 850, 1209) and once in *Poissy* (l. 1914). One also finds it in Suzanne Solente's edition of *Le Livre de la Mutacion de fortune* (*Aucuns y a qu'en desespoir / Chieent et s'occient a poir* [ll. 2269–70]; . . . *par desespoir / Ou paour de cheoir a poir / Es cruelles mains de Silla* [ll. 21489–90]).

The expression *a poir* does not appear in any of the dictionaries generally useful for this period. It is glossed, however, by Solente; she lists it as "loc., 'vivement'" (vol. 4, p. 232). In the context of the debate poems, however, a meaning of "soon" or "eventually" seems more appropriate.

567. MS *R* is the only manuscript of the seven which reads *n'a espoir* rather than *ne*. In fact, the word *n'a* appears to be a correction.

634. This line is written in the margin in MS *R*. A cross indicates where it is to be inserted in the text.

651 ff. Paris, one of the sons of King Priam of Troy and his wife, Hecuba, is the

first of a long series of examples raised by the knight to underscore the dangers of love. Paris awarded the golden apple to Venus after she promised him the most beautiful woman in the world. This woman was Helen (l. 652), Queen of Sparta and wife of Menelaus. During Menelaus's absence, Paris abducted Helen, which led to the Trojan War (l. 654). The conflict lasted more than ten years, caused great destruction in the ancient city, and resulted eventually in Greece's victory over Troy.

Either Christine or one of her sources for this story garbles the connection to Telamon (l. 661). Paris was wounded by an arrow shot by Philoctetes, with whom Telamon was closely associated in the Trojan campaigns; Paris died when his wife, Oenone, refused to heal him because he had abandoned her for Helen. Paris and Helen are mentioned again in ll. 825–33 in this poem and at l. 86 of *Trois jugemens*.

663. *Ovide* (Ovid) is the common name for Publius Ovidius Naso, a Roman poet and storyteller (43 B.C.–A.D. 17 or 18). Christine, like many other medieval authors, draws heavily for her mythological sources on two of his works, the *Metamorphoses* and the *Heroïdes*. Ovidian references in the *Debat de deux amans* include the stories of Piramus and Thisbe, Leander and Hero, Achilles and Polyxena, Aesacus and Hesperia, Iphis and Anaxerete, Jason and Medea, and Theseus and Ariadne.

671 ff. *Piramus* was a youth who fell in love with his neighbor, Thisbe (l. 673). Their parents opposed their union, so the two talked secretly through the cracks in the house wall. One night they agreed to meet at a fountain beside a white mulberry tree in the nearby woods. When Piramus arrived, he saw a lion and Thisbe's bloody veil on the ground. He mistakenly assumed that she had been killed, and in despair he took his own life. When Thisbe, in turn, arrived and found his body lying on the ground, she, too, committed suicide. Their blood turned the white mulberries a deep red.

679. The verb *quorsi*, a third-person singular preterite, is most likely a form of *accourcir* or *raccourcir* with aphaeresis of the initial syllable. The elliptical sentence in ll. 679–80 might therefore be translated as follows: "And thus grievous death shortened [the lives of] the two youngsters as a result of [their] excessive love [for each other]."

682 ff. *Lehander* (Leander) was the lover of Hero (l. 683), who lived in Sestus and was a priestess of Venus. Every night Leander swam across the Hellespont to be with Hero. Some versions say that, as he swam, he was guided by the illumination from the lighthouse in Sestus, while others suggest that the brightness was from a torch placed by Hero at the top of a tower. On a very stormy night the light was blown out by the wind, and Leander drowned. Christine does not mention that when Hero found his body washed up on the shore, she threw herself into the sea and also perished.

693 ff. *Achilles* fell in love with *Polixene* (Polyxena), one of the daughters of King Priam of Troy and his wife, Hecuba. To win his beloved in marriage, Achilles agreed to try to persuade the Greeks to make peace with Troy. While he was negotiating the marriage in the temple of Apollo, however, he was fatally wounded in

the heel when Polyxena's brother, Paris, shot him with an arrow guided by Apollo. Later, after the fall of Troy, Achilles' ghost demanded that Polyxena be sacrificed by the Greeks upon his tomb.

704 ff. *Aesacus* was the son of King Priam (l. 705) and Alexiroe, a nymph from Mount Ida. He lived alone in the remote countryside, where he fell in love with the beautiful Hesperia. One day as he spied on her, she felt his gaze, became frightened, and ran away. As he pursued her, she was bitten by a venomous snake. Aesacus blamed himself for her death and in his grief flung himself off a cliff that overlooked the sea. The sea goddess Tethys took pity on him and saved him from his fall by turning him into a bird. Aesacus, angry at being forced to continue living, dove repeatedly into the deep water, seeking death. He did not die; instead he became a lean, long-necked, sea-diving bird. In the knight's version, Aesacus threw himself into the sea in despair at having been rejected by Hesperia, bringing the story more closely into line with the surrounding tales concerning the devastating effect of rejection on lovers who fall for heartless women.

725 ff. *Ypys* (Iphis), a young Cypriot man from a humble family, loved Anaxerete, a noble lady from Cyprus. So desperate was he when she rejected his love that he hanged himself at her door. While Anaxerete was watching his funeral procession, the gods transformed her into stone as punishment for her hardheartedness.

746 ff. The Tristan legend recounts the obsessed and doomed love of Tristan for Yseut la Blonde (l. 753), the wife of his uncle, King Marc of Cornwall (l. 750). After many years of trying to keep their love secret, the lovers were discovered by Marc, who banished Tristan from his kingdom. According to the prose version of the story, Tristan died as the result of a cowardly assault by Marc himself; according to the verse romance, his death was due to a lie told by his jealous Breton wife. In the end, Yseut also died, grief-stricken, in Tristan's arms. The Tristan legend became well known in the twelfth and thirteenth centuries through a number of different versions, especially those of Béroul and Thomas. In the European Middle Ages it came to represent the theme of fatal passion and death as the ultimate union.

The squire also mentions the Tristan legend (ll. 1439–50), but in his case he uses it to underscore the ennobling aspects of love. (See note to l. 1441.)

757 ff. *Quahedins* (Kaherdin), the son of the king Hoël and the brother of Yseut, is a prominent knight in the prose romance of Tristan and in the version by Thomas.

762 ff. The Châtelain de Coucy was Guy de Thourotte, a late twelfth-century French trouvère and the titular governor of the château de Coucy (1170–1203), who died during the Fourth Crusade. At the end of the thirteenth century, a little-known author named Jakemes wrote a romance with the châtelain as its hero. He wins the heart of his lady love, the Dame de Fayel (l. 765), through his chivalric behavior and his love songs (which form part of the narrative of the romance), but he dies overseas. She dies as well, after being tricked by her jealous husband into eating the heart of her lover.

770 ff. The Châtelaine de Vergy is the main character in a tragic thirteenth-

century love story of the same name by an unknown author. In this poem, the châtelaine, a lady at the court of Burgundy, gives her love to a young knight on the condition that he reveal their liaison to no one. However, the duchess of Burgundy also declares her passion for him, and the knight, caught on the horns of a dilemma, is ultimately obliged to disclose his love for the châtelaine in order to remain near her. The lady eventually learns of his betrayal and dies. Upon finding her and discovering the reason for her death, the knight kills himself, and the duke then kills his wife in anger.

783. The word *ou* appears in MS *R* before *il y a*, but it is barred.

826 ff. For an explanation of the story of Paris and Helen, see note to l. 651. Here the knight again raises the example of Paris and Helen, including the roles Venus and Cupid play in their story, to demonstrate the strange and irrational actions even the wisest people undertake when love strikes them, and to show the unhappy end that is likely to result. Lines 834–35 summarize the knight's opinion in a nutshell: *Quieulx que soient d'amours les commençailles / Tous jours y a piteuses deffinailles* ("No matter how it begins, love always ends badly").

850. This line uses the vocabulary of falconry in a metaphor expressing how Love maintains mastery over his victims. The sense of this verse is that Love holds the lover on a leash shorter than the tether (*la longe*) restraining the sparrow hawk (*l'esparvier*).

867. Both MSS *R* and *D* read *sa art* at the end of this line (and in both manuscripts, these words are corrections). While it was possible but very unusual to retain the feminine possessive adjective *sa* before a noun beginning with a vowel, the more common tendency by far was either to elide the feminine possessive (as in the form *s'art*, to which this line has been corrected, following the reading found in the other manuscripts) or to use the masculine possessive to avoid an awkward combination of vowels in hiatus. On this point, see Marchello-Nizia, pp. 138–39; Robert Martin and Marc Wilmet, p. 125; and Peter Rickard, "The Rivalry of *m(a), t(a), s(a),* and *mon, ton, son,*" pp. 21–47 and 115–47.

879. MS *R* reads *et de servage*, which would make the line hypermetric by one syllable, but the word *de* has expunctuation marks underneath.

880. The adjective *bugle* comes from a metaphorical extension of the same word as a masculine noun, meaning "buffalo" or "steer." (Frédéric E. Godefroy cites several passages, although not this one, that rhyme *bugle* with *av[e]ugle*.) The intent seems to be to attribute a simple, stupid, bovine demeanor to this misguided lover who can no longer tell good from bad.

882. The word *cruble* is troublesome. As in the note to l. 880, the context is still that of the irrational lover blinded by the force of emotion. Godefroy lists a feminine noun, *cruble*, meaning a sort of measure for grain, but the gender does not match that of our word nor is the definition appropriate to the context. In the Supplement to his dictionary, however, he lists *cruble* as a variation on *crible*, a sieve, with our passage from *Deux amans* as his only example. Given that other vowels in this quatrain have been adapted at line's end to fit the rhyme, this solution seems

likely. The lover would thus be putting on (*se couvrir de*) a sieve as a hat against the sun he believes he sees even in cloudy weather. Such ridiculous attire would be appropriate for someone so besotted that he cannot see reason.

905. The *R* reading has been corrected here on the basis of the other six manuscripts to read *je ne croy*, while retaining *que a nul* rather than emending to *qu'a nul* because the unstressed *e* of *que* elides before *a*. In fact, however, the reading in *R* is syntactically and metrically possible. In the absence of *ne*, the syllable count can be regularized if *que* does not elide, and while *nul* most often appears with the negative particle *ne*, there are exceptions to this rule. (See Marchello-Nizia, p. 143.) It should be noted that in *R* there is a small hole in the parchment between *que* and *a*.

909. MS *R* is the only one of the seven manuscripts not to use an intermediate capital at the head of this line. (See note to l. 425, above.) Instead, it is the sole manuscript to use a capitulum mark at the preceding line (l. 908), for which there is little justification, falling as it does at the last line of the knight's speech and just before the transition to the lady's reply. It has been left in in this edition to represent accurately the decorative program in *R*.

961 ff. The *Roman de la Rose* is a thirteenth-century romance of which the first part was written by Guillaume de Lorris (in 1237) and the second by Jean de Meun (between 1275 and 1280). It was perhaps the most important vernacular allegory of the European Middle Ages. Christine's love poetry is steeped in its influence, and she engaged with it directly by launching a correspondence with some of the most learned figures of her day in protest against what she saw as the misogyny and obscenity of Jean de Meun's portion of the book. (See Hicks, *Le débat sur le Roman de la Rose*.)

In this passage of the *Debat de deux amans*, the lady is referring to the allegorical figure Reason, who attempts to dissuade the hero Lover from pursuing his quest of the rosebud with which he has fallen in love. Reason stresses the contradictions and the many dangers of passionate love, but her argument falls on deaf ears. In many ways the lady speaking here can be seen as this poem's equivalent of Lady Reason, debunking the text's predominant attitudes toward love.

969. In MS *R*, *et* is added above the line.

979. The word *s'i* in MS *R* is a correction. All other manuscripts read *y* at this spot.

981. In MS *R*, both the words *ainsi* and *ou* are corrections.

982. The oath *par saint Nicaise* refers to Nicaise, a fifth-century bishop of Rheims who was beheaded by barbarians (probably the Huns, ca. 451) at the door of his cathedral while trying to save the lives of his faithful. The barbarians also murdered his sister, Saint Eutropia, a deacon and a lector.

1002. The narrator's description of the squire speaks to the young man's cheer and youthful optimism; the phrase *ou n'ot goute d'amer* means, "In whom there is not a drop of bitterness."

1025. In MS *R*, the word *le* is added above the line.

1033–35. These three lines in MS *R*, which read very differently than in the other manuscripts, are all a correction squeezed into the space allotted for only two lines.

1073. In MS *R*, the word *grans* is a correction. All other manuscripts read *haulx* instead.

1075. In MS *R*, the word *les* is clearly a correction; a small line follows it as filler before *grans*. At this spot in the line, the *L* manuscripts read *leurs,* as does *D*. In *D*, however, *leurs* is deleted by expunctuation marks underneath the word. The *RD* reading avoids the repetition of *leurs,* with which the line begins.

1249. The relative pronoun *que* at the beginning of the line in *R* represents the subject of the verb *dites* in this line, not an unusual usage at the time. The antecedent of the pronoun is *vous* in l. 1245; the lady is saying to the knight, "What marvels I can hear you recounting (l. 1245) . . . , you who tell us that a lover who loves well is jealous" (ll. 1249–50).

1301. In both MSS *R* and *D*, a letter is scratched off the end of *Doncque*. If the word were spelled with an *s*, a common orthographic variant, the final *e* could not elide and would make the line hypermetric.

1347. In this passage describing the uncertain young lover's self-doubt, the phrase *quant il est veant* / *Jolis et gays* / *Jeunes hommes* (ll. 1347–49 means "when he sees [more literally: is seeing] handsome and lively young men." The sight of his worthy potential rivals makes him question his own appeal. He thinks he is the ugliest (*li plus lais*, l. 1350) of them all.

1358. In MS *R*, the second *de* is added above the line.

1361. MS *R* reads *cuident* rather than *cuide*, the *-nt* having been added as a correction to the singular form of the verb. (A preparation for the correction, in the form of cursive *-nt*, is still visible above the line.) While the *R* reading is possible grammatically, using *autre* as the plural pronoun subject of the verb *cuident*, the line makes better sense as found in the other six manuscripts. The subject of singular *cuide* is the noun *cuer* (l. 1358): the heart full of fear, suspicion and jealousy believes itself inferior to others (*autre ne cuide pas valoir*).

1380. Note that this pasage (ll. 1380–84) and the following (l. 1385 ff.), both of which are rhetorical questions designed to illustrate the squire's defense of love, are marked with capitulum marks. These philosophical nuggets distill his philosophy that while love, like any good thing, can be abused by those who partake of it, the damage inflicted is due to poor handling rather than to any flaw inherent in it.

1382. In MS *R*, *se* is added above the line, and an extra *la* appears before *demande* but has expunctuation marks beneath it and is also barred.

1425. A central character of Arthurian legend and romance, *Lancelot du Lac* is, of course, the best of King Arthur's knights and lover of Queen Guinevere, Arthur's wife. The squire here stresses how much Lancelot gained in strength, prowess, and reputation from his abiding love for Guinevere.

1433. The reading found in MS *R* at the beginning of this line is a correction. It is clear from the decorative filler added after *toute* that this formulation replaces a longer phrase, presumably the words *Plus qu'autre,* which are found in all other six manuscripts.

1441 ff. The squire revisits the case of Tristan, already mentioned by the knight (see note to l. 746 above), as a model of chivalry rather than as an example of tragic love. He makes the argument that Tristan undertook noble deeds because of his love for Yseut and that, although he died in grief, he is remembered for his heroism.

1455 ff. *Jason* was the king of Iolcus and leader of the Argonauts who sailed to Colchis (*Colcos,* l. 1463), an Asian country at the eastern end of the Black Sea, in search of the Golden Fleece. King Aetes of Colchis agreed to give Jason the fleece only if he could overcome a series of formidable obstacles. The challenge seemed impossible and Jason's death certain, until King Aetes's daughter, Medea (*Medee,* l. 1459), fell in love with Jason. Since she was a powerful magician, she gave him charms to protect him from danger. In turn, he vowed eternal fidelity. Some years later, however, Jason fell in love with Glauce, the daughter of Creon, king of Corinth. Medea, who had betrayed her father, killed her own brother, and left her homeland out of love for Jason, turned on him in revenge, sending Glauce a bridal gown that ignited the moment she put it on. Medea then killed her own children. The squire does not ignore the tragic aspects of the tale completely, noting in ll. 1465–66 that no matter who died as a result of this love, Jason himself was saved by it.

Medea appears elsewhere in Christine's *oeuvre.* She is invoked as an example of steadfastness in love in *Trois jugemens* (l. 855) and in the *Epistre au Dieu d'Amours* (ll. 437–44), and for her fidelity and wisdom in both the "Lai de dame" (ll. 67–84) appended to the *Cent balades d'amant et de dame,* and in the *Cité des dames* (Part I, sections 32 and 46; Part II, sections 55 and 56).

1469 ff. *Theseüs* (Theseus) was a great Athenian hero, the son of the Athenian king Aegeus. Aegeus had become the enemy of Minos (l. 1474), the king of Crete, when Minos's only son, Androgeus, was killed by a bull while on an expedition for Aegeus. In revenge, Minos had invaded and captured Athens and declared that he would destroy the city if Aegeus did not send him a yearly tribute of seven maidens and seven youths, which he would in turn give to the Minotaur to devour. One year, Theseus was sent into the labyrinth in Crete with the other youths. Minos's daughter Ariadne (*Adriane,* l. 1471) fell in love with Theseus at first sight and gave him some thread with which he made his way out of the labyrinth. He found the Minotaur asleep, killed him, and then escaped with Ariadne by sea back to Athens. The squire does not mention that on the way to Athens the ship stopped at the island of Naxos, where Theseus deserted Ariadne. Theseus is mentioned again at l. 1496.

1481 ff. *Eneas* (Aeneas), son of Anchises and Venus and ancestral hero of the Romans, showed great courage in the defense of Troy (l. 1482) during the Trojan War. After the fall of the city, he began a quest in search of a new land. Virgil's *Aeneid* describes his exploits and difficulties, beginning with his departure from Troy and ending with his arrival in Italy. At one point during these travels, he was received and helped by Dido (l. 1489), queen of Carthage. Dido fell in love with Aeneas and he with her, causing him to delay his quest. When eventually he sailed away, Dido committed suicide, overcome with grief.

1496 ff. This second mention of Theseus, first cited in l. 1469 (see note above), confuses the classical Athenian hero with the protagonist of a medieval romance concerning Theseus of Cologne. While the plots of the two tales intersect, the stories are quite independent of each other. Here, the references to Hercules and Helen again recall the Athenian, who was eager to identify himself with the Greek hero Hercules, known for his feats of valor. At one time, Theseus had also carried off Helen, later the cause of the Trojan War when she was abducted by Paris after becoming Menelaus's wife.

In this passage, Helen's kidnapping is confused and fused with the plot of a medieval romance about Theseus, son of Floridas, king of Cologne, who carried off Flore, daughter of the Roman emperor Esmeré. The original version of this Theseus story has been lost, but various reworkings survive. (See the article "Theseus de Cologne," in *Dictionnaire des lettres françaises: Le Moyen Age*, pp. 1421–22, and R. Bossuat, "Theseus de Cologne.") The reference to the golden eagle (*aygle d'or*, l. 1507) points to an episode in the medieval romance in which Theseus finds a way to meet Flore, for whom he has fallen sight unseen, by hiding inside a golden eagle taken to Flore as a gift. After she falls in love with him, he marries her secretly and takes her away by sea. Flore's father, angered (*courroucié*, l. 1510) by his daughter's defection, lays siege to Cologne and takes Theseus's father, mother, and sister to Rome as captives.

One source for the story of Theseus of Cologne in Christine's day is a section of the long romance *Le Livre du Chevalier errant* by Thomas III, Marquis of Saluzzo, longtime prisoner of the duke of Savoy. (See the critical edition of this work by Marvin James Ward.) Beginning with Chapter LXV of the *Chevalier* (Ward, p. 264 ff.), Thomas recounts the story of "Une belle damoiselle de l'empereur de Rome et de Theseus, filz au conte de Flandres." He describes in considerable detail the ruse involving the golden eagle. A very good case can be made to prove Christine knew of Theseus and the golden eagle from Thomas of Saluzzo. That they communicated is almost certain; as well as being contemporaries, they wrote on similar subject matter and their manuscripts include work by the same miniaturists. Indeed, a Paris manuscript of the *Chevalier* (ca. 1403) was possibly copied by Christine's atelier. I am grateful here, again, to Nadia Margolis, who suggested the link between Christine and Thomas and provided me with references.

With regard to the tapestry mentioned in l. 1506 ff., which depicts the eagle scene, Roy provides the following note: "La tapisserie qu'elle [Christine] nous montre devait effectivement figurer dans l'Hôtel du duc Louis qui l'avait payée, en 1389, au célèbre Nicolas Bataille la somme de 1,200 fr." He refers to Jules Guiffrey, *Histoire de la Tapisserie*, p. 34; see Roy, vol. 2, p. 307, note to ll. 1496–1512.

1521 ff. *Florimont d'Albanie* is the hero of the romance by Aimon de Varenne, *Florimont* (composed in 1188). He was the son of the duke Mataquas and of Edorie, and married the beautiful Romadanaple (*Rome de Naples*, l. 1526), daughter of King Phillip of Greece.

1526. Based on the appearance of the word in MS *R*, it is difficult to decide whether it agrees with *D*, which reads *roÿne de Naples*, or *LS*, which uses *Rome*. The adjective *grans* appears to be barred in *R*, which might indicate that the three-syllable *roïne* is intended, as in the *D* reading, rather than the disyllabic *Rome*. The latter is preferable, however, given the particulars of Florimont d'Albanie's story (see preceding note).

1532 ff. The name *le Gallois Durmas* refers to *Durmart le Gallois*, a mid-thirteenth century Arthurian romance in verse, of which Durmart is the hero. The queen of Ireland (*roÿne d'Irlande*, l. 1537) is the lady for whom he accomplishes many brave feats.

1544. *Cleomadés* (Cléomadès) is the eponymous hero of a long romance (1285) by Adenet le Roi. Cléomadès is the son of the king of Spain. His adventures take him on a magical wooden flying horse from Spain to Tuscany, where he courts the beautiful Clarmondine and takes her back to Spain. However, the evil magician who made the flying horse abducts Clarmondine in revenge against Cléomadès, who then must search far and wide for her before they can return to Spain, where they marry. Cléomadès is also mentioned in the *Dit de Poissy*; see note to l. 825 in that work.

1546. *Pallamedés* (Palamedès) first appears in the *Tristan en prose*, in which he loves Iseut but remains loyal to Tristan. The important prose romance named the *Roman de Palamède* belongs to the cycle of the Round Table and was written before 1240. It includes two parts: *Meliadus de Lennoys* and *Guiron le Courtois*. Despite his prominence in the title of the romance, Palamedès plays a minor role in the first part and an even less significant role in the second. The first part of the romance concerns the adventures of Meliadus, the father of Tristan; the second centers on the problems that Guiron le Courtois encounters while protecting his friend's wife. *Palamedès* was extremely popular in Italy, where Rusticiano da Pisa published a compilation of the work together with portions of the cyclic prose *Tristan* (1272–74). Palamedès, along with Cléomadès, is also mentioned in the *Dit de Poissy*; see note to l. 826 in that work.

1553 ff. *Artus de Bretaigne* (Bretagne) is the hero of a romance of the same name (but also known as *Le Petit Artus de Bretagne*, or *Artus le Petit*). Artus was the son of Jean, duke of Bretagne, and of the daughter of the count of Lancestre. He married Florence (*Flourance*, l. 1554) who was the daughter of the king Emandus and the queen of the Blanche Tour.

1568–69. While Christine tends to use rather fluid syntactic constructions not overly constrained by the metrical pattern of her verse, this instance of enjambment, in which the adverb *veritablement* is divided over two lines, is an extreme example.

1571 ff. *Bertran du Gueaquin, connestable de France* (ll. 1569–70), whose name in its modern version is Bertrand du Guesclin (1320–80), was a military hero who began his brilliant career in the siege of Rennes (1356–57). He was advisor to King Jean II and then high constable and commander in chief of France (1370–80) under Charles V. Du Guesclin's skill in using guerilla warfare tactics to curtail the English incursions into France and to deal with the brigands that plagued the country in the mid-fourteenth century enabled him to advance rapidly in the king's services. He is also reputed to have been a model of chivalric behavior and to have set a standard for knightly conduct.

1585 ff. *Le bon Bouisicault [l]e mareschal*: reference to Jean le Meingre, dit Boucicaut (d. 1367), maréchal of France. His two sons (mentioned in l. 1590), already well known in the early fifteenth century, were Geoffroy (d. 1429), governor of Dauphiné in 1399, and Jean II le Meingre, dit Boucicaut (ca. 1364–1421). The latter was a famous soldier who distinguished himself in numerous battles, among many others the Crusade of Nicopolis (1396) and Agincourt (1415). He died in English custody. Apart from his valor, Jean II was also known for vigorously upholding the ideals of chivalry. On April 11, 1399, upon his return from the East, he founded a society whose purpose was the protection of female honor, especially that of the wives and daughters of absent knights. This chivalric order, called "L'Ecu vert à la dame blanche," was comprised of thirteen knights who swore to defend the honor of ladies. He was also a poet and patron of the arts, and commissioned the famous illuminated book of hours that is named after him.

1591. While usually an infinitive in Old and Middle French (but not yet a noun), the word *a(d)venir* can also appear in phrases of this kind with the adjectival function of the prepositional phrase *à venir*, meaning "future," "[the time] to come."

1594 ff. *Le Connestable de Sanserre* refers to Louis de Sancerre (ca. 1342–1402), named maréchal of France in 1369 and renowned, like the preceding examples, for an illustrious military career.

1615. *Othe de Grançon* (Othon [Oton] de Granson), born between 1340 and 1350, was known in his day as both a superlative soldier and as a poet; of the two, it is his proficiency as a knight that motivates the inclusion of his name in this passage. Implicated as an accessory in the death by poisoning of Amé [Amédée] VII, count of Savoie, Granson was challenged to a duel on these charges in August 1397; he was killed in the contest. His literary production includes a considerable amount of lyric poetry as well as narrative verse, among which are the *Complainte de saint Valentin* and the *Complainte de l'an nouvel*, both known as influences for *The Book of the Duchess* by Chaucer, who regarded him highly. For more information, see Arthur Piaget, "Oton de Granson et ses poésies"; Haldeen Braddy, *Chaucer and the French Poet Graunson*, who discusses the *Deux amans* allusion to Oton; C. A. Cunningham, "A Critical Edition of the Poetry of Oton de Grandson"; James I. Wimsatt, *Chaucer and His French Contemporaries*.

1617. MS *R* reads *comment onc de*, but *onc* is barred and appears itself to be a correction.

1619. *Vermeilles Hutin* is Hutin de Vermeilles (d. 1390), who was the king's chamberlain. During his successful career, he was charged with a number of important missions for the king. He married Marguerite de Bourbon, daughter of Louis I de Bourbon, count of La Marche. Charles VI arranged for Hutin de Vermeilles's funeral rites to be celebrated in Paris in 1390 at the church of Blancs Manteaux.

1627. *Le bon Chasteau Morant* refers to Jean de Châteaumorand (late fourteenth to early fifteenth century), one of the most distinguished knights of his time. He fought with the duke Louis de Bourbon and later composed, with the help of a scribe, a chronicle of Louis's undertakings. He was also a member of the chivalric order "l'Ecu vert à la dame blanche." (See note to l. 1585.)

1641. *L'Ermite [d]e la Faye*: Like Châteaumorand, Guillaume de Montrevel, dit L'Hermite de la Faye (late fourteenth to early fifteenth century), accompanied the duke Louis II of Bourbon in his military adventures. He fought for the king of

Prussia against the Swedish, in the siege of Verteuil, at Rosebecque, against England in 1386, and in 1399 with Jean II (Boucicaut) in the service of the Greek emperor.

1653. *Monseigneur Charles d'Alebret* (Charles d'Albret), count of Dreux, son of Arnaud-Amanieu and Marguerite de Bourbon (sister of Jeanne de Bourbon, wife of Charles V), was named connétable of France in 1402. He was a member of the chivalric order founded by Boucicaut, and died in the battle of Agincourt on October 25, 1415. Christine refers to Charles d'Albret in her *Cent Balades* (II, III, XVI). She also dedicated a copy of *Deux amans* to him, as we learn in number XXI of the *Autres balades* (see Roy, vol. 1). This is manuscript *S1*, in which the same poem appears before the text of the debate (see Manuscripts, above).

1665. Jean de Werchin, seneschal of Hainaut, was both poet and knight. Treating material very similar to the *Deux amans,* he wrote an exchange of ballades with his squire, Gilbert de Lannoy, in which a mature knight and a young squire debate appropriate conduct in love. Jean also authored a longer work, *Le Songe de la barge* (1404), again similar in inspiration to Christine's debates. As a combatant, he cultivated a reputation as bold and audacious, constantly seeking out new adventures. Christine's *Trois jugemens* is dedicated to him, as is number XXXIII of the *Autres balades* (see Roy, vol. 1).

1674. Below this line in MS *R,* the catch words *n'est pas de ceulx* appear in the bottom margin in a cursive script, indicating the end of a quire in the makeup of the manuscript and corresponding to the first line at the top of the following folio (f. 68).

1677. *De Gaucourt* is Raoul de Gaucourt (d. 1417), king's chamberlain, who accompanied Charles VI on an expedition to Germany in 1388 and was later responsible for a number of other foreign missions. He died in Rouen in 1417.

1683. *Charles de Savoisi* (Savoisy) (d. ca. 1420) was prominent at the court of Charles VI, to whom he was counselor and chamberlain from 1418 to 1420.

1689. *Castelbeart* refers to Bernard de Castelbajac (late fourteenth to early fifteenth century), seneschal of Bigorre and son of Arnaud-Raymond de Castelbajac and Jeanne de Barbasan. He is mentioned also in number XII of Christine's *Autres balades* (see Roy, vol. 1).

1694. *Clignet de Breban* was Pierre de Brebant, called Clignet (d. ca. 1430). He was king's chamberlain and was named admiral of France in 1405. He was one of the seven French champions praised by Christine in *Autres balades* XXIX to XXXI (see Roy, vol. 1), which celebrates the combat of a group of seven French knights against seven from England.

1709. MS *R* reads *fuïr* rather than *suivir,* a reading rejected here because it most likely represents an inadvertent repetition of the verb in the preceding line.

1741. Two different readings appear at the head of this line, the relative subject pronoun *Qui* in *RL1L2,* and the conjunction *Que* in *DL3S.* Here the latter seems the better choice, although *qui* is possible, either as a repetition of the subject of the preceding line, or as a short form of *Qu'il.*

1751. In MS *R,* the beginning of this line is a correction, and the word *sembla* is added above the line.

152 / *Le Livre du Debat de deux amans*

1797. In MS *R*, *d'une* appears to be a correction. Note that the *L* manuscripts use the variant *une* in this spot.

1815. Following this line in MS *R*, the text repeats twelve lines, reproducing ll. 1804–15 with a few minor changes. This error may result from the similarity of ll. 1804 and 1816 (*Celle grief peine* and *Sa peine grieve*), particularly since the repetition begins with *Sa griefve peine*, an amalgam of the two. The passage was obviously not noticed as an error: the capitulum mark at l. 1809 is repeated, and there are also corrections in the passage, indicating that it was proofread as part of the text. Without these twelve lines, the poem would have ended neatly at the bottom of folio 71r°a, rather than stranding l. 2025 and the explicit at the top of the next column.

1854. In MS *R*, the word *et* is added above the line.

1958. In MS *R*, the word *tres* is added above the line.

2021. In MS *R*, the word *le* is a correction.

2023. The last five lines of the text point the reader to the anagram that appears in the form of the word *cristïenté*: rearranging its letters, one easily discovers therein the name C(h)ristine. Christine uses similar anagrams to close her other two debates. (See Notes to *Trois jugemens*, l. 1531, and to *Poissy*, l. 2075.) For critical analysis of Christine's anagrams, see references in note 70 to the introduction, above.

Le Livre des Trois jugemens

Introduction

> [I]l n'est riens qui n'ait saisons et termes
> (l. 1385)

To everything there is a season, the narrator of *Le Livre des Trois jugemens* reminds us: love, like all else, must come to an end. The repeated statement of this theme (well expressed, for example, in ll. 1293–1312) makes *Trois jugemens* the most unsentimental of Christine's three debate poems. With its condemnation of *trop amer* and *fole amour*, the text criticizes as foolish those who insist on pursuing idle intrigues and calls untrustworthy those unable or unwilling to remain faithful to the initial object of their affection.

The *trois jugemens* presented in this poem have a sharp-edged, lively, personal quality that captures the recriminating pitch of highly particularized lovers' spats. The tone is wry and cynical. The pace is brisk, even somewhat abrupt at the end, given that the third case is notably shorter than the other two. While each of the three scenarios stands as an autonomous unit, they are also all connected both thematically as an illustration of the mutability of love and structurally as a series of disagreements ostensibly in need of resolution.

Beyond this division into three distinct parts, the poem capitalizes further on the expansive capacity of the *dit* to accommodate discontinuities by introducing in the second case a correspondence between the lovers (ll. 898–1012 and 1022–92). While this written communication does not interrupt the regular flow of the narrative, which continues in its four-line rhyming blocks, both passages quite ingeniously constitute discrete letters as well as lyric *complaintes* and could be lifted out of the text as such. Quite seamlessly, therefore, Christine incorporates a variety of modes at once: for the space of those lines, the discourse shifts smoothly from narrative to lyric and from the third to the first person, while embedding written documents penned by the protagonists into the fabric of the narrator's own written account.

Who emerges unscathed from these querulous disputes? Not husbands and not lovers; only the ladies. They are slow to give in to the temptations of love and then constant once they succumb. They are most concerned with finding a faithful lover rather than a fickle one. And once deceived, they learn from experience, turning their disillusionment into a determination not to be duped again. While Christine the narrator ostensibly remains neutral in these cases, preferring not to take sides, her commentary denounces the unreliability of male lovers in general while tacitly defending women as the wiser, steadier, and more honorable of the sexes. They also raise the level of the discussion: in the exchange of *complaintes* between lovers in the second case, the lady's is the more intellectual of the two, using some of the very few allusions to mythology in this debate to make her point, while her lover's lament and advice are more prosaic. The female protagonists of the second and third cases also imply a certain solidarity among women on these topics; one states that she takes all ladies as well as loyal lovers to judge her plight (ll. 1233–34), while her sister requests that the ladies be asked to listen diligently and give their opinion before a judgment is rendered (ll. 1491–96).

Closing the poem, Christine leaves it to her chosen judge, Jean de Werchin, to add *le demourant* (l. 1521), the rest of or the ending to it. In fact, there is little to resolve. Love in its ideal mythic dimensions has been displaced by practical realities. The pernicious effect of scandal and gossip has been made manifest, the intentions of most suitors exposed as suspect, and the reaction of the female characters in situations of duress proven to be eminently reasonable, humane, and praiseworthy. Such an object lesson leaves little room for true debate.

*Le Livre des Trois jugemens**

        Cy commence le livre des .iij. jugemens
        qui s'adrece au seneschal de Haynault

Bon seneschal de Haynau, preux et sage,   [71v°a]
Vaillant en fais et de gentil lignage,
Loyal, courtois de fait et de courage,
Duit et appris   4
De tous les biens qui en bons sont compris,
Par noblece de cuer duis et appris
Es las d'amours pour accroistre le pris
De vo noblece,   8
Sage a juger du mal d'amours qui blesse,
Quieulx sont les tours, soit en force ou foiblece,
Pour ce vous ay, chier Sire, plain d'umblece,
Esleu a juge.   12
Car vo bon cuer bien sçay que le droit juge
Ou il affiert; pour ce vien a reffuge
A vous, ainsi comme ou temps du deluge
Qui tout noya,   16
Le coulomb blanc a l'arche s'avoya,
La attendi tant que souleil roya;
Auques ainsi mon cuer celle voye a
Prise sans faille,   20
Pour le debat de certaine fermaille
Qu'aucuns amans beauls de corps et de taille
Ont ensemble. Si veulent que j'en taille
Le court ou lonc,   [71v°b]   24
Mais je ne vy tel cas advenir onq
Et trop pou say pour en bien juger, donc*
Juge en soiés et je diray au lonc*
Tout leur descort   28
De mot a mot, sicom j'en ay recort,
Et a voz dis en tous cas je m'acort;
Si feront ilz, car vostre bon recort
Doit bien souffire.   32
¶ Le premier cas, ainsi comme j'oy dire,*
Fu tel qu'il a en France ou en l'empire
Une dame si belle qu'a redire
Ne scet nul ame: 36
Sage, vaillant, prisee et haulte dame,

Envoysee, loyal de corps et d'ame,
Ou n'a meffait, reprouche ne diffame.
Amer souloit   40
Un chevalier qui pour elle affolloit,
Avant qu'elle l'amast tant se douloit,
Ce disoit il, et mieulx mourir vouloit
Qu'endurer plus   44
L'amoureux mal qui le rendoit conclus,
Tant le tenoit morne, mat et reclus,*
Ne fors la mort n'attendoit au seurplus,
Se brief merci   48
Elle n'avoit de lui qui d'amer si
En grief lengour estoit taint et noircy,
Dont pour secours lui requeroit mercy
D'umble vouloir.   52
¶ Ainsi lonc temps l'ouÿ plaindre et douloir,
Mais celle tout mettoit en non chaloir;
Quanqu'il disoit, pou lui pouoit valoir
Ains qu'elle amast   56
Lui ne ses fais; en riens ne se tournast
Devers pitié, ne secours lui donnast,
Ne que pour lui nul bon point ordonnast,
¶ Tant qu'en la fin,   60
Loyal Amour, qui seult a la parfin
Aux vrays amans, qui aiment de cuer fin,
Faire secours et ayde, a celle fin
Qu'il fust amez,   [72r°a]   64
Fist que Pitié, par qui sont informez
Les gentilz cuers et pris et enfermez
Es las d'amours, fist tant qu'ami clamez
Fu de la belle,   68
Qu'Amours navra de l'ardent estincelle
Qui mainte dame et mainte damoiselle
Contraint d'amer, ou soit vesve ou pucelle*
Ou d'autre guise;   72
Quant il lui plaist soubmettre a sa devise
Qui qu'elle veult, riens n'est qu'elle n'atise.
Ainsi avint de celle a qui franchise
Fist octroyer   76
Le nom d'ami a cil qui par proyer

>
> Et bien amer ne le devoit noyer,
> Car bien l'avoit desservi en loyer,
> Comme il disoit. 80
> ¶ Dont une fois a elle devisoit
> En la priant du mal qui lui cuisoit
> Elle eust pitié, së assez souffisoit
> La grieve peine 84
> Qu'il ot souffert; si disoit, "Dame pleine
> De grant doulçour et plus belle qu'Elaine,*
> Pour vous ay eu mainte dure semaine
> Et maint meschief 88
> Pour bien amer, et n'en suis pas a chief,
> Ainçois croistra ma doulour derechef;
> Se refusé suis de vous, par mon chief,
> Je suis honnis. 92
> ¶ Dame plaisant, sans per com le phenix,*
> Desservi n'ay a tort estre pugnis
> Et ne soye maubaillis et honnis
> Par escondit, 96
> Doulce dame, ne de mon vueil desdit,
> Mais m'acordez l'amour sans contredit
> De vous, belle, car je vueil a vo dit
> Moy gouverner. 100
> Si me ferés comme droit roy regner*
> Së il vous plait vostre amour moy donner,
> Or en vueillés en tous cas ordonner
> A vo bon vueil; [72r°b] 104
> Mais garison du mal dont je me deuil
> Me promettent vo doulx vair riant oeil
> Qui en joye font remüer mon dueil*
> Souventes fois; 108
> Car leurs regars doulx, amoureux et coys
> Me garissent et blecent a la fois,
> Si que ne sçay souvent ce que je fois."*
> ¶ Par tel semblant 112
> Se complaignoit cil qui le cuer emblant
> A celle aloit par beaulx mos assemblant,
> Et tout estoit devant elle tremblant,
> Ou sembloit estre. 116
> ¶ Adont celle qui seult estre senestre

A son vouloir, par reffus qui empestre
Aux vrays amans toute joye terrestre,
Lui dist, "Amis, 120
Je ne te vueil plus tenir si soubmis,
Car il est temps que tu soies remis
Es doulx solas qui d'Amours sont promis,
Qui me commande 124
Que sans reffus a lui servir me rende.
Se j'ay meffait, que j'en paye l'amende
Et que guerdon du service te rende
Que tu as fait 128
A lui et moy, et je voy bien de fait
Que tu es mien, et de vray cuer parfait
M'aimes et crains; ne ja ne cuid meffait
En toy trouver, 132
Car par lonc temps t'ay peü esprouver,
Par quoy te puis bon et loyal trouver.
Pour ce m'amour t'ottroy sans plus rouver
A tous jours mais, 136
Car je ne cuid que tu ayes jamais
Desir d'avoir nul autre amoureux mais
Fors le mien cuer, car le tien m'est remais,
Ce sçay je bien; 140
Si suis tienne, tout aussi tu es mien.
Or soies lie, et ne pensez qu'a bien
Amours servir, et gayement te tien,
Mon doulx ami, [72v°a] 144
Car tout est tien le mien cuer sans demy.
Si soyes bon tout pour l'amour de my,
Plus ne te plains d'Amours, disant, 'Aymy!,'
Mais soiez lié." 148

¶ Adont l'amant qui ot esté lïé
Par dur refus qui l'ot contralïé,
Devant sa dame s'est humilïé
A humble chiere 152
Et liement lui dist, "Ma dame chiere,
Que j'aim et craing et ay plus que riens chiere,
Dire ne doy qu'aye comparé chiere
Si doulce amour 156
Qui tant me vault qu'elle fait sanz demour

Mon povre cuer, en qui n'avoit humour
De nul plaisir, saillir hors de cremour
De desespoir, 160
Mais par ce don d'or en avant j'espoir
Trop plus de bien que ne pensés a poir,*
Et le confort de si joyeux espoir
Bien doit garir 164
L'amoureux mal dont j'estoie au mourir.
Et puis qu'ainsi me daignez secourir,
Je prie a Dieu qu'il le me doint merir,
Ma dame gente, 168
Que je merci de toute mon entente,
Et vous promet que jamais autre attente
N'aray qu'a vous servir, car doulce rente
M'en payera. 172
C'est la doulçour qu'Amours m'envoyera
En vous servant qui me convoyera
A haulte honneur et me ravoyera
A tous bons fais." 176
¶ Aussi l'amant de cuer lye et reffais
La mercya et promist que tous fais
Foibles ou fors, et deust estre deffais,
Il porteroit 180
Pour seue amour ne ja n'arresteroit
Mais que ou paÿs ou la dame seroit
Fors pour honneur conquerre ou il pouroit,
Car pour vaillance [72v°b] 184
Yroit il hors; ja n'en eüst dueillance
Par son congié, mais de lui sanz faillance
Nouvelle orroit. Ainsi sa bien vueillance
Garder vouloit, 188
Cil qui si lié qu'a peu qu'il ne voloit
Sembloit qu'il fust, ne plus ne se doloit
Et plus joyeux seroit qu'il ne souloit
Comme il promist, 192
Et tout sembloit que de joye fremist.
¶ A brief parler, l'un a l'autre soubmist
Tout cuer et corps et sus le livre mist
Chacun sa main, 196
Et par serment promistrent, main a main,

Que loyauté tendroient soir et main;
Sanz attendre du soir a lendemain
S'entreverroient 200
A tous jours mais, tout le plus qu'ilz pourroient,
Honneur gardant, et tous jours s'aimeroient
De vraye amour, ne ja ne fausseroient
Jour de leur vie. 204
¶ Et ainsi fu ycelle amour pleuvie
Et bien sembloit que l'amant n'eust envie
Fors que par lui la dame fust servie
D'umble courage, 208
Et promettoit en lui faisant hommage
Qu'a tous jours mais seroit en son servage
Et que s'amour comme droit heritage
Vouloit garder. 212
¶ Ainsi promist, mais j'ouÿ recorder
Qu'aultrement fist sans longuement tarder
Et son faulx cuer, que l'en devroit larder,
Tost se changia, 216
Et pou a pou d'icelle s'estrangia
Qui tant l'amoit qu'a pou vive enragia
Pour son maintien qui trop le dommagia,
Sicom j'entens. 220
Non pas .ij. mois mais ancor moins de temps
Cellui l'ama qui fu pou arrestans
En celle amour; si vous diray par temps
Qu'il en avint. [73r°a] 224
¶ La dame, qui pour lui palle devint,
Maigre et lasse, car toudis lui souvint
Du dolent jour qu'elle sienne devint,
Si ne pouoit 228
Cil oublïer a qui donné avoit
Tout cuer et corps, et de certain savoit,
Dont la lasse toute vive desvoit,
Qu'il n'amoit mie 232
Elle en nul cas, car heure ne demie
Ne peu n'assez celle qui fu blesmie
Pour seue amour, et qui dame et amie
Souloit clamer, 236
N'en jouÿssoit, ne nul semblant d'amer

Ne lui monstroit, n'en recevoit qu'amer;
Et ce faisoit la dolente pasmer
Qu'il avenoit 240
Que cil a qui moult peu en souvenoit
Aucune foiz devers elle venoit
Parce qu'elle du mander ne finoit.
¶ La lasse adont, 244
Plaine de plours et de griefs souspirs dont
Son cuer fondoit, lui disant, "Lasse! et dont
Mourray je ainsi car, se Dieu me pardont,
Ne puis plus vivre 248
Se je ne suis de ce meschief delivre,
Et je vous jur et promet sur le livre
Que je ne sçay ou je suis ne que un yvre
Souvent avient. 252
Helas! amis, notre amours que devient?
Je muir de dueil certes quant me souvient
Que si tost fault, mais par moy pas n'avient.
Et qui vous meut? 256
Ne voyez vous comment mon cuer se deult?
Et je ne sçay que le vostre se veult,
Mais je voy bien que moult petit requeult
En soy mes larmes. 260
Si soit mon fait exemple a toutes dames
De croire pou ceulx qui jurent leurs armes,*
Car ce n'est tout fors pour decevoir femes.
C'est folle attente, 264
Beau doulx ami, et se je me guermente [73r°b]
Ne pensez vous que je soie dolente
Quant ne vous voy në en chemin n'en sente
Në autre part 268
Ne nouvelles n'en oy, dont mon cuer part,
Dont je puis bien de vous quitter ma part.
Je le voy bien, mais së avez a part
Autre pensee 272
Par quoy l'amour de moy en vous cessee
Soit et autre vous ayés en pensee
Et de tous poins la moye ayés quassee,
Ne le celez, 276
Mais dites moy le fait, se vous voulez,

       Car je ne sçay de quel mal vous doulez,
       Mais devers moy vous ne venez n'alez,
       Et se j'en mens,   280
       Ce savez vous, non obstant les seremens
       Que m'avez fais plains de decevemens,
       Qui me livrent au cuer trop de tourmens.
       Mais c'est pechié   284
       D'un povre cuer livrer a tel meschié
       Et quant il est pris et fort atachié
       De lui laisser durement empechié.
       Et dont me dites   288
       Se vous vouldriés de m'amour estre quittes,
       Et se j'aray tout mal pour mes merites,
       Ou se voulez la valeur de .ij. mites
       Vous amander   292
       Par devers moy, qui ne fais que mander
       Souvent vers vous sans pou en amander.
       Si m'en dites, je vous pry, sans tarder,
       Trestout le voir."   296
¶ Ainsi souvent la dame son devoir
  Faisoit vers cil qui ne vouloit avoir
  Nulle pitié, mais pour la decevoir
  Il s'excusoit   300
  Qu'il avoit trop a faire et lui nuisoit
  De mesdisans le parler qui cuisoit;
  Mais en la fin, prommettoit et disoit
  Qu'il la verroit   304
  D'or en avant souvent quant il pourroit,
  Mais non pour tant son honneur garderoit,   [73v°a]
  Mais jamais jour nul autre n'aimeroit;*
  Ce promettoit,   308
  Le desloyal qui en tous cas mentoit,
  Et celle qui a lui se guermentoit
  L'en croyoit bien et du tout s'attendoit
¶ Au mençongier,   312
  Car fole amour fait croire de leger.
  Ainsi par fois lui faisoit alleger
  Son grief tourment ou par son messager
  Lui envoyer,   316
  Mais moult souvent avoit petit loyer,

Celle qu'Amours faisoit si folloier.
Si se pouoit en doulour desvoyer
S'elle vouloit,   320
Car moult petit a cellui en chaloit
Qui pas souvent a elle ne parloit
Ne vers elle ne venoit ne aloit
Et qui loisir   324
Avoit assez, mais qu'il y eust plaisir
Et qu'il voulsist point et heure choisir,
Mais n'y avoit në amour ne desir.
¶ Ainsi dura   328
Trois ans ou plus, ainsi com me jura
Celle qui tant de maulx en endura
Que je ne sçay comment elle dura
Sans la mort traire.   332
Si ne pouoit son cuer de cil retraire
Qui par nul tour elle ne peut attraire;
Ainsi vesqui en dueil et en contraire
Un grant termine.   336
¶ Mais il n'est riens ou monde qui ne fine
Et malade quiert par droit medecine;
Et commença pou a pou la racine
A estrangier   340
De celle amour qui la tint en dongier,
Dont ot perdu repos, boire et menger.
Si n'envoya plus vers lui messagier,
Et de tous poins   344
Le frain aux dens et la bride a .ij. poins
Elle saisi, et de pres et de loings
Pour s'en oster, tant qu'elle vint aux poins
Qu'elle vouloit,   348
Et par raison, qui pas ne lui celloit
Que follement pour cellui se douloit   [73v°b]
Qui de son fait en riens ne lui chaloit.
Si s'en osta,   352
Mais du faire mie ne se hasta,
Ainçois lonc temps en l'amour arresta
Qui maint meschief et mal lui appresta.
¶ Et atant vint   356
La dame, a qui ycelle chose advint,

Que le sien cuer a raison se revint
Et assez poy de cellui lui souvint
Qui l'ot deceue, 360
Dont elle avoit mainte doulour receue,
Tout se fust elle assez tart apperceue,
Mais plus cellui n'yra a sa sceüe
Ou elle soit. 364
S i avint cas comme elle devisoit*
Qu'un autre amant durement la pressoit
Qu'il fust amez et souvent lui disoit
Qu'il l'amoit tant 368
Qu'a tous jours mais seroit sien, mais pour tant
De quanque cil lui aloit prommettant
Ne lui chaloit en riens, mais non obstant
Sans amesir 372
Cil ne finoit de lui faire plaisir
Ne pour reffus ne cessoit son desir;
Ains lui disoit que sans autre choisir
Son vray amant 376
A tous jours mais seroit en elle amant,
Ferme et loyal com pierre d'aÿmant.
Ou que cil fust François ou Allemant
Ou d'autre part, 380
Toudis avoit son penser celle part
Ne de tous biens, pour en choisir sa part,
Autre solas, n'en publique n'a part,
Ne desiroit, 384
Comme il disoit; et ainsi y paroit,
Car par le fait tout le vray apparoit
Que cil amoit, car il ne repairoit
Ne mes es lieux 388
Ou peust veoir la tres belle aux beaulx yeulx
Qu'il äouroit et servoit comme Dieux,
Se ce n'estoit es places ou de mieulx [74r°a]
Quant a valour 392
Lui peust venir, car pour nulle doulour
Qu'amours lui fist, ou fust sens ou folour,
Ne s'arrestoit quant il avoit coulour
D'aler dehors 396
Pour esprouver en vaillance son corps,

Car en honneur estoit tous ses depors.
Mais bien cuida pour amour estre mors
Ains que pitié 400
Celle eust de lui, pour laquelle amistié
Malade en fu lonc temps et dehaitié
Ains que pour lui eust pensé n'apointié
Nul bon accord, 404
Car la dame toudis avoit recort
Du faulx amant, par qui si grant descort
Fu en son cuer qu'a peu en receut mort.
Si n'ot besoing 408
Que jamais jour, ne de pres ne de loing,
Nul homme amer, car elle avoit tesmoing
Que mal venoit et meschief de tel soing,
Et pour ce attraire 412
Ne vouloit plus si penible contraire.
Si n'en pouoit l'amant nullement traire
Fors escondit, mais pour tant s'en retraire
Ne volt il mie 416
N'ycelle amour remese n'endormie
Ne fu en lui; ains com dame et amie
Il la servoit, ne heure ne demie
Il n'arrestoit 420
Qu'ou service d'elle, ou pou conquestoit,
Et moult de ses paroles y gastoit,
Mais non pour tant souvent l'amonnestoit
De sa besongne. 424
¶ Ainsi lonc temps dura par mainte alongne
Cest affaire com la dame tesmongne,
Mais il n'est riens qui bien s'en embesongne
Quë on n'acheve 428
Ne si pesant fardel que l'en ne lieve.
Au vray du fait dire en parole brieve,
Cil tant l'ama, quoy qu'il eust peine grieve, [74r°b]
Et tant servi* 432
De vray loyal cuer, subget asservi,
Que par raison il avoit desservi
Qu'il ne fust pas de joye desservi
Mais guerredonnez, 436
Et que le don d'ami lui fu donnez;*

Car tant s'estoit doulcement ordonnez
En elle amant et pour elle penez,
Qu'appercevoir 440
Quë il l'amoit de cuer sans decevoir
Elle pouoit, tant faisoit son devoir
D'elle servir, et si, qu'a dire voir,
Tort lui feïst 444
Se pitié n'eust de lui, se Dieux m'aïst,
Car n'estoit droit que son servant haÿst
Ne qu'en reffus le sien cuer envaÿst
Par fel dongier. 448
¶ Alors Amours, qui seust assouager
Les maulx crüeulx qu'en eulx fait hebreger
Qui la servent, volt adonc alleger
Les griefs ennuis 452
Qu'il ot souffert par maintes dures nuys
Dont son las cuer estoit de joye vuys.*
Si fist Pitié a Secours ouvrir l'uys
De Reconfort, 456
Et ne pot plus souffrir la dame au fort
Tenir l'amant en si grief desconfort,
Car bien savoit qu'il n'estoit rien si fort
Comme il l'amoit. 460
¶ Adont un jour l'amant se reclamoit
De ses doulours a celle qu'il cremoit,
Piteusement de l'amour l'informoit
Qui l'ot surpris 464
Par sa beauté, a qui se rendoit pris,
Et pour son los, la grace et de hault pris
Dont elle estoit, si ne l'ait en despris
Par desdaigner. 468
¶ Et adont celle, ou il n'ot qu'enseigner,
Qui tout veoit l'amant en plours baigner,
Vit qu'en sa mort ne pouoit riens gaigner.
¶ Si le retint [74v°a] 472
Pour son amant, ainsi qu'il appartint;
Et lui, qui fu loyal, si se contint
Devers celle qui son cuer ot et tint
Qu'elle l'ama 476
De tout son cuer et ami le clama.

Ainsi l'amant promist et afferma
Qu'il l'ameroit et elle conferma
Tout cest affaire. 480
Ainsi promist et ainsi le volt faire,
Car il l'ama loyaument sans meffaire,
Si bien, si bel, qu'il n'y ot que reffaire
Par lonc espace, 484
Et non obstant que tel amour tost passe,
Souventes fois cil sembla le touppasse
Qui de verdeur et de clarté trespasse
Toute autre pierre. 488
Ainsi toudis fu en lui plus vert qu'ierre
Ycelle amour, qu'il n'ot pas, par saint Pierre,
Tost acquise n'emblee comme lierre*
Qui moult tost emble; 492
Ains y souffri maint grief mal, ce me semble,*
Mais il n'est riens, quoy que descort dessemble,
Que vraye amour ne racorde et assemble
En un moument 496
Quant il lui plaist. Ainsi tres loyaument
Li duy amant s'amerent longuement
Sans nul descort et sans decevement
En tel plaisir 500
Que leurs .ij. cuers n'avoient que un desir;
Ce qu'il plaisoit a l'un ja desplaisir
Ne peüst estre a l'autre, ne choisir*
Autre solas 504
Ne voulsissent qu'estre ensemble, et ja las
Ilz n'en fussent, car tous .ij. d'un seul las
Furent lie, plaisant, sans dire, "Helas!"
¶ Et ainsi furent 508
Par moult lonc temps, mais maint scevent et sceurent
Que faulx parleurs sur les amans murmurent;
Si leur avint que mesdiseurs s'esmurent*
A parler d'eulx, [74v°b] 512
Pour les semblans qu'ilz choisirent es .ij.,
Dont ilz orent au cuer pesance et deulx.
Tout ne porent si souvent estre seulx*
A leur deport 516
Com souloient; si furent a dur port*

Lors arrivé, ou peu orent depport,
Et racompté fu par mauvais rapport
Et par envie   520
Au faulx amant premier toute leur vie
Et tout comment la dame fu servie
Du vray amant, a qui elle ot pleuvie
Et toute assise   524
L'amour d'elle du tout a sa devise.
¶ Et quant cellui ot bien par mainte guise
La verité toute sceue et enquise,
Lors a quis voye   528
Qu'il peust parler, en chemin ou en voye,
Ou en secret, si que nul ne le voye,
A celle a qui un messagier envoye
En lui priant   532
Moult chierement, non mie en maistriant,
Que parler puist a elle, et detriant*
Ne voit le jour. Lors celle en sousriant
A prins journee   536
A y parler par une matinee.
¶ Et quant furent en la place ordonnee
Adont cellui a la dame arresnee
Par tel maintien: 540
¶ "Dame, certes ne cuidasse pour rien
Que vostre cuer, que disiés estre mien,
Daignast jamais consentir fors que bien,
Ne que faulser   544
Vous daignissiés en fait në en penser.
Tant vous sceüst nul autre amant presser
Que voulsissiés vostre serment casser
Ne loyauté,   548
Que vous avez brisee, et fëauté.
Si prise pou tel grace et tel beauté
Ou il n'a foy, car serment sur l'auté
Et sur les sains   [75r°a]   552
Me jurastes Dieu, sa mere et les sains,
Que jamais jour vostre cuer n'yert deçains
De moye amour, dont il estoit ançains,
Ce disiés vous,   556
Et s'estoie vo leal ami doulx.

Et ainsi fu accordé entre nous,
Mais or vous puis faulse par devant tous
Et parjuree 560
Prouver, certes, et pou asseüree,
Puis qu'autre amour vous avez procuree.
Si est la foy que vous aviés juree
Faulse sans doubte." 564
¶ Adont respont celle, et plus ne l'escoute,
¶ "Beaulx sire, Dieux, je me merveille toute
De vostre fait et s'onques je vy goute,
Veez ci merveilles. 568
Vous me cuidez par vo tabour aux veilles
Ancor mener, mais jamais mes oreilles
N'escouteront teles ou les pareilles
Com voz paroles 572
Sont envers moy toudis toutes frivolles,
Car ne vous chault pas de .ij. poires molles
Se j'ay ami ou non, et tieulx bricoles
M'alez gitant; 576
Mais non pour tant vous en diray je ytant,
Que se je l'ay, faulse ne suis pour tant,
Car vostre cuer fu premier consentant
De moy laissier, 580
Et grans sermens feistes au commencier
Que jamais jour ne verroie plessier
L'amour de vous, qui tant a fait blecier
Mon cuer lonc temps, 584
Ce savez vous. Si ne sçay ne n'entens
Comment, puis que vous estiés consentans
De m'eslongner, que mon cuer arrestans
Y deüst estre, 588
Et a tous jours mais en douleur senestre,
Puis que veoir je pouoie vostre estre,
Car par l'euvrë on doit louer le maistre.
Et grant injure [75r°b] 592
Vous m'avez dit de m'appeller parjure
Car ne le suis, g'i mettroye gageure;
Et qui promet quoy que ce soit et jure,
Ce doit entendre 596
Cil qui reçoit le serment, s'il veult tendre

A loyauté, qu'aussi doit il entendre
A desservir le bien qu'on lui veult tendre,
Et son devoir   600
Doit faire aussi. Il est bon assavoir
Que qui promet pour autre chose avoir,
Së il ne l'a, quitte doit estre voir
De son serment.   604
¶ Ainsi a vous promis par sacrement,*
Voire en espoir que j'eusse entierement
L'amour de vous comme premierement
M'aviés promis."   608
¶ Adont respont cellui, "Certes, tost mis
M'ariés au bas, dame, et moult tost remis*
De voz raisons, mais de ce qu'entremis
Je me seroye   612
De soustenir, par tout ou je saroye,
Par devant tous proposer oseroie.
Et pour ce di, tant mentir n'en saroye,
Que vous avez   616
Vers moy faulsé, et pour riens vous sauvez
De dire que certainement savez
Qu'en moy n'avoit amour; ainsi trouvez
Vostre excusance.   620
Car se vers vous tout a vostre ordonnance
Je n'aloie, fust a feste ou a dance
Ou autre part, tout estoie en doubtance
De mesdisans,   624
Pour vostre honneur garder de mos cuisans
De leurs parlers et se fussent .x. ans
Sans vous veoir, mais quë obeïssans
Ne fusse mie   628
A autre amour ou de dame ou d'amie,
Ne deussiez vous ja heure ne demie
Pour tant faulser, mais a droite escemie*
D'amour entiere   [75v°a]   632
Et loyauté vraye en toute maniere
Vous bien garder; mais d'amour trop legiere
M'avez amé, bien en voy la maniere.
Pour ce redy   636
Que faulce estes, et de ce que je dy

                    Le jugement devant le plus hardy
                    En ose attendre et tous ceulx contredy*
                    Qui au contraire   640
                    Vouldront dire, ne vous vueille desplaire."
¶ Adont respont la dame debonnaire,
                    "Or nous doint Dieux vers loyal juge traire,
                    Mais voy cy rage   644
                    Et merveilles que de vostre lengage,
                    Qu'il soit ainsi q'une dame en servage
                    Se soit misë en recevant l'ommage
                    De son servant   648
                    Qu'elle cuidoit bon, loyal et servant,
                    Si voit aprés qui la va desservant
                    De tout plaisir, në il n'est desservant
                    Qu'amer le doye.   652
                    Et vous dites qu'elle doit toutevoye
                    En celle amour se tenir ferme et coye,
                    Mais la raison n'en voy par nulle voye.
                    Pour ce consens   656
                    Que ce debat nous mettions en tous cens
                    Dessus loyal jugë ou il ait sens,
                    Car nullement je ne voy ne ne sens
                    Vostre raison."   660
¶ Adont pristrent congié, il fu saison,
                    Et s'en tourna chacun en sa maison,
                    Et en escript chacun mist sa raison
                    Pour juge querre.   664
                    Aprés vindrent devers moy pour enquerre
                    Le mien advis, mais pou pourroie acquerre
                    De complairë a l'un pour avoir guerre
                    A la partie   668
                    Adversaire; pour ce m'en suis partie,
                    Et autre si ne sçay tout ou partie
                    De tel debat juger pou appartie
                    Y suis sans faille.   [75v°b]   672
                    Pour ce, Sire, la charge vous en baille,
                    Ne couvient ja que querre autre juge aille
                    Pour les amans, car chacun me rebaille
                    Pouoir du faire;   676
                    Si sont d'accort qu'en vous soit de l'affaire,

Car bien scevent qu'il n'y a que reffaire
En vostre bon, noble cuer, qui meffaire
Ne daigneroit. 680
¶ Ce jugement, s'il vous plait, selon droit
Vous jugerés; et ancor or en droit
.Ij. autres cas diray ou il fauldroit
Donner sentence, 684
Et sur vous tout en est mise la tence
Et le descort. Or vueil sans arrestance
Vous raconter, fust foiblece ou constance,
Ce qu'il avint 688
A .ij. amans beaulx et gens entre .xx.,
Loyaulx et bons, mais trop leur mesavint
Par Fortune, dont chacun d'eulx devint
Morne et pensif. 692
Il n'a mie des ans ancore .vj.*
Qu'une dame en qui tous biens sont assis
Un chevalier amoit, sage et rassis,
Jeune et joly, 696
Et qui toute bonne tache ot en li,
Et tout fust il mignot, cointe et joli,
Oncques ancor faulseté n'amoli
Son bon courage, 700
Ce disoit il. Aussi fu belle et sage
La dame, qui de cuer et de lengage
Ere vaillant et riche d'eritage.
Si s'entreamoient 704
Li duy amant loyaument, et clamoient
L'un l'autre amour souveraine et ne cemoient*
Fors mesdisans qui les amans esmoyent,
Et longuement 708
S'entr'amerent et si secretement
Que de leur fait ne fu grant parlement.
Si la servoit l'amant songneusement
Comme il devoit, [76r°a] 712
Et celle qui entierement savoit
Que son ami loyaument la servoit,
Le sien cuer tout entierement ravoit
En lui fichez; 716
Et souffrirent tous .ij. mains griefs meschefs

Par trop amer, qui les ot si fichez
En grant desir, qu'ilz furent tous sechez
De souffrir peine, 720
Car grant Amour, qui les amans demaine,
Trop durement mainte dure sepmaine
Leur fist avoir, car les amans a peine
Et a danger 724
S'entrepporent veoir, ne de leger
N'avenoit pas souvent, car dalmager
Ne vouloient honneur pour alleger
Leur grant desir. 728
¶ Car tant fu vray l'amant que mieulx choisir
Voulsist la mort et tout meschief saisir
Que deshonneur, ne riens qu'a desplaisir
Peust ja tourner 732
Envers celle de qui tel attourner
Le veult Amours, qu'il ne savoit tourner
De nulle part ou il peust destourner
Ne mettre jus 736
Le grief fardel qu'il porta sus et jus;
Et de trop plus grieve egreur que verjus
Lui ot Amours destrempé et fait jus
Un divers boire 740
Qu'adés avoit en cuer et en memoire,
Tant en ot beu, non en couppe n'en voirre,
Qu'il en fu tout rempli, c'est chose voire,
Et enyvré; 744
Et tel hanap ot a celle livré
Loyale Amour, qui son cuer ot livré
A si dur point que jamais delivré
Ne s'en verra, 748
Car sans partir en ses las l'enserra*
Amour ferme, qui oncques jour n'erra
Vers loyauté; si dit qu'elle querra,
Comment qu'il soit, [76r°b] 752
Voye et chemin, car trop fort l'engoissoit
Desir de cil veoir qui la pressoit
Qu'il la veïst et ainsi l'oppressoit
De toutes pars 756
Amours, desir ancor plus, les .ij. pars

Le vray amant, dont souvent les espars*
De ses doulx yeulx sur elle erent espars.
¶ Si n'en pot plus 760
Celle souffrir en qui ot amours plus
Qu'en nul autre; tout fut son corps reclus
Par fel danger qui rent amans conclus
Et desconfis. 764
Tant l'estraignoit Cupido, d'Amours filz,
Qu'elle äouroit plus que le crucefix,
¶ Qu'elle trouva, fust dommage ou prouffis,
Au paraler 768
Voye comment a celui peust parler
Que tant amoit qu'el ne pouoit celer
La grant amour qui faisoit affoller
Son cuer sans doubte. 772
Car qui d'amours affolle ne voit goute,
Ne nul peril, ne meschef, ne redoubte;
Ainsi celle, qui a l'amant fu toute,
Tant y mist peine, 776
Qu'a son ami plus d'un jour la sepmaine,
Sans le sceü de personne mondaine,
Parloit souvent, tout fust de päour plaine
Et de grant crainte 780
Pour les perilz qui aviennent a mainte
En si fait cas quant la chose est atainte.
Mais non pour tant tant fu d'amour contrainte
Qu'elle oublioit 784
Tout le meschief qu'avenir lui pouoit.
¶ Ainsi souvent son doulx ami veoit,
Si lui dura, sicomme elle disoit,
Tout un esté 788
Ce tres doulx temps, mais Fortune appresté
A mains meschiefs aux amans, et esté
Leur contraire, et souvent a arresté
Tous les depors. [76v°a] 792
¶ Ainsi, adonc, par desloyaulx rappors
Scot le mari d'icelle les accors
Des .ij. amans, tout le fait et les ports,
Le lieu, la place, 796
Ou moult souvent, a qui qu'il en desplace,

S'assembloient; si dit qu'il fault qu'il face
Tant que tous. ij. les treuve face a face
Comment qu'il aille.   800
Dont le mari, qui fu de laide taille,
Në en bonté ne valoit une maille,
Tant se muça, ou en foing ou en paille,
Qu'il esprouva   804
La verité et tous .ij. les trouva
En lieu secret; mais l'amant bien sauva
L'onneur d'elle par ce qu'il controuva
Bonne excusance,   808
Qu'il avoit loy, juste cause et aysance,
Dë y parler, ja n'en eust desplaisance,
Et la trouva cas juste ou la semblance
Par quoy raison   812
Ot de y parler en ycelle maison;*
Si n'i ot mal, peché ne desraison,
Ja n'en doubtast, car en nulle saison
Ne vouldroit faire,   816
Ce disoit il, riens qui lui deust desplaire.
¶ Et le mari, pour sa deshonneur taire,
Faisoit semblant, quoy qu'il creust au contraire,
Qu'il creoit bien   820
Ce qu'il disoit; mais oncques puis n'ot bien
La doulante, car lors sur toute rien
Lui deffendi cellui de mal merrien
Que bien gardast   824
Que jamais jour en place n'arrestast
Ou cellui fust, et que ja ne doubtast
Que la vie du corps ne lui otast
S'appercevoir   828
Jamais nul jour, par sens ne par savoir,*
Qu'a lui parlast pour nul cas, recevoir
Lui feroit mort; ce lui faisoit savoir
Par grant promesse.   [76v°b]   832
¶ Or fu tourné en dolente tristesse
L'amoureux temps qui tenoit en lëece
Les .ij. amans; or ne voyent adresce
Par nulle voye   836
De jamais jour avoir solas ne joye.

Tant ont douleur que vivre leur anoye
Ne leurs piteus regrais tous ne saroye
Compter ne dire, 840
Ne le dur temps ne le crüeux martire
Que la lasse dame ot, car tire a tire,
Son dolent cuer fondoit comme la cire
En pleurs et larmes. 844
Mais non obstant, toudis constans et fermes
Fu son las cuer en amours, dont li termes
Estoit la mort, n'attendrë autres armes*
N'avoit d'espoir 848
Qui gardassent encontre desespoir
Son dolent cuer; et choite y fust a poir*
Se grant raison, qui en a le pouoir,
Ne l'eust gardee. 852
Et le dolent amant d'autel souldee
Refu payé, mais trop griefment fraudee
Fu la lasse, plus loyal que Medee,*
De ce que point 856
N'osoit faire semblant, par nesun point,
Du mal amer qui si au cuer la point,
Dont moult souvent se mettoit en tel point
Quant seule estoit, 860
Qu'a pou ses jours et sa vie hastoit
Et son cler vis tout de lermes gastoit.
Mais en ce plour moult petit acquestoit
Car n'y ot tour 864
De son ami veoir, car une tour
Forte de mur et close d'eaue au tour
Bien la gardoit, n'il n'y avoit destour
Ne voye aucune, 868
Fust en secret ou en voye commune,
De lui veoir, ne maniere nesune,
Dont moult souvent, plourant seule a la lune,
Se complaignoit [77r°a] 872
A vraye Amour, qui si la destraignoit.
Et d'autre part, l'amant ne s'i faignoit,
Ains en griefs plours le dolent tout baignoit
En regraitant 876
La belle qui de savoureux biens tant

Faire lui seust; ore en a autre tant
De griefs doulours, dont s'en va guermentant
Piteusement. 880
Mais non pour tant enquist songneusement
D'elle, en secret et päoureusement,
Que le mari nel sceut aucunement;
Et par message 884
Bon et secret, loyal ami et sage,
Lui escripsoit souventes fois la rage
Ou ot esté puis que son doulx visage
Et son gent corps 888
Ne pot veoir, dont moult divers acors
Font en son cuer desir et les recors
Des doulx soulas, dont lui souvient ancors,
Qu'il a perdus. 892
Si s'en treuve dolent, mat, esperdus,
Et a tous jours yert du tout confondus
S'il ne la voit, et deust estre pendus,
Fault qu'il la voye. 896
¶ Et par escript tel complaint lui envoye:
¶ "Dame sans per, le chemin et la voye
Qui a vië ou a mort me convoye,
Tout mon desir, 900
Tout mon espoir, sans qui je n'ay plaisir,
Celle qu'Amours de sur toutes choisir
En remirant vo beauté a loisir
Me fist, ma dame 904
Sage, vaillant, bonne sur toute fame,
Que j'aim et sers et obeÿs, par m'ame,
Plus qu'autre riens, ne ne pourroit plus ame
Amer maistrece 908
Que je fais vous, si oyez la destresse
Ou je demour qui si le cuer maistrece*
Que je n'y voy fors de la mort l'adrece
Se ne vous voy, [77r°b] 912
Ma doulce amour, et tout vif me desvoy
Quant je pense qu'ay perdu le convoy
De vo doulx oeil. Quant m'en souvient, Avoy!,
Je muir de dueil, 916
Belle plaisant, de ma joye le sueil,

Mon paradis terrestre, autre ne vueil,
Reconforter le mal que je recueil
Vous plaise, helas! 920
Et que fera mon douleureux cuer las
Sanz vous veoir, mon gracïeux soulas,
Belle, bonne, qui me tient en ses las?
Or mettez peine 924
Que vous voye, ma dame souveraine,
S'il peut estre, car je vous acertaine
Que grant desir a desespoir me meine,
Tant me destraint, 928
Et pour ce suis du requerir contraint.
Mais non pour tant mieulx vouldroie estre estraint
Jusqu'a la mort que cil qui a restraint
Noz doulx deduis, 932
C'est le jaloux de tout mal faire aduis,
Apperceüst qu'a vous servir suis duis,
Ne qu'en appert ou en aucuns reduis
A vous parlasse, 936
Non pas pour tant que riens je le doubtasse,
Mais tout pour vous, dame, qui toutes passe,
De qui je vueil l'onneur en toute place
Tout mon vivant, 940
Garder, cherir; mieulx mourir en vivant
Vueil pour amer que ce qu'aille estrivant
A vostre honneur. Dame, a qui suis servant,
Me pardonnez 944
Se j'ay requis secours, car certenez
Suis que par vous ne peut estre donnez
A moy, qui suis a grant meschief menez;
Mais plus me poyse 948
De vostre mal, doulce dame courtoise,
Que du tourment qui si griefment me poyse,
Car je sçay bien que sans mener grant noise
Grant dueil portez, [77v°a] 952
Ne quë en riens vous ne vous deportez
Sans moy veoir, dont vous vous depportez
A grant peine, car vo cuer rapportez
A lëauté 956
Que vous porte[z] en especiaulté*

Car sur toutes portez la royaulté
De vaillance, d'onneur et de beauté
Qui vous conduit, 960
Et tous les biens font en vous leur reduit.
Si ne pourriés pour loyauté, qui duit
Vostre bon cuer, joye avoir ne deduit
Sans vostre ami. 964
Mais je vous pri, belle, pour qui gemy,
Que vous veuillés tout pour l'amour de my
Reconforter vo cuer qui sans demy
Est trestout mien, 968
Et esperer qu'encor arons du bien
Maugré le faulx jalous, desloyal chien.
Car par souffrir bonnement, vous di bien,
Le gaignerons, 972
Et l'eust juré, nous nous entramerons
Et a grant joyë ancor nous verrons
Et noz douleurs doulcement porterons
En esperant. 976
Si ne diray plus que j'aille mourant
Pour vous, belle, de qui en desirant
Nomme le nom souvent en souspirant;
Et vous tenez 980
Joyeusement, mais toudis maintenez
Foy, loyauté, ne moy qui suis penez
Point n'oublïez; s'ainsi vous ordenez
Mieulx en vauldrés, 984
N'envers Amours en riens ne deffauldrés,
Ainçois a voz desirs trop moins fauldrés
Par joye avoir, car par ce vous perdrés
Le faulx agait 988
Du desloyal mari qui en agait
Est sans cesser, car pour ce qu'en dehait
Vous voit, toudis a vous gaiter ne lait
Ne jour ne nuit. 992
Si conforter le mal qui si vous nuit
En moy amant, ne ja ne vous ennuit [77v°b]
Un peu de temps qui ne demain n'ennuyt*
Ne passera. 996
Ma doulce amour, ou mon cuer pensera

Tout mon vivant ne ja ne cessera
De vous amer tant que trespassera
L'ame du corps, 1000
Cent mile fois et plus, mes doulx depors,
Me recommand a vous et aux recors
Doulx amoureux que vous arés ancors
De voz amours. 1004
Et prie a Dieu, par devotes clamours,
Que vo gent corps, garni de bonnes mours,
En ce monde face lonc temps demours
Par bonne vie, 1008
Et puis aprés vostre ame soit ravie
Avecques Dieu ou ciel, ou n'a envie,
Et de tous biens vous soiez assouvie
A tous jours mais." 1012
¶ Ainsi l'amant, servi de divers mets,
Reconfortoit sa belle dame, mais
En son las cuer, tous maulx furent remais;
Et puis la belle, 1016
Qui conforter pour nesune nouvelle
L'amoureux mal qui dessoubs la mamelle
Trop l'engoissoit ne pot, adoncques celle
Lui rescripsoit 1020
Piteusement, et ainsi devisoit:
¶ "Beau doulx ami, en qui se deduisoit
Mon cuer, a qui vous tout seul souffisoit
Pour seule amour, 1024
Depuis le jour qu'il receut la clamour
De vo complaint qui en lui fist demour,
Sachés de vray, cil par qui en cremour
Vif en dongier, 1028
Que j'aime tant qu'il n'est riens qu'estranger
Peüst le mal qui me fait enragier
Quant ne vous puis veoir, riens alegier
Ne me pourroit 1032
Et mon las cuer de dueil ainçois mourroit
Qu'il s'esjouïst, car qui souvent orroit
Ses griefs complains, grant pitié en aroit,* [78r°a]
Në il n'est dueil 1036
Pareil au mien, ne je n'ay autre vueil

Fors de mourir et trop je me merveil
Comment je vif, car sans cesser je vueil
Ne ne repose. 1040
En ce qui m'est ancor plus dure chose,
C'est qu'il couvient que ma douleur enclose
Porte en mon cuer, ne semblant faire n'ose
De mon meschief, 1044
Ne je n'espoir jamais venir a chief
De cest ennuy, car je ne voy bon chief
De vous veoir jamais, dont par mon chief
Je mourray d'ire, 1048
Et ce sera briefment; vous l'orrés dire.
Et je desir que la mort hors me tire
De ce grief dueil, qui trop mon cuer martire
Et mal demaine 1052
Ma doulce amour, puis que je suis certaine
Qu'il n'y a tour jamais pour nulle peine
Que vous voyë, et plus que riens mondaine
Je vous desir. 1056
Et comment dont pourroye avoir plaisir
Dont me vendroit quant je ne sçay choisir
Autre soulas qui feïst amesir
Pour nul avoir 1060
Mes griefs peines? N'espoir ne puis avoir,
Car n'y a tour que peusse decevoir
Ceulx qui bien font en tous cas leurs devoir
De nous gaicter. 1064
Tres doulx amy, si n'y a nul sentier
De vous veoir, n'en chemin, n'en moutier,
Në autre part, si ne puis appointier
Nul autre tour; 1068
Si en mettez vo cuer hors de tristour,
Laissez a moy le dueil faire en destour,
Et vous prenez en faucon ou ostour
Ou en deduit 1072
De chace en bois, amis, vostre deduit,*
Car a amant pour passer temps aduit;
En ce prenoit Pyramus son reduit,*
Ou temps jadis, [78r°b] 1076
Quant pour rappors et desloyaulx mesdis,

La tres belle Thisbé, en qui toudis
Fu son vray cuer, c'estoit son paradis,
Fu mise en mue, 1080
Que pour meschief oncques ne fu desmue*
De lui amer, car droit ne se remue
Qui bien aime, ne change ne ne mue
Pour infortune. 1084
Mon vray ami, je n'y sçay voye aucune
N'autre deport. Dieux qui fist ciel et lune
Vous reconfort et moy, qui par Fortune
Suis mise au bas, 1088
Doint brief finer, car de tous les esbas
Quitte ma part, et en plourant rabas
Tous mes soulas, ne vueil autre rapas
Në autre joye." 1092

¶ Ainsi la dame a son ami renvoye
Ses griefs complains, ne n'y scet lieu ne voye
Que jamais jour par nesun tour le voye
Pour les agais 1096
De mesdisans qui plus que papegais
Vont barbetant, et tous jours firent gais;
Si ne fu plus son corps jolis ne gays
Comme ot esté. 1100
Ainsi Fortune ot tout mal appresté
Aux .ij. amans et tout leur bien osté,
Et ja par .ij. yvers et un esté
Enduré orent 1104
Ces grans ennuys, ne veoir ne se porent,
Tant traveiller ne pener ne s'i sorent,
Dont tout l'espoir avoir perdu ilz dorent
Comme il sembla 1108
A l'amant, qui gaires mais n'en troubla,
Et avec gent plus souvent assembla
Qu'il n'ot appris et son corps affubla
Plus sur le gay. 1112

¶ Et tout ainsi com le serf pour l'abay
Des chiens s'en fuit qui l'ont mis en esmay,
Cil eslongna sa dame ou mois de may
Qui renouvelle, 1116
Et oublia du tout en tout la belle [78v°a]

Et n'envoya plus messagier vers elle,
Et accointa autre dame nouvelle
Quë il ama 1120
Tant et servi quë ami le clama,
Ne l'autre plus en riens ne reclama.
¶ Dont aprés moult l'en reprist et blama
La premeraine, 1124
Que bien un an aprés en fu certaine,
Dont lui pesa si durement qu'a peine
N'en receut mort; si n'ot mais tant de peine
Des agaitans 1128
Comme el souloit, car toute riens leur temps*
Ont et saison, ne riens n'est arrestans
En un estat. Et ainsi, com j'entens,
¶ Un jour avint 1132
Qu'en certain lieu cellui amant seurvint
Ou sa prime dame fu, qui devint
Vermeille quant le vit; si lui souvint*
Du temps passé, 1136
Dont ne fu pas en son cuer effacé
Le souvenir qu'Amours ot entassé,
Si que jamais il n'en sera lassé;
Ains lui duroit 1140
Tous jours l'amour dont maint maulx enduroit
Et de rechief durement souspiroit.
Si se pensa quë a lui parleroit
Car n'y ot gent 1144
Mie foison, ne gaite ne sergent
Qui en ce cas lui fussent dalmagent.
¶ Si l'appella adont et bel et gent
Vers lui se trait, 1148
Et commença a lui dire en retrait,
"Ha! qui pensast en vous trouver faulx trait
Ne que pour riens fussiés jamais retrait
De moy amer 1152
Ne c'on vous peust faulx ne mauvais nommer!
Car tant de fois vous ouÿ affermer
Que mieulx vouldriés estre noyé en mer
Que moy laissier, 1156
Ne loyauté enfraindre ne froissier, [78v°b]

Et vous m'avez, dont moins vous doy prisier,
Deguerpie, si n'en puis appaisier
Mon cuer, par m'ame, 1160
Et faulx estes d'avoir fait autre dame
Et desloyal vers moy. C'est grant diffame
A vous, certes, a qui affiert grant blame
D'avoir ce fait." 1164
¶ Ainsi celle blama cellui de fait;*
Tout en plourant, se complaint du tort fait
Qu'il a commis; mais il dit que meffait
Il n'a vers elle 1168
En nesun cas et a tort faulx l'appelle,
Ne d'autre amer, soit dame ou damoiselle,
Il n'a mespris et de son dit appelle
Par devant tous 1172
Juges d'amours, et y fussent trestous,
Soumettre veult que son corps soit aux loups
Livré ou pris de malage ou de tous
S'il est jugié 1176
Qu'il ait mespris ne qu'il soit estrangié
De loyauté, non obstant que changié
Il ait dame sans ce qu'il eust congié
D'elle du faire. 1180
Devant juge ne pense mie a taire
Ses grans raisons et comment neccessaire
Il lui estoit de soy d'elle retraire,
Et mesmement 1184
Pour son honneur, car elle scet comment
Il ne pouoit la veoir nullement
Et le peril et grant encombrement
Ou ilz en furent, 1188
Et mesdisans, qui ancor en murmurent,
Tout ce tourment par faulx rappors esmurent,
Et tieulx parleurs aux amoureux procurent
Trop de meschief; 1192
Et elle ainsi lui manda de rechief,
Que jamais jour ne pourroit par nul chief
A lui parler, në en lonc temps n'en brief
Le veoir plus, 1196
Dont longuement en fu morne et enclus, [79r°a]

Mais n'estoit droit qu'il se rendist reclus
A tous jours mais ou du tout fust desclus
De joye avoir, 1200
Car sans amours ne pourroit recevoir
Nul jeune cuer joye, a dire le voir,
Et doncques, puis que pour nesun avoir
Ne la pouoit 1204
Veoir, certes pourchacer se devoit
En autre part, pour ce mespris n'avoit,
Ce disoit il, du faire bien savoit.
Mais se il espoir 1208
D'elle veoir eüst eü a poir,
Il eust mespris, mais elle en desespoir
Trop le mettoit, si n'avoit plus pouoir
De soustenir 1212
La grant doulour qu'i lui falu tenir*
Par trop lonc temps; doncques pour revenir
A reconfort, lui falu retenir
Dame nouvelle, 1216
Car par lonc temps il n'avoit receu d'elle*
Fors que doulour; si a tort qui l'appelle,
Pour en avoir fait une aultre nouvelle,
Faulx pour ce cas. 1220
⁋ Mais la dame qui ot le parler cas
Pour le grief plour ou elle chut a cas,*
Lui dist, "Certes ne vous fault avocas
Pour raconter 1224
Vostre raison, mais je m'ose vanter
Que se juge loyal veult escouter
Noz .ij. raisons, tort arés sans doubter,
Sicom moy semble, 1228
Car vostre cuer, qui du mien se dessemble,
Si n'a trouvé en moy riens qui ressemble
A faulceté depuis le jour qu'ensemble
Premier parlames. 1232
Si n'avez droit; juge en fais toutes dames
Et tous amans loyaulx et sans diffames,
Et si soustiens que vous n'avez .ij. drames
De cause bonne. 1236
Si soit juge trouvé, bonne personne [79r°b]

Qui de noz cas tous .ij. nous arraisonne.
Plus n'est mestier que je vous en sermonne;
Au jugement 1240
Je m'en attens du tout entierement."
꠆ Atant fina d'eulx .ij. le parlement
Et tost aprés vindrent songneusement
En ma maison. 1244
De leur debat me distrent l'achoison*
En moy priant que oÿe leur raison
J'en jugiasse, mais je dis qu'a foison
Il trouveroient 1248
Ailleurs meilleurs juges qui mieulx saroient
Droit en jugier. Si distrent qu'ilz vouloient
Que j'en jugiasse ou quë ilz me prioient
Que je leur queisse 1252
Juge loyal et bien en enqueïsse,
Et sur cellui tout le fait asseïsse.
Et je leur dis que voulentiers feïsse
Leur bon plaisir, 1256
Mais s'en tel fait je devoye choisir
Juge pour moy, ne vouldroie saisir
Autre que vous pour l'amoureux desir
Bien discerner 1260
Et pour savoir bon jugement donner;
Et lors distrent qu'en nul autre assener
Ne pourroient mieulx et pour ce ordonner,
S'il vous plaisoit, 1264
Vous vouloient leur juge et souffisoit
Vo jugement, sicom chacun disoit.
Pour ce, Sire, tout le fait sur vous soit,
S'a gre vous vient. 1268

E̱t du tiers cas sicomme il me souvient*
Je vous diray le fait; il appartient
Puis que leur vueil a juge vous retient.
Tel fu l'affaire: 1272
꠆ Un chevalier, sicom j'ouÿ retraire,
Avoit promis a tous jours sans retraire
Toute s'amour a doulce et debonnaire
Et bonne et belle 1276
Et si plaisant qu'aultre ne passoit celle
[79v°a]

Fors seulement qu'elle estoit damoiselle
Jeune d'aage, simple comme pucelle,
Jolye et gente, 1280
Et elle aussi ravoit mise s'entente
A lui amer, et de loyal entente
S'entramoient et bien, que je ne mente,
Plus de .ij. ans 1284
S'entre amerent loyaument les amans.
Ce me jura saint Julian du Mans,*
Celle qui cuer ferme ot com dyamans,
Que d'un descort 1288
En leur amour elle n'avoit recort;
Ainçois tous .ij. furent si d'un accort,
Qu'onques n'y ot un tout seul mesacort
En ce termine. 1292
¶ Mais il n'est mur si fort que l'en ne mine,
Ne si grant tas que qui veult mine a mine
L'appeticier, que l'en ne le termine;
Ne riens ne dure 1296
Sans avoir fin par le cours de nature
En ce monde, n'il n'est chose tant dure
Qui ne s'use, soit chaleur ou froidure,
Et qui ne tire 1300
A quelque fin; et ainsi tire a tire
S'usent amours souvent, s'ay je ouÿ dire,*
Et non obstant que souvent on souspire
Par trop amer, 1304
Et que les maulx d'amours soient amer,
Si ne voit on mie amours affermer
A tous jours mais, ains les voit on clamer
Et c'est souvent 1308
Fol s'i fie. Et fole amour est tout vent*
Qui peu dure et les cuers va decevant
Et un espoir dont aprés ensuivant
Sa joye vaine. 1312
¶ Ainsi fina, qui qu'en eust aprés peine,
Ycelle amour qui souloit si certaine
Estre, et puis fu desprise et incertaine
Et defaillie, 1316
Car l'amant, qui l'amour en sa baillie [79v°b]

De celle avoit, qui puis fu maubaillie
Pour lui amer et en grief dueil faillie,
Se changia tout, 1320
Et delaissa et remist en debout*
Celle qu'amer souloit et fu de tout
Leur joyeux temps qu'elle cuidast qu'a bout
Ne deust ja estre. 1324
Si lui sembla qu'il estoit trop grant maistre
Pour elle amer, et volt en plus hault estre
Mettre son cuer et bien cuida a dextre
Droit assener 1328
Pour haultement son cuer mettre et donner.
¶ Si s'acointa, com j'ouÿ raisonner,
D'une poissant dame a qui sans finer
Son cuer promist, 1332
Et tant l'ama et tant grant peine y mist,
Qu'elle l'ama. En la fin tant lui dist
Quë il l'amoit, qu'elle en grace le prist
Et le retint 1336
Pour son servant et a ami le tint.
Si ne sçay pas comment il s'i contint,
Car pou dura l'amour; a qui il tint
Ne sçay je pas. 1340
¶ Mais il n'est nul qui vous deist en nul pas
La grant douleur et le mauvais repas
Que la lasse ot qui auques au trespas
Et mise en biere 1344
En fu pour lui, la dolente premiere,
Quant elle vit et parceut la maniere
De son amant, qui se tiroit arriere
De seue amour, 1348
Et trop faisoit d'elle veoir demour,
Ne n'ot pitié de sa lasse clamour,
Non obstant ce que souvent, en cremour
Et a dongier, 1352
A lui parloit d'elle le messagier
Et lui disoit pour quoy si estrangier
Vouloit celle qui mie de legier
Ne l'oubliroit, 1356
Ains pour s'amour sanz faille se mouroit [80r°a]

S'il la laissoit, du mal qu'elle tiroit.
Il respondoit qu'au plus tost qu'il pourroit,
Yroit vers elle, 1360
Mais survenu il lui estoit nouvelle
Qui l'empeschoit pour certaine querele;
Si s'excusoit ainsi de veoir celle
Qui ne finoit 1364
De dueil mener, car bien apparcevoit
Que delaissier son ami la vouloit,
Dont trop griefment la lasse se douloit.
¶ Mais pour neant 1368
Se traveilloit et s'aloit deleant,
Car bien pouoit, s'elle estoit cler veant,
Appercevoir qu'il s'aloit retreant
D'elle sans doubte. 1372
Si en ploura en grief dueil mainte goute
Et de courroux elle se fondi toute.
¶ A brief parler du tout en tout deroute
Celle amour fu, 1376
Et la laissa et la mist en reffu
Le faulx amant, que fust il ars en fu!
Ainsi celle bien vit et apperceu
Quë autre amoit, 1380
Dont longuement dolente se clamoit
Mais n'y ot tour; pour riens le reclamoit.
¶ Si s'en souffri quant vit qu'elle semoit
Pour riens ses larmes, 1384
Car il n'est rien qui n'ait saison et termes,
Si n'estoit droit qu'a tous jours mais fust fermes
Son cuer ou dueil qui fait perdre les armes
Et corps en terre. 1388
Si appaisa son cuer de celle guerre
Au chief d'un temps, et ne volt plus enquerre
De son amant n'aucune voye querre
Pour lui veoir, 1392
Në autre part sceue amour asseoir,
Car d'amer plus ne lui devoit seoir
En son vivant, ne d'ami pourveoir
Son cuer jamais, 1396
Ce lui sembloit, car trop lui fu remais [80rºb]

Dolent penser pour amer et dur mais,
Si s'entendroit, ce disoit, des or mais.
¶ Mais escoutez
Ce qu'il avint de ce fait et nottez
Comment l'amant estoit peu arrestez,
Car ains que fust l'an passé, ne doubtez,*
Il esprouva
Grant faulceté en la dame et trouva,
Ce disoit il; car s'il le controuva
Ne sçay je pas, mais par ce se sauva*
D'elle laissier,
Et dist que cuer haultain et boubancier*
Avoit vers lui et legier a plaisier
A autre amour plus que verge d'osier.
¶ Si lui souvint
Des doulx plaisirs de celle qui devint
Palle pour lui et comment y avint.
Alors son cuer a raison se revint
Et s'avisa
Qu'il l'ameroit, car oncques n'avisa
Plus loyale, sicomme il devisa,
Ne pouoit mieulx; pour ce se ravisa
Et repenti*
Donc oncques mais loyauté lui menti
Ne dont son cuer a autre consenti.
Si a dit lors comme vray converti
Que humblement
Lui requerroit mercis piteusement
Et du meffait a son vueil vengement
Prensist sur lui, mais qu'aprés bonnement
Lui pardonnast,
Et de bon cuer loyal elle l'amast,
Si qu'en tous cas son vueil lui ordonnast
Et se jamais failloit, si le blamast
Comme mauvais.
¶ Ainsi cellui volt pourchacier sa paix
Devers la belle, a qui peu chaloit mais
De son amour, et vers elle s'est trais.
Si la raisonne
Moult doulcement et qu'elle lui pardonne

Prie humblement, et de ce la sermonne
Moult longuement, et dist qu'onques personne
N'ama plus dame 1440
Qu'il l'aimera des or mais, par son ame.
¶ Et lors celle en qui plus n'avoit la flame
De fole amour, qui deçoit homme et fame,
Prist a respondre 1444
Et dist c'on la devroit bien a seq tondre,
Puis qu'elle estoit hors du meschief qui fondre
Son cuer faisoit, pour prïer ne semondre,
S'a tel meschief 1448
Se mettoit plus; si ne l'ameroit brief
Puis que laissiee il l'avoit de rechief
Ne s'i fieroit jamais par nesun chief
Puis que deceue 1452
L'a une fois et mauvaistié perceue*
En lui; n'en quiert jamais avoir veüe
Ne plus ne veult estre d'amer meüe
Certainement; 1456
Si ne lui en tiengne plus parlement,
Car n'amera jamais jour nullement.
¶ Et cil respond et lui dit doulcement
Qu'elle aroit tort, 1460
Car repentant on ne doit mettre a mort,
Et le pecheur que conscïence mort
Dieu a merci le prent se il se remort
Com repentant. 1464
Et celle dit qu'il s'en peut bien atant
Souffrir s'il veult, car moult peu arrestant
Il y seroit, quoy qu'il voit promettant,
Mais que nouvelle 1468
Dame veïst qui lui semblast plus belle,
Si n'en veult plus ouÿr nulle nouvelle.
¶ Et cil a dit que de son dit appelle
En jugement, 1472
Car par raison veult monstrer tout clerement*
Qu'elle grant tort lui feroit s'ensement
Le guerpissoit, puis qu'a repentement
De son meffait, 1476
Et se plaindra aux amans du tort fait [80v°b]

Qu'elle lui fait, et juge veult de fait
Pour en juger; car oncques si parfait
Homs ne nasqui 1480
Qui ne meprist fors Dieu, qui tout vainqui,
Ce disoit il, ne si vaillant en qui
N'eust vice aucun, et d'estre relenqui
En tel maniere 1484
Ne seroit pas chose bien droituriere.
¶ Et pour ce veult que leal juge on quiere,*
Et s'il est dit en si faite maniere
Qu'elle nel doye 1488
Prendre a merci, aler s'en veult sa voye.
Et celle dit qu'au jugement s'octroye.
¶ Mais non obstant, elle veult toutevoye
Que ains que l'en rende 1492
Le jugement, aux dames on demande
Leur bon avis et si s'y recommande
En leur priant que chacune y entende
Diligemment, 1496
Et puis si soit donné le jugement.
¶ Ainsi greé cest accort bonnement
Ont ambedeux; a tant leur parlement
Ont affiné, 1500
Et puis aprés de cercher n'ont finé
Juge par qui il soit determiné
De leur debat, et leur procés finé.
Si sont venu 1504
Par devers moy combien qu'appartenu*
N'ait pas a mi et si se sont tenu
Sur mon avis; adont m'est souvenu
De vous, chier Sire, 1508
¶ Si leur ay dit qu'ilz vous vueillent eslire,
Car mieulx sarés de leur debat voir dire
Et droit juger que moy, car a bon mire
Doit le navré, 1512
Soy adrecier s'estre veult delivré
De son grief mal, dont par vous desevré
Le droit du tort soit; si ont recouvré
Droit justicier 1516
En vous, Sire, s'il vous plaist radrecier [81r°a]

Le grant debat dont les ouÿ tencier.*
Mais or est temps de mon oeuvre avancier
Et affiner;   1520
Le demourant commet a parfiner
A vo bon sens, car bien sarés finer
De ce qu'il fault a bien l'oeuvre affiner
Et la parfaire,   1524
Si est saison que je m'en doye taire.
¶ Mais au derrenier ver vueil dire et retraire
Quel est mon nom, qui le vouldra hors traire
Comme il deffine;   1528
Et en la fin de pensee enterine,
Qui vous octroit joye parfaite et fine,
Pri Jhesu Crist, qui ne fault ne ne fine.*
    Explicit le dit des .iij. jugemens

194 / *Le Livre des Trois jugemens*

Variants

Rubric *D omits* qui s'adrece au seneschal de Haynault, *L1L3* Cy c. le dit d. *L2 omits rubric*

1	*D* Mon s., Haynault
2	*D* et g. de l., *L* et g. en l.
3	*D* f. et de langage, *L* L. c. en fait et de langage
5	*L3* en bon s.
6	*DL* c. soubsmis et pris
9	*L omit* a.
10	*L* soit ou f.
19	*L2L3* c. telle v.
21	*L omit* Pour
27	*L* et le d.
30	*L3 omits* cas
36	*L* N'y
46	*RD* m. mate et
57	*DL* f. ne en r. se t.
59	*L1L3* l. nulle riens o., *L2* b. secours o.
75	*DL* c. en qui
95	*DL2L3* Si ne
105	*L3* g. de m.
106	*DL* vo d. r. vert o.
107	*DL* m. vueil
111	*R* que je ne
125	*L* servir entende
126	*L* q. j'en soye a l.
131	*D* ne je ne
134	*L* l. prouver
151	*R* sa d. c'est h.
161	*DL* Car p.
167	*L* D. qui le me
177	*DL2L3* Ainsi l.
185	*L3* e. doutance
187	*D* N. aroit
199	*L1L3* s. au l.
219	*L1L2* t. la d.
221	*DL* p. trois m.
238	*L* m. ne r.
243	*L* Pour ce qu'elle
246	*DL* l. disoit
262	*D* l. ames
273	*L* P. q. en moy l'a. de vous c.
275	*L2* m. arez q.
279	*DL* m. ne venez në alez
280	*L* se je m.
286	*D* p. f. et a.
287	*R* d. en peschié
298	*DL* q. n'en v.
307–9	*omitted in R*, 307 *L* Ne j.
329	*L* p. si comme me
330	*L1L3* t. ou plus en e.
339	*DL* Si c.
347	*L1L2* De s'en
357	*L* q. yceste c.
365	*R omits* Si, *L* Si a. lors comme
366	*R omits* Qu'un
374	*L3* Et p.
385	*L* et aussy y
387	*L* cil l'amoit
393	*D* Li p., *L1L3* c. par n.
394	*D* Quë on li fist ou, *L* l. feïssent feust s.
401	*L1L2 omit* de lui, *L3* e. pour l.
406	*L* si mal d.
407	*L1L3* p. recevoit m.
409	*DL* De j.
433	*L* De v. c. l.
438	*R* t. c'estoit d.
450	*DL2L3* q. ceulx f.
451	*DL* Q. le s.
457	*L* Si ne
461	*L* A. l'amant un j.
463	*L* l'a. lui fourmoit
465	*L1L2* b. acquise rendoit p.
466	*DL* et le h.
493	*DL* m. grant grief, *DL2* ce m'en s.
494	*L1L3 omit* que
502	*DL1L2* Ce qui p., *L3* Ce que p.
503	*R* Ne peut e.
511	*DL* q. mesdisans s.
515	*DL* Si ne

523	*L3* Au v.	795	*D* et le pors
533	*DL* en mescriant	809	*L* avoit lors j.
554	*R* cuert	811	*DL* Et lors t.
557	*DL* Et seroye	818	*L* p. son d.
573	*L omits* toudis	829	*DL* Pouoit jamais p. s.
577	*DL* d. je tant.	839	*L* p. regars t.
583	*DL* q. trop a	841	*L* le doulz t.
586	*L1 omits* vous	847	*DL* m. attendre n'autres a.
589	*D* A t. j. m. a d. si s., *L* A t. j. m. en d. si s.	863	*DL* p. conquestoit
		866	*L* de murs et
590	*L* v. ne p.	870	*L* v. en m.
595	*DL* Car q.	873	*L* De v. A.
602	*D* pour quelque c.	874	*D* ne se f.
605	*R* A. avoye p., *D* promis par mon serment, *L2L3* promis mon sacrement	879	*D* dont se va
		885	*D* s. certain loyal et s., *L* s. discret loyal et s.
610	*L3* M'avez au	891	*L* Les d.
611	*DL* Par v.	893	*R* d. mate e., *D* d. mat et e.
615	*DL* di car m. ne s.	910	*DL* Ou suis pour vous qui
626	*L1L2* se fusse	933	*L* de tous maux f.
630	*D omits* ja	936	*L* Qu'a v.
639	*RD omit* En	937	*DL* t. qu'en r.
641	*RD* Vouldroit d.	942	*L3* qu'a escrivant
649	*D* et fervant	950	*R omits* si
650	*DL1L3* qu'il la	957	*R* v. porter en, *DL* Qui v. conduit en
655	*D* r. n'y v.		
662	*L* s'en ala	961	*L1L3* t. ces b.
663	*L* escript ont mise leur r.	965	*L* b. par q.
675	*D* a. chascun d'eulz me	974	*DL* j. encore
685	*DL1L2* Et tout sur v. en est	980	*DL* Si v.
694	*R omits* Qu	985	*L* Ne vers A., *DL* A. de r.
697	*D* ot o ly	990	*L1L2* cesser et p.
698	*DL* cointe et poli	991	*DL2* a nous g.
703	*D* Vaillant estoit et r.	1019	*L2L3* l'e. a. ne p. c.
717	*L3* Si s., *L* m. grans m.	1027	*L* S. amis par qui vif en c.
737	*L* qu'il portoit s.	1028	*R* Vif et en d., *L* Et en d.
745	*DL* h. a c. ot relivré	1039	*L* v. et s.
749	*R* Car sen p.	1041	*DL* Et ce
761	*L* ot amer p.	1059	*L1L2* s. me f.
770	*D* a. que ne, *L* a. qu'elle ne pot celer	1070	*L3* m. de d.
		1079	*RL3* c. s'estoit s.
787	*L1L3* Si li d.	1081	*DL* Qui p.
791	*L omit* a	1085	*L3* je ne s.
792	*DL1L2* T. leurs d.	1086	*DL* D'autre d.

1097 *D* Des m.
1098 *L* j. furent g.
1109 *L1L3* m. ne t.
1121 *D* s. qu'a a.
1125 *DL* Qui b.
1135 *DL* V. ou vis q. le vit lui s.
1150 *L2* p. t. en v. f.
1177 *L2L3* m. ou qu'il
1178 *R* q. chargié
1179 *L* qu'il ait c.
1182 *DL* Ces g.
1193 *DL* e. aussi l.
1197 *L omit* en
1205 *L omit* Veoir
1213 *L* d. qu'il l.
1217–19 *DL change the order of these lines as follows: 1219, 1217, 1218*
1219 *DL* en a. quelque bonne nouvelle
1269 *R omits* Et
1302 *R* souvent sçay je
1307 *DL1L2* l. oit on
1309 *DL2L3 omit* Et, *RD* a et t.
1310 *L3 omits* les
1312 *DL* Va j.
1319 *L* et au g., *DL* d. saillie
1321 *DL* et estrangia debout
1322 *DL* f. derout
1323 *L* qu'e. cuidoit, *L1L2* qu'au b.
1333 *L* et si g.
1338 *L* il se c.
1343 *L* Qu'en la l. et q., *D* q. oncques au
1369 *L3* et aloit d.
1371 *DL* s'a. recreant
1380 *D* Q'une a.
1397 *R* Se l.
1403 *L* p. n'en d.
1409 *R* c. hault et
1442 *L omit* en
1454 *DL* l. j. n'en q. a. v.
1470 *DL* o. malle n.
1473 *DL* C. m. v. par r. c.
1486 *R* v. q. j. l. on
1494 *DL* si se r.
1499 *L* a. adont l.
1505 *R* c. qu'apparce
1506 *D* a moy et
1518 *D* dont je le oy t., *L1L3* dont j'ay oÿ t., *L2* dont je l'ou t.
1530 *L* Que v.
Explicit *D* Explicit *only*, *L1L3* Cy fine le d.

Notes

Title and rubric. The title of this poem is listed in the table of contents at the beginning of MS R as *Item le livre des .iij. jugemens qui s'adrece au Senescal de Haynau .xv.* At the top of the folios containing the text itself, that is on folios 71v° through 81r°, the formulation *Le livre des trois jugemens .xv.* appears as a running title, divided between facing pages either after *livre* or after *trois*.

26. In MS R, the word *bien* is added above the line in abbreviated form.

27. The form *soiés* demonstrates the tendency to use final *s* instead of *z* in the present indicative of second-person plural verbs (see also ll. 101, 103, 274, 275, etc.). To distinguish them from second-person singular forms, and to mark the tonic *e*, the final syllable has been marked in this edition with an acute accent.

33. The narrator's recounting of the first case is marked at this line with a capitulum mark, whereas the other two cases begin with two-line initials (ll. 693 and 1269).

46. MSS R and D both use *mate*, the feminine form of the adjective, where the masculine *mat* is required. In R, the same mistake appears at l. 893.

71. In MS R, the first occurrence of *ou* is added above the line.

86. *Elaine* refers to the beautiful Helen, wife of Menelaus, king of Sparta. She was abducted by the Trojan prince Paris, an incident that sparked the Trojan War.

93. The lover flattering his lady compares her to the phoenix, a mythological bird that consumes itself in flames only to rise again from the ashes. The characteristic in question here is that the phoenix is unique, the only one of its kind.

101. In MS R, the word *droit* is added above the line.

107. MS R reads *dueil*, whereas all others use *vueil*. The letter *d* in *dueil* is a correction, with the whole word visible as a preparation in the right margin, suggesting an authorial emendation of this passage.

111. In MS R, the word *ce* is added above the line.

162. MS R reads *penser*, but the letter *r* has an extra horizontal line through it, which corrects it to agree with the form *penses*, as found in the other manuscripts. Lines 161–65 are somewhat difficult to follow. The lover addresses his lady, who has just assured him of her devotion. He tells her that on the basis of this gift (*ce don*, l. 161), he hopes (*j'espoir*, l. 161) to have (infinitive understood rather than expressed) much more (*Trop plus de bien*, l. 162) soon (*a poir*, l. 162) than she might think (*que ne pensés*, l. 162), and the comfort of that joyful hope will cure the lovesickness of which he was dying.

262. The form *armes* is a not uncommon spelling of *ames* in Middle French, and *ames*, the reading found in MS D and phonetically the rhyme required, is likely intended as the primary meaning. Here, the spelling with *r* allows a play on words—the ladies in question are discouraged from trusting those who pledge both soul and arms—as well as an eye rhyme for *larmes* in l. 260.

307–9. These lines are missing in MS R. Line 306, which falls at the beginning of 73v°a, is followed directly by l. 310. The passage has been reinstated following MS D.

365. A two-line decorated letter appears at the head of this line in MS R, obscuring the first words of ll. 365 and 366. MSS D and L both read *Si* and *Q[ue]* at the beginning of these lines, which allows us to complete the text of MS R. The decorated initial is indecipherable; this edition uses an uppercase *S* as appropriate for the word *Si*.

The appearance of an intermediate (two-line) capital at this point in MS R constitutes an inconsistency in the decoration of the text. The major divisions in the poem fall at ll. 33, 693, and 1269, where the case histories Christine the narrator is explaining to her patron begin. All three spots are marked in MSS D and L with capitulum marks. In MS R, the beginning of the second and third cases are marked with intermediate capitals (ll. 693 and 1269; see notes for each line). One would thus have expected to find another at l. 33, but MS R places a capitulum mark there instead. Conversely, the decorated capital is unexpected here, at l. 365; while the line represents a turning point in the development of the first case (and MS D also highlights it by placing a capitulum mark at this spot), it is not as important a transition as the others. The markings for ll. 33 and 365 therefore seem to be reversed.

The explanation might lie in the formulaic phrases used in the text to introduce each of the three cases. The narrator signals their beginning with a sentence using the word *cas* (ll. 33–34, 682–83, 1269–70). Line 365, which begins *Si avint cas*, could well have been mistaken for the start of a new case and marked accordingly when the smaller details of the ornamentation of the text were planned, after the scribe's work was done.

432. In MS R, this line is written in the margin to the right of and slightly higher than l. 433.

437. In MS R, the word *le* is added above the line.

454. In MS R, the word *estoit* is added above the line.

491. The noun *lierre* is part of a complicated play on words in ll. 489–92. It means both "ivy," therefore recalling *ierre* at the end of l. 489, and "thief" in its nominative masculine singular form (of which the oblique form is *larron*). The past participle *emblee* in l. 491, meaning "stolen," is also echoed in the verb form *emble* at the end of l. 492. The passage therefore translates as follows: "And so that love was still greener in him than ivy, [a love] that he had not, by St. Peter, quickly acquired or stolen, like a thief who steals away very early."

493. In MS R, the word *mal* is added above the line.

503. The line is hypometric by one syllable as it appears in MS R unless the final *e* of *estre* is not elided. However, MS D provides the reading *peüst*, which is preferable to the R reading *peut*, because it is consistent with the context and the imperfect subjunctive *voulsissent*, which follows in l. 505. The R reading of *peut* has therefore been rejected in favor of *peüst*.

511. The word *mesdiseurs* is abbreviated in the text. The more common *mesdisans* appears in the other manuscripts, but *mesdiseurs* is an attested form, based perhaps by analogy on the word *diseur*.

515. The first word of this line, *Tout*, is clearly a correction in MS R, intruding

into the left margin and obviously longer than the word it replaces. It provides a better reading than the word *Si*, found in the other manuscripts, in that it avoids the repetition of *si* within the line.

517–19. These three lines are copied in an incorrect order in MS *R* (first *Et racompté;* next *Com souloient;* then *Lors arrivé*). The order is restored by letters in the left margin, reading *c, a,* and *b* in descending order.

534. In MS *R,* the abbreviation for *et* is inserted above the line.

605. In MS *R,* this line is hypermetric by one syllable, reading *Ainsi avoye promis par sacrement.* To correct the meter, *avoye* has been replaced with *a vous,* the reading in *D* and *L.* Another possibility is to replace *sacrement* with the *D* reading *serment,* but retaining the former allows for more variation at the rhyme.

610. MS *R* reads *au bas et dame et moult,* making the line hypermetric, but an expunctuation mark appears clearly under the first *et.*

631. *Escemie* is an orthographic variant of *escremie,* meaning "combat" or "jousting." The consonant combination *cr* is reduced to *c* in l. 706 as well (where *cremoient* is rendered *cemoient*). The word *escremie* is used here with a metaphorical or colloquial sense, meaning flirtatious behavior or granting of favors. (Giuseppe Di Stefano, in *Dictionnaire des locutions en moyen français,* lists the idioms: *jouer de l'excremie, faire le tour de l'excremie,* meaning "exercer sa malice, mais, pour une femme c'est faire la coquette.") In lines 631–34, therefore, the lady is being admonished to confine herself to (*Vous bien garder a*) decorous social interaction or seemly behavior, out of loyalty to her lover.

639. *En,* which appears in MSS *L* but not in *R* or *D,* has been added here to make up the tenth syllable in this line. It should be noted that the syllable count could also be regularized by counting unstressed final *e* in either *ose* or *attendre.*

693–94. As in l. 365, the beginning of l. 693 is marked with a two-line-high capital letter. The letter is readily recognizable as an *I,* to start the word *Il,* in which the *l* is ill aligned. Again as in l. 365, the decorated letter obscures the beginning of the following line, from which *Qu* is missing. Unlike the earlier example, however, the position of this large letter is appropriate, as it signals the start of the second case, following a short preamble by the narrator (ll. 681–92; l. 681 is marked with a capitulum mark).

706. *Cemoient* is an orthographic variant of *cremoient,* from *cremir* or *cremer,* meaning "to fear" (*craindre*).

In this line, the word *souveraine* counts as two syllables. Roy corrects it to read *souvraine,* against all manuscripts, which use *souveraine.* The correction is unnecessary, given that the interior *e* could elide. (See "Versification" in the introduction, and Marchello-Nizia, p. 82.)

749. MS *R* reads *Car sen partir.* While *sen* could be justified as a variant spelling of *sans,* it most likely represents a scribal error, reproducing the second word of the preceding line.

758–59. The word *espars* at the rhyme is used first as a noun (l. 758) and then as an adjective (l. 759). In other words, the "sparkling glances" of the lover's sweet eyes were often "bestowed" on the lady.

813. In MS R, the word *y* is faintly legible above the line.

829. In MS R, the words *nul jour* are added above the line.

847. In MS R, the *n* of *n'attendre* is added above the line. It may have been intended to precede the following word, *autres*, which would have made the line in R agree with the reading in the other manuscripts. With *n* falling before *attendre*, the final, unstressed *e* of that word must be retained rather than elided before the following vowel, in order to maintain the syllable count of the line.

850. The word *dolent* is written with a final *e* in MS R, but that *e* is clearly marked with an expunctuation mark.

855. *Medee* refers to the mythological figure Medea, who fell in love with Jason, leader of the Argonauts. While she is also commonly known for having killed her own children in a rage when Jason rejected her, she is alluded to here as an example of outstanding loyalty. Christine often uses female mythological figures in a purely positive light, choosing selectively from the legends surrounding them those aspects that best illustrate female strength and nobility of character. See note to l. 1455 in *Deux amans* for more information on both Jason and Medea and on references to Medea elsewhere in Christine.

910. In MS R, the words *je demour* are a correction, followed by a decorative filler before the word *qui*. The extra space would have allowed for the reading as found in the other manuscripts (*suis pour vous*), which is rather longer.

957. MS R reads, *Que vous porter en*, whereas MSS D and L read, *Qui vous conduit en*. In MS R, the words *porter en* are a correction. The final *r* in *porter* has been emended in this edition to *z* because the context requires the second-person plural conjugated form of the verb rather than the infinitive.

995. *Ennuyt* is an orthographic variant of *enuit* (*anuit*), meaning "this evening," "tonight."

1035. In MS R, this line is repeated, appearing once as the last line on f. 77v°b and again as the first line on 78r°a.

1073–74. These lines are reversed in MS R. Faint letters in the left margin mark the line beginning *Car a* as *b* and *De chace* as *a*.

1075. *Pyramus* and *Thisbé* (Thisbe, l. 1078) are known as ill-fated young lovers, devoted to each other in defiance of their parents' objections. On a night when they had arranged a tryst, Pyramus mistakenly thought that Thisbe had been killed by a lion, and he committed suicide in his grief. Thisbe then found the body and killed herself as well. They are invoked here as examples of constancy. In *Deux amans*, by contrast, their story is used as proof of the destructive force of love (see note to *Deux amans*, l. 671).

1081. *Que* in MS R can be read here as either a relative subject pronoun, and therefore the equivalent of DL *Qui* (a relatively common usage in Middle French; see Marchello-Nizia, p. 161), or as the conjunction *car*. The same applies to l. 1125.

1129. *El* is an orthographic variant of *elle*. The use of masculine pronouns for the feminine (especially the plural) was not uncommon in Middle French. However, the feminine *el* for *elle* is also attested, in Alain Chartier as well as Christine, for example. Christine uses singular *el* for plural *elles* in her *Dit de la Rose* (l. 105).

1135. In MS *R*, the word *si* is added above the line.

1165. In MS *R*, the word *Et* appears at the beginning of the line, but it has been barred.

1213. *Qu'i* here is an orthographic variant of *qu'il*, in accordance with Middle French usage. (See Marchello-Nizia, p. 160.) For another example, see *Poissy* l. 109 and the note to that line.

1217–19. In MS *R*, these lines appear in an order different from that in the other manuscripts. There is evidence of erasure in the margin next to them, indicating perhaps that they were meant to be labeled to indicate a correction in their sequence. While the alternate reading is perhaps preferable, the text is logical as it stands in *R* and has thus been left untouched in this edition. In l. 1219, the words *fait une aultre* are a correction; this phrase differs from the reading in the equivalent line (1217) in the other manuscripts.

1222. The lady speaks in a broken voice (*la dame . . . ot le parler cas*, l. 1221) because she has dissolved into tears. The verb *chut* is the passé simple of *cheoir*, "to fall."

1245. In MS *R*, the word *Et* appears at the beginning of the line but has been lightly barred.

1269–70. The decorated capital ornamenting these lines should, according to the pattern established by ll. 365 and 693, represent the first letter of the first word of l. 1269. In fact, however, it takes the form of an *I*, the beginning of *Je* in l. 1270 (the *e* of which has been added as a correction in darker ink before the word *vous*). The large capital obscures the first word of l. 1269, which has been restored in this edition according to the other manuscripts (*Et du tiers cas*). Whether the mistake is the result of misplacing the capital or choosing the wrong letter, it once again reminds us of the division of labor which would have dictated that the copying and the decorating of the text be done by different people. Because the third *jugemens* unmistakably begins in l. 1269 and because all the manuscripts mark that line (with a capitulum mark in manuscripts other than *R*), drawing attention to the start of the last tale, this edition corrects MS *R* to use a large *E* at that spot rather than the large *I* actually found there.

1286. *Julian* was made the patron saint of the Cathedral of Le Mans in 1158. He was sent from Rome to Gaul in the mid-third century, and his preaching and miracles are said to have converted the entire tribe of the Cenomani. In the absence of any more direct bearing of this particular saint's legend on the situation described in this passage, it is possible that Saint Julian was chosen here because *du Mans* conveniently rhymes with *amans* of l. 1285.

1302. *S'ay*. MS *R* reads *sçay*, which cannot be correct in the context of the following past participle *ouÿ*. The other manuscripts provide a suitable correction.

1309. In both MSS *R* and *D*, the verb *est* is represented by an abbreviated form that more usually resolves as the conjunction *et*. However, based on the readings of *L*, it should be spelled out as the verb form in this case.

1321. In MS *R*, the last three words of this line, which differ from the reading of the other witnesses, are definitely a correction.

1403. In MS *R*, the last two letters of the word *fust* are added above the line.

1407. In MS *R*, the word *se* is added above the line.

1409. In MS *R*, the word *hault*, which differs from *haultain*, found in the other witnesses, has been corrected to replace a longer word. The rest of the line is also a correction. As a result, however, the syllable count is short by one. The adjective *hault* has therefore been rejected in favor of *haultain*.

1420. In MS *R*, the line reads, *Et se repenti*, but *se* is lightly barred.

1453. In MS *R*, the abbreviated form of the word *et* is added above the line.

1473. In MS *R*, the word *par* is added above the line.

1486. In MS *R*, the word order of this line is somewhat different from that in the other manuscripts. It reverses the order of *juge* and *leal*, with the result that the line is hypermetric by one syllable. Moving *leal* to its position before *juge* allows the unstressed final *e* of *juge* to elide before *on*, restoring the line to ten syllables.

1505. An abbreviation appears at the end of this line in MS *R*, of which the full form, *qu'apparce*, is neither meaningful nor metrically correct. The line has therefore been adapted to agree with the reading of all the other manuscripts.

1518. In MS *R*, the words *les ouÿ*, which differ from the reading of the other manuscripts, are a correction.

1531. As in *Deux amans*, Christine again announces (ll. 1526–27) that her name can be extracted from an anagram in the last line of the text: the words *Crist* and *fine*, minus the *f*, form *C(h)ristine*. She also uses an anagram at the end of *Poissy;* see the note to l. 2075. For critical analysis of Christine's anagrams, see references in note 70 to the Introduction.

Le Livre du Dit de Poissy

Introduction

> Helas! pour Dieu, gracïeuse aux crins blois,
> Ne nous celez,
> Car nous dites vo mal, se vous voulez,
> Car pour vray croy que d'amours vous doulez.
> Mais il n'est nul qui soit plus affolez,
> Las! que j'en suis.
>
> (ll. 1015–20)

Behind the unassuming title of Christine's *Dit de Poissy* lies a remarkably fresh text that confidently pairs a courtly love debate with a vignette of life in a convent. Early critics found the apparent disjunction between the two subject matters disconcerting and read its ironic juxtaposition as demonstrating a lack of coherence. On the contrary, however, the poem contains its disparate material in a tightly controlled structure that capitalizes on the differences in register and spheres of activity to provoke reflection on the relative merits of the two. It makes an appeal to the reader by way of the structural frame to render judgment on the trite themes of love poetry.

Like *Deux amans* and *Trois jugemens*, this poem is made up of self-sufficient units. The dispute between the squire and the lady, which puts the text in the category of judgment poems, is built into the story of a day's outing to the priory of Poissy, where the narrator visits her daughter. Circumscribed by the return journey from Poissy to Paris, the laments of the isolated, lovelorn debaters contrast starkly with the representation of the productive, almost utopian community of nuns. The question of love doctrine under discussion is whether the squire's proximity to and frequent encounters with a woman who rejected him are a greater trial than that of the lady, whose separation from the knight she loves, imprisoned in foreign lands, causes her much suffering. This issue, however, is definitely secondary to the more immediate emotional crisis, namely, which of the two debaters should rightly be declared the more unhappy.

While squire and lady languish, sequestered from their peers by their self-centered despair, the religious sisters of the Dominican priory are fully integrated into a community distinguished by nobility of character and purpose as well as of social rank. By virtue of the maternal and religious devotion that motivate her visit to the priory, Christine the narrator associates herself with the realm of the priory much more than with the world of the debaters. Her involvement in the debate is limited strictly to that of spectator and reporter. Although the point is never taken up as a didactic or moralizing element in the text, life at the priory emerges as infinitely preferable over the trials of love; through the eyes of Christine and her friends, the reader sees the convent as a haven for virtuous women, one in which, moreover, they sacrifice none of the material comforts and refinement to be had in privileged, secular, courtly circles.

Both components of this *dit* contain remarkable passages clothed in conventional terms. The account provided of the grounds, architecture, routines, and inhabitants corroborates and augments archival sources on the Dominican order and its house at Poissy. Christine demonstrates a keen interest in and eye for detail, describing with relish the plumbing system that brings running water to various parts of the priory, the splendid ornamentation of the chapel, the living quarters of the nuns, and the degree of their interaction with the outside world. She lavishes even greater attention here on a community of religious women than on the Parisian town house with which she sets the scene for *Deux amans*. The vocabulary and aesthetic in both reflect secular, aristocratic, courtly ideals; the nuns are every bit as comely and desirable as the ladies at the party, for example. But beneath the familiar veneer lies a report of documentary value, giving to the realistic setting common in late medieval *dits* a much greater specificity of time and place than is usual.

Likewise, the seemingly unexceptional passages in which the squire and lady describe their respective situations include, on the woman's part, a rather bold reworking of well-rehearsed material. The unusual aspect to her portion of the argument is quite simply the parallelism between her part and the squire's. First of all, she is given three hundred lines to his five hundred (ll. 1071–1372; 1390–1876), much closer to parity than in similar debates (such as Guillaume de Machaut's *Jugement dou roy de Behaigne*, for example). In other words, she is allowed a much more extended speech than the lady usually enjoys.

Furthermore, and most surprising, the portrait she gives of her lover matches point for point that given by the squire of his lady. While the adjectives and order of elements—working from head down to toe—are commonplace, we know them from portraits of *women* spoken in a *male* voice. None of the physical attributes standard in those early *blasons* are overlooked in the lady's description of her knight, and she speaks frankly of her attraction to him. The portrait disturbs normative gender expectations of the period by reversing the traditional gaze of male suitor on female beloved, inverting the subject and object of desire. In so doing, it draws fresh attention to its physicality and sensuality, revealing a side of female desire which rarely works its way into courtly texts.

The *Dit de Poissy* rejuvenates old structures with topical references and a larger speaking role for the female protagonist. Of Christine's three debates, this text most strikingly illustrates that convention need not be a constraint. She deftly employs convention, instead, to provide a point of entry into new territory and newly meaningful variations on old themes.

*Le Livre du Dit de Poissy**

    Cy commence le Livre de Poissy qui s'adrece a un estrange
Bon chevalier vaillant, plain de savoir,*   [81r°b]
    Puis qu'il vous plaist a de mes diz avoir
    Et le m'avez par escript fait savoir
    De vostre humblece,   4
Non obstant ce que ma povre foiblece
Ne soit digne que vostre gentillece
S'encline a ce, je tendray la promesse
Que je promis   8
Au messagier que vous m'avez tramis
De loings de ci, et comme a vrays amis
Me recommand a vous de cuer soubmis.
A vo command   12
¶ Si vous envoy faire ce jugement
Dont .ij. amans contindrent durement.
Si m'ont prïee et requis chierement*
Que je leur quiere   16
Juge loyal et que bien en enquiere
Pour droit juger leur descort en maniere*
Qu'i leur en doint sentence droituriere*
Selon raison.   20
Et non obstant qu'en France ait grant foison
Des bons et beaulx qui en toute saison
Saroient droit juger, pour achoison
Du bien de vous   24
Vous ay choisi a juge dessus tous,
Tout non obstant soiés vous loing de nous;
Si en vueillés, s'il vous plaist, Sire doulx,
Le droit jugier.*   28
Et s'il vous plaist a du fait vous charger,
Je vous diray le cas pour abriger;
Comme il avint vous orrés sans targer
Et en quel temps,   32
La ou ce fu vous sera dit par temps,
Car il n'a pas ne mille ne cent ans,
Non pas un mois; ains fu en l'esbatans
Gracïeux mois   36
D'avril le gay, ou reverdissent bois,

¶ Ce present an mil .cccc. ainçois
La fin du mois. Il avint une fois
Que j'os vouloir 40
D'aler jouer; si volz aler veoir
Une fille que j'ay, a dire voir,
Belle, gente, jeune et de bon savoir,
Et gracïeuse 44
Au dit de tous; si est religïeuse
En abbaÿe riche et precïeuse,
Noble, royal et moult delicïeuse;
Et est assise 48
Loing de Paris .vj. lieues celle eglise,
Qui moult faite est de gracïeuse guise.
Poyssi a nom la ville ou elle est mise
Et celle terre. 52
Si apprestay a un lundi mon erre;
Compaignie plaisant envoyay querre
Qui tout plaisir me vouldroient pourquerre
Sans delayer. 56
¶ Si y avoit maint jolis escuyer
Qui de leur bien me vindrent convoyer
Pour esbatre, non pour autre loyer.
Lors a grant joye 60
Nous partismes de Paris; notre voye
Chevauchames et moult joyeuse estoye;
Si furent ceulx qu'avecques moy menoye*
Et toutes celles, 64
Ou il avoit de gentilz damoiselles,
Doulces, plaisans, gracïeuses et belles. [81v°b]
Lors lïeement devisions des nouvelles
Et des estours 68
Qui moult souvent aviennent en amours.
En chevauchant, gayement de maints tours
Nous parlames; n'y ot müés ne sours
Ne nul taysant, 72
Ainçois chacun y aloit devisant
Ce que le mieulx lui estoit aduisant.
¶ La n'avoit dit ne sonné mot cuisant,
Mais tous joyeux; 76
Si y chantoit qui chanter savoit mieulx,

Si hault, si bien, que souvent tous li lieux
Retentissoit, et ainsi qui mieulx mieulx
S'esjouïssoit 80
Chacun en soy et moult resjouïssoit
Le temps nouvel, qui adont commençoit.
¶ Et le souleil clerement reluisoit
Sur l'erbe vert; 84
Tout le chemin y fu plain et couvert
De flourettes, chacune a l'ueil ouvert
Vers le souleil qui luisoit descouvert.
Ne en l'annee 88
Il n'avoit fait si doulce matinee
Et toute fu la terre enluminee
De rosee que le ciel ot donnee,
Qui resplandir 92
Fist l'erbe vert pour tous cuers esbaudir.
La n'avoit riens pour la terre enlaidir;
Tout estoit bel pour amans enhardir
A bien amer. 96
¶ Par mi ces pres, Nature ot fait semer
Marguerites et flours qu'on sieust nommer
Flour de printemps; par tout veist on germer
Maintes diverses 100
Herbes et flours qui a la terre aherses
Encor furent, vertes, rouges et perses,*
Jaunes, yndes, qui males ne diverses
Ne furent mie. 104
La ot la flour de ne-m'oublïez-mie,
Souviengne-vous-de-moy, qui n'est blesmie
Mais vermeille, dont amant et amye [82r°a]
Font chappellés 108
Et qu'i mettent souvent en anelés*
Par devises et autres jouuelés
Qu'ilz se donnent jolis et nouvellés
Par drüerie. 112
¶ Ainsi adont fu la terre flourie,
Mais il n'est nul qui deist la chanterie
Des oysillons qui de voix tres serie
Nottes nouvelles 116
Chantoient hault, et ces alloes belles

En l'air seri disoient les nouvelles
Du doulx printemps, chantans a voix isnelles
Et a haulx sons.   120
Sur ces arbres et par my ces buissons
Ces oysillons disoient leurs chançons;
La pouïst on ouÿr maintes leçons
De rossignolz*   124
Qui disoient leur virelais mignos.
Et pastoures, qui gardoient aigneaulx,
Leur chappellés faisoient a lignos
Par my ces champs,   128
Tous purs de flours, en escoutant les chans
Des oysillons et par buissons crochans.
Pres de Saine venismes approchans
A lie chiere;   132
Si fist plus bel ancor sur la riviere,
Car oysillons de plus lie maniere
Par ces isles a haulte voix planiere
Se deduisoient   136
Si liement que tous esjouïssoient
Les cuers de nous, et trop fort nous plaisoient
Arbres et prez qui par tout verdissoient
¶ Et ces saussayes   140
Reverdissans et les jolies voyes
Souef flairans, ces buissons et ces hayes
Ou rossignolz disoient chançons gayes,
Et le doulx bruire   144
De l'eaue qui en courant faisoit bruire
Ces gors, ces pieux, pour noz cuers plus deduire,*
Si qu'il n'est dueil qui la ne deüst fuire
N'estre remis.   [82r°b]   148
Adont d'errer nous sommes entremis
Pour estre la a l'eure qu'os promis.*
Alors fiché s'est entre nous et mis
Un ventelés   152
Doulx et plaisant, qui noz cours mantelés
Nous souslevoit, souef et frechelés.
C'est zephirus qui boutons nouvellés
Fait espanir   156
Et ces belles, doulcetes flours venir

Et aux amans donne maint souvenir
De leurs amours; pour ce voult survenir
En celle place   160
Que le souleil ne gatast notre face.
Ce fist Amours, ce croy je, de sa grace,
Qui l'envoya ainsi en cel espace.
¶ Par le serain   164
Chevauchames tant que tous main a main
Arrivames, ancor ert assez main,
Au bel chastel qui a nom Saint Germain
Qu'on dit en Laye.   168
Adont entrer nous couvint en la gaye
Doulce forest, mais ou monde n'a laye
Gent ne letrez qui nel scet ou essaye,
Qui peüst croire   172
Le doulx deduit du lieu, car j'ay memoire
Que tout ainsi comme a marché ou foire,
S'assemblent gent a tas, c'est chose voire.
Avoit a tant   176
De rossignolz en cellui lieu chantant,
Qui ça et la aloient voletant,
Qu'onques, je croy, ensemble on n'en vid tant
Comme il ot cy,   180
Qui disoient: "Ocy! ocy! ocy*
Le faulx jaloux së il passe par cy,
Sans le prendre n'a pitié n'a mercy*
En no pourpris."   184
Et la forest espece que moult pris
Reverdissoit, si qu'en hault furent pris
L'un a l'autre les arbres qui repris
Sont, et planté   188
Moult pres a pres li chesne a grant planté   [82v°a]
Hault, grant et bel, non mie en orphanté;
Ce scevent ceulx qui le lieu ont hanté,
Si que souleil*   192
Ne peut ferir a terre a nul recueil
Et l'erbe vert, freche et belle a mon vueil,
Est par dessoubs; n'on ne peut veoir d'ueil
Plus belle place   196
A mon avis, et qui peut face a face

La ses amours veoir ou les embrace,
Je ne cuide mie que pou lui place,
Car c'est deduit 200
Trop avenant que d'estre en ce reduit
Ou doulx printemps ou oysillons sont duit
De demener leur solas et leur bruit
Ou temps d'esté. 204
Si croy pour vray qu'Amours ot appresté
A cellui jour toute gaye honnesté;
Aussi croyent ceulx qui orent esté
O moy le jour, 208
Car d'esbatre ne cessames tousjour,
Rire et jouer et chanter sans sejour
Ou deviser d'aucun parti d'amour.
Et la forest 212
Nous passames et veismes sans arrest*
Droit a Poissi, ou tost trouvames prest
Quanqu'il couvint et tout ce qui bon est
A droit souffire. 216
⁋ Quant dessendus fusmes, chacun s'atire
Le mieulx qu'il peut de vesture et se mire
Si qu'en l'atour il n'y ait que redire.
Et puis alames 220
En l'abaÿe ensemble vers les dames
Au parlouer, et puis dedens entrames,
Tout non obstant que portes a grans lames
Y ait moult fortes; 224
Mais par congié on ot ouvert les portes.
La trouvasmes dames de belles sortes,
Car il n'y ot contrefaites ne tortes,
Mais moult honnestes 228
Des vestemens et des atours des testes, [82v°b]
Simples, sages et a Dieu servir prestes.
La nous firent noz amies grans festes
Et lie chiere. 232
Adont celle que j'aim moult et tiens chiere
Vint devers moy, de tres humble maniere
S'agenoilla, et je baysay sa chiere
Doulcete et tendre, 236
Puis main a main alames sans attendre

En l'eglise pour service a Dieu rendre.
Si oÿmes la messe et congié prendre
Vosmes aprés, 240
¶ Mais les dames si nous prïerent tres
De boire un coup, et ylec assez pres
Nous menerent en lieu bel, cler et fres
Pour desjuner, 244
Car n'estoit pas ancor temps de disner.
Mais n'osmes pas loisir de sejourner
La longuement ne gaires de resner,
¶ Quant la songneuse 248
Et tres vaillant, noble religïeuse,
Ma redoubtee dame gracïeuse,
Marie de Bourbon, qui est prïeuse*
De celle place, 252
Tante du roy de France, en qui s'amasse
Toute bonté et qui tout vice efface,
Si nous manda de sa benigne grace
Quë aillissions 256
Devers elle, ne point ne laississions,
Joyeux fusmes de ce, ne voulsissions
Que sans veoir elle nous yssissions
De ce pourpris. 260
Si nous sommes .ij. a .ij. entrepris
Et alames vers la dame de pris.
Par les degrez de pierre que moult pris
En hault montasmes 264
Ou bel hostel royal que nous trouvasmes
Moult bien paré, et en sa chambre entrasmes
De grant beauté, si nous agenoullames
Lors devant elle, 268
Et la tres humble dame nous appelle [83r°a]
Plus pres de soy et de mainte nouvelle
Nous aresna doulcement, comme celle
En qui humblece 272
A et bonté et tout sens et noblece.
¶ Et tost aprés, la tres noble princesse,
Fille du roy, qui venoit de la messe
Et est rendue 276
En cellui lieu et voilee et vestue,

A Dieu servir donnee et esleüe,
A qui honneur est donnee et deüe,
Entre en la chambre.   280
C'est ma dame Marie, jeune et tendre;*
Mais ne fu pas seule, bien m'en remembre,
Ains mainte dame ot o soy, dont la mendre
Fu gentil femme,   284
Noble, poissant, et avec celle dame
Fu la noble fille de bonne fame*
Du conte de Harecourt, ait son ame
Dieu qui ne fine,   288
Qui pres estoit sa parente et cousine.
Et adont ma dame, sans plus termine,
La prïeuse se lieve et si l'encline,*
Si fimes nous   292
Tres humblement; si nous receut trestous
Si doulcement que ja ne fussions saoulz
D'elle veoir, tant a le maintien doulx
Et humble chiere.   296
¶ Si nous plut moult a veoir la maniere
Du bel estat royal qui leans yere,
Toutes dames, car en nulle maniere
N'y entreroit   300
Pour les servir nul homme; on n'y lairoit,
Ne a elles aucun ne parleroit,
S'il n'est parent ou ceulx qu'il y menroit
Avecques lui;   304
N'on n'y lairoit jamais entrer nullui
Fors par congié, a dongier, n'a par lui
N'entre dedens seul, n'il n'y a cellui
Non en couvent.   308
Ne je ne sçay së il leur va grevant,
Mais jamais jour pour pluye ne pour vent   [83r°b]
De la n'istront et ne voient souvent
Les gens estranges.   312
Et de belles plusieurs y a comme anges.*
Si n'y vestent chemises, et sus langes
Gisent de nuis; n'ont pas coustes a franges
Mais materas   316
Qui sont couvers de beaulx tapis d'Arras

Bien ordenez, mais ce n'est que baras,
Car ilz sont durs et emplis de bourras;*
Et la, vestues, 320
Gisent de nuis celles dames rendues,
Qui se lievent ou elles sont batues*
A matines. La leurs chambres tendues
En dortouer 324
Ont pres a pres, et en refretouer
Disnent tout temps, ou a beau lavouer;
Et en la court y a le parlouer
Ou a treillices 328
De fer doubles a fenestres coulices,
Et la endroit les dames des offices
A ceulx dehors parlent pour les complices
Et neccessaires 332
Qu'il leur couvient et fault en leurs afaires.
¶ Si ont prevosts, seignouries et maires,*
Villes, chasteaulx, rentes de plusieurs paires
Moult bien assises; 336
Et riches sont, ne nulles n'y sont mises
Fors par congié du roy, qui leurs franchises
Leur doit garder; et maintes autres guises
A la endroit 340
Dont me tairay, car qui compter vouldroit
Toutes choses longuement y mettroit.
¶ Si tourneray a parler or endroit
Comment prenimes 344
De noz dames congié et nous en veismes,*
Mais ne l'osmes mie quant le requismes,
Tout non obstant notre devoir en feismes.
Ains voult, ainçois 348
Que partissions, que beussions une fois
Ma dame la prïeuse; a basse vois
Moult nous pria, par doulx maintien courtois, [83v°a]
De desjuner, 352
Car en ce lieu nullui n'ose disner.
Si nous couvint son vueil enteriner,
Et par plusieurs dames nous fist mener
En une chambre 356
Belle, plaisant, la ou ot fait estendre

Nappes blanches, flairans, et tapis tendre,
Vins, viandes apporter sans attendre,*
A grant largece,   360
En vaisseaulx d'or et d'argent, par noblece.
Et les dames plaines de gentillece,
Ou voulsissions ou non, de leur humblece
S'entremettoient   364
De nous servir et les mes apportoient
Delicïeux, et goute n'en goustoient,
Dont nous pesoit fort, et moult se penoient
D'umble maniere   368
De nous servir; Dieux leur rende la chiere
Qu'ilz nous firent liement, sanz enchiere.
¶ Et aprés ce, devers ma dame chiere
Nous retournasmes   372
Prendre congié et la remerciasmes,
Puis les degrez du palais avalasmes;
Vers le couvent de rechief nous alasmes*
Pour congié prendre   376
Des dames de leans, car point mesprendre
Ne voulsissions; et lors nous vindrent prendre
Par my les mains et nous voldrent aprendre
Le tres bel estre   380
De cellui lieu qui fu fait de bon maistre,
Car ce semble droit paradis terrestre.
Si nous firent devaler en leur cloistre
Qui tant est bel   384
Que plus plaisant depuis le temps Abel
Ne fu veüs, car maint jolis chambel
Y a ouvré, et sur maint fort corbel
Sont soustenues   388
Les grans voultes haultes devers les nues,
Et par dessoubz pavees de menues
Pierres faites a ouvrages, et nues
Luisans et belles,   392
Et tout entour a haultes colombelles   [83v°b]
Bien ouvrees a fueillage et tourelles
D'entailleure de pierre; ainsi sont elles
En tous les lieux   396
Du cloistre grant, largë et spacïeux

Qui est quarré; et affin qu'il soit mieulx,
A un prael ou milieu gracïeux,
Vert, sans grappin, 400
Ou a planté ou my un tres hault pin,
Ne fu veüs plus bel depuis Pepin,
Si est fueillu et plus droit qu'un sappin;
Bien y avient. 404
Aprés ou refrestouer on revient
Qui tant est bel que pas ne me souvient
Qu'onques si bel lieu visse, et si contient
Moult grant espace. 408
Hault, grant et cler est et luisant com glace,
Les voirrieres y sont de belle face,
Et de menus carreaulx par la terrace
Est tout pavé 412
Et si tres net qu'il semble estre lavé.
Et pres de la le chapitre est trouvé
Qui est moult bel et gentement ouvré.
¶ A brief parler, 416
Par tant de lieux beaulx on nous fist aler
Que du veoir ne poions säouler,
Ne nulle part n'y a que regaler,
Tant sont plaisans, 420
Et en esté delitable et raisans.
Mais de compter ne doy estre taysans
Comment par tout pour estre plus aysans
Vient la fontaine 424
Clere, freche, doulce, plaisant et saine,
Quë en ce lieu sourt de dois et de veine*
Et par tuyaulx vait par leans, n'a peine
A il reduit 428
Nezun leans, grant ne petit, je cuid,
Ou ne voise fontaine par conduit.
Es cuisines es grans pierres y bruit
Toudis et chiet 432
A grans gorgions, ne nul temps n'y dechet;*
Ainsi par tout leans ou il eschiet [84r°a]
Est assise, dont moult bien en enchiet
A mains affaires 436
Qui sont ou lieu qui de repos n'ont gaires.

Tonnes a vin, celliers de plusieurs paires,
Fours, despences et autres neccessaires
Tous a compas 440
Y sont assis, car en ce lieu n'a pas
Petit couvent, mais plus grant qu'au Hault Pas.*
Ainsi par tout nous trassames maint pas
Et par grans cours 444
Larges, longues plus d'un cheval le cours,
Ou grans chantiers de buche furent sours,
Bien pavees et belles a tous tours.*
Mais ancor vorent 448
Plus nous monstrer les dames qui moult sorent,
Car leur dortoir ordonné comme ilz l'orent
Et leurs beaulx lis qui sus cordes fait orent
Ilz nous monstrerent; 452
Mais en ce lieu de noz hommes n'entrerent
Nul quel qu'il fust, car hommes ne monterent
Oncques mais la; par droit s'en deporterent
A celle fois. 456
Si est moult bel, grant, large, cler et coys,
Bien ordonné et fait en tous endrois,
Si qu'il pert bien qu'il fu fondé de roys
Et de grant gent 460
Qui espargné n'orent or në argent.
¶ Aprés tout ce, li degré bel et gent
Descendismes; trouvasmes notre gent
Et de rechief 464
Vosmes aler au moustier, ou maint chef
A de maint saint; si vosmes en tout chef*
Considerer le lieu, mais ja a chef
Je ne venroye 468
De deviser la beauté qu'i veoye,
Car tant est bel, hault, cler, se Dieu me voye,
Que sa beauté retraire ne saroye
Entierement, 472
Et ce semble estre fait tout nouvelment,
Tant est fin blanc, et le maçonnement [84r°b]
Et ens et hors fait si joliement,
C'on ne pourroit 476
D'or ne d'argent ouvrer en nul endroit

Mieulx c'ouvrees sont pierres la endroit.
A brief parler, a souhaitier fauldroit
Qui vouldroit mieulx; 480
Et si est grant et large, se m'ayst Dieux,
Et hault voulté a pillers gracïeux
Qui soustiennent l'edifice et li lieux
Moult bien ouvrez. 484
¶ Et le moustier est en .ij. decevrez
Affin que homme d'elles ne soit navrez;
N'y entreroit nezun pour dire, "Ouvrez!,"
Ne d'aventure, 488
Car ou milieu il a une closture
Qui le moustier separe sans rousture;
Ceulx qui disent la messe et l'escripture
De l'euvangile 492
Si sont dehors et les gens de la ville,
Et en la nef sont les dames sans guille
Qui respondent de haulte voix abille
A ceulx dehors, 496
Et de leurs voix femenines accors
Font gracïeux, et vigilles de mors,
Nonne, vespres, matines et recors
Chantent leans. 500
¶ Mais il n'est nul, tant fust il cler veans,
Qui racontast, et tout seroit neans,
Comment toutes choses y sont seans,
Ne je n'en mens; 504
Car il y a tant de beaulx aournemens,
Riches, nouveaulx, et nobles paremens
Sur les autelz et tous estoremens,
Et ces dorures 508
Sur chappitiaulx et pommiaulx a pointures
D'or et d'asur, et tant belles paintures,*
Biaulx ymages et propres pourtraitures
Selon la guise 512
Quë il couvient a paremens d'eglise,
Qu'il n'est chose qui n'y soit a droit mise, [84vºa]
Dont les dames et le lieu chacun prise
En tous affaires, 516
Car devotes, sages et debonnaires,

Simples, doulces sont; et portent .ij. paires*
De vestures, car fros et capulaires,
Et leur gonnelle, 520
Qui est dessoubz, blanche est quom noif nouvelle,
Large, flotant, çainte soubz la mamelle;
Mantel de noir ont dessus, n'y a celle
Qui autre arroy 524
Ait de vestir, nez la fille du roy;
Et de ventres de connins, sanz desroy,
Sont leurs manteaulx fourrez de bon conroy,
Mais bien ont robes 528
De bon fins draps, ce ne sont mie lobes,
Tout ne soient ne mignotes ne gobes,
Blanches, nettes, sans ordures ne bobes,
Et cuevrechiefs* 532
Blans comme noif delïez sur leurs chefs,
Et un voile noir dessus atachez.
Sans cointise, simplement, sans pechez
Sont atournees, 536
¶ Et en tous cas si bien sont ordonnees
Que je les tiens pour de bonne heure nees
D'estre ensement a servir Dieu donnees.
Si leur souffit? 540
Ouÿl, je croy, car c'est leur grant prouffit,
Në oncques mais nulle ne si meffit
Et bien leur plaist servir Dieu qui les fit
En celle guise. 544
¶ Quant nous osmes bien remiré l'eglise,
Clere com jour et couverte de bise
Pierre ardoise, bien taillee et assise
Comme il couvient, 548
Et tout le lieu qui grant place contient,
Encor dïent que veoir nous couvient
Leurs beaulx vergiers, la ou maint bon fruit vient.
Si nous menerent 552
En leurs jardins, celles qui se penerent
De nous faire plaisir, et ne finerent [84vºb]
Tant que lëens fumes, ne s'en tanerent;
Mais pour voir dis 556
Que ce semble estre un tres doulx paradis,

Et y est on tout d'oysiaulx essourdis,
Car la, je croy, plus de .lx. et dix
Y a de paires 560
D'abres portans fruis, et est cilz repaires*
Tout de beaulx murs bien clos, në il n'est gaires
Choses estans en jardins neccessaires
Qui la ne soient. 564
Et un beau clos y a que moult prisoient
Ceulx et celles qui en la place estoient;
La y a dains a cornes qui couroient
Moult vistement, 568
Lievres, connins y sont habondanment,
Et .ij. viviers la sourdans proprement,
Bien façonnez de tout estorement,
Plains de poisson; 572
Chevriaulx y a sauvages a foison.
Qu'en diroie? Ja en nulle saison
Ne fussions las d'estre en celle maison,
¶ Se Dieux me gart, 576
Tant y fait bel. Mais ja estoit moult tart
Temps de disner au couvent ou sa part*
Celle perdroit qui y vendroit a tart,
Et durement 580
Reprise fust, et adont haultement
Ont le timbre sonné; departement
Couvint faire lors bien hastivement
A grant reclaim, 584
Et ma fille, qui toudis par la main
M'aloit tenant, de cuer de desir plain
Moult me prioit a jusque a lendemain
De sejourner, 588
Et retourner leans aprés disner
Nous voulsissions; adont falu finer
Nostre parler et notre erre ordener.
Et la portiere, 592
Bonne et sagë, et de doulce maniere,*
¶ Et celles qui tant nous firent grant chiere, [85r°a]
Merciasmes; adont la clacelliere
A desserrees 596
Les grans portes fortes et bien barrees,

Hors yssimes, puis les ont reserrees.
Mais de celles qui la sont demourees
Et de la place 600
N'y a cellui qui grant compte ne face.
Tout en parlant vimmes en pou d'espace
Ou lieu qu'on dit Bourbon, ou gent s'amasse*
Pour bien logier; 604
La trouvasmes tout prest notre mengier,
Si assismes au disner sans targer,
Mais n'avions pas besoing de nous charger
De grant viande. 608
¶ Mais on feroit bien une grant legende
Du lonc parler, de la chiere tres grande
Qu'on nous ot fait, et du lieu ou lavande
Croit et rosiers 612
A grant foison, sans façon de closiers,
C'est es jardins ou a maint cerisiers,
Et du beau lieu qui n'est pas cloz d'osiers,
Mais de cloison 616
Fort et belle, pour oster l'achoison
Des maulx qu'on fait au monde a grant foison.
¶ Ainsi fu la dicte mainte raison,
Et puis lavames 620
Aprés disner noz mains et nous levames,
Et tout en piez une piece parlames,
Puis reposer un petit nous alames,
¶ Tant qu'il fust temps 624
De retourner ou lieu si delitens,
Car, quant a moy, me sembloit bien .c. ans
Que g'i fusse, mais gueres arrestans
N'y fumes mie 628
Aprés disner, je croy, heure et demie
Quant celle qui et maistresse et amie*
De ma fille est, nous manda; endormie
Ne fus lors pas 632
Et de dormir oz ja fait mon repas.
Si esveillay les autres et le pas [85r°b]
Nous alames, en devisant tout bas,
Jusques aux lices 636
De la grant court dehors ou edefices

            A grans et beaulx pour les gens des offices
            Qui sont au lieu neccessaire et propices.
            De la nous vimmes   640
            Au parlouer; longuement nous y times,
            Car d'entrer ens a peine nous chevimes
            Et requerir de grace le feÿmes
            A la tres sage   644
            Ma dame la prïeuse au grant courage,
            Car d'entrer ens .ij. fois n'est pas usage,
            N'a estrangiers në a ceulx du lignage,
            Non en un jour.   648
        ¶ Mais bien estrë y voulsissions tousjour,
            Car aux hommes trop plaisoit la doulçour
            De ces dames qui de moult simple atour
            Furent voillees,   652
            Si ne furent ne noires ne hallees,
            Mais comme lis blanches et potellees.
            Si sont de nous les nouvelles alees
            Devers ma dame   656
            Qui l'enter ens souffry; ce fu, par m'ame,
            A grant peine, car pour tant s'elle est fame
            De tel honneur, si craint elle le blame
            Des ancïennes.   660
        ¶ Quant ens fumes, les dames tres humaines
            Nous menerent ou jardin vers fontaines;
            La nous simes et de choses mondaines
            Pou devisames: 664
            Ne parlames d'amours ne ne dansames,
            Ains enquismes tout et leur demandasmes
            De leur ordre les poins, et n'y pensasmes
            Decepcion;   668
            La n'ot parlé fors de devocion,
            De Dieu servir en bonne entencion,
            Et d'oroisons et de la Passion
            Et de tieulx choses,   672
            Car les belles, plus frechetes que roses,
            Qui moult jeunes furent ou lieu encloses,   [85v°a]
            N'oyent parler fors de si faites proses
            En nul endroit,   676
            Et grant pechié feroit qui leur touldroit

Leur bon propos. Et quant fu temps et droit
De nous partir, lors nous levames droit
Pour congié prendre, 680
Car demourer la trop on peut mesprendre.
Mais nous couvint le vin ainçois atendre,
Si mengiames et bumes, et reprendre
De leurs joyaulx 684
Il nous couvint: non fermilles nouviaulx,
Mais boursettes ouvrees a oysiaulx
D'or et soye, çaintures et las biaulx
Moult bien ouvrez, 688
Quë autre part ne sont tieulx recouvrez.
¶ Si leur deismes: "Dames, or nous ouvrez,
Temps est d'aler; a peine decevrez
De vous serons, 692
Mais guerredonner jamais ne vous pourons
Ne mercïer assez, et ou sarons
Voz bons servans estre toudiz vouldrons,
Et commander 696
Vous nous pouez et au besoing mander
Com les vostres, s'il vous plait demander."
Ainsi parlant venimes sans tarder
Tout a loisir 700
Vers la porte; lors failli mon plaisir,
Si que des yeulx couvint larmes issir
Quant je baisay celle ou j'ay mon desir,
Qui m'est prochaine. 704
En la baysant lui dis "a Dieu" a peine,
En l'ennortant qu'a Dieu servir se peine;
Et de toutes pris congié, mate et veine,
Et par pitié. 708
Mais ceulx qui la furent de m'amistié
Me blasmerent, dont j'oz cuer dehaitié,
Et a parler prirent d'autre dictié
Pour m'oublïer 712
Et moy tollir a merencolïer,
Dont je les dos de leur bien mercïer.*
Ainsi parlant alions sans detrïer [85v°b]
A voix serie, 716
¶ Tant qu'au logis a notre hostellerie

Fumes venus, ou une gallerie
A par dessoubs une place flourie,
Moult belle et gente, 720
Et un jardin joli ou a mainte ante;
Lors d'entrer ens nous meismes a la sente.*
Quant y fumes, adoncques sanz attente,
A chiere lie 724
Une belle damoiselle jolie
Jeune, gente, gaye, fresche et polie,
Qui fu o nous, dist sans merencolie:
"Si que ferons?* 728
Se vous me creez, trestous nous danserons
Et la quarole ci commencerons."
Lors dirent tous: "Ne vous en desdirons."
¶ Si commença 732
La danse adonc et chacun se pensa
De sa chançon dire; si s'avança
Celle qui au premier les empressa
Et sa chançon 736
Dist haultement et de gracïeux son,
Ou il avoit en la prime leçon:
"Tres doulx ami de bien amer penson."
Et puis aprés, 740
Un escuyer qui d'elle fu emprés,
Qui moult courtois est et bel et doulx tres,
Et voulentiers de chanter est engrés,
Voix enrouee 744
Il n'avoit pas, mais doulce et esprouvee,
Si a dit lors, ne sçay s'il l'ot trouvee,
"Gente de corps et de beauté louee."
Et de renc puis 748
Chacun chanta tant qu'il fu pres de nuis,
¶ Car le dancier ne tournoit a anuis
A nul qui fust. Si fu le soupper cuis,
Ce nous dist on, 752
Adonc de la dance nous departon
Ou il avoit maint joli valeton,
Mainte belle pucelle a doulx menton,
Mignote et gente; [86r°a] 756
N'estions pas seuls, mais bien, que je ne mente,

Y avoit la, ce croy je, plus de .xxx.,
Tous jeune gent et de joyeuse entente,
Que de noz gens 760
Que d'autre gent, trestous mignos et gens,
Qui de servir deduit sont diligens
Et bien semblent d'Amours estre sergens
Moult amiables. 764
¶ Congié prirent, adont seismes aux tables
Qui ou jardin soubz treilles delitables
Furent mises. Adont les mets notables
Nous apporterent 768
Noz meisgnees, mais ne se deporterent
Mië atant, ainçois nous presenterent
Celles que Dieux et noblece ennorterent
A tous bien fais, 772
Car ma dame la prïeuse un beau mais
Nous envoya et de son bon vin, mais
De meilleur vin ne bura homs jamais
De Saint Poursain,* 776
En pos dorez largement et a plain.
Pour ce le fist qu'o nous avoit tout plain
Des gens du roy, vaillans et de sens plain,
Tres noble gent. 780
Si rendismes les beaulx vaisseaulx d'argent,
Humble merci en nous moult obligent
A ma dame, et mercy a son sergent
Qui l'aporta. 784
Mais le couvent pas ne se deporta,
Car de par les dames nous ennorta
Un messagier salu et rapporta
Bonnes goyeres 788
Bien sucrees, bien faites et legieres,
Pommes, poires de diverses manieres.
Lors de leurs biens et de leurs bonnes chieres
Les merciasmes. 792
Et aprés ce d'autre chose parlames
Et en propos de plusieurs cas entrasmes
Et d'un et d'el la endroit devisames,
Tant qu'il avint 796
Quë a parler des chevaliers on vint; [86r°b]

De ce royaume et d'autres plus de .xx.
Furent nommez et de plusieurs souvint,
En celle place, 800
Qui ont bonté, sens et valour et grace.
Qui plus a fais de beaulx fais et qui passe
Autres en pris fu dit en cel espace,
Et qui se porte 804
Se vaillamment que renom on lui porte
En toutes pars, tant est de gentil sorte,
Et ou prouece et valour n'est pas morte
Fu racompté. 808
Et ceulx qui plus ont les armes hanté
Et les hantent, et qui plus seurmonté
Ont en beaulx fais, et ceulx qui voulenté
Ont et desir 812
De faire bien, et qui ont leur plaisir
De voyager ne ne prennent loisir
De nul repos et ne veulent choisir
Autre deport, 816
Li quieulx sont bel et li quieulx jeune et fort
Et qui le mieulx se revenche de tort.
Ainsi de ceulx lors devisames fort
A lonc sermons. 820
¶ Et adonc vous, Sire, que je semons
Du jugement juger, entre les bons
Fustes nommé, pour tant s'oultre les mons
Estes adés, 824
Car voyager plus que Cleomadés,*
Vray fin amant comme Palamedés,*
Fustes nommé, et bien leur souvint des
Beaulx vassellages 828
Quë avez fais plusieurs fois en voyages
Et corps a corps rabatus les oultrages
De mains autres et portez les grans charges
En mainte guerre; 832
Et la fu dit qu'il ne couvenoit querre
Nul chevalier meilleur en nulle terre,
Ce savoit on en France et Engleterre
Et oultre mer, 836
Et en mains lieux ailleurs, ainsi nommer

Vous ouÿ bon et pour voir affermer [86v°a]
Que plus loyal oncques es fais d'amer
Ne fu de vous, 840
Bel, gracïeus, franc, amiable et doulx;
Ce disoient plusieurs qui avec nous
Furent venus, et noble gens trestous,
Qui congnoissoient 844
Vous et voz fais et de bien en disoient,
Si largement que voulentiers louoient
Ceulx et celles qui en la place estoient,
Et de dicter, 848
Meisme en françois, et gayement chanter
Vous louoient, et voulentiers hanter
Dames d'onneur, pour plus en vous enter
Toute noblece. 852
¶ Lors quant j'ouÿ parler de vo sagece,
Comme autre fois aye de vo prouece
Oye parler, je fis une promesse
Que je feroye 856
Aucun beau dit et si l'envoyeroye
A vous, Sire, quant messagier aroie,
Car voulentiers vostre acointe seroie
En tout honneur,* 860
Car a tous bons on doit avoir amour.
Adont ot un lors qui dit sanz demour
Quë ou paÿs ou vous estes un tour,*
Et sans targier, 864
Devoit aler, et se de ce charger
Le vouloie, voulentiers messager
Il en seroit. Et adonc du menger
Sommes levé, 868
Dites graces aprés qu'osmes lavé;
Tout en parlant par dessus le pavé
Sommes alez jouer tant que trouvé
Avons les champs, 872
Ou grant deduit prenions d'oÿr les chans*
Des rossignolz quant fumes approchans
Des islettes sur Saine ou accrochans
Engins avoit, 876
Res et fillez pour prendre la endroit

Le gros poisson se celle part venoit.* [86v°b]
Et moult jolis paÿs entour soy voit
Qui la demeure, 880
Car pres et boys et saussois qu'on labeure
On peut veoir, et vignes par desseure.
La chantasmes et jouasmes une heure
Tant qu'il fu nuit; 884
Si laissames atant notre deduit,
Car il fu temps de soy traire au reduit;
Lors devisant, sans riens qui nous ennuit,
Nous en tournasmes 888
¶ A nostre hostel ou a joye couchames.
Et au matin la messe ouÿr alames,
Prismes des dames congié puis montasmes
Sur haquenees 892
Grosses, belles, gentement ordenees,
Qui ains partir furent bien desjunees,
Si fumes nous pour ce que matinees
Furent longuettes. 896
Lors au chemin par ou croiscent herbetes
Nous sommes mis, et de fleurs nouvelletes
Osmes chappiaulx, et parlant d'amourettes
Chevauchions fort 900
Par la forest plaine de grant deport
Dont oysillons font maint divers accort,
Qui aux amans fist plus poignant recort
De leurs amours. 904
¶ Lors s'avança en chevauchant tous jours
La plus belle de toutes, et le cours
Bien d'un cheval fu loing, et par destours
Aloit pensive. 908
Mais les autres chantoient a l'estrive
Et quant je vy celle si ententive
A fort penser, doubtay que maladive
Fust ou dolente, 912
Car pallie trop estoit et moult lente
A soulacier, peu y avoit s'entente.
Pour ce oz paour que d'aucun mal en sente
Fust ou troublee 916
Pour quelque cas. Lors un de l'assemblee

Qui voulsist bien avoir amour emblee, [87r°a]
Ce croy je bien, et aucune affublee
D'amour entiere, 920
Vois appeller. Në en la place n'yere
Nul escuyer de plus gente maniere,
Ne plus gentil ne de meilleure chiere,
Mais souspirant 924
Aloit souvent; bien croy qu'en desirant
Avoit maint mal. Lors dis en lui tirant:
"Beau sire, veez com celle retirant
Se va lontaine 928
De nous; certes, je me doubt qu'elle ait peine
De quelque ennuy, ou qu'elle ne soit saine.
Vers elle alons, qu'elle ne soit trop veine
Ou a mal aise, 932
Car ne cuid pas que sans cause se tayse."
Et cil respont et dit: "Par saint Nicaise,*
Aler y fault, car elle n'est pas ayse,
Ce croy je bien." 936
Lors son cheval brocha et je le mien;
En peu d'eure aconsuivismes le sien.
¶ Si lui dis lors: "Quel chiere? Avez vous rien
Qui bon ne soit 940
Qui si pensez?" Et celle demussoit*
Son visagë, et pour ce le baissoit,
Que trop grief plour durement la pressoit;
Ne vouloit mie 944
Qu'apperceussions que lerme ne demie
De l'ueil gitast, ne qu'elle fust blesmie.
Et quant celle qui moult estoit m'amie
Je vy plourer, 948
Trop m'en pesa, et lors sans demourer
M'en tiray pres, car moult volz labourer
A ce savoir qui si fort acourer
Fist la dolente. 952
Si lui priay de toute mon entente
Que l'achoison me deïst sans attente
Qui la troubloit, et pour quoy se demante
Si durement. 956
Adont celle prist plus parfondement

A souspirer et pleurer tendrement.
¶ Quant l'escuyer perceust le plourement, [87r°b]
Tant en ot dueil 960
Que les lermes lui en vindrent a l'ueil,
Et com cellui ou tout bien ot recueil,
Tres doulcement lui dist et de bon vueil:
"Ma damoiselle 964
Doulce, plaisant, tres gracïeuse et belle,
Ne nous celez desplaisir ou nouvelle
Que vous ayés, car je vous jur, par celle
Vierge Marie 968
Qui Dieu porta, qu'en vous sera tarie
La grief doulour dont je vous voy marrie
Se c'est chose qui puist estre garie
Par mon labour. 972
Si vous requier et pri par grant amour,
Ne nous celez vostre tres grant doulour,
Car bien savez qu'en tous cas votre honnour
Vouldrions garder. 976
Si nous dites vostre cas sans tarder,
Et puis vous plaise a dire et commander,
Se nullement il se peut amander,
¶ Je le feray, 980
Sachés de vray, et secret vous tenray."
Et je lui dis: "Amie de cuer vray,
Ne nous celez vostre ennuy ou seray
Trop courroucie[e],* 984
Car ne croyez qu'il me plaise ne siee
Dont si vous voy estre mal appaysiee;
Si vous suppli que soiés accoisee
Et nous comptez 988
Pour quoy adés si grant doulour sentez."
Et lors cellui de rechef presentez
S'est a elle, si lui dist: "N'en doubtez,
Doulce courtoise, 992
Que l'amender vouldray comment qu'il voise."
Et lors celle respont, a basse noise:
"Votre mercy, mais riens n'est qui racoise
Mon grief ennuy 996
Qui n'est mie commencié në hyer n'uy.

Mais laissez moy plourer; a nul ne nuy,
Ne vous doit point chaloir de fait d'autruy.
Laissiez m'ester, [87v°a] 1000
Car ne pourriés ma grief pesance oster;
Ce poyse moy dont m'oyez guermenter,
Mais le grief plour ne puis ore arrester
Qui si me point, 1004
Dont me desplait, car il vient mal apoint.
Mais de pieça, sachez, suis en ce point,
Non obstant ce que je n'en vueille point
Faire semblant 1008
Devant les gens, combien qu'aille tremblant
Souventes fois du mal qui si troublant
Va mon las cuer; mais je me vais emblant
Souventes fois 1012
D'entre les gens, et lors mon grief dueil fois."
¶ Adont respont cellui qui fu courtois:
"Helas! pour Dieu, gracïeuse aux crins blois,
Ne nous celez, 1016
Car nous dites vo mal, se vous voulez,
Car pour vray croy que d'amours vous doulez.
Mais il n'est nul qui soit plus affolez,
Las! que j'en suis, 1020
Quelque chere que je face, et ne truis
Nul bon repos et de joye suis vuis,
Dont je me doubt qu'amours a ouvert l'uis
De ma grief mort. 1024
Ne point n'est tant grande, je m'en fais fort,
Vostre doulour com le mal que je port,
Car il n'est nul qui peust plus grief effort
De dueil sentir 1028
Sans mort souffrir, car souvent consentir
Me vueil a mort, com d'amours vray martir,
Et d'entre gent m'esteut souvent partir
Pour dueil mener. 1032
Si vueillés donc vostre grief plour finer;
A moy laissez le grant dueil demener,
Qui plus en ay et dont me fault pener
Toute ma vie." 1036
¶ Adonc celle qui n'ot de riens envie

Fors de plourer, dont n'estoit assouvie,
Revint a soy un pou et com ravie
Et dist: "Helas! [87v°b] 1040
Comment peut cuer avoir moins de solas
Que le dolent mien, doulereux et las?
Et puis qu'il faut que descueuvre le las
Qui si me lye, 1044
Par quoy je suis en tel merencolie
Que de dueil muir ou soit sens ou folie,
Et la cause pour quoy ne suis pas lye,
Je vous diray 1048
De mot a mot, ne ja n'en mentiray,
Et la chose qu'onques plus desiray
Et pour quoy plus de mal tire et tiray
Ja si lonc temps; 1052
Car a vo dit souffrés, sicom j'entens,
Plus mal que moy, mais ne suis consentans
De croire que nul ait pis, et partemps
Le voir sarés. 1056
Mais avant tout vo foy me baillerés
Que tout le voir vous me regehirés
De vostre ennuy et le mien cellerés."
⁋ Adont respont 1060
Cil qui maint mal dedens son cuer reppont:
"Tenez ma foy, car cil qui fist le mond
Me puist grever quant chose diray dont
Soiés dolente, 1064
Et tout le mal qu'il couvient que je sente
Par trop amer vous diray sans atente;
Mais qu'ayés dit le vostre et la tourmente
Qui si vous tient." 1068
Adonc celle qui trop d'ennuy soustient
Un grant souspir gita, qui du cuer vient,
Et puis a dit: "Or diray dont me vient
La grant doulour 1072
Dont j'ay pallie et tainte la coulour,
Ne que oublïer ne puis de ma folour,
Et qui mon las dolent cuer noye en plour
Souventes foiz. 1076
⁋ Sire, il a bien .vij. ans et plus .j. mois*

Que je donnay m'amour au plus courtois*
Et au meilleur chevalier, a mon chois,
C'om peust trouver   [88r°a]   1080
En ce monde, car par soy esprouver
En tous bons fais on le pouoit prouver
Pour le meilleur de tous; ainsi sauver
Me vueille Dieux   1084
Com je ne cuid qu'il soit jone ne vieulx
Homme de lui plus parfait soubz les cieulx,
Car on ne peust esgarder de .ij. yeulx
En nul endroit   1088
Nul plus tres bel, car lonc corps grant et droit
Et si bien fait, qu'a souhaitier fauldroit
Qui vouldroit mieulx, en riens ne l'amendroit.
¶ Et se corsage   1092
Il avoit bel et droit, aussi visage,
Car cheveleure ot crespe et de plumage*
Sus le brunet; mais sur tous l'avantage
Ot de biauté   1096
Son tres beau front karré en loyauté
Car grant et large en especiaulté
Fu. Avec ce portoit la royauté
Des beaulx sourcilz,   1100
Loncs, ennarchez, bruns, graisles furent cilz
Sur les doulx yeulx qui des maulx plus de .vj.
M'ont fait et font et livre mains soucis
Et maint grief dueil,   1104
Car oncques homs ne porta plus doulx oeil:
Brunet, rÿant, persant de doulx accueil,
Qui ont occis mon cuer. Mais son entreoeil
Fu large et plain,   1108
Et son regart tant fu de doulçour plain
Qu'il m'a donné le mal dont je me plain,
Car quant sur moy l'espart venoit a plain,
Je vous dy bien,   1112
Contenance n'avoye ne maintien,
Car a mon cuer sembloit qu'il deist: "Ça vien,"
Tant le tiroit a soy comme tout sien.
Nez tres bien fait,   1116
Longuet a point, traitis sans nul meffait,

Droit et selon le vis si tres parfaict
Que le viaire en grant beauté reffait.
Mais a merveilles 1120
Ses tres belles levres furent vermeilles, [88r°b]
Grosses sans trop, non pas jusqu'aux oreilles
Bouche grande, mais petite et com fueilles
De vert laurier, 1124
Souef flairant com rose de rosier;
Li dent fin, blanc, net, petit et entier,
Menton rondet, ancor ot pou mestier
De barbe faire, 1128
Car jeune estoit et son tres doulx viaire,
Qui de beauté fu le droit exemplaire,
Sanguin et plain, riant pour a tous plaire,
Estoit sans faille. 1132
Et col bien fait, gros par la chevesaille,
Mais espaules ot de trop belle taille:
Larges, plaines, droictes, et ou qu'il aille,
Croy que son per 1136
Ne trouvera de bras a coups frapper
Plains de force, legiers pour agrapper
Contre ces murs pour ces chastiaulx happer
Et prendre a force, 1140
Si les ot loncs, gros, bien fais; n'ot pas torse
Sa belle main de tout bien faire amorse,
Droite, longuë et plus dure qu'escorce,
Ferme et ossue. 1144
Mais la beauté est en mon cuer consceue
De son beau pis; quant m'en souvient j'en sue
De grant doulour, car maintes fois receue
Par amour fine 1148
G'i ay esté, car sa belle poitrine
Large, longue, bien faite en tout termine,
Passe toutes de beauté; c'est la mine
De toutes graces. 1152
Ventre ot petit, basset, et hanches basses,
Gent par les flans, rains rondes, non pas quasses,
Grosses cuisses qui onq ne furent lasses
De souffrir peines 1156
En fait d'armes; jambes longues et pleines,

De ners seches, droites depuis les aines,
Grosses assez, en bas graisles, sans veines,
Bien façonnees. 1160
Mais ses beautés de nature ordenees
Tres parfaictes ne furent pas finees, [88v°a]
Ains en ses piez furent enterinees;*
Ne furent pas 1164
Grans ne petis trop, mais fais par compas
Selon le corps, drois, loncs, pour faire pas
Bien mesurez et pour saillir trespas
A la barriere. 1168
Sa charneure ferme, dure et entiere,
Soueve au tast et de bonne maniere,
Clere, brune, plaisant et si belle yere
Que plus ne peust. 1172
¶ Ainsi fu bel, si qu'a peine le creust
Nul se veü avant sa beauté n'eust,
Cil qui mon cuer avoit; droit fu qu'il l'eust,
Car desservi 1176
Bien le m'avoit puis que premier le vy.
Mais ne crai pas qu'onques plus assouvi*
Chevalier fust ou mond, je vous pleuvy,
En toute grace, 1180
Car de prouece avoit en toute place
Sur tous renom du jeune aage et espace
Qu'il ot d'armer, et si estoit la masse
De gentillece, 1184
De ligneë attrait de grant noblece,
Riche d'amis, d'avoir et de sagece,
Et si estoit ancor de tel jeunece
Qu'a mon advis 1188
Vint quatrë ans n'ot ancore assouvis
L'eure et le jour que premier je le vis
Et que mon cuer fu par ses yeulx ravis
En son amour. 1192
Et son gent corps de beauté fait a tour,
Tant fust aysié qu'il n'estoit si fort tour,*
Fust en armes pour conquester honnour
Ou a jouster, 1196
Lancier barres, lances, baston oster,

Saillir, luter, legieretez hanter,*
Nul ne pouoit devant lui arrester
En toutes choses. 1200
A brief parler, toutes graces encloses
Furent en lui, n'en diroie les closes
Jamais nul jour në en rimes n'en proses. [88v°b]
Mais son arroy 1204
Jolis, gay fu, cointe sans nul desroy*
Et de maintien vous semblast filz de roy,
Tant fu plaisant et de gentil conroy;
Et humble et doulx 1208
Fu entre gent et gracïeus sur tous,
Joyeux, riant, envoysié sans courrous,
Et belle voix ot et haulte sur tous,
Et entre dames 1212
Franc et courtois, et servant toutes fames
A son pouoir; mais n'en ouÿst diffames
Pour riens qui fust, et qui en deïst blames,
Ne le souffrist, 1216
Certes son corps ainçois a mort offrist.
¶ Et s'a feste venist ou il se prist
A la dance, je vous jur Jhesu Crist
Que le dancier 1220
Et le chanter, ou a soy envoysier,
Tant lui seoit, ou a gieux commencier,
Qu'il n'estoit nul qui le voulsist laisser,
Tant fu amé, 1224
N'oncques de riens, je croy, ne fu blamé.
En fais, en dis estoit tres affermé,
Et ja s'estoit en tant de lieux armé
Que renommee 1228
Estoit de lui ja en maint lieux semee,
Tant vaillamment s'estoit en mainte armee
Bien esprouvé. Mais de lui si amee
Fu par lonc temps, 1232
Tres qu'il n'avoit pas ancore .xx. ans,
Qu'onques ancor homs ne fu plus constans
En nulle amour, loyal, në arrestans,
Qu'il fu en celle. 1236
¶ N'oncques ne fu dame ne damoiselle

Mieulx servie d'amant, non tant fust belle,
Qu'il me servi ainçois que sa querelle
Voulsisse entendre; 1240
Et en griefs plours sa belle face tendre
Souvent moulloit, priant qu'a mercy prendre
Le voulsisse, tant qu'Amours me fist rendre [89r°a]
Et recevoir 1244
Sa doulce amour. Mais tant fist son devoir
De moy servir qu'onques, a dire voir,
Plus loyauté ne pot amant avoir
Envers sa dame; 1248
Si m'amoit tant et moy lui, par mon ame,
Que n'avions soing ne d'omme ne de fame
Ne d'autre riens fors d'amer sans diffame
Tres loyaument. 1252
Ainsi .ij. ans regnames doulcement
Sans avoir grief ne nul encombrement,
Si n'avions soing ne autre pensement
Qu'a bien amer. 1256
¶ Lasse, dollente! or fault dire l'amer
Qui mon dolent, triste cuer fait pasmer
Et qui me fait tant de lermes semer
Plaine de rage. 1260
Ce fu le mal et doulereux voyage*
De Honguerie, ou tant ot grant damage,
Qui me toli le bel et bon et sage
Que tant amoye; 1264
Il a .v. ans et plus que celle voye
Fu emprise, dont mon cuer en plours noye,
Et qui me met de desespoir en voye,
Tant suis marrie. 1268
Ha! voyage mauvais de Honguerie,
La ou peri tant de chevalerie,
Et Turquie, puisses estre perie
Lonc et travers, 1272
Qui fis aler Le Conte de Nevers*
En ton paÿs desloyal et divers,
A qui Fortune ala trop a revers
A celle foiz,* 1276
Ou moururent tant de vaillans François

Et d'autre gent bons, gentilz et courtois,
Dont le dommage est et fu de grief pois
Et trop grevable. 1280
La s'en ala cil qui tant agreable
Mon cuer avoit, dont j'ay dueil importable,
Et le Basac, l'ame en soit au deable,*
L'emprisonna; 1284
Ne le fist pas occire, ains rençonna [89r°b]
Lui et d'autres, sicomme raisonna
Un sien parent qui de la retourna
Bien d'aventure. 1288
Si n'est pas mort cil en qui j'ay ma cure,
Mais ancore est en grieve prison dure.
Il n'a pas moult que le vid, sicom jure,
Un vaillant homme 1292
Qui du dit lieu vint pelerin a Romme,
Puis en France, si rapporta la somme
C'om lui demande, et la guise et la forme
De sa rançon. 1296
Ainsi le bel et bon en tel façon
Des Sarrasins est tenu en prison,
Dont mon las cuer seuffre tel cuisançon
Qu'il derve d'ire. 1300
Et ce qui plus ancor mon mal empire
Est qu'il m'est vis qu'il n'y a qui l'en tire,
Car leur devoir en font mal, a voir dire
Comme il me semble, 1304
Tous ses parens, dont mon cuer de dueil tremble,
Car leurs terres deussent tous vendre ensemble
Ains qu'ilz n'eussent cil qui ange ressemble*
De beauté fine. 1308
¶ Et plust a Dieu qui ne fault ne ne fine
Que traire hors en peusse en brief termine
Par tout vendre ma chevance enterine
Et mon vaillant, 1312
Et moy meismes alasse traveillant
Jusques au lieu ou est le bon vaillant.
Certes mon cuer ne lui seroit faillant
Jour de mon aage; 1316
N'y querroie trametre autre message

Pour viseter le bel et bon et sage,
Et se la mort me prenoit ou voyage,
De par Dieu fust, 1320
Durast mon corps tant comme durer peust
Et se Fortune vouloit et lui pleust
Que jusques la alasse, et il y fust,
Et tant feïsse* 1324
Qu'en la prison ou il est me meïsse,
Ne cuidez pas que la durté haÿsse [89v°a]
Non pour mon corps, du lieu, et l'en treÿsse,
Ce m'est advis. 1328
Ainsi seroit mon desir assouvis
Qui du veoir est si tres alouvis
Qu'il n'en craindroit peine, je vous plevis,
Pour prendre mort. 1332
Et qui saroit le dueil et le remort
Que j'ai souffert pour lui tant grief et fort,*
Merveille aroit comment je suis si fort
De le souffrir, 1336
Car bien cuiday mon cuer a mort offrir
Quant la nouvelle je ouÿ descouvrir
Du grant meschief ou il couvint perir
Tant de vaillans, 1340
Car mon las cuer je senti si dueillans
Que je ne sçay qu'il ne me fu faillans
Ou que mon corps de griefs couteaulx taillans
N'alay occire, 1344
Ne le grief dueil tout ne saroie dire
Qu'ay eu depuis, car ne saroie eslire
Quel m'est meilleur, ou le plourer ou rire:
Trestout m'est un. 1348
Et pour tant se bonne chiere en commun
Je fois, certes mon cuer n'a bien nesun
Et moult souvent plourer devant chacun
Il me couvient, 1352
Quant grant desir trop fort sur moy survient,
Car sans cesser de cellui me souvient
Qui a mon cuer, qu'en prison on retient
Si durement, 1356
Et quant plus suis en grant esbatement

Lors me souvient plus de son grief tourment
Qui ma joye rabat trop durement.
¶ Ainsi vous ay 1360
Dit mon meschief et puis quant commençay;
C'est la cause pour quoy je vous laissay
Et pour plourer devant je m'avançay.
Doncques ne dites 1364
Jamais nul jour que plus soient petites
Que les vostres mes griefs doulours despites,
Car ce ne sont fors que roses eslites [89v°b]
Envers les moyes. 1368
Mais les vostres, s'il vous plait toutevoyes,
Vous me dirés et les tours et les voyes
Dont vous viennent tristes pensees coyes
Et si grief yre." 1372
Lors a finé son parler sans plus dire,
Mais oncques mais raconter n'ouÿ lire
N'ouÿ parler d'autre qui tel martire
Alast menant, 1376
Car en parlant s'aloit si demenant
Qu'il couvenoit que cellui soustenant
Alast son corps et a force tenant,
Ou du cheval 1380
Choëte fust plus de .c. fois aval.
Si nous faisoit a tous .ij. si grant mal
Que les lermes couroient contreval
De notre face, 1384
Et de bon cuer nous confortions la lasse.
Mais tant souffroit de tristece grant masse
Que de plourer ne pouoit estre lasse
Et de dueil faire. 1388
¶ Adonc le doulx escuyer debonnaire
Lui dist tout bas: "Pour Dieu, vueillés vous taire
De ce grief plour qui tant vous est contraire.
Vous vous tüez 1392
Et vo beau corps tout changez et müez;
Si n'est pas sens dont si vous argüez
Et un petit tristece loing rüez.
Si m'escoutez 1396
Et vous orrés comment suis assotez

Par trop amer. Plus ne vous guermentez;
Laissez a moy le dueil car n'en doubtez,
Trop plus en ay. 1400
¶ Si vous diray le fait de mon esmay:
Il a .v. ans ou ara en ce may
Que m'embati en lieu que trop amay
En ma male heure, 1404
Mais Fortune, qui sans cesser labeure
Pour nuire aux gens me volt lors courir seure,
Car je n'avoye ains, se Dieux me sequeure,
Soing ne trisstour; [90r°a] 1408
Jolis et gay estoie en mon atour,
Et jeunement je vivoye a tout tour,
Ne congnoissoie alors d'amours le tour
Ne sa pointure 1412
Qui m'a depuis esté diverse et dure.
Si m'embati par ma mesaventure
Un jour en lieu ou Amours sa droiture
Vouloit avoir 1416
Des jeunes gens, dont la a dire voir
Avoit assez qui moult bien leur devoir
En lui servir mettoyent et savoir
Entierement. 1420
En un jardin fu, plain d'esbatement,
Ou de mon mal vint le commencement,
Car en ce lieu me prist trop doulcement
Le grief malage 1424
Que puis m'a fait et fait trop de damage,
Car par regart m'en yvray du beuvrage
Qu'Amours livre, qui met au cuer la rage
De dueil comblee. 1428
En ce jardin avoit une assemblee
Belle et plaisant ou joye estoit doublee,
Mainte dame de beauté affublee
Et mainte belle 1432
Et avenant, jolie damoiselle.
Il y avoit mainte doulce pucelle,
Son chevalier par la main n'y ot celle
Qui ne tenist 1436
Ou escuyer, se pres d'elle venist.

La dançoient, mais il vous souvenist
Que Dieu y fust qui si les soustenist
En grant lëece,   1440
Car onc ne vy de joye tel largece.
Et en ce lieu ot mainte grant maistresse
Et mainte autre paree de noblece
Et maint jolis   1444
Gay chevalier, car de la flour de lis
Noble et royal ou lieu plain de delis
Avoit aucuns, et d'autres si polis
Que ce sembloient   [90r°b]   1448
Dieux, dëesses, qui ou lieu s'assembloient,
Dont l'un a l'autre les cuers s'entre embloient
Moult soubtilment, et du mal s'affubloient
Qui a grant joye   1452
Est commencié et puis en griefs plours noye.
Ou lieu entray ou Fortune la voie
Lors m'adreça qui a mort me convoye
Sans departance.   1456
Quant je fus pres pour veoir l'ordenance,
Une dame qui de ma congnoissance
Estoit adonc me va prendre a la dance,
Voulsisse ou non;   1460
Lors de plusieurs fu nommé par mon nom,
Si disoient que de chanter renom,
Bien voulentiers, avoie, dont de non*
Je ne deïsse.   1464
Si fu raison que je leur obeÿsse,
Ou bien ou mal que mon chant aseÿsse,
Villenie fust se ne le feïsse;
Adont chantay,   1468
Sicom je sço, un rondel que dictay.
Quant j'oz chanté, la gaires n'arrestay
Q'une dame chanta; mais n'escoutay
Jour de mon aage   1472
Chant si bien dit de voix ne de lengage,
Ne si plaisant a ouÿr; l'avantage
Celle en avoit sur toutes par usage
Et de nature.   1476

¶ Quant le doulx chant oÿ dit par mesure
Mes yeulx haulçay, regarday par grant cure
De celle qui chantoit la pourtraiture
Et le viaire   1480
Qui tant fu bel, doulcet et debonnaire,
Que je ne sçay com nature pourtraire
Pot si bien fait, n'autel beauté parfaire
Ne mettre a chief;   1484
Car elle avoit comme fin or le chief,
Blonc, crespelet, et d'un blanc cueuvrechief
Bien delïé le couvert de rechief
Mignotement;   [90v°a]   1488
Mais a son front ne fault amendemment,
Car grant et plain, honny, blanc, proprement
Commë yvoire ouvré, poliement
Est façonné,   1492
Et si sourcilz par nature ordonné,
Grailles, longues, basses et affiné,
De grant beauté, brunes; n'ymaginé
Plus bel entrueil   1496
Ne peut estre, large, onny et si oeil
Vers et rians; plaisans et sans orgueil
Fu son regart, et de tres doulx accueil.
Beau nez traictifs   1500
Et non trop grant, trop lonc ne trop petis,
Mais droit, bien fait, odorant et faitis,
Selon le vis gracïeux et gentilz.
Et ses tres belles,   1504
Doulces, plaisans jonettes et macelles,
Ce sembloit lis avec roses nouvelles
Entremeslé, n'autre beauté a celles
Ne s'appareille,   1508
Car grassetes de beauté non pareille
Furent et sont; et sa petite oreille,
Assise a point et de coulour vermeille.
Souef flairant   1512
La bouchette ot, petiote et riant,
Grossette a point, et quant en sousriant
Elle parloit, come perle d'Oriant

Ses dens menus* 1516
On voyoit blancs et serrez plus que nulz,
Onnis, doulces, en santé maintenus,
Bien arrengez, en tous lieux beaulx tenus.
Et .ij. petites 1520
Fosses plaisans, de grant doulçour eslites,
En sousriant es jouetes escriptes
Ot bien seans; mais les doulçours escriptes
Du mentonnet, 1524
Rondet, plaisant, gracïeux, sadinet
Et fosselu, vermillet, mignonnet,
Ne pourroient, tant est fin, doulcinet,
Et au doulx vis [90v°b] 1528
Bien respondant, qui fu tout assouvis
De grant beauté, rondelet a devis,
Le plus doulcet et plus bel qu'onques vis
Mieulx façonné. 1532
Et son beau col, par mesure ordené,
D'un collier d'or entour avironné,
Fu rich et bel, que le roy ot donné,
Sur sa gorgette 1536
Moult avenant, qui fu blanche et bien faite,
Et de petis fillez semble estre traicte.
Mais Nature, qui mainte euvre a parfaite,*
Ne fist ouvrage 1540
Oncques plus bel, je croy ne dis oultrage,
Que sa plaine, polie, blanche et large
Poitrine; fu sans os ne veine ombrage,
C'est chose voire, 1544
Blanche com lis, polie comme yvoire,
Et le tetin tout ainsi q'une poire,
Poignant, rondet ot ou sain; onc memoire,
Bien dire l'ose, 1548
N'ay d'avoir veu oncques si doulce chose.
Helas, eureux est qui la se repose!
Mais plus tendrete et plus freche que rose,
Je vous asseure; 1552
Ferme, clere fu sa belle charneure,
Et ses beaulx bras loncs, graisles par mesure.
Plus belle main oncques n'ot creature,

Longuette et lee, 1556
Ne pot avoir, n'est pas chose celee,
Blanche et loncs, dois grassette et potelee,
Bien faite, onnie, droite et bien dolee.
Et corselet 1560
Graislet, longuet, droit, appert, grassellet,
Hanches basses, rains voultis, rondelet,
Le ventre avoit fin, doulcet et mollet,
Sicom je tiens, 1564
Car Nature qui en lui mist tous biens,
Ou demourant, je croy, n'oublia riens,
Ainçois la fist, ainsi com je maintiens,
Toute parfaicte [91r°a] 1568
En grant beauté; si ot jambe graislete
Et petit pié, de guise nouvellette
Doulcetement chaussiee. Et ainsi faite
¶ Par moult grant cure 1572
L'ot cree[ë] et formee Nature,
Belle, plaisant sur toute creature;
Et avec ce en bonté fu si pure,
Qu'il n'y ot vice 1576
En son bon cuer, qui fu vuit de malice;
Et en tous cas elle fu si propice
Qu'elle n'estoit de riens faire novice
Qui a valable 1580
Dame d'onneur soit faire raisonnable,
Et de lignee attraitte moult notable.
Mais en tous fais elle est tant agreable,
En doulx maintien 1584
Et en parler, et en tout autre bien,
Qu'il n'est tresor qui s'acompare au sien;
Rire, jouer, dancer sur toute rien
Bien lui avient, 1588
Et ses plaisans doulçours mon cuer retient;
Comment ou lieu la vi, bien me souvient,*
Rire, jouer, parler comme appartient
A noble dame, 1592
Par si tres doulx maintien que, par mon ame,
Tant lui seoit qu'il n'y avoit nul ame*
Qui ne deïst qu'onques si doulce fame

N'avoit veüe, 1596
De gayeté par a point si meüe,
Lie, jouant et de sens pourveüe.
Si ot vestu adont la tres esleue
Un vert corset 1600
De fin samit, ou son beau corps doulcet
Estoit estroit cousu a un lasset
A son coste rondelet et grasset,
Qui gentement 1604
Lui avenoit; ainsi songneusement
La regarday ne ne pos nullement
D'elle mes yeulx retraire aucunement,
Tant me plaisoit. [91r°b] 1608
¶ Mais Amours, qui tout ce faire faisoit,
Apperceut bien que mon cuer y musoit
Et pour ce l'arc que souvent entesoit,
Treÿ de poche 1612
Et fleche prist poignant et mist en coche,
Tire vers moy et roidement descoche.
Par my le cuer m'assena de la floche
De Doulx Regart; 1616
Or fus navrez, ne fery pas en dard,
Car en tel point fu mis, se Dieux me gart,
Ains que partis fusse de celle part,
Qu'en moy n'avoit 1620
Sens në avis. Mais ancor pou grevoit
La navreure qu'Amours faite m'avoit;
Ne savoye la force qu'elle avoit,
Ains agreable 1624
Me fu ce trait ne me sembla grevable,
Mais si tres doulx et si tres savourable,
Qu'il m'iere avis qu'il me seroit valable
En tous endrois 1628
Et seroie par ce trop plus adrois
Et plus jolis et plus gay; c'estoit drois.
Et si fus je, car j'en devins plus drois
Et trop plus cointe. 1632
¶ Ainsi devins adonc d'Amours accointe
Et me plut bien au de premier la pointe*
Qui m'a esté depuis d'amertume ointe

Diverse et dure. 1636
Ou lieu me tins jusqu'a la nuit obscure,
Car de veoir celle en qui mis ma cure
Ne fusse las jamais, je le vous jure.
Mais par raison 1640
De deppartir il fu temps et saison,
Si s'en ala chacun en sa maison.
Mais ne cuidiez que dormisse foison
Celle nuitee; 1644
Tant doulcement s'est adont delitee
Ma pensee qui toute a rescitee
La grant beauté qui en celle habitee
A, qui largece* [91v°a] 1648
En a. Ainsi pensant a sa noblece
Fu maintes nuis et mains jours en simplece,
Sans sentir mal ne chose qui me blece.
Ainçois estoie 1652
Gay et jolis plus qu'onques et hantoye
Souvent les lieux ou ma dame sentoye.
Si jouoyë et dansoye et chantoye
Par grant revel 1656
Moult liement comme amoureux nouvel,
Et du gay temps le tres doulx renouvel
Lié me tenoit et ainsi me fu bel,
Par un espace, 1660
Le temps ainçois quë eusse pensé lasse.
¶ Mais vraye amour qui les amans enlasse
Souffrir ne veult plus que me deportasse.
D'ardant desir 1664
D'elle estre amé cellui me vint saisir
Par mi le cuer, tellement que plaisir
Ne poz oncques puis avoir ne choisir
Autre soulas 1668
Qu'elle veoir, dont oncques ne fu las.
Mais ce veoir plus estraignoit le las
De mon desir dont souvent dire, "Helas!"
En regraittant 1672
Me couvenoit, desirant s'amour tant
Que n'estoye nulle part arrestant
Qu'el service de ma dame; et pour tant

⁋ Je m'acointay 1676
De ses amis et souvent les hantay,
Plaisir leur fis, et servi et portay
Leur grant honneur et si me presentay
Du tout a eulx. 1680
Ainsi tant fis par promesses et veulx
Et par servir ses amis en tous lieulx,
Que je pos bien sans blasme aler tous seulz
En son hostel 1684
Quant me plaisoit, dont j'en os plaisir tel
Que n'en voulsisse avoir autre chetel;
Et moult souvent parloye d'un et d'el
Avecques elle. [91v°b] 1688
Et par tel sens tous temps hantay la belle
Que mesdisans n'en esmurent nouvelle,
Car sagement me gouvernoie en celle
Amour qu'avoye 1692
Et ay ancor et aray ou que soye
Tout mon vivant, quoy qu'avenir m'en doye.
Ainsi souvent m'esbatoie et jouoie
D'umble maniere 1696
Avec celle que tant aim et tiens chiere,
Et elle aussi me faisoit bonne chiere*
A toute heure liement, sans anchere,
⁋ Et me mandoit 1700
Souventes fois et son vueil commandoit.
Si faisoie comme amant faire doit
Tout son command; assez bien m'en rendoit,
Ce m'iere avis, 1704
Le guerredon, quant de son tres doulx vis
Avoie un ris, tous estoie assouvis,
Ou un plaisant regart; quant vis a vis
A lonc loisir 1708
La pouoie veoir, autre plaisir
Ne sceüssë en ce monde choisir.
Mais ne cuidez que mon ardant desir
J'osasse dire 1712
Ne racompter comment pour lui martire,*
Car trop doubtoie encheoir en son yre;
Mais bien pouoit congnoistre mon martire

     A mon semblant, 1716
     Car moult souvent estoie tout tremblant
     Devant elle, tant m'aloient troublant
     Souspirs et plours et mon vis affublant
     Par grant destresse. 1720
❡ Mais non pour tant ma tres dure tristece
     Ne gehissoie a ma doulce maistresse
     Qui me veoit souvent par grant aspresse
     Müer coulour 1724
     Devant ellë, et ainsi ma doulour
     Je lui celay, bien croy que c'ert folour.
     Et quant tout seul demenoye mon plour
     Par grant aÿr, [92r°a] 1728
     Lors pensoie a elle tout regehir,
     Mais la päour qu'elle m'en peust haÿr
     Et que mon plaint ne daignast point oÿr
     Si me touloit 1732
❡ Forse et vigour du mal qui me douloit
     Devant elle dire; si s'en aloit
     Tout mon propos et de moy s'en voloit
     Tout hardiment. 1736
     En ce point fus et souffri longuement
     Sanz requerir nul autre alegement.
     Si me sembla que trop petitement
     Desservi eusse 1740
     D'elle estre amé, et que digne ne fusse
     D'elle prïer ne qu'a dame l'eslusse
     Pour tant que pou valoye; pour ce en Prusse
     Et oultremer 1744
     Et en mains lieux me volz pour elle armer.
     Pour moy vanter ne le dis, car amer
     Faisoit tout ce dont louer ne blamer
     On ne m'en doit. 1748
     Par son congié d'elle mon corps partoit,
     Mais le vray cuer point ne s'en departoit;
     Au retourner elle me recevoit
     A lie chiere. 1752
❡ Ainsi l'amay de vraye amour entiere,
     Sans lui oser dire en nulle maniere,
     Ne d'autre riens songneux en nul temps n'yere

Que de servir 1756
Elle qui tant me pouoit desservir
Qu'il m'iere avis qu'y mon cuer asservir
Ne pouoyë assez pour assouvir
Son bon vouloir. 1760
¶ Mais autrement m'avint, dont tant douloir
Il m'en esteut que tout en non chaloir
Ma vie met souvent; mais pou valoir
Me pot mon dueil, 1764
Car la belle doulce, en qui j'ay mon vueil,
Ne sçay pour quoy, se changia: në accueil
Plus ne me fist ne de chiere ne d'ueil
Ne de maintieng, [92r°b] 1768
Et tout m'osta l'esperance du bien
Que j'avoye, et si me monstra bien
Qu'elle n'amoit moy ne mes fais en rien;
Ne sçay pour quoy, 1772
Mais tout a coup me planta la tout quoy,
Sanz moy vouloir n'en appert n'en requoy
Plus regarder ne veoir entour soy,
Tant me fu fiere. 1776
Et quant je vy et perceu la maniere
Et que tant me faisoit diverse chiere,
Se j'en oz dueil, nul nel demand n'enquiere,
Car esbahis 1780
Si me trouvay d'estre d'elle haÿs
Et sans savoir pour quoy, qu'onq fol naÿs
Plus enragiez ne fu, et s'envaÿs
Et dechaciez 1784
De tout le mond fusse, en exil chaciez;
Ne me fust pas tant de mal pourchaciez,
Ce m'iere avis, com le mal qu'enchaciez
Fu et fichié 1788
En mon las cuer a tort et a pechié;
N'oncques depuis il n'en fu relachié,
¶ Dont j'ay souffert et ay trop de meschié.
Mais qu'avint il 1792
Quant je me vi getté en tel exil?
Trop bien cuiday ouvrer comme soubtil

De lui compter mon tres mortel peril
Et la grief peine 1796
Que j'oz souffert pour lui mainte sepmaine.
Si la trouvay un jour en une plaine,
Vers elle alay a chiere triste et veine,
Et hardiment 1800
Je pris en moy de dire ouvertement
Ma grief doulour; si dis couvertement
La grant amour et le grant marrement
La ou j'estoye, 1804
Et en plourant, en grant doulour comptoye
Tout mon estat et si me guermentoye
Pour quoy d'elle si estrangié estoye,
Et pour quel cas [92v°a] 1808
Elle m'avoit ainsi flati a cas
Et de mon bien si estrangié et cas,
Ne qui m'avoit esté tel avocas
Ne si contraire. 1812
Car ne cuiday oncques dire ne faire
A mon pouoir riens qui lui deust desplaire,
Mais la servir en tous cas et complaire
A mon pouoir, 1816
Ce pouoit bien de vray appercevoir.
¶ Ainsi lui dis de tout mon fait le voir,
Mais quant li oz mon cas fait assavoir
Or valu pis, 1820
Car responce si plaine de despis
Me fist, et fus d'elle si racropis,
Que bien cuiday mortellement ou pis
Tout devant elle 1824
M'aler ferir, car la responce d'elle
Me poigni trop; n'oncques n'ouÿ nouvelle
Si desplaisant, certes, comme fu celle.
A brief parler, 1828
Elle me dist plainement, sans celer,
Ne lui plaisoit ne mon venir n'aler
Ne, se pour lui mourir ou affoller
Or en devoye, 1832
Ne m'ameroit jamais par nulle voye,

Si n'y pensasse, ains alasse ma voye,
Car autre riens jamais d'elle n'aroye
Par son serment, 1836
Et que je l'en creüsse seurement.
Si s'en parti mal de moy durement.
Je demouray plus noircy quarrement
De grant doulour 1840
Et comme mort, sans poulx et sanz coulour,
Un mien compains me trouva sanz chalour
La enroidi, qui de ma grant folour
Trop me reprist; 1844
Si m'enporta et a force me prist,
Et bien cuida que dure mort surprist
Mon povre corps qui fu, par Jhesu Crist,
Si tourmenté [92v°b] 1848
Que maintes fois me vint en voulenté
De moy tolir la vie ou la santé,
Si que je fusse en tres dure orphanté
Trestout mon aage. 1852
¶ Ainsi me fu celle dame sauvage;
Mais ne cuidez qu'onques puis son courage
Vers moy changiast, mais toudis si ombrage
Et si tres dure 1856
De pis en pis; et ancor ainsi dure
Que je ne sçay veoir comment je dure
Si grant meschief ne si cuisant ardure
Ne tel contraire 1860
Comme j'en ay, et ne m'en puis retraire,
Ne tant ne sçay de mal pour elle traire
Que je m'en puisse eslongner n'en sus traire
Pour l'oublïer. 1864
Ainçois la voy souvent pour plus lïer
Mon dolent cuer, ne par humilïer
Las! je ne puis son cuer amolïer;
Ains est plus dur 1868
Encontre moy que de marbre un gros mur.
Si seuffre mal et meschief pesme et sur
Ou je n'espoir fors la mort, je vous jur
Dieu et les sains; 1872

Et pour ce di que vous avez trop mains
De mal que moy et que vo cuer est sains
Envers le mien, qui de mal est ençains
Et de pesance." 1876
¶ Ainsi cellui ot dit sa mesaisance
Et comme il ert de mort en grant balance.
Adont respont celle sans arrestance
Et dist: "Ay lasse! 1880
Que dites vous? Certes, sauf vostre grace,
J'ay plus de mal en un tout seul espace
Que vous n'avez tant que tout un mois passe,*
Et c'est raison 1884
Në il n'y a point de comparoison,
Car quant je pense a la dure prison
Ou mon ami a ja mainte saison*
Esté en mue, [93r°a] 1888
Et qu'il est la comme une beste mue,
N'ay si bon sens que tout ne se remue.
Et comment donc pourroie estre desmue
D'avoir la rage 1892
Doulereuse qui trop me fait d'oultrage?
Mais vous avez sur moy grant avantage,
Car vous vëez la belle au cler visage,
Souvent avient; 1896
Et si avez espoir qui vous soustient,
Car s'a present vostre dame se tient
Dure vers vous, certes, mon cuer maintient
Que desservir 1900
Pourrés ancor s'amour par bien servir;
Si vous pourra et donner et pleuvir
Toute s'amour, ainsi pourrés chevir
Tout a vo gre; 1904
Et peut estre qu'elle fait tout de gre
Pour essayer vous, et, se tout en gre
Prenez son vueil, ancor en hault degré
Vous pourra mettre. 1908
Si vous en di tout le voir a la lettre.
Helas! mais moy, et quel confort m'empetre
Nul bon espoir fors ma vie desmettre

Par desespoir." 1912
¶ Et cil respont: "Dites vous donc qu'espoir
Ay qui me dit que bien aray a poir,
Certes non ay, ains du tout me despoir
D'avoir jamais 1916
L'amour d'elle, car ja lonc temps remais
Suis en ce point, mais oncques n'en eus mais
Que tout meschief et divers entremais
Trop doulereux. 1920
Et si la voy, dont je suis eüreux,
Ce dites vous, mais pou m'est savoureux
Cellui veoir, las, dolens, meseureux!
C'est vision 1924
Que trop me vient a grant confusion,
Car j'alume ma grant destruccion
Et le grief feu qui mon entencion
Ne lait changer; [93r°b] 1928
Car quant la voy si tres belle, estranger
Je ne m'en puis, mais vif doy enrager
Quant ses semblans voy, pour moy dalmager
Si tres contraire 1932
A mon vouloir. Et si ay plusieurs paire
De grans doulours, car trop me fait contraire
Jalousie, dont ne me puis retraire,
Car trop ay doubte 1936
Que ma dame d'elle tant me deboute
Pour autre amer, a qui ne plaisoit goute
Qu'entour elle j'alasse, somme toute,
Car n'a raison 1940
De moy haÿr pour nulle autre achoison.
¶ Et dont, se bien entendez ma raison,
J'ay plus de mal que vous; si nous taison,
Atant souffise, 1944
Car bien savez qu'en vous est toute assise
De vostre ami la vraye amour et mise,
Et moy, j'aime celle qui me desprise
En grant content; 1948
Dont vostre cuer ne pourroit avoir tant
De grans ennuis comme je vois sentant.

Je ne di pas que n'en ayés pour tant
A grant planté,   1952
Mais vostre ami, a qui Dieux doint santé,*
Pourrés veoir brief, car son parenté
Ne le larroit mie en ce lieu planté
Par lonc termine;   1956
Et si n'est dueil ne meschief qui ne fine,
Car il a ja lonc temps que ce fu, si ne*
Peut estre que l'amour ne se decline,
Car qui est d'oeil   1960
Moult eslongné, pou lui dure son dueil.
Et si pouez avenir a vo vueil
Prochainement, et tout en autre fueil*
Soy attourner,   1964
Fortune qui a voulu bestourner
Vo bien en mal, si se pourra tourner
Si que verrés vostre ami retourner*
Et tost mander."   [93v°a]   1968
¶ Adonc le prist ycelle a regarder
Et respondi: "Dieu le doint sans tarder!
Mais s'il y meurt, Dieux l'en vueille garder,
Comment ravoir   1972
Le pourray je? Il est bon a savoir
Qu'a grant peine vif eschappera voir,
Et c'est ce qui me fait trop recevoir
De grief martire.   1976
Et je vous ay ci endroit ouÿ dire
Que qui est loings d'ueil, le cuer loings s'en tire;
Helas, aymy! Dieux scet que je desire
Plus ou autant   1980
Mon doulx ami et l'aim tout autrement
Com quant de moy estoit pres arrestant,
Ne jamais jour tant que l'ame batant
Me voit ou corps   1984
Ne l'oubliray; et vous diray ancors
Ce qui me fait ancor plus durs recors:
C'est que je sçay qu'il a de moy remors
Et grant pitié,   1988
Car il scet bien que pour son amistié

J'ay cuer dolent et triste et dehaitié.
Et vous dites que j'en ay la moitié
Mains de doulour 1992
Pour ce que sçay que j'ay toute s'amour,
Mais, sauve soit vo paix, ainçois mon plour
En est plus grant et en ay plus favour
A sa personne, 1996
Car plus trouvé ay sa doulce amour bonne
Et tant plus l'aim; mais celle que felonne
Est envers vous droite achoison vous donne
D'avoir moins dueil 2000
De son refus, et par ce prouver vueil
Que mille fois et plus que vous recueil
De pesant mal et ay moins de recueil
Et moins reffuge 2004
¶ A bon espoir, et de ce requier juge
Sage et loyal, qui de no debat juge."
Et cil respont: "Et de tel acort su ge.*
Or soit trouvé [93v°b] 2008
Juge loyal, par qui il soit prouvé
Et droit jugé, car par moy reprouvé
Ne sera ja puis que l'avez rouvé.
¶ Or advison 2012
Qui il sera, et si soit gentilz hom
Qui sache bien entendre no raison
Et en juger le droit selon raison,
Et si soit sage 2016
En fais d'amours par sens et par usage.
Si en mettrons sur lui toute la charge
Et nous tendrons de fait et d'arbitrage
Au jugement 2020
Qu'il en donra sans nul descordement."
Ainsi greé l'ont tous .ij. bonnement,
Et puis ilz m'ont prié moult chierement
Que j'avisasse 2024
Qui seroit bon et que leur devisasse.
¶ Lors y pensay un bien petit d'espace,
Si me souvint de la tres bonne grace
Et bon renom 2028
De vous, chier Sire, ou il n'a se bien non;

Si leur dis lors et vous nommay par nom
Mais qu'il vous pleust ne leur dire de non,
Qu'il m'iert avis 2032
Qu'ilz aroient en vous juge a devis
Sage et loyal, et de tout bon advis.
Ce leur plut moult et furent assouvis
De leur vouloir, 2036
Car tant orent oÿ, a dire voir,
Dire de vous de bien et de savoir
Qu'autre juge ja ne quierent avoir;
Mieulx ne demandent, 2040
Së il vous plaist, et si se recommandent
A vous, Sire, a qui supplient et mandent
Que voz pensers un petit y entendent,
Non obstant qu'armes 2044
Vous occuppent. Et de leurs dures larmes
Me prïerent que les cas meisse en termes
Pour envoyer a vous dedens brief termes
Pour droit juger [94r°a] 2048
Lequel par droit doit avoir plus legier
Mal apporter ou en doit plus charger,
Et qui plus vit en peine et en donger
Des .ij. parties. 2052
¶ Atant se sont noz parolles parties,
Car de Paris approchions les parties,
Et de noz gens, dont estions departies,
Nous approchames; 2056
Et liement ensemble chevauchames
Tant que cheus moy a Paris arrivames,
Ou a grant joye et a feste disnasmes.
Et quant mengié* 2060
Et solacié omes, prendre congié
Voldrent trestuit, mais bien m'ont enchargié
Li duy amant que tost fust abregié
De leur affaire, 2064
¶ Dont tost aprés je commençay a faire
Ce present dit, sicom l'oyez retraire.
Mais or est temps que je m'en doye taire,
¶ Et en la fin 2068
Du derrenier ver de cuer loyal et fin*

Me nommeray, et Dieu pry au deffin
Que bonne vie et puis a la parfin
Son paradis   2072
Il vous ottroit et a tous les gentilz
Vrays fins loyaulx amans et non faintis
Que vraye amour tient subgés et creintis.*
                        Explicit le dit de Poyssy

Variants

Rubric *D adds* L. du dit de P., *DL1L3 omit* qui s'adrece a un estrange, *L2 omits rubric.*

7	*DL* ce j'en tendré
15	*L* m. prië
19	*DL* Qu'il l.
22	*DL* De b.
27	*L* Bien v.
43	*DL* B. et g.
55	*L1L3* p. si me voldrent, *L2* p. me voldrent
62	*L1L3* Chevauchoye
63	*RDL2* qu'avec
77	*DL* q. savoit chanter
88	*D* Mais en
93	*DL* p. les c., *L1L3* c. resbaudir
102	*R* Encore f.
109	*D* Et qu'il m., *L* Et qu'ils m.
110	*D* Pour d.
115	*R* orillons
117	*R* et ses a.
119	*DL* c. de v.
121	*D* S. les a.
129	*L1L3* en estoient l.
135	*R* P. ses i.
140	*R* Et ses s.
141	*DL* et ces j.
154	*L* s. souvent et
163	*L* Q. l'envoyoit
174	*D* a marche ou a f.
179	*L* on ne v.
181	*D* d. Aussi aussi aussi
183	*R* p. a p.
198	*L2* v. et l.
201	*L omit* que
215	*R omits* et
221	*DL* Ensemble en l'abaÿe v.
224	*L* Y ot m.
229	*DL* De v.
235	*R* S'agelongna
262	*D* a. a la
264	*L3* Et h.
291	*D* si s'encline
302	*D* e. homme ne
303	*DL* c. quë il m.
313	*L1L3* b. y a p. c. a., *DL* c. angelz
314	*DL* Si ne v., *L* et sans l.
325	*L* et ou r.
331	*R* l. compices
358	*DL* N. f. b. et
359	*DL* v. apportent
360	*L* De g.
378	*DL* Ne v. l. n. pristrent a prendre
386	*L1L3* c. moult
393	*D* t. autour
397	*D* large et espacïeux
401	*DL* p. en my, *L* t. bel p.
403	*DL* d. que s.
415	*D* b. ce puet estre prouvé
418	*R* ne pouoit, *L3* ne nous p.
426	*DL* Qui
431	*L1L2* c. en g.
437	*L1L3* r. n'a g.
439	*L* F. et d.
447	*R* t. cours
452	*L3 omits* nous
461	*R* Q. espargé, *DL* e. n'y ont or
468	*L3* ne verroye
473	*DL* Et s. e. f. t. nouvellement
474–75	*reversed in R*, 475 *L3 omits* si
478	*L* M. que ouvrees
486	*L* d. n'osoit n.
505	*DL omit* de
510–11	*reversed in R*, 510 *DL* D. et d. t. b. pourtraitures
514	*L* N'il n.
521	*L1L3 omit second* est
525	*DL* A. a v.
527	*D* S. ces m., *L* S. les m.
536	*L3* Vont a.
537	*D* c. sont si b. o.
540	*DL1L2* S'il l.

544 L En telle g.
551 DL b. jardins la
558 L Et la e.
559 L C. croy que bien p.
562 DL de haulz m.
570 D Et un vivier la sourdant p.
578 R Tant d.
582 DL s. le partement
587 L p. ains quë a l.
593 D omits first et
596 R Et d.
601 D c. n'en f.
621 D d. et de table nous l.
628 D Ne f.
630 DL q. est m.
631 L1L3 omit est
633 L d. oz je f.
636 D J. au lices
645 DL au franc c.
663 L1L3 et des c.
665 DL N'y p.
685 DL f. n'aniaulx
689 DL Qui a.
703 DL je laissay c. ou est m.
706 L En la notant q.
707 D t. c. p. m.
718 L1L3 v. en u.
719 DL A et d.
721 L omit a
722 D L. d'entre eulx n., L3 omits ens
726 L J. g. fresche gaye et p.
728 DL Cy q.
729 DL v. m'en c.
730 DL q. yci c.
741 L1L3 e. delez elle fu pres, L2 e. qui delez elle fu e.
744 L V. esrouee
749 L fu presque n.
751 D n. qu'y f., L n. qui y f.
761 L omit trestous
763 L2 Qui b., DL s. estre d'Amours s.
797 DL p. de c., L2 c. en v.
803 L en tel e.
805 R r. en l.

813 DL2 l. desir
819 D de ce l.
820 R Et l.
845 D et du b.
851 L3 D. d'amour, DL v. planter
855 D f. veu et p.
862 D un q. l. d. s., L un q. d. l. s.
873 R l. champs
879 D s. voioit
881 DL b. saulsoies q.
887 L n. ait nuit
891 R c. et p., DL P. c. d. d. p. m.
902 DL Ou o.
903 L a. font p.
907 L omit fu
913 L omit trop
916 L1L3 omit ou
918 DL Q. b. v.
919 R Se c., L b. ou a.
928 D S'en va
932 L Ou en m.
938 DL Et en p. d. aconsumes le s.
939 L3 l. Que c.
949 L T. me p.
950 L1L3 Me t.
955 R q. ce d.
967 D v. avez
984 RDL T. courroucié
991 R C'est a
997 L1L3 h. ne huy
998–99 reversed in L1L3, 999 L c. du f.
1000 R Laissier m.
1001 L ma grant p.
1002 L1L3 m. vous m.
1006 L en tel p.
1017 DL Mais n.
1037 R A doulce c.
1039 D R. un p. a s. comme r., L R. un p. a s. et
1041 R a. maint de
1042 L le m. d. d. et maz
1051 L et tray
1052 DL Ja a l.

1075	*L* l. c. d. n.	1251	*L* f. amer s.
1077	*L1L3* b. un an et, *DL* et plusieurs m.	1262	*RL* De Hongrie, *D* ou trop ot
1081	*L* c. pour s.	1269	*DL1L3* de Hongrie
1082	*DL* A t.	1273	*DL* a. Monseigneur de
1086	*DL* Homs p. p. adés dessoubz l. c.	1297	*L* A. le bon et bel de t.
1092	*L* Et le c.	1302	*DL* C'est q., *L3* a qu'il l'en
1093	*DL* b. a droit a.	1303	*L1L3* m. au v.
1094	*D* c. crespe ot et p., *L omit* ot *and* de	1307	*DL* q. angel r.
1098	*L* l. fu en e.	1309	*L* He p., q. ne ment ne
1100	*DL* De b.	1310	*DL* h. l'en p.
1102	*L* q. de m.	1311	*DL* Pour t.
1109	*L1L3* r. f. t. de	1317	*L* Ne q.
1118	*D* si tres bien fait	1319	*L* p. en v.
1122	*DL* t. n'ot p.	1324	*R* Certes t.
1123	*L omit* et	1329	*L* m. devoir
1125	*D* f. ou r.	1331	*L2* Q. ne c.
1126	*DL* b. p. n. et	1337	*DL* m. corps a
1135	*DL* L. d. p. et	1339	*D* c. mourir, *L* Du grief m.
1139	*R* C. ses m.	1341	*D* c. senti si deffaillans
1145	*L* M. en m. c. e. la b. c.	1353–54	*reversed in R*
1147	*R* d. qu'ay m.	1357	*L2* en grief e.
1163	*DL* Car en	1361	*L* p. q'en c.
1167	*omitted in R*	1370	*L1L3* l. cours et
1171	*L1L2* b. p. si tres plaisant yere, *L3* b. et si tres plaisant yere	1372	*L* Et grief martire
1174	*L* se a. v. sa	1374	*L* m. ne raconter ne lire
1175	*R* qu'il eust	1377	*DL* en plourant si s'aloit d.
1178	*D* ne cuid p., *L* M. je ne cuid p.	1390	*DL* d. Helas pour D., *L* v. v. traire
1183	*L* ot d'armes et	1393	*L* t. chargiez et
1189	*L1L3* V. et quatre	1413	*L* m'a esté depuis d.
1196	*R* Ou adjouster	1419	*RD* m. leur s.
1197	*L* L. b. et dars, b. o.	1425	*DL* Qui
1198	*D* l. l. haster, *L* l. legierement h.	1426	*L* r. je pris trop du b.
1204	*R* M. sans a.	1430	*DL omit* et
1205	*DL* J. et g, *omit* nul	1441	*R* j. tele
1206	*L* f. d'un r.	1450	*L* Et l'un
1211	*D* h. sans toux	1463	*R* de nom
1219	*R* d. se v., *L1L3 omit* jur	1470	*DL* c. g. la n'a
1233	*DL* n. a. p.	1473	*DL* v. et de
1235	*DL* a. plus loyal n'arrestans	1486	*DL* d'un seul c.
1236	*L3 omits* fu	1491	*L* y. onny
1249	*L* et je l.	1498	*D* Vairs et
		1501	*D* Ot n.
		1504	*L3 omits* ses

1505 D Et tres p.
1509 R grassete
1513 DL ot petite et
1523 L1L3 Et b., DL d. descriptes
1525 L R. doulcet g.
1528 DL Et a d.
1529 D B. respondent
1537 D M. avenoit
1539 L omits a
1541 L p. beau
1546 L a. comme p.
1547 DL s. ne m.
1555 DL Et p. b., omit n'ot
1558 DL B. a l., L d. grossette
1566 D Ou demouroit
1569 D j. grassette
1573 RDL L'ot creé
1580 D a sa v.
1581 L3 D. d'amour s.
1586 L q. se compare au
1590 DL b. m'en s.
1591 DL R. p. j. c.
1593 L t. bel m.
1594 DL a. nulle ame
1596 R N'avoient
1597 DL p. esmeüe
1598 L L. joyant et
1611 RD l. qui s.
1616 L Le d.
1631 L c. je d.
1635 DL m'a depuis esté d'a.
1645 RD d. c'est a.
1646 L a resistee
1647 R Sa g.
1649 R En va
1655 L Et j.
1660 L P. une e.
1661 DL De t., D e. pensee l., L qu'eusse pensee
1667 DL p. avoir onques puis ne c.
1670 L p. estrangoit le
1675 L Qu'ou s.
1678 DL f. les s.
1686 L Q. ne v.

1687 D p. et d'un
1689 DL s. long t.
1698–99 reversed in L
1699 omitted in D
1707 R En un
1713 R l. me atire, D l. ma tire
1718 R t. m'aloye t.
1721 DL d. destrece
1726 R que s'ert, DL ce ert
1729 RD a lui t.
1733 L Le hardement du, D omits me
1742 L d. je l'eusse
1743 RD v. et p., R en Peusse
1745 DL l. aillours me voulz a.
1758 DL a. que m.
1759 DL N'y p.
1782 L2 p. q. ne onc f., L1L3 p. q. n'onc f.
1787 R a. quon le
1802 DL g. languour, d. couardement
1805 L p. a g.
1809 L3 a. plati a, L a tas
1829 D Celle
1830 L p. en m.
1846 D b. cuidoit q.
1858 DL c. j'endure
1862 DL s. p. e. de m. t.
1863 L e. ne s.
1878 L il est de
1881 R C. sauf vo, D sauve vostre g.
1883 R v. m'avez t.
1890 DL s. qui t.
1910 DL moy quel reconfort m.
1912–15 omitted in L3
1915 L1L2 me desespoir
1925 DL Qui
1931 R Q. ces s.
1963 R a. sueil
1967 L q. vers v.
1975 D f. plus r.
1978 D d'u. que le c. s'en t.

1979 *L* s. si je
1981 *D* t. autretant
1999 *DL* E. si vers vous
2006 *D omits* et
2007 *DL* de cel a., *D* a. suis je
2013 *L* et qu'il soit
2023 *DL* puis si m.
2034 *D omits the first* et
2038 *L* Sire de
2042 *R* q. prient
2046 *DL* q. le c.
2063 *D* Lui d.
2069 *L* Au d.
2074 *DL* f. a. l. et
Explicit *L1L3* Cy fine le d. de P.

Notes

Title and rubric. In the rubric, the phrase *qui s'adrece a un estrange* (which appears only in MS *R*) alludes to the poem's patron and recalls the rubric of *Trois jugemens*, which runs as follows: *Cy commence le livre des .iii. jugemens qui s'adrece au Seneschal de Haynault*. It refers most likely not to Jean de Werchin, the seneschal honored in *Trois jugemens*, but to either the marshal Boucicaut or to Jean de Châteaumorand. Willard arrives at that conclusion, pointing out that Werchin was not absent from France at the time *Poissy* was written (April 1400, according to ll. 35–39), whereas Boucicaut and Jean de Châteaumorand were in Constantinople in the spring of that year. See Willard, *Christine de Pizan: Her Life and Works*, pp. 64–65.

The table of contents in MS *R* gives the same information, listing the poem as *Item le Livre de Poissy qui s'adresce a ung chevalier estrangier .xvi.* The running title above the text reads simply: *Le livre de Poissy .xvj.*

1. As in the other two debate poems, the first letter of the first word, *Bon*, is a four-line-high, elaborately decorated capital executed in pink with white filigree, from which springs ivy foliage extending along the left margin. Similar to the others, the inside of the letter contains a vine decoration in pink, blue, white, and black on a gold background. A mistake was made with the capital letter beginning the text in MS *D*; it is an uppercase *M*, making the first word of the text *Mon* rather than *Bon* as in MSS *L1, L2*, and *R*. (In *L3*, the first letter of the first word was never added.) Upon close inspection, a small *b* is apparent in the left margin, obviously a preparation for either the execution or the correction of the letter. The text of *Poissy* contains none of the two-line capitals that mark major transitions in *Deux amans* and *Trois jugemens*.

15. *Priee*: although MS *D* agrees with MS *R*, Roy corrects to *prié*, following the *L* reading, perhaps to standardize the past participles in this line (*priee* and *requis*). I have chosen to leave the reading as it stands, on the grounds that agreement was very flexible in the fourteenth and fifteenth centuries (see Marchello-Nizia, p. 325). In similar constructions elsewhere in *Poissy*, where a feminine direct object precedes the passé composé, treatment of the past participle varies; for example, it does not take the feminine ending in ll. 2023 or 2062 but does in l. 1147. Line 1573, like l. 15, uses one past participle with a masculine ending and one with the feminine. Given the inconsistencies found in this text as in the others, I have not attempted to make usage uniform. (In l. 1573, however, the masculine past participle has been changed to *cree[ë]*, because the line is hypometric without the additional *e*, which must be counted even though it falls before a vowel.)

18. *Descort:* not to be confused with the genre found in classical troubadour poetry, this term seems to be used here more generally in its meaning "désaccord" or "dispute." It is used similarly in *Trois jugemens*, at ll. 494–95: *Mais il n'est riens, quoy que descort dessemble, / Que vraye amour ne racorde et assemble*; and at ll. 498–99: *Li duy amant s'amerent longuement / Sans nul descort et sans decevement*. Elsewhere in Christine's judgment poems, however, it seems to constitute a synonym of *débat* and *tence* (or *tençon*). This is well illustrated in the prologue of *Deux amans: Si vous*

diray / Le grant debat, ne ja n'en mentiray, / De .ij. amans que je moult remiray, / Car leur descort a ouÿr desiray / Et leur tençon / Gracïeuse, non mie en contençon (ll. 76–81). In *Trois jugemens* one reads: *Et sur vous tout en est mise la tence / Et le descort* (ll. 685–86). The word is used again in *Deux amans* at ll. 1934 and 1950 and in *Trois jugemens* at l. 28.

19. *Qu'i:* Here, as in l. 109 below and in *Trois jugemens,* l. 1213, for example, the form *qu'i* can be read as *qu'il* (or *qu'ilz*). I have therefore retained the *R* reading.

28–31. While MSS *D* and *L* maintain the *-ier* ending for each of the infinitives found at the rhyme in this quatrain, the *R* reading, which rhymes *er* with *ier,* is quite acceptable in Middle French practice. The ending of *targer* is abbreviated in MS *R* and could have been resolved either way. (The verb occurs twice more in the text, fully written out, once with *-ier* [l. 864], and once with *-er* [l. 606].)

63. *Qu'avecques:* MSS *R, D,* and *L2* read *avec;* the *L1* and *L3* has been adopted here because the one added syllable restores what is otherwise a hypometric line. While not indicating it as such, Roy makes the same correction. I have used the spelling of the long form as it appears in MS *R* at ll. 304 and 1688.

102. *Encor:* the reading *encore* in MS *R* gives a hypermetric line. Spelling of this adverb, like others, is flexible: the shorter form occurs in MS *R* at l. 550; other orthographic variants in MS *R* are *ancore* (ll. 1189, 1233, 1290) and *ancor* (ll. 133, 166, 245, passim).

109. *Qu'i* can be read as an orthographic variant of *qu'ilz.* The *D* and *L* readings are, respectively, *qu'il* (retained by Roy) and *qu'ilz.* See *Poissy,* l. 19, and *Trois jugemens,* l. 1213, for other examples. Another possibility in this instance is that the form represents *qu'y,* with *ils* unexpressed as a subject pronoun.

124–27. This rhyme with its considerable variations in spelling is regularized in the *L* MSS, perhaps simply for the eye, so that all four words in final position end in *-oz.*

146. *Ces gors, ces pieux:* the word *gort* (modern French *gord*) refers to a kind of fishery known in English as a kiddle or stake net. It consists of two converging rows of posts (the *pieux* mentioned here) that are planted in a river bottom and funnel fish into a net. The river water makes a pleasant rushing or gurgling noise as it passes through this arrangement of poles and net.

150. *Os:* several developments in the evolution of preterites are evident in this first-person singular preterite form of *avoir.* In Middle French, verbs with a past perfect in *oi/eüs* were changing in the first- and third-persons singular and the third-person plural to be consistent with the other forms. At the same time, the final *i* was disappearing from first-person singular perfects in *ui* and *oi,* while an *-s* was being added. (See Marchello-Nizia, pp. 225–26, 213–14). In this instance, the first change is not yet manifested here, but the second and third are. The form occurs again in l. 1685 and is spelled *oz* in ll. 633, 710, 915 passim. The same explanation applies to the verb *dos (devoir)* in l. 714.

181. *Ocy:* Christine draws directly on ll. 25–27 of Machaut's *Jugement dou roy de Behaigne,* where the narrator goes into the woods, following one of the singing birds he hears: *Si en choisi en l'air un voletant / Qui dessus tous s'en aloit gla-*

tissant: / *'Oci! Oci!'* Christine's passage elaborates on the pun involved, where *ocy* can be read as the second-person singular imperative of *occire*.

This onomatopoeic imitation of the nightingale's song (which MS *D* spells *aussi*) is attested to in texts as early as the late twelfth century. While Ovid's nightingale story (*Metamorphoses* 6) does not use the same precise rendering of the bird call, Christine certainly recalls the Ovidian style of oblique, poignant communication with this brief but richly signifying cry. Her bird also certainly evokes its well-known predecessors in Marie de France's lai *Laüstic* and in the tale *Philomena* attributed to Chrétien de Troyes.

183. *N'a:* adding *n'* as found in all four manuscripts other than *R* makes *prendre* count as two syllables, restoring both the meter and a parallel construction in the second half of the line.

192. The rhyming of *eil* with *ueil* that occurs in this quatrain is not unusual in Middle French; see Marchello-Nizia, p. 70.

213. The verb form *veismes* is the first-person plural preterite of *venir* and is also used in l. 345. See the discussion of verb forms in the Introduction, in the section "Language."

251. *Marie de Bourbon* was the daughter of Pierre I, duke of Bourbon, and sister of Jeanne of Bourbon, wife of Charles V. This did indeed make her *Tante du roy de France* (l. 253). She entered the convent at Poissy in 1351 at the age of four and took her vows when she was seventeen. In 1380 she was elected the seventh prioress of Poissy and held that position until her death on January 10, 1401. She was the only prioress in the history of that religious house to belong to the immediate royal family. One of the few pieces of sculpture from the priory that survive is a statue of Marie de Bourbon done in black-and-white marble. It originally stood in the choir of the church, to the right of the great screen, close to an altar (see Bories, p. 45). The statue was apparently kept at the church in Saint-Denis for some time (according to Noël, whom Roy cites for this information), but Moreau-Rendu, a more recent source, gives its location as the Louvre.

281. This *Marie* was the daughter of Charles VI and Isabeau de Bavière. Born in August 1393, she was only four years old when she joined the community at Poissy in 1397 and would therefore still have been a little girl at the time Christine's *Dit* was written. According to Pougin, she died of the plague in 1438 (p. 539, note 2).

286. *La fille du comte de Harecourt:* Pougin identifies this young woman as the daughter of Jean VI, count of Harcourt, and Catherine of Bourbon, sister of Jeanne of Bourbon, wife of Charles V. Her relationship to the princess (see l. 289) was therefore *grand'tante* (Pougin 539, note 4). Roy supplies her name, Catherine d'Harcourt, and the following information:

> Entrée au couvent de Poissy en 1380, on lui reconnut 200 liv. de rente le 8 août 1396. Sa soeur Blanche, d'abord religieuse à Sainte-Marie de Soissons, était, depuis 1391, abbesse du célèbre monastère de Fontevrault (B.N., *Pièces orig. 1479* et P. Anselme, vol. 5, 133). (Roy, vol. 2, p. 312)

291. *L'encline:* Although often used with a reflexive meaning, *encliner* can also be transitive, meaning "saluer en s'inclinant." Here *ma dame . . . La prieuse* is bowing to the princess Marie, introduced in l. 274.

313. *Anges:* MS R reads *angles,* but the *l* of this word is crossed out and expunctuated with a mark below the line. The removal of *l* regularizes the rhyme, which remains, in MSS D and L, at least orthographically irregular. See also the note to l. 1307.

319. This description is used in Georges Duby, ed., *A History of Private Life,* as an example of the kinds of beds found in various sorts of medieval residences. The passage reads:

> Some monastic beds were beautiful in appearance yet still austere. Christine de Pisan tells us that the nuns in the dormitory at Poissy slept fully dressed, without sheets, and on flocked rather than down mattresses. Nevertheless, their beds were covered by elegant woven spreads: "There were no nightgowns or lingerie and their beds have no frilly down *coutes* but rather *materas* covered with beautiful Arras tapestries, well made, but this is just decoration, for [the mattresses] are hard and filled with flocking." (p. 493)

The translation is a fairly accurate rendering of ll. 314–19 (unlike the translations given earlier of ll. 443–47 [p. 436] and ll. 448–56 [p. 487], which both contain serious errors), although a more literal reading of the first part of the passage would be: "they do not wear nightdresses there, and they lie on rough woolen blankets at night; they have no featherbeds, but rather mattresses covered with beautiful Arras tapestries. . . ." Hinnebusch states that the beds to be found in Dominican monasteries were hard and rough: "Friars could have a matting of straw, wool, or sacking but not a mattress." According to their Constitution, the friars were required to sleep in a tunic and underclothing (Hinnebusch, p. 358); this precept explains why the ladies slept clothed (*vestues,* l. 320) rather than in nightgowns. See also the reference to the ladies' beds in l. 451.

322. *Batues:* Pougin provides an interesting interpretation of this phrase: "Peut-être doit-on interpréter ce mot dans le sens de 'appelées par une cliquette'" (p. 540, note 3). While Pougin apparently questions the implication that the sisters were subjected to rather rigorous discipline, the tone of the passage reinforces precisely this interpretation by showing how the nuns forgo creature comforts. See also ll. 577–82, which provide both another example of stringent rules (any nun who is late for dinner loses her share) and a description of the way in which the nuns were called to assemble.

334. In MS R, a space before *maires* has been filled with a decorative box and diagonal strokes. The vellum appears to have been patched at this spot. See the note to l. 375, which is exactly overleaf from l. 334.

345. *Nous en veismes:* There is no compelling reason to make *en veismes* one word, as Roy did. The verb *veismes* is the first-person plural preterite of *venir* (also used in l. 213), and the phrase translates as "nous nous en allâmes."

359. *Apporter:* keeping the infinitive instead of adopting *apportent*, the third-person plural present indicative found in the other manuscripts, makes *apporter* depend, like *estendre* and *tendre*, on *ot fait* (l. 357); rather literally, "There where one had had white, sweet-smelling cloths laid out and carpets spread, wine and food brought without delay."

375. This line in MS R is written in the margin. The vellum has been patched at this spot. (See the note to l. 334.)

426. *Quë:* while MSS D and L use *Qui* at the beginning of this line, the form *que* was not uncommon as a subject pronoun in Middle French and has therefore been retained. (See Marchello-Nizia, p. 161.) Other examples occur at ll. 689, 1425, 1925.

433. *Dechet:* MSS D and L use *dechiet*, thus preserving the rhyme in *-iet*.

442. *Hault Pas:* the most probable identification for this place name appears to be the Hospital of Saint-Jacques-du-Haut-Pas, situated at what is today number 252, rue Saint-Jacques, in Paris. The 1949 Michelin *Guide de Paris* provides the following entry for this address:

> Institut national des Sourds-Muets. Il fait le coin de la rue de l'Abbé-de-l'Epée. A cet endroit s'était installé, au 14e s., un hôpital qui donnait assistance aux nombreux pèlerins faisant route vers St.-Jacques-de-Compostelle ou en revenant. Les religieux qui assuraient le service venaient du couvent d'Alto-Passo (Haut Pas), près de Lucques. Ils s'appelaient, ici, frères de St.-Jacques-du-Haut-Pas. (p. 110)

Gustave Pessard, *Nouveau dictionnaire historique de Paris*, says that the first chapel was built on this site in 1350, although the church there now was not begun until 1630 (pp. 1350–51). L'Abbé Lebeuf, *Histoire de la ville et de tout le diocèse de Paris*, places the Hospitaliers du Haut-Pas, originally from Luca, Italy (on the Arno), in Paris as early as the reign of Philippe le Bel. On the origins of the order, see also Jeremiah F. O'Sullivan, ed., *The Register of Eudes of Rouen*, p. 553, note 31.

An institution of this sort that catered to a large number of travelers would need considerable facilities and supplies, much like the wine cellars, ovens, and other *neccessaires* at Poissy described in the preceding passage (ll. 438–42). Christine, as a Paris resident, would certainly have been aware of the existence of such a shelter. It is also conceivable that she knew about the mother house in Italy.

447. *Cours* for *tours* in MS R is likely a scribal error, influenced by the endings of ll. 444 and 445. Furthermore, the letters *c* and *t* look much alike in the manuscripts containing the debate poems and can easily be confused. The *DL* reading has been adopted here.

466. In MS R, *de* is added above the line between A and *maint*, in abbreviated form and with a flourish.

510. In MS R, the second *et* is added above the line, to the right of *d'asur*, in its abbreviated form.

518–23. This description of the Dominican habit is quite accurate. It consisted of a white tunic and scapular, a leather belt, and black mantle. The requisite black veil and white wimple are mentioned in ll. 532–34. The one puzzling item in the list of garments is *fros* (l. 519), (*carfroc* in Roy). One definition for this word as it was used in the Middle Ages is "ce qui dans l'habit du moine couvre la tête, les épaules, [et] la poitrine" (*Le Robert: Dictionnaire historique de la langue française*). It is possible, therefore, that the word refers to the "capuce" (in English, the "capuche"), a hood or cowl originally joined to the scapular at the neck opening but made a separate garment in the mid-fourteenth century. It, too, would have been white. (See Hinnebusch, p. 340.)

532. The *f* in *cuevrechiefs* and in *chefs*, l. 533, would certainly not have been pronounced before final *s*, therefore assuring the rhyme. See Marchello-Nizia, p. 85.

561. *D'abres* is an orthographic variant of *D'arbres*. This *R* reading, which has lost its first *r* through the process of dissimilation, is not unusual.

578. *Temps:* the homonym *Tant* found in *R* is in all likelihood a scribal error influenced by the beginning of l. 577. The *DL* reading has therefore been adopted here.

593. In MS *R*, the catchwords *Et celles qui* appear below l. 593, in the lower margin. They are the first words of a new quire that begins with folio 85.

603. *Bourbon:* Pougin was unable to identify this proper name, stating that "Il n'y a pas aujourd'hui d'endroit à Poissy dont le nom rappelle celui-là" (p. 548, note 2). Bories, however, notes with regard to this line that "la cour Bourbon était une grande hôtellerie qui se trouvait sur la place où se tient aujourd'hui le petit marché" (p. 65).

630. In MS *R*, the first *et* has been corrected. It is written over a word that was longer by at least one letter and the *e* itself appears to be untouched, suggesting that *R* may have originally have read *est* just as the other four manuscripts do. With the correction, ll. 630–31 thus read: "When she who is both mistress and friend to my daughter. . . ." The *D* and *L2* readings are incorrect, as both repeat *est* (*qui est maistresse . . . De ma fille est*). MSS *L1* and *L3* have solved the problem by omitting *est* from l. 631.

714. *Dos* is the first-person singular preterite of *devoir*.

722. *Meismes* is disyllabic in MS *R*, but the readings in MSS *D* and *L3* require that it be counted as three syllables, still the more usual form in the fourteenth and early fifteenth centuries. (See Marchello-Nizia, p. 57.)

728. Given the tendency in MS *R* to confuse *s* and *c*, it is possible that *Si* was meant as *ici*, in agreement with the *DL* reading *Cy*. Nevertheless, the particle *si* is acceptable here; the line as given translates more or less as "So, what shall we do?" as opposed to the *DL* variant, "What shall we do here [in this garden]?"

776. This *vin de Saint Poursain* must refer to the product of the well-known vineyards at what is today Saint-Pourçain-sur-Sioule, in the canton of Allier. In his history of Saint-Pourçain, A. Laforêt states: "Les vins de Saint-Pourçain bénéficièrent depuis les temps les plus reculés d'une fort bonne réputation. D'après les documents, ils alimentèrent la table royale du XIIIe au XVe siècle" (p. 245). Apparently Charles VI received two barrels of this wine at Beauvais as a gift in 1387. For further information, consult Laforêt's chapter "Les vins de Saint-Pourçain," pp. 245–64.

825. *Cleomadés* (Cléomadès) is the hero of a courtly romance of the same name written by Adenet le Roi in 1285. In the story, Cléomadès fights battles, overcomes various obstacles to his love for Clarmondine, and travels through Europe by means of a magic flying wooden horse. Adenet's work is mentioned in Froissart's *L'Espinette amoureuse:* the protagonist comes upon a young lady reading a *rommanc.* When he asks her what it is called, she replies, *De Cleamodés* [sic] / *Est appellés. Il fu bien fes / Et dittés amoureusement* (Anthime Fourrier, ed., ll. 703, 705–7).

826. *Palamedés* (Palamedès) first appears in the *Tristan en prose.* He is a Saracen knight in love with Iseut but loyal to Tristan. There exists a work called the *Roman de Palamède,* which was composed after the first version of the prose *Tristan* and before 1240; it concerns primarily the fathers of well-known heroes (including Tristan and Palamedès himself).

Like Cléomadès, Palamedès belongs to the late medieval compendium of useful literary examples of knightly virtue. Christine also uses them in tandem in *Deux amans,* in a passage describing heroes to whom love brought fame (ll. 1544–50; see the notes to ll. 1544 and 1546). No doubt the rhyming quality of their names is as much a link between them for Christine's purposes as any resemblance in their stories.

860. *Honneur:* On the quality of the vowel at the rhyme in this quatrain, see Marchello-Nizia, pp. 69–70. The spelling *honnour* in MSS *D* and *L* maintains the eye rhyme better than the *R* reading, but the difference between the two is purely orthographic.

863. The noun phrase *un tour* depends on *Devoit aler* (l. 865), with the infinitive *faire* understood. Thus ll. 862–65 read: "Then there was a man who said at once that he was supposed to take a trip to the country where you are, without delay...."

873. *Chans:* the *R* reading of *champs,* a homonym of the word expected, was likely copied under the influence of the ending of l. 872. The *DL* reading has been substituted here.

878. In MS *R, se* is a correction, for which a preparation remains above the line.

934. The oath *par saint Nicaise* refers to a fifth-century Christian martyr. See the note to *Deux amans,* l. 982.

941. *Qui* is in this case an orthographic variant of the oblique case relative pronoun *cui* used in the absolute, that is, without a preposition. It therefore means *à qui,* where *qui* represents an inanimate object, the antecedent of which is *rien,* l. 939. The sense of the narrator's question to the lady (ll. 939–41) is therefore, "Is there [Have you] anything unpleasant about which you are thinking?" On *qui* as *cui* and as a relative pronoun referring to either an person or a thing, see Marchello-Nizia, p. 160.

984. *Courroucie[e]:* the correction is necessary to ensure the feminine rhyme in this quatrain. In MS *R,* l. 984 is the only line in this group of four that lacks the final *e,* while MSS *D* and *L* have *sié* in final position in l. 985 and MS *L* ends l. 987 in *accoisié.*

1077. MSS L_1L_3 read *un an* instead of the seven years mentioned in MS *R, D,* and *L2*. While possible in terms of the meter of this line, the length of time is incorrect in light of ll. 1253 and 1265, which state that the lady's knight was captured more than five years before and that he and she had already loved each other for two years prior to his capture.

1078. In MS *R*, the word *courtois* is split between *t* and *o*, around a hole in the vellum. Another word is split in this fashion in l. 2000. Consistent with the high quality of production in this manuscript, there are few instances where holes in the support have not been repaired. Most have been filled with patches of similarly colored parchment, the edges of which were beveled to ensure a smooth join. The holes are often difficult to detect unless the folio is seen against a light source, which reveals the darker double thickness where the two surfaces are glued.

1094. In MS *R, de* is added above the line.

1163. In MS *R*, a correction has been made to the word *Ains*; the *a* is a lowercase letter rather than the capital normally found at the beginning of a line.

1178. *Crai* is an orthographic variant of *croi*. The spellings *ai* and *oi* were often interchangeable at this time (Marchello-Nizia, p. 64).

1194. In MS *R*, the *st* of *fust* is added above the line.

1198. *Hanter* here is used in the sense of "practiquer" (as found in Edmond Huguet's *Dictionnaire de la langue française du seizième siècle*), and *legieretez* means "légèreté" or "facilité." The phrase therefore translates roughly as "exercise his agility" or "demonstrate his nimbleness."

1205. MS *R* has a mark added above the line between *jolis* and *gay* that appears to be the abbreviation for *et*. This reading would correspond with that in MSS *D* and *L*. It is left out here because, given the *R* reading of *nul desroy*, the addition of *et* would result in a hypermetric line.

1261. The phrase *mal et doulereux voyage / De Honguerie* (ll. 1261–62) refers to the crusade to Nicopolis, which took place when Sigismund, king of Hungary, appealed to western Europe for help against the Turkish forces of Sultan Bajazeth. (See the note to l. 1283.) The Franco-Burgundian army that went to the aid of Sigismund was led by Jean, count of Nevers. (See the note to l. 1273.) So many men responded to the summons to join the crusade that only the elite were admitted. Aziz Suryal Atiya, in *The Crusade of Nicopolis*, puts the number of participants at 1,000 knights plus at least an equal number of squires. The battle took place on September 25, 1396, and proved disastrous for Jean and Sigismund's forces. Their armies were decimated, and many of the captives taken were killed. The news of the disaster reached Paris with some of the survivors who straggled back late in 1396.

Meanwhile, among the captives, a handful of the most highly born leaders of the expedition had been spared (including Jean de Nevers, Philippe d'Artois, Jacques de Bourbon, Jean de Bourgogne, Henri de Bar, and Guy de la Trémouille), in the hope of exchanging their lives for large ransoms. Once these sums had been paid, Nevers and some of his companions arrived home safely to a hero's welcome.

Some points of Christine's account here are inconsistent with the facts. She states in ll. 1265–66 that the voyage to Hungary was undertaken *Il a .v. ans et plus*, whereas the crusaders did not leave until 1396, four years prior to the year given as the date for the events of the *Dit de Poissy* (1400). (One might conceivably resolve this problem of dating by reading the words *celle voye* in l. 1265 more figuratively as meaning "course of action" rather than "voyage"; the crusade was preached as early as 1394, and negotiations were concluded in 1395.) As to the notion that her fictional knight's return was prevented by the inability of his family to raise the necessary money (l. 1301 ff.), this obstacle to love is a convenient invention. In fact, the responsibility did not actually devolve on each prisoner's relations. According to Atiya, "The deadweight of the ransom and of the accumulated expenses fell, not on the various individual prisoners, but mainly on the shoulders of the Duke of Burgundy" (p. 110).

For further historical detail in modern sources, see Sir Steven Runciman, *History of the Crusades*, vol. 3, pp. 458–62; and Atiya, especially the chapters "The Battle of Nicopolis" and "The Aftermath." Numerous descriptions of this crusade also exist in sources contemporary with Christine. See, for example, Lalande's edition of *Le Livre des Fais du bon messire Jehan le Maingre, dit Bouciquaut*, pp. 88–128; the following passages from Kervyn de Lettenhove's *Oeuvres de Froissart: Chroniques:* vol. 15, particularly pp. 216–31, 242–53, 262–69, 309–52, 355–60, and 392 ff.; "Relation de la Croisade de Nicopoli, par un serviteur de Gui de Blois," appended in two parts to Froissart's *Chroniques* (part 1, vol. 15, pp. 439–508, and part 2, vol. 16, pp. 413–43); excerpts from Philippe de Mézières, "L'Epistre lamentable sur la desconfiture du roy de Honguerie," also appended to the *Chroniques* (vol. 16, pp. 444–525). Finally, one should mention the poems by Eustache Deschamps that make reference to Nicopolis and the crusade. In the *Oeuvres complètes d'Eustache Deschamps*, Auguste H. E. de Queux de Saint-Hilaire and Gaston Raynaud, eds., these are: Balade XLIX, "Exhortation à la croisade" (vol. 1, pp. 138–39); Balade DCCLXIX, "Sur l'expédition de Barbarie" (vol. 4, pp. 266–67); Balade MCCCIX, "Contre la Hongrie et la Lombardie" (vol. 7, pp. 66–67); Balade MCCCXVI, "Pour les Français morts à Nicopolis" (vol. 7, pp. 77–78); Balade MCCCCXXVII, "Faicte pour ceuls de France quant ilz furent en Hongrie" (vol. 8, pp. 85–86).

1273. In MS *R*, the words *Le Conte* are a correction. They contain the first capital letters used inside a line, and they are written in letters larger than normal. Whatever *Le Conte* replaces was longer than the corrected title. One might speculate that MS *R* originally read *Monseigneur* like the other four manuscripts, which raises the intriguing question of why it was changed. The count in question is Jean sans Peur (1371–1419), who became duke of Burgundy in 1404 after the death of his father, Philippe le Hardi.

1276. In MS *R*, this line is written in the margin, and small marks in the shape of a cross or an *X* both precede the line and indicate where it should be inserted in the text. The first word, *A*, is barely legible and is written as a lowercase letter.

1283. The title *le Basac* refers to Bajazeth [Bayezid] (1354–1403), sultan of the Ottoman Turks from 1389–1402. He led the Turkish forces against the Western crusaders at Nicopolis. (See the note to l. 1261.)

1307. In MS R, a final letter has been erased at the end of the word *ange*, where MSS D and L have *angel*. Cf. l. 313, where the *l* of what was *angles* has been expunctuated.

1324. In MS R, which diverges from the other witnesses here, the whole line has been scratched out and corrected.

1334. In MS R, the *i* of *j'ai* is added above the *a*. This is the only occurrence of this spelling in MS R, where *ay* is the standard form for the first-person singular indicative present of *avoir*. (See ll. 25, 42, 173, 703, 1035, 1073, passim.)

1463. The R reading of the final word, *nom*, has been rejected in favor of the DL spelling *non*, so as to make it immediately recognizable as a negation and to mirror the word at the end of l. 1460.

1516. In MS R, the second *e* has been scratched out of what was *menues*. In Old and Middle French, the noun *dent* could be either feminine or masculine.

1539–47. This sentence is a good example of an "apo koinou" construction, in which two independent phrases are linked into a single sentence by a shared word that functions as a different part of speech in each. The overlap in sense makes the sentence difficult to punctuate by modern rules. In this example, the first part of the sentence concerns Nature's handiwork: *Nature . . . Ne fist ouvrage / Oncques plus bel . . . Que sa . . . Poitrine*. The second describes the knight's admirable chest: *Sa . . . Poitrine fu sans os ne veine ombrage. . . .* The shared words, *sa poitrine*, are the object of the first phrase but the subject of the second.

1590. In MS R, the word *me* is added above the line in lighter ink.

1594. The noun *ame* can be either masculine or feminine in Middle French; note that MSS D and L read *nulle ame*, which does not change the syllable count.

1634. In MS R, the word *de* is inserted above the line in lighter ink. The expression *au de premier* means "au début," "at first," treating the adverbial phrase *de premier*, which itself usually means "d'abord," as a noun phrase.

1648. In MS R, the letters A and l in this line, which is the first line of 92v°a, are written very large and extend through the upper margin. The tops of them have been cut off, evidence that the folio had its upper edge trimmed at some point in the manuscript's history.

1698–99. Roy reverses these lines, presumably on the strength of the L reading. MS D is missing what in this edition is l. 1699, with no indication whether the missing line belongs before or after l. 1698. The order here follows the R reading, with l. 1699 modifying the lady's warm reception of the squire (l. 1698). In translation, the R reading says: "And she also welcomed me warmly / At all hours, gladly, without delay, / And asked for me / Often . . . " (ll. 1698–1701). The meaning of *anchere* (*enchiere*, in the L manuscripts) is not immediately clear. The definitions "enchère" and "renchérissement" found in Old French dictionaries do not seem appropriate in this context. The translation offered here uses as a guide an entry in Huguet's dictionary, which lists the phrase "sans faire grand enchere" as "sans tarder" (vol. 3, p. 398b).

1713. The L reading *martire* is more logical than either the R reading, *me atire*, or the D reading, *ma tire*. It is used here as an intransitive verb meaning "souffrir le martire." Roy also uses it, although without listing the rejected D reading in the variants. The *D* reading does pose a problem, in that one can clearly see that *ma* and *tire* were once joined. A letter has been erased, and from traces left it may well have been an *r*. Using *martire* at the end of l. 1713 also has the advantage of providing, in the form of a conjugated verb, a rich rhyme for the noun *martire* in l. 1715.

1883. The *R* reading of *m'avez* is likely a case of scribal error, where perhaps one more minim than required was added. It has been corrected from the readings in MSS *D* and *L*.

1887. Below this line in MS *R*, one finds the catchwords *Esté en mue*, which begin a new quire on folio 93r°.

1953. In MS *R*, the verb *doint*, which is abbreviated, has two nasal bars above it. This may be to fill in the space left by the short line preceding it. Open space is often filled in MS *R* by using larger or more ornate letters than usual in the line above or below. For example, *y* often has a dot above it when it occurs in the top line of a column (ll. 107, 310, 838, 959, 1728) or below the space following a four-syllable line (ll. 181, 1465). See also the note to l. 1967.

1958. This line as it scans is actually hypermetric, but *si ne* has to be contracted, when read aloud, from two syllables to one in order to rhyme with *fine*, etc. See a similar construction in l. 2007.

1963. The long *s* of *sueil* in MS *R* is missing the crossbar that would make it the *f* of *fueil*. It has been corrected from the readings in MSS *D* and *L*.

1967. In MS *R*, the word *ami* ends in a long *i*, unusual in word-final position, which descends into the space following the short l. 1968.

2007. *Su ge* is an orthographic variant of *suis je*. The *D* variant *suis je* is easier for the reader to understand than the *R* and *L* equivalents (*su je* and *su ge*, respectively), but the contracted form was certainly meant as an eye rhyme. The meter depends, as in l. 1958, on the contraction of *su ge* / *suis je* into one syllable. MSS *R* and *L* represent this contraction phonetically.

2060. The phrase *Et quant mengié* / *Et solacié omes* (ll. 2060–61) means, "When we had eaten and amused ourselves." Having finished their dinner at the house of Christine, the narrator, the travelers will now take leave of her, after the debaters ask her to write up their story quickly (ll. 2062–64).

2069. *Derrenier* must count for only two syllables; otherwise, the line is hypermetric. Although various orthographic variants exist, all five manuscripts spell the word the same way here. While in Middle French an *e* between consonants in a middle syllable can be either elided or pronounced (see Marchello-Nizia, p. 82), it is generally pronounced in the *Poissy* manuscripts, this particular case notwithstanding.

2075. *Creintis* unscrambled gives *Cristine*, the anagram announced in ll. 2068–70. Both other debates likewise end in anagrams. (See the notes for *Deux amans*, l. 2023, and for *Trois jugemens*, l. 1531.) For critical analysis of Christine's anagrams, see references in note 70 to the Introduction.

Glossary

This glossary is by no means intended to be comprehensive. Rather, it lists words that are used in the debate poems but are not readily found in a standard, widely available reference source such as A. J. Greimas's one-volume *Dictionnaire de l'ancien français*. These words may be archaisms, neologisms, idiomatic usages, orthographic variants, or other unusual items. My major sources have been F. E. Godefroy, A. Tobler and E. Lommatzsch, G. Di Stefano, and E. Huguet (see the bibliography for complete references).

Standard abbreviations are used to indicate parts of speech: *adj.* = adjective; *adv.* = adverb or adverbial; *conj.* = conjunction; *f.* = feminine; *fut.* = future; *imper.* = imperative; *impf.* = imperfect; *imps.* = impersonal; *ind.* = indicative; *inf.* = infinitive; *interj.* = interjection; *m.* = masculine; *n.* = noun; *p.* = past; *part.* = participle; *p.c.* = passé composé; *pl.* = plural; *pr.* = present; *prep.* = preposition; *p.s.* = passé simple; *pron.* = pronoun; *refl.* = reflexive; *subj.* = subjunctive; *v.* = verb. The numbers 1 through 6 refer to persons of finite verb forms.

Not all occurrences are listed for items which appear repeatedly.

An asterisk refers the reader to further information in the notes following each poem.

abay, *n.m.*, TJ1113, barking
acolie, *n.f.*, DA127, a flower, named ancolie or columbine
aconter, *v.*, to attach importance to, give credence to: **aconte**, *3pr.ind.*, DA939
aconsuyvre, *v.*, to reach, to catch up with: **aconsuivismes**, *4p.s.*, P938
acort, *n.m.*, P497, P902, harmony; TJ794, TJ1498, arrangement, agreement; P2007, opinion; **mettre accort**, DA1945, to settle, resolve
acourer, *v.*, to suffer, to grieve: *inf.*, P951
adés, *adv.*, DA1611, P824, at the moment, still
adjouster, *v.*, to attribute to, associate with: **adjoustez**, *5pr.ind.*, DA1259
aduire, *v.*, to befit, to please: **aduit**, *3pr.ind.*, TJ1074; **aduisant**, *pr.part.*, P74
aduis, *adj.*, DA1650, TJ933, inclined, prepared (to do something)
adviser, *v.*, to consider, to decide: **advison**, *4pr.ind.*, P2012
affait(i)er, *v.*, to educate, teach: **affaite**, *3pr.ind.*, DA1089
affubler, *v.*, to put on, wear, to cover (hide) a part of the body: **affubla**, *3p.s.*, TJ1111; **affublant**, *pr.part.*, P1719; **s'affubloient**, *3refl.pr.ind.*, P1451

agait, agaitant, *n.m.*, TJ1096, trap; DA541, DA1211, TJ988, TJ1128, spy; **en agait**, TJ989, on the lookout
agaitier, *v.*, to spy, to keep watch: *inf.*, DA1218, DA1355
agus, *adj.*, DA744, sharp, pointed
a(h)erdre, *v.*, to be attached to: **aherses**, *p.part.*, P101
alloe, *n.f.*, P117, lark
alongne, *n.f.*, TJ425, delay
amesir, *v.*, to lessen: **sans amesir**, TJ372, without flagging
anchere, enchiere, *n.f.*, bid; **sans anchere/enchiere**, P370, P1699, without bargaining, wholeheartedly
anoier, *v.*, to vex, annoy: **anoit**, *3pr.ind.*, DA343; **anuyé**, *p.part.*, DA213, sad
anoye, *n.m.*, TJ838, torment, unhappiness
anui, *n.m.*, P750, boredom, tedium
äourer, *v.*, to adore: **äouree**, *p.part.*, DA829; **äouroit**, *3imp.ind.*, TJ390, TJ766
appert, en appert, *adv.*, P1774, openly
aresner, *v.*, to speak to, address: *inf.*, DA300; **aresna**, *3p.s.*, P271; **arraisonne**, *3pres.ind.*, TJ1238
arremens, *n.m.*, DA758, ink
arroy, *n.m.*, P524, P1204, outfit; DA1730, action, condition
assener, *v.*, to strike, aim: *inf.*, DA1769, TJ1328; to succeed: *inf.*, DA302, DA2017
assesmé, *adj.*, DA 98, DA1699, outfitted, adorned, well turned out
assis, *adj.*, P336, well placed, provided for; DA789, situated, located
attrait, *adj.*, P1185, P1582, descended (from), born (of)
attrét, *n.m.*, provision, preparation; welcome; **faire attrét**, DA579-80, to make welcome, to be receptive to
auté, *n.m.*, TJ551, altar
avoy, *interj.*, TJ915, [reinforces distress]
aymy, *interj.*, TJ147, P1979, [exclamation of pain]
aÿrer, *refl.v.*, to become angry, irritated: **s'aÿre**, *3pr.ind.*, DA462
baudour, *n.f.*, DA1164, joy, fervor
bault, *adj.*, DA1587, DA1834, joyful, emboldened
besillier, *v.*, to harm, mistreat: **besillant**, *pr.part.*, DA1430
bigne, *n.f.*, DA1388, raised bump, goose egg, caused by a blow
bobe, *n.f.*, P531, (dirty) spot
boubancier, *adj.*, TJ1409, arrogant, prideful
bouter, *v.*, to place, push, put: **boutees**, *p.part.*, DA494; **en sus bouté**, DA11, rejected; **se bouter**, *refl.v.*, to engage in, to undertake: **se boute**, *3pr.ind.*, DA847
bugle, *adj.*, DA880*, stupid, simple
capulaire, *n.m.*, P519, scapular [see note to P523]
cas, *adj.*, TJ1221, broken (voice)
cas, *n.m.*, fall, accident; **a cas**, TJ1222,* suddenly, completely; **flati a cas**, DA1206, P1809, knocked down, crushed

cault, *adj.*, DA1586, prudent, wise
cemoient, see **cremer**
certené, *adj.*, TJ945, certain
chambel, *n.m.*, P386, cornice or transom
chantier, *n.m.*, P446, heap, pile
chapitrer, *v.*, to blame, to reprimand: **chapitre**, *3pr.ind.*, DA965
charneure, *n.f.*, P1169, P1553, flesh, skin
chetel, *n.m.*, P1686, return (from an investment), recompense
cheus = **chez**, *prep.*, P2058, at the house of
chevance, *n.f.*, P1311, livelihood, possessions
chevir, *v.*, to succeed in, finish: *inf.*, P1903, **chevimes**, *4p.s*, P642; **se chevir**, *refl.v.*, to manage, cope: *inf.*, DA567, DA890
chevesaille, *n.f.*, P1133, collar(bone)
clacelliere, *n.f.*, P595, (woman) keeper of the keys
cloison, *n.f.*, P616, enclosure, fence
closier, *n.m.*, P613, porter, gardener
colombelle, *n.f.*, P393, small pillar or column
compoindre, *v.*, to bite or sting: **compoint**, *p.part.*, DA1306
conroy, *n.m.*, DA304, P1207, state, disposition; DA1731, condition; **de bon conroy**, P527, in good order, of good material
corbel, *n.m.*, P387, bracket, beam
corde, *n.f.*, rope; **sus cordes**, P451, (a mattress) supported by ropes
corsage, *n.m.*, P1092, body, torso
coulice, *n.f.*, runner, slide; **fenestres coulices**, P329, sliding windows
couste, *n.f.*, featherbed, bedcover; **coustes a franges**, P315, fringed bedcovers
couvertement, *adv.*, P1802, discreetly
couvine, *n.f.* or *n.m.*, DA542, secret agreement, understanding
cremer, cremir, to fear: **cremoit**, *3impf.ind.*, TJ462; **cemoient**, *6impf.ind.*, TJ706*
cruble, *n.m.*, DA882,* sieve
cueuvrechief, *n.m.*, P1486, kerchief; P532, kerchief worn as a wimple
daintié, *n.m.*, pleasure, joy; **a grant daintié**, DA763, with great pleasure
deffin, deffiner, *n.m.*, P2070, DA2019, end
deguerpir, *v.*, to abandon, to leave: **deguerpie**, *p.part.*, TJ1159
dehaitié, *adj.*, DA253, TJ402, P710, P1990, unhappy, miserable
delayer, *refl.v.*, to delay, slow down: **se deleant**, *pr.part.*, TJ1369
deliter, *refl.v.*, to rejoice, to take delight: **s'est delitee**, *3p.c.*, P1645;
    delitable, delitens, *adj.*, P421, P625, P766, charming, delightful
demour, *n.m.*, DA71, stage; TJ1007, stay
demucier, *v.*, to hide: **se demussent**, *6refl.pr.ind.*, DA1354; **demussoit**, *3impf.ind.*, P941
departance = **deportance**, *n.f.*, delay; **sans departance**, P1456, directly, without delay

278 / Glossary

deporter, *refl.v.*, to spare oneself: **se deporterent**, *6p.s.*, P769; **se deporta**, *3p.s.*, P785; to enjoy oneself, to have fun: **se depporte**, *3pr.ind.*, DA1220; **vous depportez**, *5pr.ind.*, TJ953; **me deportasse**, *1impf.subj.*, P1663; to refrain, to deprive oneself: **vous depportez**, *5pr.ind.*, TJ954; **se deporterent**, *6p.s.*, P455
deport, *n.m.*, TJ398, TJ1001, P816, P901, pleasure, joy; sport, diversion
derout, *p.part.* of **derompre**, TJ1375, destroyed, spoiled
derrenier = **dernier**, *adj.*, TJ1526, last
derver, *v.*, to go mad: **derve**, *3pr.ind.*, DA620, DA1250, P1300
desceindre, *v.*, to untie, to free: **deçains**, *p.part.*, T554
descort, *n.m.*, DA79, DA1934, TJ28, TJ494, P18, disagreement or dispute
despences, *n.f.pl.*, P439, provisions
detrïer, *v.*, to delay: *inf.*, P715; **detriant**, *pr.part.*, TJ534
dextre, *n.m.*, DA209, right; **a dextre**, TJ1327, directly, adroitly
dongier, *n.m.*, peril, difficulty; **a dongier**, P306, with difficulty
duire, *v.*, to lead, to instruct, govern: **duit**, *3pr.ind.*, DA311, TJ962
duit, *adj.*, DA3, DA1659, TJ4, P202, given to, with a propensity for
el = **elle**, *pron.*, TJ1129,* she
embatre, *refl.v.*, to participate in: *inf.*, DA330; **s'embatent**, *6pr.ind.*, DA1295
embler, *v.*, to steal, sneak away: **emble**, *3pr.ind.*, TJ492; **emblant**, *pr.part.*, P1011; **emblee**, *p.part.*, TJ491; to conceal: **emblant**, *pr.part.*, TJ113;
emblee, *adj.*, P918, secret, hidden
embesongner, *refl.v.*, to apply oneself diligently: **s'embesongne**, *3pr.ind.*, TJ427
embronchier, *refl.v.*, to hide or cover oneself: **s'embrunchant**, *pr.part.* DA237
empestrer, *v.*, to restrain, shackle, hinder: **empestre**, *3pr.ind.*, DA518, TJ118
en sus, *adv.*, P1863, away, aside; **en sus bouté**, DA11, see **bouter**
ençains, *adj.*, P1875, surrounded, burdened (figuratively)
enchiere, see **anchere**
encheoir, *v.*, to fall into: **encheoir en**, *inf.*, P1714, to bring upon oneself, fall prey to: **encheoir de**, derive from, be due to: **enchiet**, *3pr.ind.*, P435
encliner, *v.*, to bow to someone: **encline**, *3pr.ind.*, P291*
encuser, *v.*, to make known, tell about: **encusé**, *p.part.*, DA710
endroit, *adv.*, [reinforces adverbs of time or place]; **la endroit**, DA1918, immediately; P340, there in that place
engigner, *v.*, to trick: **engigne**, *3pr.ind.*, DA1390
engrés, *adj.*, P743, enthusiastic, willing
engriger, *v.*, to make worse, aggravate: **engrige**, *3pr.ind.*, DA1803
ennuyt, *adv.*, TJ 995,* tonight
enserre, *n.f.*, DA549, constraint, barrier
entente, *n.f.*, DA93, TJ1281, TJ1282, P759, P914, intention, thought; **de toute mon entente**, TJ169, P953, with all my heart
enter, *v.*, to implant, attach: *inf.*, P851
enterin, *adj.*, DA1830, DA1847, TJ1529, P1311, entire, complete

enteser, *v.*, to bend, draw (a bow): **entesoit**, *3imp.ind.*, P1611
entremettre, *refl.v.*, to undertake: **s'entremettoient**, *6imp.ind.*, P364;
    entremettant, *adj.*, DA219, enterprising, skilled
entreveche, *n.f.*, DA114,* a dance movement [?]
erre, *n.m.* or *f.*, voyage, path; **apprester son erre**, P53, to prepare for one's trip; **ordener [son] erre**, P591, to prepare one's departure
esbattre, *v.*, to amuse, have fun: *inf.*, DA328, P59, P209; **esbatant**, *pr.part.*, DA216; **m'esbatoie**, *1refl.impf.ind.*, P1695; **s'esbatent**, *6refl.pr.ind.*, DA1294;
    esbatant, *adj.*, DA42, P35, pleasing, enjoyable;
    esbat, *n.m.*, DA325, TJ1089, **esbatement**, *n.m.*, P1357, P1421, game, entertainment
esbaudir, *v.*, to bring joy to: *inf.*, P93;
    esbaudi, *adj.*, DA250, cheerful, joyful
escemie = **escremie**, *n.f.*, TJ631,* jousting; flirtatious behavior
esmouvoir, *v.*, to incite, spread (rumor), to provoke, trouble: **esmoyent**, *6pr.ind.*, TJ707; **esmurent**, *6p.s.*, TJ1190, P1690
espardre, *v.*, to dispense, bestow: **s'espart**, *3refl.pr.ind.*, DA1167;
    espart, *n.m.*, DA515,* portion, part
    espar, *adj.*, TJ759,* granted, bestowed
espart, *n.m.*, TJ758,* spark, darting glance
espovente, *adj.*, DA1027, frightened, afraid
estancher, *v.*, to quench (thirst), satisfy (hunger): **estanchee**, *p.part.*, DA290
estorement, *n.m.*, P571, fittings, furnishings, embellishments
estour, *n.m.*, P68, verbal skirmish, attack
estrang(i)er, *v.*, to estrange, to push away: *inf.*, TJ340, TJ1354; **s'estrangia**, *3refl.p.s.*, TJ217; **estrangié**, *p.part.*, TJ1177, P1807, P1810
estriver, *v.*, to oppose, cause trouble: **estrivant**, *pr.part.*, TJ942
esture, *n.f.*, **tout a esture**, DA347, suddenly
faitis, *adj.*, P1502, elegant, pretty, well-formed
fermille, *n.f.*, P685, buckle or clasp
flairant, *adj.*, P358, perfumed; **souëf flairant**, P142, P1125, P1512, sweet-smelling
flatir, *v.*, to strike, throw down: **flati**, *p.part.*, DA1206, P1809 [see **cas**]
foison, *n.f.*, P1643, adundance, great quantity
fosselu, *adj.*, P1526, dimpled
froc, *n.m.*, P519* [see note to P518-23], (part of) the head covering in nuns' and monks' robes
fuer, *n.m.*, price, rate; **a tous fuers**, DA1527, at any price
gaigner, *v.*, to win over: **gaigné**, *p.part.*, DA1767
gaite, *n.m.* or *f.*, TJ1145, spy
gesir *v.*, to lie down: **gieu**, *p.part.*, DA991
gibet, *n.m.*, DA1298,* gibet, gallows
gieu = **jeu**, *n.m.*, DA142, DA183, P1222, game

gisarme, *n.f.*, DA498, spear, thrusting weapon
gobe, *adj.*, P530, sumptuous, frivolously fashionable
gonnelle, *n.f.*, P520, robe, tunic
gort, *n.m.*, P146,* stake net, for fishing
goyere, *n.f.*, P788, type of tart
grappin, *n.m.*, P400, a bit of straw
guerdonner, guerredonner, *v.*, to recompense, reward: *inf.*, P693; **guerredonnez**, *p.part.*, TJ436;
    guerdon, guerredon, *n.m.*, DA596, DA1188, TJ127, P1705, reward, compensation
guermenter, *refl.v.*, to lament, bewail: *inf.*, P1002; **me guermente**, *1pr.ind.*, TJ265; **vous guermentez**, *5pr.ind.*, P1398; **se guermentant**, *pr.part.*, TJ879; **me guermentoye**, *1impf.ind.*, P1806; **se guermentoit**, *3impf.ind.*, TJ310
guerpir, *v.*, to leave, abandon: **guerpissoit**, *3impf.ind.*, TJ1475
haid, *n.m.*, joy, desire; **a son haid**, DA1773, to one's liking, as one likes
haitié, *adj.*, DA762, happy, joyful
hanter, *v.*, to frequent, visit often: *inf.* P850; to practice or engage in frequently: *inf.*, P1198; **hanté**, *p.part.*, P809, **hantent**, *6pr.ind.*, P810
happer, *v.*, to seize, take possession of: *inf.*, P1139
haÿ, *interj.*, DA493 [exclamation of grief]
hutin, *n.m.*, DA1573, battle, combat
ierre, *n.m.*, TJ489, ivy
las, *interj.*, P1020, P1867, alas
las, *n.m.*, DA231, TJ506, snare, trap; P687, laces (for tying)
las, *adj.*, DA230, DA471, TJ505, weary; unhappy
lay, *adj.*, secular, lay; **laye gent**, P170, laypeople, the unschooled
lëens, *adv.*, P555, in that place
lierre, *n.m.*, TJ491,* thief; ivy
lobe, *n.f.*, P529, trick, lie
loustre, *n.f.*, DA1479, otter
macelle, *n.f.*, P1505, cheek
mais = mets, *n.m.*, DA146, dish, course of a meal (used literally and figuratively)
maistrier, *v.*, to govern, dominate, to torment: **non mie en maistriant**, *pr.part.*, TJ533, without harrassing
malage, *n.m.*, DA240, TJ1175, P1424, illness, suffering
marrastre, *n.f.*, DA877, (cruel) stepmother
marri, *adj.*, P970, P1268, afflicted, sorrowful
martireer, *v.*, to suffer martyrdom: **martire**, *1pr.ind.*, P1713*
mauvaistié, *n.f.*, TJ1453, badness, weakness of character
merrien, *n.m.*, substance, nature (in a moral or material sense); **mal merrien**, TJ823, bad character
mesdiseur = mesdisant, *n.m.*, TJ511, gossip, slanderer

mesprendre, *v.*, to offend, to commit an offence: *inf.*, P377; **meprist**, *3p.s.*, TJ1481; **mesprison**, *n.f.*, DA823, DA1183, fault, insult
meüe, see **mouvoir**
mignot, *adj.*, P530, affected, vain
mite, *n.f.*, TJ291, a small coin
mouvoir, *v.*, to move, to (a)rouse: **meut**, *3pr.ind.*, TJ256;
   meüe, *p.part.*, TJ1455, P1597, affected, moved
musart, *adj.*, DA864, simple, dreamy
muser, *v.*, to amuse oneself: **muse**, *3pr.ind.*, DA1217; to reflect on: **musoit**, *3impf.ind.*, P1610
nasquier, *v.*, to be born: **nasqui**, *3p.s.*, DA607, TJ1480
nerf, *n.m.*, P1158, ligament
nuble, *n.m.* or *f.*, DA883, cloud
ocy, *interj.*, P181,* [onomatopoeic imitation of the nightingale's call]; also *2imper.* of **occire**, to kill
ombrage, *adj.*, P1543, dark; P1855, taciturn, unfriendly
ort, *adj.*, DA1298,* disgusting, dirty
ouvrage, *n.m.*, (piece of) work; **pierres faites a ouvrages**, P391, stones arranged in a mosaic
paistre, *v.*, to give sustenance to: **paist**, *3pr.ind.*, DA1173
päour, *n.f.*, TJ779, fear; **päourousement**, *adv.*, TJ882, fearfully
partemps, *adv.*, P1055, soon
paraler, *v.*, to go, reach: **au paraler**, TJ768, finally, after all
parceux = **paresseux**, *adj.*, DA1669, lazy
parfiner, *v.*, to complete: *inf.*, TJ1521;
   parfin, *n.f.*, DA751, DA941, DA1051, TJ61, P2071, end
pesme, *adj.*, P1870, very bad
planter, *v.*, to abandon: **planta**, *3p.s.*, P1773
plantureux, *adj.*, DA1140, fertile
ploit, *n.m.*, DA201, situation, disposition
poir, **a poir**, *adv. expression*, DA565,* TJ162,* TJ850, TJ1209, P1914, soon, eventually
pourpris, *n.m.*, DA1657, enclosure, courtly setting
prael, *n.m.*, P399, courtyard, open space
quarole = **carole**, *n.f.*, P730, a dance
quom = **com(me)**, *conj.*, P521, like
quorsir = **(r)accourcir**, *v.*, to shorten: **quorsi**, *3p.s.*, DA679*
rabattre, *v.*, to cast down: *inf.*, DA331; **rabat**, *3pr.ind.*, P1359; **rabatus**, *p.part.*, P830
racois(i)er, *v.*, to quiet, stifle: **racoise**, *3pr.ind.*, DA390; **racoise**, *3pr.subj.*, P995
racropi, *adj.*, P1822, humiliated, belittled
raisonner, *v.*, to address, plead with: **raisonne**, *3pr.ind.*, TJ1436; to recount: *inf.*, DA1770, TJ1330; **raisonna**, *3p.s.*, P1286

ramenter, ramentevoir, *v.*, to remember, recall, to evoke: **ramenteü (-teu)**, *p.part.*, DA1409, DA1658, DA1980; **ramentoit**, *3imp.ind.*, DA1082

ravaller, *refl.v.*, to fall away: **se ravalle**, *3pr.ind.*, DA1839

regehir, *v.*, to reveal, admit: **regehirés**, *5fut.ind.*, P1058

relenquir, *v.*, to abandon, betray: **relenqui**, *p.part.*, DA604, TJ1483

remerir, *v.*, to reward, recompense: *inf.*, DA1763

remirer, *v.*, to consider, examine closely, to admire: **remire**, *3pr.ind.*, DA1754; **remirant**, *pr.part.*, DA171, TJ903; **remiré**, *p.part.*, P545; **remiray**, *1p.s.*, DA78

requoy, *n.m.*, calm; secluded spot; **en requoy**, P1774, in private, in secret

rescripsier, *v.*, to write back, reply in writing: **rescripsoit**, *3impf.ind.*, TJ1020

resner = **raisnier**, *v.*, to converse: *inf.*, P247

retraire, *v.*, to describe, recount: *inf.*, P471; **retrait**, *p.part.*, DA1609, DA1757; to retreat: **se retreant**, *refl.pr.part.*, TJ1371; **retrait**, *p.part.*, TJ1151

retrait, retret, *n.m.*, DA138, retreat, refuge, dwelling;
  en retrait, TJ1149, privately, in an aside

rompre, *v.*, to break: **ront le lengage**, *3pr.ind.*, DA1825, put an end to the discussion

rousture, *n.f.*, P490, breach, opening

sachant, *adj.*, DA238, wise, knowledgeable, knowing

sade, *adj.*, DA1142, DA1381, charming, agreeable

sadinet, *adj.*, P1525, diminutive of **sade**

samit, *n.m.*, P1601, a fine, imported silk

sault, *n.m.*, DA114, a leap, a kind of dance

saussaye, *n.f.*, **saussois**, *n.m.*, P140, P881, a grove of willows

seche, *adj.*, P1158, without flesh or fat

semondre, *v.*, to invite: **semons**, *1pr.ind.*, P821; to admonish: **semont**, *3pr.ind.*, DA1523

sequeurre, *v.*, to help: **sequeure**, *3pr.ind.*, P1407

serain, *n.m.*, P164, serenity, calm (here, of the early morning)

seraine, *n.f.*, DA459, siren, mythical seductive woman

sergent, *n.m.*, TJ1145, P763, P783, servant, follower

seri, *adj.*, P118, P716, calm; P115, harmonious

solacier, *v.*, to amuse, rejoice: *inf.*, DA87; **solacié**, *p.part.*, P2061

souëf, *adj.*, DA1165, P154, P1170, sweet, pleasant; *adv.*, sweetly, gently [see **flairant**]

souldee, *n.f.*, TJ853, wages, recompense

sourdre, *v.*, to run, flow: **sourdans**, *pr.part.*, P570; **sourt**, *3pr.ind.*, P426; to arise, result: **sourdent**, *6pr.ind.*, DA813, DA1230

soy, *n.f.*, DA289, thirst

taner, *refl.v.*, to become tired or bored: **se tanerent**, *6p.s.*, P555

tarïence, *n.f.*, DA1287, churlish, irritating nature

tarir, *v.*, to make disappear, to take away: *inf.* DA1760; **tari**, *p.part.*, P969

tencier, *v.*, to debate, quarrel: *inf.*, DA51, TJ1518;
  tence, *n.f.*, DA1945, TJ685, dispute, quarrel

tors, tort, *adj.*, DA467, circuitous, indirect; P1141, deformed, lame; DA1105, DA1335, twisted, distorted
touppasse, *n.m.*, TJ486, topaz
tourteau, *n.m.*, type of cake; DA1926, (figuratively) rewards, treats
traictif, *adj.*, P1500, well-turned, pleasing
travailler, *refl.v.*, to torment oneself, try one's best: **se traveilloit**, *3impf.ind.*, TJ1369
tresche, *n.f.*, DA112, a dance, ball, or gathering
tresmuer, *v.*, to transform: **tresmüé**, *p.part.*, DA454, DA712; **se tresmuer**, *refl.inf.*, to change one's facial expression: **se tresmuoit**, *3imp.ind.*, DA274
vaillant, *n.m.*, P1312, fortune, possessions
veant, *pr.part.* of **veoir**, DA1347*;
 cler veant, TJ1370, P501, perspicacious, insightful
ventelés, *n.m.*, P152, breeze
verjus, *n.m.*, TJ738, acidic juice of unripe raisins
vermillet, *adj.*, P1526, pink
verve, *n.f.*, DA523, caprice, folly; DA928, discourse, speech
vouacarme, *n.m.*, DA497, lamentation
ynde, *adj.*, P103, dark blue

Bibliography of Works Cited

This bibliography consists of works cited in the introduction or the notes accompanying the texts. For further references concerning Christine de Pizan's corpus, see the bibliographies by Angus J. Kennedy and Edith Yenal, listed below.

Adams, Carol, Paula Bartley, Hilary Bourdillon, and Cathy Loxton, eds. *From Workshop to Warfare: The Lives of Medieval Women*. Cambridge: Cambridge University Press, 1984.
Altmann, Barbara K. "L'art de l'autoportrait littéraire dans les *Cent Balades* de Christine de Pizan." In *Autour de Christine de Pizan*, eds. Liliane Dulac and Bernard Ribémont, 327–36. Orléans: Paradigme, 1995.
———. "Christine de Pizan's Livre du Dit de Poissy: An Analysis and Critical Edition." Ph.D. diss., University of Toronto, 1988.
———. "Diversity and Coherence in Christine de Pizan's *Dit de Poissy*." *French Forum* 12.3 (September 1987): 261–71.
———. "Reopening the Case: Machaut's *Jugement* Poems as a Source in Christine de Pizan." In *Reinterpreting Christine de Pizan*, ed. Earl Jeffrey Richards, Joan Williamson, Nadia Margolis, and Christine Reno, 137–56. Athens: University of Georgia Press, 1992.
Atiya, Aziz Suryal. *The Crusade of Nicopolis*. London: Methuen, 1934.
Badel, Pierre-Yves. "Le débat." In *La littérature française aux XIVe et XVe siècles. Grundriss der romanischen Literaturen des Mittelalters* 8.1, 95–110. Heidelberg: Winter, 1988.
———. *Introduction à la vie littéraire du moyen âge*. Paris: Bordas/Mouton, 1969.
Binias, A. M. "Glossaire des vieux mots employés par Christine de Pisan dans le *Livre du dit de Poissy*." M.A. thesis, University of Leeds, 1926.
Bloch, R. Howard. *Medieval French Literature and Law*. Berkeley: University of California Press, 1977.
Bories, Edmond. *Histoire de la ville de Poissy*. Poissy: Champion, 1925; Marseille: Laffitte Reprints, 1978.
Bossuat, R. "Theseus de Cologne." *Le Moyen Age* 65 (1959): 97–133, 293–320, 539–77.

Bossy, Michel-André, ed. and trans. *Medieval Debate Poetry: Vernacular Works.* New York: Garland, 1987.

Bozzolo, Carla, Hélène Loyau, and Monique Ornato. "Hommes de culture et hommes de pouvoir parisiens à la cour amoureuse." In *Pratiques de la culture écrite en France au XVe siècle: Actes du Colloque international du CNRS, Paris, 16–18 mai 1992, organisé en l'honneur de Gilbert Ouy par l'unité de recherche "Culture écrite du Moyen Age tardif,"* ed. Monique Ornato and Nicole Pons, 245–78. Textes et études du Moyen Age 2. Louvain-la-Neuve: Fédération Internationale des Instituts d'Etudes Médiévales, 1995.

Braddy, Haldeen. *Chaucer and the French Poet Graunson.* Baton Rouge: Louisiana State University Press, 1947.

Brownlee, Kevin. *Poetic Identity in Guillaume de Machaut.* Madison: University of Wisconsin Press, 1984.

———. "Romance Rewritings: Courtly Discourse and Auto-Citation in Christine de Pizan." In *Gender and Text in the Later Middle Ages,* ed. Jane Chance, 172–94. Gainesville: University Press of Florida, 1996.

Bruins, J. E. *Observations sur la langue d'Eustache Deschamps et de Christine de Pisan.* Amsterdam: De Dordrechtsche Drukkerij, 1925.

Bruzelius, Caroline A., and Constance H. Berman. Introduction to special edition on Women. *Gesta* 31.2 (1992): 73–75.

Burgess, Glyn S., ed., with Robert A. Taylor et al. *The Spirit of the Court: Selected Proceedings of the Fourth Congress of the International Courtly Literature Society.* Dover, N.H.: Brewer, 1985.

Burgess, Glyn S., et al., eds. *Court and Poet: Selected Proceedings of the Third Congress of the International Courtly Literature Society.* Liverpool: Cairns, 1981.

Calin, William. *The French Tradition and the Literature of Medieval England.* Toronto: University of Toronto Press, 1994.

———. *A Poet at the Fountain: Essays on the Narrative Verse of Guillaume de Machaut.* Lexington: University Press of Kentucky, 1974.

Cappelli, Adriano. *Dizionario di abbreviature latine ed italiane.* Milano: Ulrico Hoepli, 1985.

Cerquiglini, Jacqueline. "1401, St. Valentine's Day: The Charter of La Cour Amoureuse Is Read Aloud in the Hôtel d'Artois; Trials of Eros." In *A New History of French Literature,* ed. Denis Hollier, 114–18. Cambridge: Harvard University Press, 1989.

———. "Le clerc et l'écriture: le 'voir dit' de Guillaume de Machaut et la définition du 'dit'." In *Literatur in der Gesellschaft des Spätmittelalters,* ed. Hans Ulrich Gumbrecht. Grundriss der romanischen Literaturen des Mittelalters, Begleitreihe 1, 151–68. Heidelberg: Winter, 1980.

———. "Le Dit." In *La littérature française aux XIVe et XVe siècles. Grundriss der romanischen Literaturen des Mittelalters* 8.1, 86–94. Heidelberg: Winter, 1988.

———, ed. *Cent ballades d'amant et de dame.* Bibliothèque médiévale 10/18. Paris: Union Générale d'Editions, 1982.

Cerquiglini-Toulet, Jacqueline. "L'amour des livres au XIVe siècle." In *Mélanges de philologie et de littérature médiévales offerts à Michel Burger,* 333–40. Geneva: Droz, 1994.

———. *La couleur de la mélancolie: la fréquentation des livres au XIVè siècle, 1300–1415.* Paris: Hatier, 1993.

———. "Des emplois seconds de la rime et du rythme dans la poésie française des XIVe et XVe siècles." *Le Moyen Français* 29 (1991): 21–31.

Chaurand, Jacques. *Introduction à la dialectologie française.* Paris: Bordas, 1972.

Cockshaw, Pierre. *Miniatures en grisaille.* Brussels: Bibliothèque Royale Albert 1er, 1986.

Coleman, Joyce. *Public Reading and the Reading Public in Late Medieval England and France.* Cambridge: Cambridge University Press, 1996.

Combettes, Bernard. "Une notion stylistique et ses rapports avec la syntaxe. Narration et description chez Christine de Pizan." In *Le génie de la forme. Mélanges de langue et littérature offerts à Jean Mourot,* 51–58. Nancy: Presses Universitaires de Nancy, 1982.

Cunningham, C. A. "A Critical Edition of the Poetry of Oton de Grandson, Ms. L." Ph.D. diss., University of North Carolina at Chapel Hill, 1987.

Curnow, Maureen. "The *Livre de la Cité des Dames* of Christine de Pisan: A Critical Edition." Ph.D. diss., Vanderbilt University, 1975.

de Lettenhove, Kervyn, M. le baron, ed. *Oeuvres de Froissart: Chroniques.* 25 vols. Brussels: Devaux, 1867–77.

de Winter, Patrick M. *La bibliothèque de Philippe le Hardi, de Bourgogne (1364–1404): Etude sur les manuscrits à peintures d'une collection princière à l'époque du "style gothique international."* Paris: Editions du Centre national de la recherche scientifique, 1985.

———. "Christine de Pizan, ses enlumineurs et ses rapports avec le milieu bourguignon." In *Actes du 104e Congrès National des Sociétés Savantes (1979),* 335–75. Paris: Bibliothèque Nationale, 1982.

Deschaux, Robert. "Le lai et la complainte." In *La littérature française aux XIVe et XVe siècles. Grundriss der romanischen Literaturen des Mittelalters* 8.1, 70–85. Heidelberg: Winter, 1988.

Di Stefano, Giuseppe. *Dictionnaire des locutions en moyen français.* Montreal: Editions CERES, 1991.

Dictionnaire des lettres françaises: Le Moyen Age. Paris: Fayard, 1992.

Dogaer, Georges, and Marguerite Debae. *La librairie de Philippe le bon. Exposition organisée à l'occasion du 500e anniversaire de la mort du duc.* Brussels: Bibliothèque Royale Albert 1er, 1967.

Doutrepont, Georges. *La littérature française à la cour des ducs de Bourgogne: Philippe le Hardi, Jean Sans Peur, Philippe le Bon, Charles le Téméraire.* Paris: Champion, 1909.

Duby, Georges, ed. *A History of Private Life: II. Revelations of the Medieval World.* Trans. Arthur Goldhammer. Cambridge: Belknap Press of Harvard University Press, 1988.

Dulac, Liliane. "Christine de Pisan et le malheur des 'vrais amans'." In *Mélanges de langue et de littérature médiévales offerts à Pierre Le Gentil*, 223–33. Paris: Société d'édition d'enseignement supérieur, 1973.

———. "Dissymétrie et échec de la communication dans les *Cent ballades d'amant et de dame* de Christine de Pizan." *Lengas* 22 (1987): 133–46.

———. "*Le Livre du dit de Poissy* de Christine de Pizan: poème éclaté ou montage signifiant." In *Ecrire pour dire: études sur le dit médiéval*, ed. Bernard Ribémont, 9–28. Sapience 3. Paris: Klincksieck, 1990.

Faral, Edmond. *Recherches sur les sources latines des contes et romans courtois du moyen âge*. Paris: Champion, 1913.

Fenster, Thelma S., ed. *The Book of the Duke of True Lovers*. Trans. Thelma S. Fenster and Nadia Margolis. New York: Persea, 1991.

———, ed. *Le Livre du Duc des vrais amans*. By Christine de Pizan. Medieval and Renaissance Texts and Studies 124. Binghamton, N.Y.: Center for Medieval and Early Renaissance Studies, 1995.

Fenster, Thelma S., and Mary Carpenter Erler, eds. *Poems of Cupid, God of Love*. Leiden, Netherlands: Brill, 1990.

Foulet, Alfred, and Mary Blakely Speer. *On Editing Old French Texts*. Lawrence, Kans.: Regents, 1979.

Fourrier, Anthime, ed. *Jean Froissart: 'Dits' et 'Débats.'* Geneva: Droz, 1979.

———, ed. *Jean Froissart: L'espinette amoureuse*. Paris: Klincksieck, 1963.

Gaspar, Camille, and Frédéric Lyna. *Les principaux manuscrits à peintures de la Bibliothèque royale de Belgique*. 2ème partie. Paris: Société française de reproductions de manuscrits à peintures, 1945.

Gay, Lucy M. "On the Language of Christine de Pisan." *Modern Philology* 6.1 (1908): 70–96.

Gellrich, Jesse M. *Discourse and Dominion in the Fourteenth Century: Oral Contexts of Writing in Philosophy, Politics, and Poetry*. Princeton: Princeton University Press, 1995.

Godefroy, Frédéric E. *Dictionnaire de l'ancienne langue française et de tous les dialectes*. 10 vols. Paris: Vieweg, 1881–1902; reprint, Kraus Reprint, Nendeln/Liechtenstein, 1969.

Greimas, Algirdas Julien. *Dictionnaire de l'ancien français jusqu'au milieu du XIVe siècle*. Paris: Larousse, 1968.

———, and Teresa Mary Keane. *Dictionnaire du moyen français: la Renaissance*. Paris: Larousse, 1992.

Guiffrey, Jules. *Histoire de la tapisserie*. Tour: A. Mame, 1886.

Haidu, Peter. "Making It (New) in the Middle Ages: Towards a Problematics of Alterity." *Diacritics* 4 (Summer 1974): 2–11.

Hamburger, Jeffrey F. "Art, Enclosure and the Cura Monialium: Prolegomena in the Guise of a Postscript." *Gesta* 31.2 (1992): 108–34.

Hicks, Eric. *Le débat sur le Roman de la Rose*. Paris: Champion, 1977.

Hicks, Eric, and Gilbert Ouy. "The Second 'Autograph' Edition of Christine de Pizan's Lesser Poetical Works." *Manuscripta* 20 (1976): 14–15.

Hindman, Sandra L. *Christine de Pizan's "Epistre Othéa": Painting and Politics at the Court of Charles VI.* Toronto: Pontifical Institute of Mediaeval Studies, 1986.

———. "The Composition of the Manuscript of Christine de Pizan's Collected Works in the British Library: A Reassessment." *British Library Journal* 9.2 (Autumn 1983): 93–123.

———. *Sealed in Parchment: Rereadings of Knighthood in the Illuminated Manuscripts of Chrétien de Troyes.* Chicago: University of Chicago Press, 1994.

Hinnebusch, William A., O.P. *The History of the Dominican Order.* 2 vols. Staten Island, N.Y.: Alba House, 1965–73.

Hoepffner, Ernest, ed. *Oeuvres de Guillaume de Machaut.* 3 vols. Paris: Firmin-Didot [SATF], 1908–21.

Hollier, Denis, ed. *A New History of French Literature.* Cambridge: Harvard University Press, 1989.

Huguet, Edmond. *Dictionnaire de la langue française du seizième siècle.* 7 vols. Paris: Champion, 1925–66.

Imbs, Paul. *Le Voir-Dit de Guillaume de Machaut: étude littéraire.* Paris: Klincksieck, 1991.

Jauss, Hans Robert. *Toward an Aesthetic of Reception.* Trans. Timothy Bahti. Minneapolis: University of Minnesota Press, 1982.

Jodogne, Omer. "Povoir ou Pouir? Le cas phonétique de l'ancien verbe 'pouoir'." In *Mélanges de linguistique et de philologie romane offerts à Monseigneur Pierre Gardette,* 257–66. Strasbourg: Travaux de linguistique et de littérature 4.1, 1966.

Jung, Marc-René. *Etudes sur le poème allégorique en France au moyen âge.* Berne: Francke, 1971.

Kells, Kathleen E. "Christine de Pisan's *Le dit de Poissy*: An Exploration of an Alternative Life-Style for Aristocratic Women in Fifteenth-Century France." In *New Images of Medieval Women: Essays Towards a Cultural Anthropology,* ed. Edelgard E. DuBruck, 103–19. Lewiston, N.Y.: Mellen, 1989.

Kelly, Douglas. "Amitié comme anti-amour: Au-delà du *fin amour* de Jean de Meun à Christine de Pizan." In *Anteros: Actes du colloque de Madison (Wisconsin), March 1994,* 75–97. Orléans: Paradigme, 1995.

———. *Medieval Imagination: Rhetoric and the Poetry of Courtly Love.* Madison: University of Wisconsin Press, 1978.

Kennedy, Angus J. *Christine de Pizan: A Bibliographical Guide.* London: Grant and Cutler, 1984.

———. *Christine de Pizan: A Bibliographical Guide, Supplement 1.* London: Grant and Cutler, 1994.

———. "A Selective Bibliography of Christine de Pizan Scholarship, circa 1980–1987." In *Reinterpreting Christine de Pizan,* ed. Earl Jeffrey Richards, Joan Williamson, Nadia Margolis, and Christine Reno, 285–98. Athens: University of Georgia Press, 1992.

Kibler, William W., and James I. Wimsatt, eds. Music edited by Rebecca A. Baltzer. *"Le jugement du roy de Behaigne" and "Remede de fortune."* Athens: University of Georgia Press, 1988.

Kittay, Jeffrey. "Utterance Unmoored: The Changing Interpretation of the Act of Writing in the European Middle Ages." *Language in Society* 17.2 (1988): 209–30.

Krueger, Roberta. *Women Readers and the Ideology of Gender in Old French Verse Romance*. Cambridge: Cambridge University Press, 1993.

Laennec, Christine. "Christine Antygrafe: Authorial Ambivalence in the Works of Christine." In *Anxious Power*, ed. Carol J. Singley and Susan Elizabeth Sweeney, 35–49. Albany: State University of New York Press, 1993.

Laforêt, A. *Saint-Pourçain, cité historique et carrefour du Bourbonnais*. Moulins: Pottier, 1961.

Laidlaw, J[ames] C. "Christine de Pizan—An Author's Progress." *Modern Language Review* 78 (1983): 532–50.

———. "Christine de Pizan—A Publisher's Progress." *Modern Language Review* 82 (1987): 35–75.

———. "Christine de Pizan, the Earl of Salisbury and Henry IV." *French Studies* 36 (1982): 129–43.

———. "The *Cent Balades:* The Marriage of Content and Form." In *Christine de Pizan and Medieval French Lyric*, ed. Earl Jeffrey Richards. Gainesville: University Press of Florida, forthcoming.

Lalande, Denis, ed. *Le Livre des Fais du bon messire Jehan le Maingre, dit Bouciquaut*. Geneva: Droz, 1985.

Långfors, Artur. *Recueil général des jeux-partis français*. Paris: Champion [SATF], 1926.

Langlois, Ernest. *Recueil d'arts de seconde rhétorique*. Paris: Imprimerie Nationale, 1902.

Lawson, Sarah, trans. *Christine de Pisan: The Treasure of the City of Ladies (or The Book of the Three Virtues)*. New York: Penguin, 1985.

Le Gentil, Pierre. "Christine de Pisan, poète méconnu." In *Mélanges d'histoire littéraire offerts à Daniel Mornet*, 1–10. Paris: Nizet, 1951.

———. *Littérature française du moyen âge*. Paris: Colin, 1963.

Lebeuf, L'Abbé. *Histoire de la ville et de tout le diocèse de Paris*. Paris: Féchoz et Letouzey, 1883.

Lecoy, Félix. "Note sur quelques ballades de Christine de Pisan." In *Fin du moyen âge et renaissance: mélanges de philologie française offerts à Robert Guiette*, 107–14. Anvers: De Nederlandsche Boekhandel, 1961.

Lops, R.L.H. "*Le Livre du Dit de Poissy* van Christine de Pizan." *Rapports-Het Franse Boek* 61.4 (1991): 146–56.

Lorcin, Marie-Thérèse. "Mère nature et le devoir social: la mère et l'enfant dans l'oeuvre de Christine de Pizan." *Revue Historique* 282 (1989): 29–44.

Lote, Georges. *Histoire du vers français*. 2 vols. Paris: Boivin, 1951.

Marchello-Nizia, Christiane. *Histoire de la langue française aux XIVe et XVe siècles*. Paris: Bordas, 1979.

Margolis, Nadia. "Christine de Pizan: The Poetess as Historian." *Journal of the History of Ideas* 47 (1986): 361–75.

———. "Clerkliness and Courtliness in the *Complaintes* of Christine de Pizan." In

Christine de Pizan and Medieval French Lyric, ed. Earl Jeffrey Richards. Gainesville: University Press of Florida, forthcoming.

———. "Elegant Closures: The Use of the Diminutive in Christine de Pizan and Jean de Meun." In *Reinterpreting Christine de Pizan*, ed. Earl Jeffrey Richards, Joan Williamson, Nadia Margolis, and Christine Reno, 111–23. Athens: University of Georgia Press, 1992.

Martin, Robert, and Marc Wilmet. *Manuel du français du moyen âge: 2. Syntaxe du moyen français*. Bordeaux: SOBODI, 1980.

McLeod, Enid. *The Order of the Rose: The Life and Ideas of Christine de Pizan*. London: Chatto and Windus, 1976.

Meiss, Millard. *French Painting in the Time of Jean de Berry: The Boucicaut Master*. London: Phaidon, 1968.

———. *French Painting in the Time of Jean de Berry: The Late XIV Century and the Patronage of the Duke*. 2 vols. London: Phaidon, 1967.

———. *French Painting in the Time of Jean de Berry: The Limbourgs and Their Contemporaries*. 2 vols. New York: Braziller, 1974.

Meiss, Millard, and Sharon Off. "The Bookkeeping of Robinet d'Estampes and the Chronology of Jean de Berry's Manuscripts." *The Art Bulletin* 53 (1971): 225–35.

Meyer, Paul. "Note sur le manuscrit offert par Christine de Pisan à Isabeau de Bavière (Musée Britannique, Harley 4431)." In *Oeuvres poétiques de Christine de Pisan*, ed. Maurice Roy, 3:xxi–xxiv. Paris: Firmin Didot, 1886–96.

———. "Notice du ms. 25970 de la Bibliothèque Phillipps (Cheltenham)" and "Melior et Ydoine." *Romania* 37 (1908): 209–35, 236–44.

Millet, Hélène. "Qui a écrit *Le Livre des Fais du bon messire Jehan Le Maingre, dit Bouciquaut?*" In *Pratiques de la culture écrite en France au XVe siècle: Actes du Colloque international du CNRS, Paris, 16–18 mai 1992, organisé en l'honneur de Gilbert Ouy par l'unité de recherche "Culture écrite du Moyen Age tardif,"* ed. Monique Ornato and Nicole Pons, 135–49. Textes et études du Moyen Age 2. Louvain-la-Neuve: Fédération Internationale des Instituts d'Etudes Médiévales, 1995.

Mombello, Gianni. *La Tradizione manoscritta dell'"Epistre Othea" di Christine de Pizan*. Memorie dell'Accademia delle Scienze di Torino, classe di Scienze Morali, Storiche e Filologiche. Series 4a, no. 15. Torino: Academia delle Scienze, 1967.

Moreau, Thérèse, and Eric Hicks, trans. *La Cité des dames*. Paris: Stock, 1986.

Moreau-Rendu, S. *Le Prieuré royal de Saint-Louis de Poissy*. Colmar: Alsatia Colmar, 1968.

Mühlethaler, Jean-Claude. "'Les poètes que de vert on couronne': En marge du nouveau *Dictionnaire du moyen français:* Réflexions sur quelques changements dans le champ lexical de la création poétique au XVe siècle." *Le Moyen Français* 30 (1992): 97–112.

Noël, Octave. *Histoire de la ville de Poissy*. Poissy: Marchant, 1869.

Nouvet, Claire. "Writing in Fear." In *Gender and Text in the Later Middle Ages*, ed. Jane Chance, 279–305. Gainesville: University Press of Florida, 1996.

Ong, Walter J. *Orality and Literacy: The Technologizing of the Word*. New York: Methuen, 1982.

———. "Orality, Literacy, and Medieval Textualization." *New Literary History: A Journal of Theory and Interpretation* 16.1 (Autumn 1984): 1–12.
Ornato, Monique, and Nicole Pons, eds. *Pratiques de la culture écrite en France au XVe siècle: Actes du Colloque international du CNRS, Paris, 16–18 mai 1992, organisé en l'honneur de Gilbert Ouy par l'unité de recherche "Culture écrite du Moyen Age tardif."* Textes et études du Moyen Age 2. Louvain-la-Neuve: Fédération Internationale des Instituts d'Etudes Médiévales, 1995.
O'Sullivan, Jeremiah F., ed. *The Register of Eudes of Rouen*. Trans. Sydney M. Brown. New York: Columbia University Press, 1964.
Oulmont, Charles. *Les débats du clerc et du chevalier dans la littérature poétique du moyen-âge*. Paris: Champion, 1911.
Ouy, Gilbert, and Christine Reno. "Les hésitations de Christine: Etude des variantes de graphies dans trois manuscrits autographes de Christine de Pizan." *Revue des langues romanes* 92.2 (1988): 265–86.
———. "Identification des autographes de Christine de Pizan." *Scriptorium* 34 (1980): 221–38.
Palmer, R. Barton, ed. and trans. *Guillaume de Machaut: The Judgment of the King of Bohemia (Le Jugement dou Roy de Behaingne)*. New York: Garland, 1984.
Paradis, Françoise. "Une polyphonie narrative: Pour une description de la structure des *Cent ballades d'amant et de dame* de Christine de Pizan." *Bien Dire and Bien Aprandre* 8 (1990): 127–40.
Paris, Gaston, ed. "Un poème inédit de Martin Le Franc: *La Complainte des dames.*" *Romania* 16 (1887): 383–427.
Paris, Paulin. *Les manuscrits françois de la Bibliothèque du roy*. 7 vols. Paris: Techener, 1836–48.
Parkes, M. B. *Pause and Effect: An Introduction to the History of Punctuation in the West*. Berkeley: University of California Press, 1993.
Pessard, Gustave. *Nouveau dictionnaire historique de Paris*. Paris: Eugène Rey, 1904.
Piaget, Arthur. "La cour amoureuse dite de Charles VI." *Romania* 20 (1891): 417–54.
———. "Oton de Granson et ses poésies." *Romania* 19 (1890): 237–59, 403–48.
———. "*Le songe de la barge* de Jean de Werchin, Sénéchal de Hainaut." *Romania* 38 (1909): 71–110.
Picherit, Jean-Louis. "Christine de Pisan et le *Livre des Faicts du bon messire Jean le Maingre, dit Boucicaut, mareschal de France et gouverneur de Gennes.*" *Romania* 103 (1982): 299–331.
Pinet, Marie-Josèphe. *Christine de Pisan, 1364–1430: étude biographique et littéraire*. Paris: Champion, 1927; Geneva: Slatkine Reprints, 1974.
Poirion, Daniel. *Le moyen âge: 1300–1480*. Paris: Arthaud, 1971.
———. *Le poète et le prince. L'évolution du lyrisme courtois de Guillaume de Machaut à Charles d'Orléans*. Paris: Presses Universitaires de France, 1965.
———. "Traditions et fonctions du 'dit poétique' au XIVe et au XVe siècle." In *Literatur in der Gesellschaft des Spätmittelalters*, ed. Hans Ulrich Gumbrecht. Grundriss der romanischen Literaturen des Mittelalters, Begleitreihe 1, 147–50. Heidelberg: Winter, 1980.

Pope, Mildred K. *From Latin to Modern French.* 2d ed. Manchester: Manchester University Press, 1952.
Pougin, P. "Le Dit de Poissy de Christine de Pisan: Description du prieuré de Poissy en 1400." *Bibliothèque de l'Ecole des chartes* 18 (1857): 535–55.
Pugh, Annie Reese. "Le *Jugement du roy de Behaigne* et le *Dit de Poissy* de Christine de Pisan." *Romania* 23 (1894): 581–86.
Queux de Saint-Hilaire, Auguste H. E. de, and Gaston Raynaud, eds. *Oeuvres complètes d'Eustache Deschamps.* 11 vols. Paris: Firmin Didot, 1878–1903.
Richards, Earl Jeffrey. "Christine de Pizan and the Question of Feminist Rhetoric." *Teaching Language Through Literature* 22.2 (April 1983): 15–24.
———, ed. *Christine de Pizan and Medieval French Lyric.* Gainesville: University Press of Florida, forthcoming.
———, ed., with Joan Williamson, Nadia Margolis, and Christine Reno. *Reinterpreting Christine de Pizan.* Athens: University of Georgia Press, 1992.
———, trans. *Christine de Pizan: The Book of the City of Ladies.* New York: Persea, 1982.
Rickard, Peter. *Chrestomathie de la langue française au quinzième siècle.* Cambridge: Cambridge University Press, 1976.
———. "The Rivalry of *m(a), t(a), s(a),* and *mon, ton, son* Before Feminine Nouns in Old and Middle French." *Archivum Linguisticum* 11 (1959): 21–47, 115–47.
Rimmon-Kenan, Shlomith. *Narrative Fiction: Contemporary Poetics.* New York: Methuen, 1983.
Le Robert: Dictionnaire historique de la langue française. Paris: Robert, 1992.
Robineau, E.-M.-D. *Christine de Pisan: sa vie, ses oeuvres.* Saint-Omer: Fleury-Lemaire, 1882.
Roques, Mario. "Etablissement de règles pratiques pour l'édition des anciens textes français et provençaux." *Romania* 52 (1926): 243–49.
Roy, Maurice, ed. *Oeuvres poétiques de Christine de Pisan.* 3 vols. Paris: Firmin Didot [SATF], 1886–96.
Runciman, Sir Steven. *A History of the Crusades.* 3 vols. Cambridge: Cambridge University Press, 1951–54.
Schäfer, Lucie. "Die Illustrationen zu den Handschriften der Christine de Pizan." *Marburger Jahrbuch für Kunstwissenschaft* 10 (1937): 119–208.
Schilperoort, Johanna Catharina. *Guillaume de Machaut et Christine de Pisan, étude comparative.* Ph.D. diss., University of Leiden. The Hague: Mouton, 1936.
Scully, Terence Peter. "The Love Debate in Mediaeval French Literature with Special Reference to Guillaume de Machaut." Ph.D. diss., University of Toronto, 1966.
Shahar, Shulamith. *The Fourth Estate: A History of Women in the Middle Ages.* New York: Methuen, 1983.
Sinnreich-Levi, Deborah M., ed. and trans. *Eustache Deschamps: L'Art de dictier.* East Lansing, Mich.: Colleagues Press, 1994.
Solente, S[uzanne]. "Christine de Pisan." *Dictionnaire des lettres françaises: le moyen âge,* ed. Robert Bossuat et al., 183–87. Paris: Arthème Fayard, 1964.

———. "Christine de Pisan." *Histoire littéraire de la France* 40: 335–422. Paris: Imprimerie Nationale, 1974.

———, ed. *Christine de Pisan: Le Livre de la Mutacion de Fortune*. 4 vols. Paris: Picard [SATF], 1959–66.

Stock, Brian. *The Implications of Literacy: Written Language and Models of Interpretation in the Eleventh and Twelfth Centuries*. Princeton: Princeton University Press, 1983.

Tobler, A., and E. Lommatzsch. *Altfranzösisches Wörterbuch*. 10 vols. Berlin: Weidmannsche Buchhandlung; Wiesbaden: Franz Steiner, 1925–76.

Towner, Sister Mary Louis, ed. *Lavision-Christine: Introduction and Text*. Catholic University of America, 1932; reprinted, New York: AMS, 1969.

Varty, Kenneth. *Christine de Pisan's Ballades, Rondeaux, and Virelais: An Anthology*. Leicester, England: Leicester University Press, 1965.

Wagner, Robert-Léon. *L'ancien français: Points de vue, programmes*. Paris: Larousse, 1974.

Walters, Lori. "The Woman Writer and Literary History: Christine de Pizan's Redefinition of the Poetic Translation in the *Epistre au dieu d'amours*." *French Literature Series* 16 (1989): 1–16.

Ward, Marvin James. "A Critical Edition of Thomas III, Marquis of Saluzzo's 'Le Livre du Chevalier errant'." Ph.D. diss., University of North Carolina at Chapel Hill, 1984.

Wharton, Susan, ed. *René d'Anjou: Le Livre du Cuer d'amours espris*. Paris: Union Générale d'Editions, 1980.

Willard, Charity Cannon. "Christine de Pizan: *Cent ballades d'amant et de dame*: Criticism of Courtly Love." In *Court and Poet: Selected Proceedings of the Third Congress of the International Courtly Literature Society*, ed. Glyn S. Burgess et al., 357–64. Liverpool: Cairns, 1981.

———. *Christine de Pizan: Her Life and Works*. New York: Persea, 1984.

———. "Concepts of Love According to Guillaume de Machaut, Christine de Pizan, and Pietro Bembo." In *The Spirit of the Court: Selected Proceedings of the Fourth Congress of the International Courtly Literature Society*, ed. Glyn S. Burgess, Robert A. Taylor, et al., 386–92. Dover, N.H.: Brewer, 1985.

———. "Jean de Werchin, Seneschal de Hainaut: Reader and Writer of Courtly Literature." In *Courtly Literature: Culture and Context: Selected Papers from the Fifth Triennial Congress of the International Courtly Literature Society*, ed. Keith Busby and Erik Kooper, 595–603. Utrecht Publications in General and Comparative Literature 25. Amsterdam: Benjamins, 1990.

———. "Lovers' Dialogues in Christine de Pizan's Lyric Poetry from the *Cent Ballades* to the *Cent ballades d'amant et de dame*." *Fifteenth Century Studies* 4 (1981): 167–80.

———. "A Visit to the Dominican Abbey of Poissy in 1400." Paper presented at the Fifteenth Annual Sewanee Mediaeval Colloquium, University of the South. Sewanee, Tennessee, April 1988.

Wimsatt, James I. *Chaucer and His French Contemporaries: Natural Music in the Fourteenth Century.* Toronto: University of Toronto Press, 1991.

Yenal, Edith. *Christine de Pizan: A Bibliography.* 2d ed. Scarecrow Author Bibliographies 63. Metuchen, N.J.: Scarecrow, 1989.

Zenker, Rudolf. *Die provenzalische Tenzone, eine literarhistorische Abhandlung.* Leipzig: Vogel, 1888.

Zumthor, Paul. "Rhétorique et poétique latines et romanes." In *Grundriss der romanischen Literaturen des Mittelalters* 1, 57–91. Heidelberg: Winter, 1972.

———. "Le texte médiéval entre oralité et écriture." In *Exigences et perspectives de la sémiotique: Recueil d'hommages pour Algirdas Julien Greimas / Aims and Prospects of Semiotics: Essays in Honor of Algirdas Julien Greimas,* ed. Herman Parret and Hans George Ruprecht, 827–43. Amsterdam: Benjamins, 1985.

www.ingramcontent.com/pod-product-compliance
Lightning Source LLC
Chambersburg PA
CBHW022105150426
43195CB00008B/272